Informing America's Policy on Illegal Drugs

What We Don't Know Keeps Hurting Us

Committee on Data and Research for Policy on Illegal Drugs

Charles F. Manski, John V. Pepper, and Carol V. Petrie, editors

Committee on Law and Justice and Committee on National Statistics

Commission on Behavioral and Social Sciences and Education

National Research Council

NATIONAL ACADEMY PRESS
Washington, D.C.

NATIONAL ACADEMY PRESS 2101 Constitution Avenue, N.W. Washington, D.C. 20418

NOTICE: The project that is the subject of this report was approved by the Governing Board of the National Research Council, whose members are drawn from the councils of the National Academy of Sciences, the National Academy of Engineering, and the Institute of Medicine. The members of the committee responsible for the report were chosen for their special competences and with regard for appropriate balance.

The study was supported by Contract/Grant No. DC 8C01 between the National Academy of Sciences and the White House Office of National Drug Control Policy. Any opinions, findings, conclusions, or recommendations expressed in this publication are those of the author(s) and do not necessarily reflect the view of the organizations or agencies that provided support for this project.

Suggested citation: National Research Council (2001), *Informing America's Policy on Illegal Drugs: What We Don't Know Keeps Hurting Us.* Committee on Data and Research for Policy on Illegal Drugs. Charles F. Manski, John V. Pepper, and Carol V. Petrie, editors. Committee on Law and Justice and Committee on National Statistics. Commission on Behavioral and Social Sciences and Education. Washington, DC: National Academy Press.

Library of Congress Cataloging-in-Publication Data

Informing America's policy on illegal drugs : what we don't know keeps hurting us / Charles F. Manski, John V. Pepper, and Carol V. Petrie, editors.
    p. cm.
Includes bibliographical references and index.
    ISBN 0-309-07273-5 (cloth)
  1. Narcotics, Control of—United States—Evaluation. 2. Drug traffic—Research—United States. 3. Drug abuse—Research—United States. 4. Drug abuse—United States—Prevention—Evaluation. 5. Evaluation research (Social action programs)—United States. I. Manski, Charles F. II. Pepper, John, 1964- III. Petrie, Carol.
    HV5825 .I547 2001
    363.45'0973—dc21
    2001003168

Additional copies of this report are available from National Academy Press, 2101 Constitution Avenue, N.W., Lockbox 285, Washington, D.C. 20055.

Call (800) 624-6242 or (202) 334-3313 (in the Washington metropolitan area)

This report is also available online at **http://www.nap.edu**

Printed in the United States of America

THE NATIONAL ACADEMIES

National Academy of Sciences
National Academy of Engineering
Institute of Medicine
National Research Council

The **National Academy of Sciences** is a private, nonprofit, self-perpetuating society of distinguished scholars engaged in scientific and engineering research, dedicated to the furtherance of science and technology and to their use for the general welfare. Upon the authority of the charter granted to it by the Congress in 1863, the Academy has a mandate that requires it to advise the federal government on scientific and technical matters. Dr. Bruce M. Alberts is president of the National Academy of Sciences.

The **National Academy of Engineering** was established in 1964, under the charter of the National Academy of Sciences, as a parallel organization of outstanding engineers. It is autonomous in its administration and in the selection of its members, sharing with the National Academy of Sciences the responsibility for advising the federal government. The National Academy of Engineering also sponsors engineering programs aimed at meeting national needs, encourages education and research, and recognizes the superior achievements of engineers. Dr. Wm. A. Wulf is president of the National Academy of Engineering.

The **Institute of Medicine** was established in 1970 by the National Academy of Sciences to secure the services of eminent members of appropriate professions in the examination of policy matters pertaining to the health of the public. The Institute acts under the responsibility given to the National Academy of Sciences by its congressional charter to be an adviser to the federal government and, upon its own initiative, to identify issues of medical care, research, and education. Dr. Kenneth I. Shine is president of the Institute of Medicine.

The **National Research Council** was organized by the National Academy of Sciences in 1916 to associate the broad community of science and technology with the Academy's purposes of furthering knowledge and advising the federal government. Functioning in accordance with general policies determined by the Academy, the Council has become the principal operating agency of both the National Academy of Sciences and the National Academy of Engineering in providing services to the government, the public, and the scientific and engineering communities. The Council is administered jointly by both Academies and the Institute of Medicine. Dr. Bruce M. Alberts and Dr. Wm. A. Wulf are chairman and vice chairman, respectively, of the National Research Council.

Contents

Preface

This is the final report of the Committee on Data and Research for Policy on Illegal Drugs. Here, and in its earlier Phase I Report, the committee assesses the knowledge available and needed to inform national drug control policy. I believe that our committee has completed its mission in a manner that does credit to the National Research Council consensus committee process, which strives to provide reasoned, scientifically grounded analyses of issues of national significance.

Drug control policy is a matter of enormous controversy. Perhaps the hardest challenge that our committee faced throughout its three years of work was to remain dispassionate about a subject that engenders strong views. Committee members had to always be conscious that our charge was to inform drug policy, not to recommend policy. We had to keep in mind that an absence of evidence about the merits of current drug policy implies neither that this policy should be abandoned nor that it should be retained. An absence of evidence implies only uncertainty about the merits of current policy relative to possible alternatives.

The absence of evidence came to be the focal concern of the committee, as we gradually concluded that the nation possesses little information about the effectiveness of current drug policy, especially of drug law enforcement. Viewing the unending public debate about drug policy, the committee became painfully aware that what we don't know keeps hurting us. It troubles the committee that we are not able to offer the nation a conclusive or even suggestive basis for choosing among alternative portfolios of prevention, treatment, and enforcement. Some, believing that present knowledge does support one policy or another, may find this report unpalatable. We hope that Americans will take the report as a call to action to initiate data collection and research that will enable more informed policy making in the years ahead.

The committee could not have completed its work without the assistance of many scholars and policy officials who gave unstintingly of their time and shared their resources, their work, and their thinking with us. To gather information on a variety of subjects from a diversity of perspectives, we held four public workshops: Workshop on Cost-Effectiveness Studies, June 23-24, 1998; Workshop on Measuring the Prevalence, Dynamics, and Effects of Illegal Drug Use, November 19-20, 1998; Workshop on Enforcement Activities and the Operation of Drug Markets, May 19-20, 1999; and Workshop on Drug Data Organization, February 17-18, 2000. We thank all of the individuals who served as presenters and discussants at these meetings. They are listed here alphabetically, and with their affiliations at the time of each workshop: Douglas Anglin, University of California at Los Angeles; Steven Belenko, Columbia University; Jonathan Caulkins, Carnegie Mellon University; Jan Chaiken, Bureau of Justice Statistics; Barry R. Crane, Institute for Defense Analyses; Richard Curtis, John Jay College of Criminal Justice; John Eck, University of Cincinnati; Phyllis Ellickson, RAND Corporation; Susan S. Everingham, RAND Corporation; Jeffrey Fagan, Columbia University; Graham Farrell, Rutgers University; Thomas Feucht, National Institute of Justice; Arthur Fries, Institute for Defense Analyses; John Geweke, University of Minnesota; Meyer Glantz, National Institute on Drug Abuse; Don Goldstone, Substance Abuse and Mental Health Services Administration; Jeffrey T. Grogger, University of California, Los Angeles; Lana Harrison, University of Delaware; Jared Hermalin, U.S. General Accounting Office; Jeff Hill, Office of Management and Budget; Ed Hunter, National Center for Health Statistics; Ram Jain, Drug Enforcement Administration; Bruce Johnson, National Drug Research Institute; Lloyd Johnston, University of Michigan; Robert Kaestner, National Bureau of Economic Research; Mark A.R. Kleiman, University of California at Los Angeles; Mike Klein, Food and Drug Administration; George Koob, Scripps Research Institute; Judith Lessler, Research Triangle Institute; Steven Levitt, University of Chicago; Deborah Liederman, Food and Drug Administration; Robert Moffit, Johns Hopkins University; Daniel Nagin, Carnegie Mellon University; Mangai Natarajan, John Jay College of Criminal Justice; David Nelson, Centers for Disease Control and Prevention; Jacques Normand, National Institute on Drug Abuse; Janet Norwood, formerly, Bureau of Labor Statistics; Rafael Perl, Congressional Research Service; Peter Reuter, University of Maryland; Rex A. Rivolo, Institute for Defense Analyses; Lee Robins, Washington University; Christy Schmidt, U.S. Department of Health and Human

Services; Christopher A. Sims, Yale University; Ed Sondik, National Center for Health Statistics; Ken Stark, Washington State; Miron Straf, National Research Council; Patrick Tarr, U.S. Department of Justice; Wendy Taylor, Office of Management and Budget; Jeremy Travis, National Institute of Justice; Craig Uchida, Twenty-first Century Solutions; Tom Vischi, U.S. Department of Health and Human Services; Katherine Wallman, Office of Management and Budget.

The committee is especially grateful to John V. Pepper, University of Virginia, whose work as a consultant to the committee throughout its period of operation was truly invaluable. John contributed greatly through his analyses of critical questions and through his participation in the writing and editing of both this final report and the earlier Phase I Report. We are grateful to Dan Melnick, private consultant and formerly at the Substance Abuse and Mental Health Services Administration and the National Science Foundation, who did much to develop the Workshop on Drug Data Organization and who provided expert advice on issues related to the organization of drug data collection in the federal statistical system. We are also grateful to Bobby Charles, Counsel, U.S. House of Representatives, who provided important information on interdiction issues and who wrote a paper for the committee on the potential for linking data from diverse sources.

We would like to thank the following National Research Council staff: Barbara Boyle Torrey, executive director, Division on the Behavioral and Social Sciences and Education, and Faith Mitchell, deputy director, for their continuous, sound advice and assistance in support of the committee's work; Eugenia Grohman, associate director for reports, for her advice on developing the report and for steering this and the Phase I Report through the National Research Council review process; Christine McShane, for her excellent editorial work at several stages of manuscript preparation; Yonette A. Thomas, who served as study director until July 2000; Kathleen Frydl, research associate, who came late into the project but made important contributions to our response to review and managed the review and final manuscripts; Karen Autrey, senior project assistant, who ably managed the logistics from meeting space to food to finances for the project's first two years; Lecia Quarles, a new project assistant, who proofread the manuscript; and Ralph Patterson, senior project assistant, also new to the project, who managed final travel logistics, project finances, and handled what seemed to be the endless mailing of draft final reports to the committee and reviewers.

This report has been reviewed in draft form by individuals chosen for their diverse perspectives and technical expertise, in accordance with procedures approved by the Report Review Committee of the National Research Council (NRC). The purpose of this independent review is to provide candid and critical comments that will assist the institution in making the published report as sound as possible and to ensure that the report meets institutional standards for objectivity, evidence, and responsiveness to the study charge. The review comments and draft manuscript remain confidential to protect the integrity of the deliberative process.

We thank the following individuals for their participation in the review of this report: David S. Cordray, Institute for Public Policy Studies, Vanderbilt University; Dean Gerstein, National Opinion Research Center, Washington, DC; Arthur S. Goldberger, Department of Economics, University of Wisconsin; Adele Harrel, Director, Justice Policy Center, Urban Institute, Washington, DC; Bob Hoffman, New York City Poison Center; Herbert D. Kleber, Department of Psychiatry, Columbia University College of Physicians and Surgeons; Pamela K. Lattimore, Research Triangle Institutes, Research Triangle Park, North Carolina; Lester Lave, Graduate School of Industrial Administration, Carnegie Mellon University; Philip R. Lee, Institute for Health Policy Studies, University of California, San Francisco; Daniel S. Nagin, H.J. Heinz School of Public Policy, Carnegie Mellon University; Irving Piliavin, Institute for Research on Poverty, University of Wisconsin; Thomas C. Schelling, School of Public Affairs, University of Maryland; Richard Schmalensee, Sloan School of Management, Massachusetts Institute of Technology; Fay Taxman, Department of Criminal Justice, University of Maryland; and Larry Wasserman, Department of Statistics, Carnegie Mellon University.

Although the reviewers listed above have provided many constructive comments and suggestions, they were not asked to endorse the conclusions or recommendations nor did they see the final draft of the report before its release. The review of this report was overseen by Stephen Fienberg, Department of Statistics, Carnegie Mellon University, and Henry Riecken, University of Pennsylvania School of Medicine (emeritus). Appointed by the National Research Council, they were responsible for making certain that an independent examination of this report was carried out in accordance with institutional procedures and that all review comments were carefully considered. Responsibility for the final content of this report rests entirely with the authoring panel and the institution.

Charles F. Manski, Chair
Committee on Data and Research
For Policy on Illegal Drugs

Informing
America's
Policy on
Illegal Drugs

Executive Summary

The consumption of illegal drugs and the design of efforts to control drug use pose some of the most difficult and divisive problems confronting the American public. As a public health and social problem, illegal drugs are responsible for numerous ills, including the premature death of some drug users. The country has borne the weight of the violence and crime that seem to inevitably accompany illegal drug distribution. As a practical problem, recurring drug epidemics have overwhelmed the nation's treatment resources and plagued police forces and a judicial system struggling to maintain order and credibility.

It is little wonder, then, that Americans have turned to public officials at all levels—local, state, and federal—to reduce illegal drug use and mitigate its effects. The most recent figures available from the Office of National Drug Control Policy (ONDCP) indicate that, in 1999, federal expenditures on control of illegal drugs surpassed $17 billion; combined expenditures by federal, state, and local governments exceeded $30 billion. What is more, the nation's so-called "drug war" is a protracted one. The country has spent roughly this amount annually throughout the 1990s. (In comparison, the United States contributed a total of $7.5 billion to the allied effort in the war in the Persian Gulf in 1991.)

Adequate data and research are essential to judge the effectiveness of the nation's efforts to cope with its illegal drug problem. Given the importance of the illegal drug problem and the continuing controversy about how best to confront it, there is a pressing need for the nation to assess the existing portfolio of data and research and to initiate stronger efforts where necessary. Accordingly, at the request of the U.S. Office of National Drug Control Policy, the National Research Council established the Committee on Data and Research for Policy on Illegal Drugs. The committee was given the charge to:

1. assess existing data sources and recent research studies that support policy analysis;
2. identify new data and research that may enable the development of more effective means of evaluating the consequences of alternative drug control policies; and
3. explore ways to integrate theory and findings from diverse disciplines to increase understanding of drug abuse and the operation of drug markets.

The committee's general findings are presented in this, its final report. An earlier Phase I report presented the committee's technical assessment of two studies of cocaine control policy that have played prominent roles in recent policy discussions.

Some of the committee's recommendations, discussed below, are addressed to specific government agencies; it is important to understand, from the outset, how the committee went about assigning responsibility to certain agencies in some instances. As the committee formulated each of its many recommendations, we deliberated about how the recommendations might best be implemented. In particular, we considered which of the numerous existing federal statistical and research agencies might most appropriately be charged with the task of implementing the recommendations. The committee was informed in these deliberations by the presentations of agency representatives in committee-sponsored workshops as well as by the familiarity of committee members and staff with the operation of the relevant agencies. In some cases, the committee had sufficient institutional understanding to be able to recommend that a particular agency or group of agencies be charged with a particular task. In other cases, the committee has not named implementing agencies because it would be too speculative and perhaps even counterproductive for it to do so.

Overall the committee finds that the existing drug use monitoring systems and programs of research are useful for some important purposes, yet they are strikingly inadequate to support the full range of policy decisions that the nation must make. The central problem is a woeful lack of investment in programs of data collection and empirical research that would enable evaluation of the nation's investment in drug law enforcement. We begin with this most critical matter and then turn to other important aspects of drug data and research. A complete list of the committee's recommendations appears in Table 1.1 at the end of Chapter 1.

IMPROVING DATA AND RESEARCH ON ENFORCEMENT

Enforcement activities include enforcement of domestic drug laws that prohibit the manufacture, sale, possession, or use of illegal drugs. They also include international efforts to reduce the supply of drugs through crop eradication and disruption of drug transport. Measured by spending, enforcement activities now constitute the major component of U.S. drug control policy; between 1981 and 1999, expenditures on enforcement increased more than tenfold. The escalation in domestic enforcement is manifest in an inventory of criminal justice processing facts: in 1998, 1.6 million people were arrested for drug offenses, 3 times as many as in 1980, and 289,000 drug offenders were incarcerated in state prisons, 12 times as many as in 1980 (23,900). The benefits and costs of current law enforcement policy and the possibility of alternative strategies continue to be the subject of heated public debate. Yet, because of a lack of investment in data and research, the nation is in no better position to evaluate the effectiveness of enforcement than it was 20 years ago, when the recent intensification of enforcement began.

The committee concludes that the nation's ability to evaluate its enforcement activities is severely hampered by two major data deficiencies: the absence of adequate data on drug consumption and reliable data on drug prices. Current estimates of illegal drug consumption are derived from simple measures of prevalence and frequency of use. Current information on price is derived from data collected for the purpose of providing evidence in criminal trials. As this report demonstrates, these data do not suffice for evaluating enforcement policy.

Consumption data are critical to assess the responsiveness of drug use to enforcement. **The committee recommends that work be started to develop methods for acquiring consumption data.** Existing surveys of drug use collect information on frequencies of use but not on the quantity of drugs that users consume. Data on drug consumption are essential for understanding the operation of drug markets; the dynamics of initiation, intensification, and desistance; the response of drug users to changes in price; and the public health and economic consequences of drug use.

A second key gap in existing data is information on drug prices. It may seem that the accuracy of estimates of the prices of illegal drugs is a technical concern of importance only to a small community of researchers. But accurate drug price data are critical for measuring the success of enforcement policy, a primary aim of which is to increase the retail price of drugs and, thereby, to reduce consumption. Existing price information is collected by the Drug Enforcement Administration and other law enforcement agencies for operational purposes and does not provide reliable indicators of retail price movements in actual drug markets. Nor does it provide an adequate foundation for analysis of the causes and consequences of price changes.

For example, there is a broad consensus that current enforcement policy has increased drug prices relative to what they would be otherwise. However, the country does not know the magnitude of this increase, which aspects of current policy have had this effect, the amount by which it has decreased consumption, or which consumers have been most affected. Similarly, the nation is poorly informed about trends in the prices of illegal drugs, short-run fluctuations in prices, and the effects on prices of law enforcement operations and other policy interventions. All of these questions must be answered if the United States is to judge the effectiveness of its drug control policies or develop policies of greater effectiveness.

The committee recommends that work be started to develop methods for improving existing data and acquiring more reliable drug price data. Until accurate price data are constructed, the nation will be poorly informed about long-term trends and short-term fluctuations in prices of illegal drugs, about the magnitude of expenditures on illegal drugs, and about the efficacy of interventions. In the committee's view, planning activities for better data and research on drug consumption and drug prices could be begun immediately and implemented as soon as a suitable infrastructure and level of funding is in place.

Improved consumption and price data alone will not suffice to strengthen the country's understanding of drug enforcement policy. New empirical research will also be required. Inquiry into supply reduction aspects of enforcement policy has used two methodologies: *impulse-response analysis*, which strings together events to connect a hypothesized cause (the impulse) to the suspected effect (the response), and *systems research*, which develops a formal model of a complex system and then applies the model to predict outcomes.

The committee concludes that the complex dynamics connecting enforcement to domestic drug prices, compounded by the severe limitations of existing data, creates difficult obstacles for the successful use of impulse-response analysis to measure the effects of supply-reduction policies. Even if, as the committee hopes, adequate data should be obtained, the multiplicity of events that affect drug prices, coupled with other forces that affect the time path from a given enforcement action to a response in drug price, makes this type of analysis untenable except in very tightly controlled circumstances.

The committee recognizes that thus far systems research has had to rely on fragile empirical foundations. Scrutiny of current systems models reveals particularly strong needs for empirical research on three questions:

1. *Geographic substitution*: To what extent can producers and traffickers thwart enforcement in one geographic area by moving production or smuggling routes elsewhere?
2. *Deterrence*: How can the deterrent effects of supply-reduction activities be measured? How large are they?
3. *Adaptation*: What is the time lag between successful enforcement operations and adaptive responses on the part of producers and traffickers?

While answers to these questions will not come easily, it is the committee's judgment that systems research has potential to inform supply-reduction policy and should therefore be fortified with research support. **The committee recommends that the Office of National Drug Control Policy should encourage research agencies to develop a sustained program of information gathering and empirical research aiming to discover how drug production, transport, and distribution respond to interdiction and domestic enforcement activities. The committee strongly recommends that empirical research address the three critical issues of geographic substitution, deterrence, and adaptation.**

Not all of enforcement policy is directed toward reduction of the supply of illegal drugs. An important component of such policy, especially recently, has been to attempt to reduce the demand for drugs by deterring use and by incapacitating users. Using sanctions to reduce demand can also facilitate treatment of arrested users. A rational drug control policy must take appropriate account of the benefits and costs of enforcing sanctions against drug users. Here too, research is sorely lacking. **The committee recommends that the National Institute of Justice and the National Institute on Drug Abuse collaboratively undertake research on the declarative and deterrent effects, costs, and cost-effectiveness of sanctions against the use of illegal drugs. Particular attention should be paid to the relation between severity of prescribed sanctions and conditions of enforcement and the rates of initiation and termination of illegal drug use among different segments of the population.**

The committee recognizes that improvement of data on drug consumption and prices, strengthening the empirical foundation for systems research, and assessment of enforcement policy aimed at drug users pose a set of challenging tasks whose accomplishment will require new resources. However, we view these enhancements of data and research as neither impossible to accomplish nor prohibitive in cost. It is worth keeping in mind how little is currently spent on drug data and research relative to the country's expenditure implementing its drug policy. The federal government, according to the ONDCP, currently invests approximately $780 million each year to monitor illegal drug use and conduct research on drug policy, but less than 15 percent of this amount goes for research on enforcement. Funding for research on enforcement policy is minimal, particularly when compared with the amount spent on carrying out enforcement policy. In 1999, only $1 was spent on enforcement research for every $107 spent on enforcement itself. Moreover, in any given year, the greater part of enforcement research funds go to support criminal justice system operations (i.e., crop eradication research, crime analysis for investigations, analysis of case-loads in the federal courts) technology development, and drug testing, rather than data collection and social science research (Office of National Drug Control Policy, 2000).

The committee has concluded that effective research on enforcement policy requires not only the necessary funding but also creation of the appropriate research infrastructure. Other government examples are relevant here. The Department of Labor is called on to make sophisticated projections regarding the economy and employment. In order to do so, it created the Bureau of Labor Statistics (BLS). The BLS is a statistical agency separate from the operational programs of the department, a circumstance that enables it to concentrate on its charge and command the services of the relevant academic researchers. In the drug treatment research arena, the National Institute on Drug Abuse (NIDA) serves a similar purpose. In the committee's view, creating an infrastructure to support enforcement research is essential to the design of sound data collection systems and to the development of an integrated research program. Yet we understand the difficulty of creating a new agency to perform even this very important work.

Therefore, in order to facilitate collection of better drug enforcement data and the implementation of a strong research program, **the committee recommends that the National Institute of Justice, the National Science Foundation, and the Bureau of Justice Statistics should be assigned joint responsibility and given the necessary funding to build the scientific infrastructure for research on illegal drug markets and the effects of drug control interventions.**

The suggested organization takes advantage of the specific expertise of the National Institute of Justice in law enforcement research, the statistical expertise of the Bureau of Justice Statistics, and of the specific expertise of the National Science Foundation in economic research. In our judgment, Congress should provide new funds for this effort. While determining specific costs was beyond the committee's charge, funding levels provided to NIDA for data and research on treatment may serve as an instructive example.

In sum, the committee recommends a four-part approach for improving data and research on drug law enforcement: (1) development of new data collection systems on illegal drug consumption and the price of illegal drugs, (2) support for strengthening the empirical foundations of systems research, (3) support for research on the effectiveness of enforcement policy aimed at drug users, and (4) establishment of an infrastructure to facilitate the work.

OTHER MAJOR RECOMMENDATIONS

The committee was asked to review the entire range of data and research that might inform policy on illegal drugs. The discussion above identifies the most obvious shortcomings of the present portfolio. Existing programs that monitor the prevalence of drug use and those that study treatment and prevention receive more resources and are therefore further developed. Still, the committee makes a number of major recommendations whose implementation should further strengthen the nation's data and research on illegal drug use and policy. We arrived at these recommendations through a review of selected data collection systems and research literature and through analysis that revealed limitations in present knowledge.

Monitoring Drug Use

The committee examined the four major systems that collect annual data on large samples to monitor patterns and trends in drug use in the United States. Two of these, the National Household Survey of Drug Abuse (NHSDA) and Monitoring the Future (MTF), are national surveys based on probability samples of known populations, respectively: people who live in households and people who attend schools. The two other data systems sample events rather than people: arrests in the Arrestee Drug Abuse Monitoring program (ADAM) and emergency room visits and some deaths in the Drug Abuse Warning Network (DAWN). We draw several conclusions regarding data gaps and the need to improve these programs.

First, the committee concludes that the subpopulations established by research to be at highest risk for drug abuse that causes serious harm—people in prisons and jails, hospitals, residential treatment centers, homeless people, and school dropouts—are not adequately covered by any of these four surveys. **The committee recommends that methods be devel-**

oped to supplement the data collected in the National Household Survey of Drug Abuse and Monitoring the Future in order to obtain adequate coverage of subpopulations with high rates of drug use.

Second, the chronic problem in survey research of inaccurate response is particularly acute in surveys of drug abuse, since illegal drug use is a stigmatized behavior and respondents are reluctant to report it accurately. Without a better estimate of inaccurate response, researchers and policy makers can not be confident in the inferences drawn from existing data monitoring illegal drug use. The committee is encouraged by a recent project to evaluate inaccurate response in the NHSDA, but this project is only a first step. **The committee strongly recommends a systematic and rigorous research program (1) to understand and monitor inaccurate response in the national use surveys and (2) to develop methods to reduce reporting errors to the extent possible.**

Third, longitudinal data—examining a set of variables in the same subjects or population over time—regarding causes and patterns of drug use, the effects of drug use on behavior, and the effects of policies on drug use are critical to an assessment of drug policy. Existing data that are federally supported in the Monitoring the Future survey have not been shared with the research community because of unresolved problems of protecting the confidentiality of such data. Therefore, the quality of the data cannot be assessed objectively, nor can judgments about whether to collect additional longitudinal data be made. In the committee's judgment, these data must be made available to the broader research and policy community. **The committee recommends that the Office of National Drug Control Policy and the granting agency (currently the National Institute on Drug Abuse) establish an oversight committee of statisticians and other experts, knowledgeable in procedures for balancing the needs for public access with the goal of confidentiality, to establish guidelines for providing access and for monitoring whether access to the data is quickly and easily provided.**

Prevention of Drug Use

Prevention encompasses an array of noncoercive activities intended to prevent, reduce, or delay illegal drug use. The committee reviewed the research literature on the effectiveness of a wide range of prevention activities and found mixed results. Some prevention activities appear to be effective at delaying the initiation or reducing the frequency of marijuana use, as well as tobacco and alcohol use by minors. However, because most evaluations are of school-based approaches, the success of many other approaches is unknown. Popular programs, such as "zero tolerance" strategies, have not been evaluated at all, or as in the case of project D.A.R.E., have been found to have little impact on illegal drug use. Large amounts of public funds are therefore being allocated to programs whose effectiveness is unknown or known to be limited.

In light of these findings, **the committee recommends a major increase in current efforts to evaluate drug prevention efforts. Further research is needed to better understand (1) effects of the entire spectrum of plausible approaches to prevention proposed or in use, rather than those that are most easily evaluated; (2) effects of drug prevention programs implemented under conditions of normal practice, outside the boundaries of the initial tightly controlled experimental tests of program efficacy under optimal conditions; (3) effects of different combinations of prevention programs, for example, how they complement each other or detract from one another when used in combination, as they most often are; and (4) the extent to which experimentally induced delays in tobacco, alcohol, and marijuana use yield reductions in later involvement with cocaine and other illegal drugs specifically, and long-term effects of prevention programming more generally.**

Treatment of Drug Use

Official guidelines for research-based treatment, as well as numerous scholarly reviews of drug treatment programs, have been published over the past decade. Their findings are not repeated here. Rather, this report presents recommendations for improvement in the science of drug treatment evaluation. In particular, there is a need for better information on the potential benefits and costs of drug treatment as an adjunct or alternative to criminal justice sanctions and coercive treatment policies.

In the committee's view, development of more effective treatments, as well as more accurate information on variations in treatment effectiveness for different groups of recipients, would be facilitated by performance of successive, randomized controlled clinical trials. A sequence of studies featuring random assignment of clients to different treatment conditions would increase the likelihood and rapidity with which improved treatments could replace less effective ones, and it would help avoid introducing costly innovations that may later be found to be ineffective or even cause harm.

Because treatment availability is limited and some drug users lack motivation, only a small proportion of all drug-dependent individuals receive treatment. Moreover, results derived from self-selected patients who remain in treatment optimistically skew findings in favor of effectiveness. Because of ethical problems with randomly assigning patients requesting treatment to a no-treatment condition, existing studies do not provide data on addiction in the absence of any treatment. In our judgment, researchers miss opportunities for randomized trials with no-treatment controls in settings in which such trials would be practical and ethical—for example, criminal justice settings, in which many drug-involved offenders otherwise go untreated. **The committee recommends that treatment researchers take greater advantage of possible opportunities for randomization to no-treatment control groups. For example, we strongly encourage studies of incarcerated and postincarcerated prisoners as outlined in this report. The committee urges federal and state agencies and private institutions to minimize organizational obstacles to such studies, within ethical and legal bounds.**

Organizational Improvements

In our review of data and research on drug use and drug policy, the committee found important gaps. Some data are missing altogether, while other data need improvement in order to be truly useful for supporting policy design and evaluation.

Many of these problems emanate from a lack of funding support and from the fragmentation of drug data collection over a large number of federal agencies. Each of the major statistical collections reviewed herein is managed by a different agency, none of which has statistical reporting as its major focus. We reiterate our concern regarding the lack of data and research on drug enforcement policies and, in conclusion, we dwell especially on a need overall for strengthening the professional staffs and capabilities of organizations responsible for data collection and analysis, and for increasing the independence of their operations.

The numerous substantive recommendations in this report cannot be implemented without improvements in the practices of statistical agencies and a consolidation of the federal effort. In particular, two key steps are necessary for improving the quality of data on illegal drugs:

1. Efforts should be taken to strengthen the professional staffs and capabilities of the organizations responsible for data collection and analysis and to increase the independence of their operations.

2. Data collection should over the long run be consolidated into a small number of statistical agencies, perhaps two, which would take a leadership role in organizing and collecting statistical data at the federal level.

Upgrading collection efforts in existing agencies and consolidation of data collection are essential tasks for improving the scope and quality of data on illegal drugs. Unless these organizational goals are achieved, the nation will continue to be poorly informed and policies on illegal drugs will be operating largely in the dark. But the committee recognizes that these steps require determined and effective leadership. Our final recommendation therefore concerns the need for leadership in organizational improvements and reorganization. **The committee recommends that the Office of National Drug Control Policy place organizational improvements for data high on its agenda in the immediate future. If it does not move quickly to implement the changes required to improve statistical data the President and Congress should find other ways to ensure that the substantive and organizational changes are swiftly and effectively achieved.**

THE CHALLENGE AHEAD

Three decades ago, Congress decided to diversify the federal response to drug problems, investing in surveillance, biobehavioral and etiological research, and education and treatment. As a result, the nation has the data systems and research infrastructure needed to assess the effectiveness of preventive and therapeutic interventions. Although further improvements are needed in these areas, as explained in this report, the data and research capacity are in place. In stark contrast, neither the data systems nor the research infrastructure needed to assess the effectiveness of drug control enforcement policies now exists. It is time for the federal government to remedy this serious deficiency. It is unconscionable for this country to continue to carry out a public policy of this magnitude and cost without any way of knowing whether and to what extent it is having the desired effect.

REFERENCES

National Research Council
   1999   *Assessment of Two Cost-Effectiveness Studies on Cocaine Control Policy.* Committee on Data and Research for Policy on Illegal Drugs. C. Manski, J.V. Pepper, and Y. Thomas, eds. Washington, DC: National Academy Press.
Office of National Drug Control Policy
   2000   *National Drug Control Strategy: Performance Measures of Effectiveness; FY 2001 Budget Summary.* Washington, DC: Government Printing Office.

Part I

Introduction and Background

1

Introduction

Our nation employs a variety of means to reduce the consumption of illegal drugs and mitigate their adverse consequences. Choosing the right mix of instruments presents a complex policy decision; there are many different lines of attack. To manage this complexity, policy makers and the public have often adopted simple dichotomies, contrasting law enforcement approaches with medical approaches and supply-reduction approaches with demand-reduction approaches. Everyone seems to agree that the nation ought to use a portfolio of instruments that appropriately balances these broad categories, yet views on how close the nation now is to the optimal balance differ a great deal.

The sharp disagreements about drug control policy that persist in U.S. society have both normative and empirical components. On the normative side, people in America vary in their moral judgment of drug use and in their concern with the collateral consequences of drug control activities. On the empirical side, people vary in their assessment of the effectiveness of the drug abuse prevention, drug treatment, domestic law enforcement, and foreign interdiction activities that have formed the elements of U.S. drug control policy. The continuing debate about drug control policy manifests itself in many ways, among which is an annual battle within the federal government on the allocation of funding across different instruments.

Data and research cannot resolve disagreements about the morality of drug use, but they may be able to narrow the divergence of views on the effectiveness of drug control policy today and contribute to the formation of more effective policy tomorrow. With this in mind, the White House Office of National Drug Control Policy (ONDCP) requested the National Research Council (NRC) to convene a committee to study the data and research needed to inform national policy on illegal drugs. The Committee on Data and Research for Policy on Illegal Drugs was formed in early 1998 under the aegis of the NRC's Committee on Law and Justice and Committee on National Statistics. Its charge was to:

1. assess existing data sources and recent research studies that support policy analysis;
2. identify new data and research that may enable the development of more effective means of evaluating the consequences of alternative drug control policies; and
3. explore ways to integrate theory and findings from diverse disciplines to increase understanding of drug abuse and the operation of drug markets.

This report represents the results of the committee's work.

As part of its work, the committee earlier assessed in depth two studies that evaluated the cost-effectiveness of alternative drug control instruments in reducing domestic consumption of cocaine—one by analysts at RAND (Rydell and Everingham, 1994) and the other by analysts at the Institute for Defense Analyses (IDA) (Crane, Rivolo, and Comfort, 1997). These two studies, which have drawn considerable attention, used very different methodologies and drew sharply different conclusions. The committee's evaluation of the two studies was transmitted to the Office of National Drug Control Policy in April 1999 as its Phase I report, *Assessment of Two Cost-Effectiveness Studies of Cocaine Control Policy*.[1] The Executive Summary of the Phase I report, which describes the committee's main findings, is included in this volume as Appendix C.

CHANGING PERSPECTIVES ON DRUG CONTROL POLICY

As a prelude to discussion of the scope and themes of the report, we think it helpful to review how the prevailing perspectives on drug control

---

[1]Points of view different from that of the committee regarding its Phase I Report are expressed in comments received from some of the authors of the Institute for Defense Analyses (IDA) and RAND studies. These comments are available to the public in the NRC public access file for this project. All references in both the Phase I and final reports to the IDA analysis or findings are based solely on the 1997 IDA report by Crane, Rivolo, and Comfort. All references to the RAND analysis or findings are based solely on the 1994 RAND report by Rydell and Everingham.

policy came to be. A constructive way to do so is to look historically at the evolution of drug policy and the language that has been used to discuss it.

Law Enforcement and Medical Approaches

Current drug policy has its roots in the adoption of the Harrison Narcotics Act in 1914.[2] Although framed as a tax measure, the goal of the statute was to suppress the nonmedical use of what are called narcotic drugs (a classification that encompassed morphine, heroin, and other opiates, as well as cocaine). The effect was to criminalize the manufacture, sale, and possession of these drugs outside medical channels. An aggressive campaign of enforcement by federal authorities was deployed in the 1920s to terminate the practice of opiate maintenance by physicians and clinics. Eventually, the prohibitory approach was extended by Congress to marijuana in 1937, and during the 1930s and 1940s all state legislatures enacted a parallel set of laws. Penalties for narcotics offenses were increased in the 1950s, and new psychoactive pharmaceutical products were brought under federal control in the 1960s in an effort to suppress nonmedical use of these drugs. This accumulation of federal and state antidrug statutes was replaced in 1970 by the federal Controlled Substances Act and by parallel acts at the state level.

Until the 1970s, enforcement of this comprehensive array of drug prohibitions was the predominant instrument of the nation's antidrug policy. What was called the law enforcement approach was generally understood as a relatively complete policy: drugs are dangerous to the social order. Therefore, it is both just and useful to prosecute those who supply drugs and those who use them. By setting out laws against these activities and enforcing them, individuals would be dissuaded and deterred from supplying and using drugs. If some persisted despite the prohibition, it would be both just and effective to incapacitate them as threats to society.

In the late 1950s and 1960s, however, the dominance of this law enforcement model was challenged by some influential lawyers and physicians who wanted to respond to drug addiction with medical methods (including civil commitment) rather than prosecution and punishment. In their view, chronic drug use was not a wholly voluntary choice but rather a disease to which some helplessly succumbed. The disease may have had its roots in biology, in the social conditions in which people lived, or in the dependence-producing power of the drugs themselves. But whatever

---

[2]For a historical summary of drug policy predating the Harrison Act, see Institute of Medicine (1990: Volume 1, Chapter 2).

the sources, once these factors are present, an individual's ability to act independently is undermined. Given this fact, it seemed both unjust and ineffective to respond to drug use among individuals as a crime. It seemed unjust because addicts were unable to decide to stop using drugs; ineffective because deterrence would fail, and incapacitation would work only as long as the restraint continued.

What they proposed as an alternative was the medical treatment of drug users. The most radical version of the approach called for drugs now banned to be legally available to addicts, their use to be regulated by physicians who could prescribe the drugs to patients under their care. For much of the 1960s, drug policy was locked in a debate between "cops and docs." Should society continue its commitment to law enforcement, or should it shift to the medical approach?

Steps were taken in the 1970s to combine the law enforcement and medical approaches into a single framework. In 1972, Congress enacted legislation embracing one of the core positions of the proponents of the medical approach—that people with drug problems should be given incentives and assurances of confidentiality to encourage them to enter treatment. In addition, the federal government supported programs to use criminal prosecution as a lever for treatment participation. Congress also appropriated funds to support drug treatment programs. The debate between cops and docs receded in a policy environment in which both approaches were used simultaneously.

Supply-Reduction and Demand-Reduction Policies

In the late 1960s and early 1970s, drug policy analysts began talking in somewhat different terms. Influenced by economic theory, they now referred to supply-reduction and demand-reduction policies. These terms became particularly prominent in the 1980s when the ONDCP was created, with its deputy directors for demand and supply reduction.

Supply-reduction strategies focused on limiting the supply of drugs that might flow to illegal markets, while demand-reduction strategies focused on reducing the demand for drugs. To some, the new idea of supply and demand policies was almost indistinguishable from the old idea of cops and docs. Supply-reduction strategies looked like law enforcement, and demand-reduction strategies looked like drug treatment. However, there were important differences in thinking about drug policy in terms of supply and demand rather than in terms of enforcement and treatment.

First, in the new conception that distinguished supply and demand approaches, law enforcement was divided into two parts. Enforcement efforts directed at drug producers and distributors were considered supply-reduction strategies, and enforcement efforts directed at drug users were considered demand-reduction strategies.

Second, new supply-reduction instruments emerged that were not enforcement activities. The idea took hold that those now engaged in the production of heroin and cocaine in Asia, South America, and elsewhere might be persuaded to stop not by the threat of crop eradication and arrest, but through subsidies supporting efforts to shift production to other, less profitable crops. Similarly, programs to improve the labor market conditions of disadvantaged youth might induce street-level drug dealers to move into legitimate employment. In addition, it was an explicit strategy of major multimodality treatment programs in the early 1970s to reduce local heroin supplies by recruiting user-dealers into treatment. Thus, crop substitution programs, youth employment programs, and programs treating user-dealers became part of the nation's portfolio of drug control instruments.

Third, a new demand-reduction strategy, drug abuse prevention, assumed a more important place in thinking about drug policy. Of course, law enforcement already aimed to prevent drug use. Drug laws put society on notice that use of certain drugs is deviant, and enforcement of these laws sought to deter potential drug users by threatening arrest and incarceration. The new notion of drug abuse prevention brought into play efforts by schools, neighborhood groups, and parents to persuade youth and other populations at risk that drug use is bad and dangerous. It also brought into play efforts by the military, civilian employers, and schools to deter drug use by initiating drug-testing programs and by levying noncriminal sanctions (e.g., fines, suspensions, dismissal) on soldiers, employees, and students found to use drugs.

Box 1.1 displays these different policy instruments in the form of a matrix that shows how the original ideas of the law enforcement and

BOX 1.1 Matrix of Drug Control Instruments

	Supply Reduction	*Demand Reduction*
Law enforcement	Crop eradication Disruption of transport Domestic enforcement	Criminal sanctions for possession/use Coerced treatment
Medical	Regulation of pharmaceuticals	Drug treatment
Socioeconomic	Crop substitution Youth employment programs	Drug education and persuasion Noncriminal sanctions

medical approaches are related to the newer ideas of supply-reduction and demand-reduction policies. There is also a third dimension to this matrix: it is useful to distinguish federal efforts from state, local, and community efforts to deal with drug use, and think of national drug control policy as being the sum of efforts that are undertaken at these different levels of government.

Complementarities

Perhaps the most important advance in thinking about drug policy has been the idea that instruments drawn from the different categories may complement one another in a constructive manner. Thinking in terms of complementarities leaves behind the simple dichotomies of past conceptualizations of drug policy, opening new possibilities for combining instruments in innovative ways. Complementarities can also appreciably complicate the already difficult problem of assessing the effectiveness of alternative drug-control strategies.

One aspect of thinking about complementarities combines law enforcement directed at drug users with treatment of those users. For many years it was thought that law enforcement approaches conflicted with treatment approaches. At a philosophical, ideological, or political level, this may still be true. That is, the politics of drugs tends to align those who favor law enforcement approaches as the just and effective response to drug abuse, against those who favor treatment and prevention approaches to drug abuse. Operationally, however, it is increasingly recognized that different instruments may complement one another, in the sense that each one allows the other to perform better than it could alone.

For example, law enforcement may help treatment by putting pressure on drug users to seek and remain in treatment, or by providing a direct referral source for drug users who have not yet decided to volunteer for treatment. Drug treatment may help law enforcement succeed by providing a lower cost, more effective response to drug-using offenders than jail or prison, and by softening the harsh consequences of drug law enforcement that would otherwise apply. These positive complementarities between enforcement and treatment, however, must be balanced against the possibility that efforts to coerce drug users into treatment may widen the reach and deepen the intensity of punishment.

Complementarities may also exist among drug control instruments operating at different levels of government. It may be that international and federal enforcement efforts create conditions under which local efforts to control street-level drug markets can plausibly succeed in reducing the local availability of drugs. Conversely, effective local law enforcement may provide some of the leads that are necessary to allow federal law enforcement efforts to become effective. In a different vein, federal financing of research on treatment may allow for more effective treatment efforts than localities could mount on their own.

Moreover, as society has learned to see drug use in epidemic as well as endemic terms, people have begun to realize that the value of a particular policy instrument in a broader portfolio of drug control instruments may vary with time. At the early stage of an epidemic, it may be wise to combine drug abuse prevention activities with law enforcement so as to minimize its spread. At later stages, when rates of initiation of drug use have slowed, it may be that the emphasis should shift to treatment. Thus, thinking about complementaries among drug control instruments should recognize the dynamics of drug problems.

SCOPE AND THEMES OF THE REPORT

The charge to the committee requested a study of data and research to inform drug control policy. In one very important sense, this charge set a clear limit on the scope of the committee's work. Our mandate was the positive task of informing drug policy, not the normative task of recommending policy. Thus the reader of this report will not find policy prescriptions herein. In particular, the report neither endorses nor condemns current drug control policy.

Yet the charge as stated is very broad. It was clear at the outset that achievement of a useful, well-grounded consensus report would require that the committee limit the scope of its work. As does every NRC committee, we had to confront the reality that, however pressing and important the problem of public policy may be, a time-limited committee of volunteers assisted by a small staff needs to choose its themes carefully if it is to contribute at all.

Considering how best to use our time and resources, we were mindful that earlier committees of the National Academies had previously investigated some aspects of the nation's drug problems, although not the broad question of how data and research might inform policy. Box 1.2 lists these recent reports on drug problems. We have aimed to build on and complement this work, not duplicate it. We also were aware that our own efforts to inform drug control policy would undoubtedly be followed by those of others, who may in turn build on our work.

With these thoughts in mind, the committee reached several strategic decisions on scope and themes that ultimately shaped this report. We call attention to these decisions here, so that readers will better anticipate what to expect and not expect in the chapters that follow.

**BOX 1.2   Recent Reports of the National Academies
on Drug Problems**

Institute of Medicine

1990   *Treating Drug Problems*, Volume 1. Committee for the Substance Abuse
        Coverage Study. Dean Gerstein and Henrick J. Harwood, editors. Wash-
        ington, DC: National Academy Press.

1992   *Treating Drug Problems*, Volume 2. Committee for the Substance Abuse
        Coverage Study. Dean R. Gerstein and Henrick J. Harwood, editors.
        Washington, DC: National Academy Press.

1995   *The Development of Medications for the Treatment of Opiate and Co-
        caine Addictions: Issues for the Government and Private Sector.* Com-
        mittee to Study Medication Development and Research at the National
        Institute on Drug Abuse. Carolyn E. Fulco, Catharyn T. Liverman, and
        Laurence E. Earley, editors. Committee to Study Medication Develop-
        ment and Research at the National Institute on Drug Abuse. Washing-
        ton, DC: National Academy Press.

1996   *Pathways of Addiction: Opportunities in Drug Abuse Research.* Commit-
        tee on Opportunities in Drug Abuse Research. Washington, DC: Nation-
        al Academy Press.

1997   *Dispelling the Myths About Addiction: Strategies to Increase Under-
        standing and Strengthen Research.* Committee to Identify Strategies to
        Raise the Profile of Substance Abuse and Alcoholism Research. Wash-
        ington, DC: National Academy Press.

1999   *Marijuana and Medicine: Assessing the Science Base.* Janet E. Joy,
        Stanley J. Watson, Jr., and John A. Benson, Jr., editors. Washington,
        DC: National Academy Press.

National Research Council

1993   *Preventing Drug Abuse: What Do We Know?* Committee on Substance
        Abuse Prevention Research. Dean R. Gerstein and Lawrence W. Green,
        editors. Washington, DC: National Academy Press.

1993   *Under The Influence? Drugs and the American Work Force.* Jacques
        Normand, Richard O. Lempert, and Charles P. O'Brien, editors. Com-
        mittee on Drug Use in the Workplace. Washington, DC: National Acad-
        emy Press.

Illegal Drugs

The first major decision that the committee made was to focus on substances whose sale or use is illegal in America today, taking the legal status of drugs as given. A more expansive scope for our work could easily have been justified. From a public health perspective, addiction to such legal substances as tobacco and alcohol may constitute problems more severe in their adverse consequences than addiction to such illegal drugs as cocaine, heroin, or marijuana. From a behavioral perspective, complementaries in the use of legal and illegal drugs have been conjectured in the "gateway hypothesis," which posits that the early use of tobacco and marijuana is usually a precursor to the use of hard drugs, while the substitutability of legal and illegal psychoactive drugs has been emphasized by economic models that focus on the role of prices in determining drug use. From a legal perspective, it is useful to keep in mind that the legal status of addictive substances is not immutable; drug laws are made by and can be changed by society.

All of these considerations notwithstanding, the committee made a pragmatic decision to focus its attention on the illegal drugs that are the targets of present-day drug control policy. We decided that any attempt to confront the public health problems posed by alcohol and tobacco would make the task entirely unmanageable. We do, however, cite data and research on alcohol and tobacco when they may offer lessons for analysis of illegal drugs, for example, when studying the drug use of minors. We decided that changes in the legal status of addictive substances, such as the prohibition of alcohol and the legalization of marijuana, are not sufficiently under active consideration by policy makers for this committee to contemplate what data and research may have to say about these policy options.

Indeed, the committee has for the most part focused on a subset of illegal drugs. This report dwells on cocaine, with lesser attention to heroin, and still less to other drugs. Giving primacy to cocaine may be natural in light of the "crack" cocaine crisis that gripped American society in the 1980s and the continuing position of cocaine as a focus of research and a flash point in the public debate about drugs. Yet the committee is aware that patterns of drug use may change with time. Twenty years ago it would have been natural to give primacy to heroin, and this may again be the case in the near future. Or one of numerous synthetic addictive substances may pose the overriding drug threat of tomorrow. Be this as it may, the broad substantive concerns and methodological issues addressed in this report will remain germane to drug policy.

Chapter 2 of this report summarizes the state of knowledge about the determinants of use of illegal drugs, and the consequences for users and society. This chapter is not concerned with drug control policy per se. Rather, it provides basic background for consideration of policy.

Data for Monitoring Drug Problems

A second major decision was to choose the types of data to consider in depth. The committee decided to focus substantial attention on data regularly collected by the federal government, which are widely used to monitor the nation's drug problems. Two annual population surveys, the National Household Survey of Drug Abuse (NHSDA) and Monitoring the Future (MTF), form the country's main sources of information on trends and cross-sectional patterns in drug use. The government also supports regular data collection on the drug use of persons who experience certain events—including arrest, incarceration, and hospital emergency room treatment. The Arrestee Drug Abuse Monitoring Program collects drug use data on arrestees; various Bureau of Justice Statistics surveys collect such information on prisoners; and the Drug Abuse Warning Network collects information on hospital emergency room visits related to drug use.

The Drug Enforcement Administration's System to Retrieve Information from Drug Evidence (STRIDE) is the main existing source of information on drug prices. These and other data collection activities of the federal government provide the primary descriptive information that policy makers and the public presently use to gauge the overall dimensions of the nation's drug problems. These data collection systems are described and evaluated in detail in Chapter 3.

The committee views accurate description of trends and cross-sectional patterns in drug use, prices, and other relevant variables as essential to informed development of drug control policy. Hence the committee decided not only to scrutinize the various data collection systems now in place but also to consider principles for regular collection of drug-related data in the federal statistical system. We examine the various data collection systems in Chapter 3 and make recommendations for the federal statistical system in Chapter 4.

This report focuses on the structure of the various data collection systems, not their findings. The annual report on the National Drug Control Strategy of the Office of National Drug Control Policy draws on these data sources in an effort to provide a comprehensive portrait of drug problems in the United States.

Modes of Research

A third decision, reflecting the committee's charge, was to consider research that bears directly on drug policy, not basic research on drug addiction. Chapters 5 through 8 report the committee's assessment of the research currently available to support analysis of drug control policy and make recommendations for improvements. Chapter 5 examines supply-reduction policy in totality, ranging from foreign interdiction to local policing strategies. Chapters 6, 7, and 8 examine the three main elements of demand-reduction policy: sanctions against use of illegal drugs (Chapter 6), drug education, persuasion, and other prevention activities (Chapter 7), and treatment of drug users (Chapter 8).

As the committee went about its work, it found very different modes of research in use to evaluate different instruments of drug control policy. At one extreme, establishment of the National Institute on Drug Abuse in the 1970s has fostered the development of a considerable body of research on drug treatment that has sought to adhere to the model of medical research. Here the units of analysis are individuals, and randomized clinical trials are considered to be the "gold standard." Observational studies of samples of individuals receiving different treatments are viewed as expedients that may have to serve until randomized trials can be performed.

At another extreme, the few studies of foreign interdiction performed to date have employed either the observational approach of impulse-response analysis or the theory-oriented approach of systems research. These modes of research reflect the difficulty of the problem. The units of analysis for study of interdiction policy are large geographic regions within which the interactions of many distinct actors determine drug production and distribution. Moreover, interdiction studies have had to make do with hardly any data at all on the behavior of these agents. After all, it is very difficult to obtain evidence about illegal enterprises, especially those operating in foreign countries.

The committee does not see much prospect for convergence to a common mode of research on different aspects of drug control policy. Hence Chapters 5 through 8 vary considerably in the tenor of their discussions and in the foci of their recommendations. The committee acknowledges that the effectiveness of drug treatment, prevention, and law enforcement activities cannot be evaluated with equal ease or rigor. However, a common standard of proof can and should be applied to assess the credibility of all research aiming to inform policy. The strength of the policy conclusions drawn in a study should always be commensurate with the quality of the evidence. For a complete list of the committee's recommendations, see Table 1.1 at the end of this chapter.

The Nation's Investments in Data and Research:
Focus on Enforcement

As the committee went about its work, it discovered that the research available to evaluate different instruments of drug control policy varies as dramatically in magnitude as in mode. We found the central problem to be a serious lack of investment in programs of data collection and empirical research that would enable evaluation of the nation's investment in drug law enforcement.

Existing programs of data and research on drug treatment and prevention receive more resources and are therefore further developed. The committee does make recommendations whose implementation should further strengthen the nation's understanding of treatment and prevention, but these recommendations are mainly meant to improve programs of data and research that are already in place. It is the committee's view that to inform enforcement policy will require initiation of entirely new programs, as well as development of appropriate organizational infrastructure to support them.

Between 1981 and 1999 the nation's expenditures on enforcement increased more than tenfold. The escalation in domestic enforcement is manifest in an inventory of criminal justice processing facts: in 1998, 1.6 million people were arrested for drug offenses, 3 times as many as in 1980, and 289,000 drug offenders were incarcerated in state prisons, 12 times as many as in 1980 (23,900). The benefits and costs of current law enforcement policy and the possibility of alternative strategies continue to be the subject of heated public debate. Yet, because of a lack of investment in data and research, the committee has reluctantly concluded that the nation is in no better position to evaluate the effectiveness of enforcement now than it was 20 years ago, when the recent intensification of enforcement began.

Collection of the data and performance of the research needed to inform enforcement policy will require new resources. The committee has not attempted to determine the specific costs of the initiatives recommended in this report. To explain the absence of cost estimates, it may suffice to observe that the task of producing them lay beyond the charge to the committee. However, the more basic reason why the committee does not provide cost estimates is that any such estimates would be too speculative to be useful. Our recommendations for new data and research to inform enforcement policy call for the nation to begin the process of developing a coherent body of knowledge. The proper time to produce specific cost estimates will be when that process is under way.

What the committee can say is that we view the recommended enhancements of data and research as neither impossible to accomplish nor prohibitive in cost. It is the committee's view that Congress should provide new funds for this effort. Consider how little is currently spent on drug data and research relative to the country's expenditure implementing its drug policy. The federal government, according to the ONDCP, currently invests approximately $780 million each year to monitor illegal drug use and conduct research on drug policy, but less than 15 percent of this amount goes for research on enforcement. Funding for research on enforcement policy is minimal, particularly when compared with the amount spent on carrying out enforcement policy. In 1999, only $1 was spent on enforcement research for every $107 spent on enforcement itself. Moreover, in any given year, the greater part of enforcement research funds go to support criminal justice system operations (i.e., crop eradication research, crime analysis for investigations, analysis of caseloads in the federal courts), technology development, and drug testing, rather than data collection and social science research. [3]

Implementation of Recommendations

As the committee formulated each of its many recommendations, it deliberated about how they might best be implemented (Table 1.1 lists all of the recommendations at the end of this chapter). In particular, we considered which of the numerous existing federal statistical and research agencies might most appropriately be charged with the task of implementing the recommendations. The committee was informed in these deliberations by the presentations of agency representatives in committee-sponsored workshops as well as by the familiarity of committee members and staff with the operation of the relevant agencies. In some cases, the committee had sufficient institutional understanding to be able to recommend that a particular agency or group of agencies be charged with a particular task. In other cases, the committee has not named implementing agencies because it would be too speculative and perhaps even counterproductive for us to do so.

The committee deliberated especially fully on how the nation might best implement its recommendations on data collection for monitoring

---

[3]In 1991, the federal investment in enforcement research was $111.6 million, or 2.5 percent of federal domestic enforcement expenditures and 0.5 percent of the total expenditure on drug control. By 1999, federal funds alone for enforcement had increased to $12.3 billion, reflecting a near doubling in spending on domestic enforcement over 1991 levels, yet enforcement research funding remained essentially stable at $113.2 million (Office of National Drug Control Policy, 2000).

drug problems. A full chapter of this report (Chapter 4) examines this question.

Present-Oriented and Forward-Looking Analysis of Drug Policy

Early in its deliberations, the committee found it essential to distinguish between two senses, one present-oriented and the other forward-looking, in which data and research can inform drug policy. We recognize that an analysis may be of value to decision makers today if it makes the best use it can of whatever data are currently available in order to furnish advice or reach conclusions about actions that must be taken now, before better data can be gathered and interpreted. The premises of such an analysis should be explicit, and the logic that links its steps should be transparent. Its conclusions should appropriately convey the uncertainty that is inevitable given the limitations of the existing data. But more than this should not be asked of it.

Our report looks mainly to the future. The committee has been asked to explore how new data might enable research that yields much more definitive assessments of drug policy than are possible at present. It may take several years, a decade, or more to gather and interpret crucial data that are now unavailable—during which policy makers must continue to make do as they have in the past. But in the longer run, a sustained and systematic effort to develop firm empirical foundations for drug policy is necessary if the nation is to have any hope of improving the quality of its decision making.

It makes no sense to continue to argue about drug policy for additional decades, as we have so often in the past, in terms of plausible but unverified assumptions about the nature of drug production, distribution, and use. If society is to make wiser decisions in the years ahead, we must now decide on a strategy to identify the critical empirical questions for drug policy and take the steps needed to answer these questions. Initiating this process is the important task addressed in this report.

REFERENCES

Institute of Medicine
  1990   *Treating Drug Problems*, Volume 1. Committee for the Substance Abuse Coverage Study. Dean Gerstein and Henrick J. Harwood, editors. Washington, DC: National Academy Press.
Office of National Drug Control Policy
  2000   *National Drug Control Strategy: Budget Summary February 2000*. Washington, DC: U.S. Government Printing Office.

TABLE 1.1 Committee Recommendations Listed By Chapter

Recommendation	Page Number	Agency or Agencies	Research	Data	Procedure or Infrastructure
Data Needs for Monitoring Drug Problems: Chapter 3					
The committee recommends that the Office of National Drug Control Policy and the granting agency (currently the National Institute on Drug Abuse) establish an oversight committee of statisticians and other experts, knowledgeable in procedures for balancing the needs for public access with the goal of confidentiality, to establish guidelines for providing access and for monitoring whether access to the data is quickly and easily provided.	83	ONCDP NIDA			X
The committee recommends that the granting agency require that the contractors who gather data for Monitoring the Future move immediately to provide appropriate access to the longitudinal data. The committee recommends that if access is not provided in accordance with the guidelines of the oversight committee, the Office of National Drug Control Policy and the granting agency consider whether the public interest requires relocating the grant in another organization that will provide the level of access necessary for the data to be most useful for purposes of informing public policy on illegal drugs.	84	ONCDP NIDA		X	
The committee recommends that work be started to develop methods for acquiring consumption data.	86	NIJ NSF BJS		X	

continues

TABLE 1.1 Continued

Recommendation	Page Number	Agency or Agencies	Research	Data	Procedure or Infrastructure
The committee recommends that methods be developed to supplement the data collected in the National Household Survey of Drug Abuse and Monitoring the Future in order to obtain adequate coverage of subpopulations with high rates of drug use.	88	SAMHSA ONDCP NIDA BJS		X	
The committee recommends a systematic and rigorous research program (1) to understand and monitor nonresponse and (2) to develop methods to reduce nonresponse to the extent possible.	95	NIDA SAMSHA	X		
The committee strongly recommends a systematic and rigorous research program (1) to understand and monitor inaccurate response in the national use surveys and (2) to develop methods to reduce reporting errors to the extent possible.	100	NIDA SAMSHA	X		
The committee recommends that the Office for National Drug Control Policy and the Centers for Disease Control and Prevention undertake to develop principles and procedures for information and surveillance systems on illegal drug-taking and its associated hazards.	105	ONCDP CDC	X		
The committee recommends that work be started to develop methods for improving existing data and acquiring more reliable drug price data.	111	NIJ BJS NSF		X	
The committee recommends that a major effort be devoted to "importing" standard procedures on constructing price indices into the development of price indices for illegal drugs. This effort should take place in collaboration with federal statistical agencies that specialize in this area, particularly the Bureau of Labor Statistics.	116	NIJ BJS NSF BLS	X		

Recommendation	Page	Agency	
The committee recommends that consideration be given to constructing a set of satellite accounts that track the flows in sectors comprising legal and illegal drugs. This set of accounts would be called the National Drug Accounts. These satellite accounts would not enter into the current core national income and product accounts.	117	BJS NIJ NSF	X

Drug Data Organization: Chapter 4

Recommendation	Page	Agency	
The committee recommends that public-use files of all major statistical series should be deposited in a data library. On a broader level, every agency sponsoring the collection of population-based data related to illegal drugs should require in their contracts and grants the timely deposit of public-use files in an appropriate data library or its dissemination in other ways.	129	ONDCP NIDA BJS SAMSHA CDC	X
The committee recommends the formation of an executive branch board to review proposed data collection protocols that might be used as a part of a research effort to design, collect, report, and validate statistical series on economic data, such as prices, expenditures, and consumption. It may be necessary to have rules or legislation enabling the board to exercise its functions in a manner that clearly separates law enforcement from this research enterprise.	130	ONDCP	X
The committee recommends that the Office of National Drug Control Policy place organizational improvements for data high on its agenda in the immediate future. If it does not move quickly to implement the changes required to improve statistical data the President and Congress should find other ways to ensure that the substantive and organizational changes are swiftly and effectively achieved.	135	ONCDP	X

TABLE 1.1 Continued

Recommendation	Page Number	Agency or Agencies	Research	Data	Procedure or Infrastructure
Supply-Reduction Policy: Chapter 5					
The committee recommends that the Office of National Drug Control Policy should encourage research agencies to develop a sustained program of information gathering and empirical research aiming to discover how drug production, transport, and distribution respond to interdiction and domestic enforcement activities. The committee strongly recommends that empirical research address the three critical issues of geographic substitution, deterrence, and adaptation.	157	ONDCP NSF BJS NIJ	X	X	
The committee recommends research on how illegal drug prices are determined. Much law enforcement activity is aimed, at least in part, at increasing the price of drugs. Without reliable knowledge of how retail prices are determined, one can only speculate about the effectiveness of such programs.	166	BJS NSF NIJ	X		
The committee recommends survey research on the labor supply of illegal drug dealers.	169	BJS NIJ NSF	X		
The committee recommends that state and local governments be encouraged to explore and assess alternative approaches to law enforcement, including decreases as well as increases in the intensity of enforcement. Organizational arrangements should be made to ensure that the resulting changes in law enforcement measures and policy are well designed and that the data needed to evaluate their consequences are acquired and analyzed.	178	BJS NIJ NSF			X

Sanctions Against Users of Illegal Drugs: Chapter 6

			X
The committee recommends that the National Institute of Justice and the National Institute on Drug Abuse collaboratively undertake research on the declarative and deterrent effects, costs, and cost-effectiveness of sanctions against the use of illegal drugs. Particular attention should be paid to the relation between severity of prescribed sanctions and conditions of enforcement and the rates of initiation and termination of illegal drug use among different segments of the population.	195	NIJ NIDA	X
The committee recommends that the National Institute of Justice and the National Institute on Drug Abuse collaborate in stimulating research on the effects of supplemental sanctions, including loss of welfare benefits, driver's licenses, and public housing, on the use of illegal drugs.	197	NIJ NIDA	X
The committee recommends that the Bureau of Labor Statistics monitor the measures taken by employers to discourage use of illegal drugs by their employees, including drug testing, and that the National Institute on Drug Abuse support rigorous research on the preventive effects and cost-effectiveness of workplace drug testing.	201	BLS NIDA	X
The committee recommends that the National Institute on Drug Abuse and the Office of Educational Research and Improvement support rigorous research on the preventive effects, costs, and cost-effectiveness of drug testing in high schools, with a particular emphasis on the relationship between drug testing and other formal and informal mechanisms of social control.	203	NIDA OERI	X

TABLE 1.1 Continued

Recommendation	Page Number	Agency or Agencies	Research	Data	Procedure or Infrastructure
Preventing Drug Use: Chapter 7					
The committee recommends additional research to assess the effectiveness of social competency skill development and normative education approaches, which emphasize conveying correct information about the prevalence of drug use and its harmful effects.	227		X		
The committee recommends additional research on prevention practices implemented under conditions of normal practice so that variability in effects from study to study may be better understood. The committee recommends further research on alternative methods and targeting mechanisms for teaching social competency skills.	227		X		
The committee recommends a major increase in current efforts to evaluate drug prevention efforts. Further research is needed to better understand (1) effects of the entire spectrum of plausible approaches to prevention proposed or in use, rather than those that are most easily evaluated; (2) effects of drug prevention programs implemented under conditions of normal practice, outside the boundaries of the initial tightly controlled experimental tests of program efficacy under optimal conditions; (3) effects of different combinations of prevention programs, for example, how they complement each other or detract from one another when used in combination, as they most often are; and (4) the extent to which experimentally induced delays in tobacco, alcohol, and marijuana use yield reductions in later involvement with cocaine and other illegal drugs specifically, and long-term effects of prevention programming more generally.	234	X			

Treatment of Drug Users: Chapter 8

The committee recommends that priorities for the funding of treatment evaluation research should be changed; large-scale, national treatment inventory studies should not be conducted at the expense of greater funding for randomized controlled clinical trials.	249	NIDA	X
The committee recommends greater scientific attention to now-missed opportunities to conduct randomized trials of drug treatments with no-treatment control conditions.	258	NIDA	X
The committee recommends that treatment researchers take greater advantage of possible opportunities for randomization to no-treatment control groups. For example, we strongly encourage studies of incarcerated and postincarcerated prisoners as outlined in this report. The committee urges federal and state agencies and private institutions to minimize organizational obstacles to such studies, within ethical and legal bounds.	263	NIDA	X
The committee strongly recommends that treatments intended to benefit people be evaluated in carefully conducted randomized controlled experiments.	263	NIDA	X
The committee recommends broader use of meta-analytic techniques for cumulating and comparing findings across treatment outcome studies.	265	NIDA	X

TABLE 1.1 Continued

Recommendation	Page Number	Agency or Agencies	Research	Data	Procedure or Infrastructure
Final Thoughts: Chapter 9					
The committee recommends that the National Institute of Justice, the National Science Foundation, and the Bureau of Justice Statistics should be assigned joint responsibility and given the necessary funding to build the scientific infrastructure for research on illegal drug markets and the effects of drug control interventions.	277	NIJ NSF BJS			X

NOTE:
BJS= Bureau of Justice Statistics
BLS= Bureau of Labor Statistics
CDC= Centers for Disease Control and Prevention
NIDA= National Institute on Drug Abuse
NIJ= National Institute of Justice
NSF= National Science Foundation
OERI= Office of Educational Research and Improvement
ONDCP= Office of National Drug Control Policy
SAMHSA= Substance Abuse and Mental Health Services Administration

2

Determinants and Consequences
of Drug Use

I n this chapter, the committee provides a general overview of the ex-
tant research on the determinants and consequences of drug use, with
special emphasis on methodology and integration among research tra-
ditions. In it we do not make recommendations; rather, this chapter provides relevant background material for analyses of illegal drug policy.

DETERMINANTS OF DRUG USE

A basic understanding of the determinants of drug use, especially of
abuse and addiction, is a prerequisite to serious discussion of drug control policy. Different research disciplines, from neuroscience to economics
to social psychology, offer distinct perspectives. These perspectives are
not mutually exclusive, but, in practice, each discipline has investigated
some determinants of drug use to the exclusion of others. Efforts to integrate the various disciplines will enhance understanding of drug use and
help to inform drug policy.

Advances in neuroscience suggest that the addiction process involves
multiple factors that vary across drugs, individuals, and the environment
(O'Brien, 1995). To focus only on one of these elements is to oversimplify,
yet research on drug use has often isolated certain variables to the exclusion of others. For example, economic research tends to focus on the price
of illegal drugs as a general measure of the incentives faced by consumers
(Becker and Murphy, 1988; Orphanides and Zervos, 1995; Hung, 2000).
Other nonpecuniary costs undoubtedly also influence drug use, but they

have been hard to quantify, so economic research into these areas has been scant. Little is known about the incentives provided by legal and social sanctions aiming to deter drug use (discussed in Chapter 6). Moreover, economists have generally not considered environmental, family, or peer influence on drug use. Conversely, social psychologists have studied individual, family, peer, neighborhood, and social risk factors for drug use but have generally neglected the economic costs of using drugs.

The first section of this chapter summarizes what is known about the determinants of drug use and describes methodological and data-related problems in evaluating these determinants. It begins with a review of the neuroscience perspective, with an emphasis on how the effects of drug use vary across drugs, individuals, and their circumstances. It then examines economic research on the price sensitivity of drug use. Finally, it summarizes what is known about how individual and social factors may influence drug use.

This survey is intentionally brief. The literature on the determinants of drug use is enormous in volume and scope. Researchers in criminology, economics, sociology, psychology, biochemistry, neurobiology, and epidemiology have sought to understand the determinants of illegal drug use. Since a comprehensive survey of this large literature is beyond the purview of this report, this section attempts to summarize key features of the knowledge base that may be important to evaluate the effectiveness of drug control policies. For a contemporary and more comprehensive review of what is known about the addictive process, see the recent Institute of Medicine reports, *Pathways of Addiction* (1996) and *Dispelling the Myths About Addiction* (1997).

The Neuroscience Perspective on Addiction

Many medical researchers view addiction as a disease similar to other chronic and relapsing conditions, such as asthma, diabetes, and hypertension (Institute of Medicine, 1995, 1996, 1997; O'Brien and McLellan, 1996; Leshner, 1997). According to this perspective, the physical dependence created by some drugs plays a relatively minor role. Treating the pain and suffering that starts when drug use stops is straightforward, while effective intervention to prevent relapse into drug-taking is quite complex. Long-term changes to the brain circuitry and the emotional cues that can trigger this circuitry may last a lifetime (Institute of Medicine, 1997). As with any chronic relapsing disease, understanding the dynamic processes of initiation, escalation, reduction, persistence, and relapse are especially important and difficult challenges. The processes that affect initiation of drug use are not identical to those that promote persistence of drug use or development of drug dependence (e.g., see Tsuang et al., 1999; Stallings et al., 1999; Kendler et al., 1999; Bucholz et al., 2000). Similarly, the processes that influence relapse are not necessarily identical to either of these earlier processes (e.g., see Siegel, 1984; Childress et al., 1993; Brewer et al., 1998; Robbins et al., 2000).

Advances in the neuroscience of addiction are beginning to provide a strong scientific basis for drug abuse treatment and prevention programs as well as other drug control policies (Institute of Medicine, 1996). Neuroscientists have long linked drug addiction with some disruption of the brain reward system (Olds and Milner, 1954; Wise, 1978; Cooper et al., 1996). Many drugs, including illegal drugs, can change feeling-states and may induce pleasurable feelings through actions within the central nervous system. This can happen in a number of different ways, depending on the drug, and often involves the neurotransmitter dopamine (Institute of Medicine, 1997). Normally, after release, a "transporter" returns dopamine back to the neuron that released it.[1] Cocaine causes a buildup of dopamine by effectively blocking the transporter and preventing the neurotransmitter from deactivating. Amphetamine causes the neuron to release more dopamine by essentially putting the transporter into "reverse." Heroin, alcohol, and other drugs also affect an array of reward and neurotransmitter pathways, some (but not all) linked to the dopamine transporter mechanisms (e.g., see Ritz et al., 1987, 1988; Maldonado et al., 1997; Self, 1998; Yoshimoto et al., 2000).

An important feature of the addictive process is that the feeling-states induced by drug use can be affected by past consumption. The mechanisms are different for each category of drug: nicotine, opioids (heroin), sedatives (alcohol), and stimulants (cocaine, amphetamines). Some research on the stimulant drugs suggests a sensitization model. According to this model, repeated use of stimulants sensitizes certain aspects of the reward system so that a small amount of the drug or even an environmental cue previously associated with the drug can precipitate renewed drug use. Desensitization, or tolerance, involves a different model, in which exposure to a drug causes less response than was previously caused. This phenomenon is particularly prominent with opiates, such as heroin, and sedatives, such as alcohol. Tolerance can be explained in part by the response of the nervous system acting to maintain a constant balance of neural activity in spite of major changes in stimulation. The nervous system integrates attempts to keep the body in a state of equilibrium.

These neuro-adaptive changes are critical for producing addiction. Taken with adequate dose and frequency, addictive drugs produce long-

---

[1]Recent evidence points to other potential pathways of reinforcement-related neurotransmission (e.g., see Cornish et al., 1999; Cornish and Kalivas, 2000; Koob, 2000).

lasting changes in brain functioning that continue after the last dose of the drug (Leshner, 1997; O'Brien, 1995).[2] While all illegal drugs affect brain systems, they do so in different ways and thus have different behavioral effects. Table 2.1 displays nine general classes of drugs by functional or behavioral activity. In terms of behavioral responses, alcohol and marijuana are sedating, whereas cocaine and amphetamines are powerful stimulants. Opiates such as heroin have multiple effects, including stimulation, relaxation, and analgesic actions. Nicotine stimulates and relaxes different systems. All of these are associated with the development of dependence, and all can lead some users to report craving, obsession-like thinking about drug use, and compulsion to use drugs, even when the degree of stimulation or sedation is minimal.

Other drug-related conditions and processes also come into play, including the purity and efficacy of one drug relative to another. Similarly, the route of administration appears to influence the addictive properties. Drugs that are smoked or injected reach the brain more rapidly than those that are ingested; these routes of administration are associated with more rapid onset and produce more powerful effects. The importance of purity and mode of administration can be demonstrated in considering the coca plant. Crack cocaine is far more addictive than chewed coca leaves, although both come from the same source. Crack cocaine is smoked, thereby producing volatized pure drug in the lungs' surface area. This process is far more fast-acting and addictive than occurs when powder cocaine absorbed via the nasal passage (Institute of Medicine, 1997).[3]

The potency and form of administration may also play important roles in the initiation and intensification process. Smoking and injecting drugs cause discomforts that may discourage use and intensification. In contrast, ingesting drugs in either liquid or tablet form is not likely to cause similar physical discomfort.

---

[2]There is a recent line of neuroscience research on the mechanisms that govern sensitization and tolerance, including research on postsynaptic signaling mechanisms. Through this research, it has been possible to discover pathways by which exposure to cocaine and other drugs can provoke neural and behavioral plasticity. It appears that the plasticity occurs in response to a cocaine-associated alteration in the expression of genes within the nucleus of the neuron postsynaptically. This cocaine-modulation of gene expression is linked to development of sensitivity to the drugs, possibly contributing to the drug dependence process (e.g., Kelz et al., 1999).

[3]It would be unethical to expose cocaine-naïve human subjects to crack cocaine and to powder cocaine in order to determine which form of cocaine is more "addictive," but the presently available evidence suggests most rapid and pronounced development of cocaine dependence symptoms when crack cocaine is smoked or when powder cocaine HCl is injected intravenously (e.g., see Gossop et al., 1994; Hastukami and Fischman, 1996).

TABLE 2.1   Classification of Abusive and Additive Drugs

Class	Description
Caffeine	Produces wakefulness, mild central nervous system (CNS) and cardiovascular stimulation, Mild tolerance, dependence following chronic use.
Alcohol	Produces dose-dependent relaxation, disinhibition, mild euphoria, inebriation, intoxication, CNS depression, liver damage. Significant tolerance and dependence-withdrawal following chronic use; intense craving, alcoholism.
Nicotine	Produces mild CNS and cardiovascular stimulation. Tolerance and dependence-withdrawal following chronic use; intense craving; nicotine addiction.
Depressants (sedatives, hypnotics, anxiolytics): barbiturates, methadqua-lone, diazepam, and other benzodiazepines	Produce dose-dependent relaxation, disinhibition, mild euphoria, inebriation, intoxication, CNS depression. Significant tolerance and dependence withdrawal following chronic use; craving; addiction.
Cannabinoids (marijuana, hashish: tetrahydrocan-nabinol (THC)	Produce dose-dependent relaxation, disinhibition; alterations of mood, emotion and behavior; inebriation, intoxication. Mild tolerance.
Opiates (opioids) and related analgesics: heroin, codeine, morphine, synthetic opioids.	Produce dose-dependent analgesia, euphoria, disinhibition, anesthesia, CNS depression. Significant tolerance and dependence-withdrawal following chronic use; intense craving; opioid addiction.
Stimulant: cocaine, amphetamine, methamphetamine, methylphenidate	Produce dose-dependent mild-strong CNS stimulation, behavioral hyperactivity, adverse cardiovascular effects, euphoria. Tolerance and dependence withdrawal following chronic use; intense craving; addiction.
Hallucinogens: lysergic acid diethylamide (LSD), mescaline, psilocybin, dimethyltryptamine (DMT), dimethoxymethyl-amphetamine (DOM), MDA, MDMA ("ecstasy"), phensyclidine (PCP; "angel dust") ketamine	Symptoms vary depending on which drug: visual distortions, hallucinations, mood changes, arousal, euphoria, anxiety, agitation, emotional withdrawal, thought disturbances, aggressive behavior, panic, catatonia. Mild tolerance with chronic use; little or no withdrawal.
Inhalants: solvents, aerosols, acetone, benzene, nitrous oxide, amyl nitrate	Produce dose-dependent relaxation, mild euphoria, dizziness, disinhibition, inebriation, intoxication, anesthesia, CNS depression, liver damage, cardiovascular depression.

Source: Institute of Medicine (1997:Table 1.1).

Why do some people who experiment with drugs become addicted, while others do not? The answer to this question is quite complicated. The ways in which a particular drug activates, reinforces, and desensitizes pleasure can vary with dose, frequency, and chronicity of use; drugs also vary in their effects across individuals and environments. Medical researchers often view the contraction of a disease as an interaction of an agent, a host, and the environment. Applying this framework to drug use, the agent is the drug taken. As described above, drugs differ in effect. The host refers to the characteristics of the individual drug user, including genetic makeup, family history, traits of temperament or personality (e.g., openness to experience, or to risk-taking behavior), affiliation with drug-using peers who provide models for drug-taking behavior, and expectations about the drug effects. Individuals respond to the same drug in the same dose in different ways. The last piece of this disease contraction sequence, the environment, refers to availability of the drug and the sociocultural context surrounding its use. Experience and social context exert powerful effects on the brain and thus on behavior. Environmental cues also alter the effects of use. Thus the addiction process involves multiple simultaneous factors that vary across drugs, individuals, and environments (O'Brien, 1995).

Economic Research on Price Sensitivity

Economic research on the determinants of drug use focuses on the relationship between quantity consumed and price. In particular, a demand function relates consumption of a commodity to its price. The price elasticity of demand is the percentage change in consumption that is caused by a 1 percent change in the price. For example, if a 1 percent increase in the price causes a 0.5 percent decrease in consumption, then the price elasticity of demand is –0.5. It may seem that demand for an addictive substance is likely to be insensitive to price, so that the price elasticity of demand is close to zero, but this is not necessarily the case. The demand for cigarettes provides an illustration. The many studies of the price elasticity of demand for cigarettes have found that the long-run price elasticity of demand is in the range –0.27 to –0.79 for the population as a whole and –0.9 to –1.3 for college students (Chaloupka, 1991; Becker et al., 1994; Chaloupka and Wechsler, 1997).

Demand functions and price elasticities must be understood to formulate effective drug policies. In particular, many antidrug policies are aimed at increasing the price that consumers must pay for a drug. If demand does not change when the price increases, then such policies will have little effect on consumption but will increase drug sellers' earnings. These policies may also increase property crimes by consumers who need more money to buy higher-priced drugs. A policy that has such effects is counterproductive. In contrast, if demand is highly sensitive to price, then policies that increase drug prices will cause desirable decreases in consumption and sellers' earnings.

Recent estimates of price elasticities of demand for cocaine and heroin vary widely, although several studies report elasticities that are quite high (that is, the elasticities may have large negative values).[4] Caulkins (1995) obtained price elasticity estimates of –2.5 and –1.5 for cocaine and heroin, respectively. Saffer and Chaloupka (1995) estimated the price elasticity of participation (that is, the fraction of individuals who use an illegal drug) to be in the range –0.8 to –0.9 for heroin and –0.4 to –0.6 for cocaine. Grossman et al. (1996) estimated the long-run price elasticity of participation in cocaine use to be in the range –1.3 to –1.6, and estimated the long-run price elasticity of frequency of use conditional on participation to be –0.5. Chaloupka et al. (1998) obtained estimates of cocaine participation elasticities by youths in the range –0.2 to –1.0. The elasticity of frequency of use conditional on participation was in the range –0.3 to –0.5, and the estimated elasticity of demand was in the range –0.6 to –1.5. In summary, recent estimates of the price elasticity of demand for cocaine span a range of –0.6 to –2.5.

It is difficult to know how one should judge the various estimates of price elasticities of demand for cocaine and heroin. In addition to spanning a very wide range, they all suffer from a variety of severe conceptual and data-related difficulties, which are described below. The effects of these problems on estimation accuracy are unknown. Accordingly, existing estimates of demand functions and price elasticities should be treated as only suggestive. Certainly, none can be extrapolated to an environment in which prices for illegal drugs are much lower than they are now (due, for example, to a reduction in the penalties for possession, distribution, or sale).

Why Estimating Demand Functions and Price Elasticities Is Difficult

In the committee's judgment, the severe, unsolved conceptual and data-related problems involved in the estimation of demand functions for illegal drugs mean that no persuasive demand function for cocaine or other illegal drugs has yet been estimated. The problems with existing estimates include:

---

[4]Caulkins and Reuter (1998) and Saffer and Chaloupka (1995) review earlier elasticity estimates. These vary widely but tend to be closer to zero than are more recent estimates.

1. Lack of reliable price data. The development of a demand function consists of using statistical methods to relate observed price changes to changes in consumption. Price data that indicate what consumers *really* pay are needed to do this. The committee found that existing data on the prices of illegal drugs do not represent actual drug prices in cities.

2. Price dispersion. The prices of illegal drugs vary greatly among transactions. The same dealer may charge different prices to different buyers, and prices may vary greatly over the distance of a few city blocks. In addition, the prices paid by different buyers may change in different ways over time. Moreover, a buyer may have some control over the price he pays. One way of controlling the price is by choosing the amount to purchase. There is substantial quantity discounting of cocaine and heroin, even within the range of quantities found in retail transactions. Thus, the price per unit purchased is likely to be lower if the quantity purchased is large than if it is small. A consumer may also be able to influence the price by his choice of seller. In particular, a consumer may choose to familiarize himself with several sellers and may choose not to buy from a high-priced seller if he knows that a lower-priced one is nearby. The committee knows of no model of demand for illegal drugs that takes account of potential price dispersion. All studies that have come to our attention use a price index as a proxy for sale prices. The price index typically is an estimate of the cost of one gram of pure cocaine or heroin in a city. The index is constant over all transactions in a given city and year (see Chapters 3 and 5 for a detailed discussion).

3. Other costs. The sale price is only one of the costs that a consumer pays for an illegal drug. There are also search costs (the time spent looking for a seller), the costs associated with any legal penalty that may be incurred if the consumer is arrested, and, possibly, psychological costs associated with committing an illegal act. The committee found no source of data on search costs and no demand model that attempts to incorporate these costs.[5] Data are available on legal penalties for possessing illegal drugs (see Chapter 6 for further discussion of this issue). The committee knows of three studies that have incorporated these into a model of de-

---

[5]ADAM (Arrestee Drug Abused Monitoring) asks arrested drug users whether there was a time during the 30 days preceding the interview when they attempted to buy drugs and had the cash but were unsuccessful. ADAM also asks the reasons for lack of success. The answers to these questions provide crude indicators of the search costs experienced by ADAM respondents. It is not known whether the difficulties in buying drugs experienced by ADAM respondents are representative of difficulties experienced by consumers in general. No study that the committee knows of has used information from ADAM to construct an indicator of search costs for a demand model.

mand for an illegal drug (Saffer and Chaloupka, 1995; Chaloupka et al., 1998; DeSimone, 1998).

4. Lack of quantity data. Data on the quantities of drugs that consumers buy do not exist. To be most useful, a dataset should give quantities purchased in individual transactions, but even city-level aggregate consumption data might be useful.[6] Because quantity data are not available, existing demand models use proxies. One common proxy is participation; this is a binary indicator (or a yes/no measure) of whether an individual has used a specified drug in a specified time period such as the past 30 days. Another proxy is the frequency of use (the number of times that an individual has used a drug in a specified time period). Some studies use both proxies—for example, Grossman et al. (1996) and Chaloupka et al. (1998)—estimate models of participation and of frequency of use conditional on participation. The accuracy of participation and frequency of use as proxies for quantity consumed is unknown (see Chapter 3 for further discussion of quantity data).

5. Addiction. The utility that a consumer obtains from current consumption of an addictive drug depends on his past consumption (Becker and Murphy, 1988). Therefore, in a demand model for an addictive drug, current consumption depends on past consumption in addition to the price. If the consumer is foresighted, then current consumption also depends on future consumption (Becker et al., 1994). The dependence of current consumption on past and (possibly) future consumption increases the difficulty of obtaining suitable consumption data. Specifically, longitudinal consumption data measuring the quantity consumed over time are needed.[7] The Monitoring the Future (MTF) survey provides longitudinal data on participation and use frequency by youths. Grossman et al. (1996) used these data to estimate a demand function for cocaine that takes account of the effects of addiction. No other consumption study reviewed by the committee was longitudinal. Instead, studies employed a

---

[6]Aggregate consumption in the U.S. as a whole has been estimated by combining estimates of numbers of consumers, expenditure estimates obtained from arrested consumers interviewed by DUF (the predecessor of ADAM), and price estimates obtained from STRIDE (Office of National Drug Control Policy, 1997). The resulting consumption estimates are not available for individual cities and, in any case, are probably too crude for use in estimating demand functions.

[7]Becker et al. (1994) estimated a model of the demand for cigarettes by using state-level aggregate consumption data (a time-series of cross-sections) instead of panel data. They assumed that state-level aggregates can be treated as consumption by a representative consumer. Becker et al. (1994) did not discuss the accuracy of this assumption. The assumption is problematic for cocaine, because cocaine consumers are highly heterogeneous. The representative consumer assumption cannot account for differences between the consumption patterns of casual and heavy users of cocaine.

cross-sectional model, relating an indicator of current consumption to the current price, which does not take the effects of addiction into account.

6. Heterogeneity of consumers. Cocaine consumers include casual and heavy users. These two groups face similar prices (or distributions of prices) but have very different consumption patterns. The levels of the demand functions of casual and heavy users are obviously different. It is possible that the slopes (the changes in consumption due to a unit change in price) are also different. For example, casual users may be more responsive to changes in prices than are heavy users. If so, the high elasticities of participation found in recent studies of demand may mainly reflect responses of casual users to price fluctuations. In addition, the finding that frequency of use (conditional on participation) is less responsive to price than the number of users may be strongly influenced by the behavior of heavy (high frequency) users who are relatively insensitive to price changes. No demand model that the committee has seen allows for the possibility that casual and heavy users have different price sensitivities.

7. Cross-elasticities. Some illegal drugs may be substitutes or complements for others. If so, the demand for one drug may depend on the price of another. Most studies have ignored such cross-elasticity effects. Two exceptions are models of demand for heroin and cocaine by Caulkins (1995) and a model of marijuana participation by DeSimone (1998). Moreover, possible complementarities are the focus of research on what has been called the gateway effect (see Chapter 7 for further discussion).

8. The dynamics of drug use. No existing empirical model of demand for drugs describes the process by which individuals initiate and make transitions among different levels of drug use (for example, from nonuse to casual use, from casual use to nonuse or heavy use). Everingham and Rydell (1994), Rydell and Everingham (1994) and Everingham et al. (1995) propose a conceptual framework for modeling such transitions. However, the data that are required for empirical study of drug use dynamics and their dependence on prices and other costs of drug use are not available to researchers. Implementation of such a study would require a longitudinal dataset that describes drug use by individuals over time. The Monitoring the Future survey gathers longitudinal data on participation and frequency of use by youth, but it rarely makes the data available to researchers.

9. Heterogeneity of drugs. Cocaine is sold in several chemically distinct forms (mainly cocaine base and powder cocaine). These forms have different prices, and consumers consider them to be different products. It is therefore likely that different forms of cocaine have different demand functions and price elasticities. The committee is aware of no study that has estimated separate demand functions or price elasticities for different forms of cocaine.

The lack of suitable data is the most serious obstacle to developing better demand functions and estimates of price elasticities. It is unlikely that significantly better estimates can be developed without better data on retail prices, quantities transacted and consumed, and search costs. Improved data on quantities and search costs will be most useful if they are longitudinal. Without reliable price and consumption data, it is not possible to predict the outcomes of policy measures aimed at influencing the price or availability of illegal drugs, and it is not possible to evaluate the effects of these policies after they have been implemented.

Individual and Social Risk Factors

Some research explores the statistical association of drug use with risk factors, which characterize individuals or their environment. Risk factors are conditions and processes that, when present, signal an increased likelihood that individuals will develop a behavior or a health-related condition (Garmezy, 1983).[8] A large literature provides a wealth of information on the risk factors associated with drug use: children growing up with addicted parents are more likely to use and abuse, deviant adolescents are more likely to use as adults, individuals residing in high-crime areas are more likely to use, etc. These and other risk factors are sometimes taken to be "candidate causes" of drug use—suspected causal influences for which there may not be enough evidence to make a firm claim of causation.

Other risk factors, in contrast, signal a reduced likelihood of a behavior or condition, such as drug use or drug dependence. Some are thought to act by offering direct resistance to ill health or maladaptation. The gene-linked enzymes involved in alcohol and nicotine metabolism, which encourage drowsiness or another symptom that discourages further use, are of this type. Others are thought to act by canceling or modifying the negative effects of risk-increasing factors. For example, frequent participation in church-related activities may reduce the risks associated with living in neighborhoods with street-level drug markets (Crum et al., 1996). Some may directly reduce a dysfunction, lessen the effect of the risk-increasing factors, disrupt the process through which certain factors operate to cause a dysfunction, or prevent the initial occurrence of deleterious factors (Coie et al., 1993).

---

[8]In the prevention field, no single theoretical model has been embraced, although most organized prevention activities rely on a risk and protective factor framework (Van Etten and Anthony, 1999; Institute of Medicine, 1994). Hansen and O'Malley (1996) identify eight different theoretical models that have dominated prevention activities.

BOX 2.1   Categories of Risk Factors

Individual Predisposing Factors:
> Early and persistent antisocial, aggressive, or rebelliousness behavior
> Impulsiveness, low self-control, sensation-seeking
> Low levels of social and emotional competency

Informal Controls:
> Attachments to parents and other individuals
> School success/attachment to school/commitment to education or work
> Belief in rules in general

Social Influences to Use:
> Association with/exposure to drug-using models: parents, siblings, or
> peers
> Low levels of parental supervision and monitoring
> Parental/sibling attitudes favorable to drug use
> Psycho-social work environment

Perceived Norms Favoring Drug Use:
> Lax or inconsistently enforced laws limiting the possession, use or sales
> of drugs
> Unclear or inconsistent messages about substance use
> Inconsistent application of consequences for use
> Incorrect perceptions of the prevalence of use

Suspected risk factors can be organized into the clusters shown in Box 2.1.[9] Early-established personality characteristics (e.g., irritable temperament, harm-avoidant personality traits, social anxiety, maladaptive or aggressive behavior in early elementary school) may predispose some individuals to seek dangerous thrills or constrain their capabilities for recognizing and avoiding risky situations. People with psychiatric disorders, including depression, attention deficit disorder, and anxiety disorders, have higher risks of using and abusing drugs. Individuals with these characteristics may be more likely to experiment with drugs, to continue using drugs, and to fail to reduce drug use in the face of persistently harmful consequences.

Certain individuals may also be at higher risk of becoming drug users due to inherited traits. While not definitive, a mounting body of evidence suggests that the genetic pathways are related to the adverse conse-

---

[9]These characteristics, conditions, and processes are reviewed in detail elsewhere (Anthony and Helzer, 1995; Gottfredson, 2000; Gottfredson, et al., 1996; Hansen and O'Malley, 1996; Hawkins et al., 1992; 1995; Institute of Medicine, 1994, 1996, 1997) and are not repeated here.

quences of drug-taking and possibly initiation and continuation of use (Institute of Medicine, 1996, 1997). Studies of families show that children of alcoholics are at much higher risk of developing the disorder even if adopted at birth and raised by nonalcoholic adoptive parents. Studies of twins and adopted children suggest that early onset of alcoholism is strongly influenced by genetic factors, while later onset seems more strongly influenced by environmental and emotional factors. Some Asians with a specific genotype are biologically protected from becoming alcoholics. Caucasians are not known to have this genotype, but there is evidence of genetic influence on early tolerance to alcohol and with it an increased vulnerability to alcoholism (Institute of Medicine, 1996; Yoshida et al., 1991). Animal studies have demonstrated strong genetic influences over both use and intensification, and while specific genes and combinations of genes have not yet been identified, there is evidence for the inheritance of a variety of alcohol-related traits, including preference, sensitivity, tolerance, and withdrawal (e.g., see Argawal and Goedde, 1990; Yoshida et al., 1991; Uhl et al., 1995; Institute of Medicine, 1996, 1997; Merikangas et al., 1998b; Tsuang et al., 1998; Kendler and Gardner, 1998; Kendler and Prescott, 1998a, 1998b; Foroud and Li, 1999; Adams et al., 1999; Uhl, 1999; True et al., 1999; Kendler et al., 1999; Sellers and Tyndale, 2000).

In addition to individual risk factors, social factors may also play an important role. Sociologists and social psychologists have long sought to determine how social interactions and environment more generally may affect drug use. Suggestive statistical associations have frequently been reported. Risk-associated characteristics of families and communities, which may be constant (e.g., multigenerational family history of drug dependence), or time-varying conditions (e.g., harmful processes of abusive or coercive social interaction within families) are related to subsequent use. Children of addicts are more likely than their counterparts to use and abuse drugs as adults. Neighborhood and community drug use patterns and crime rates are correlated with use (Luthar and Cushing, 1999; Petronis and Anthony, 2000). Association with substance-using peers is also highly predictive of substance use. Adolescent use generally takes place among peers and most individuals also experience some peer influence to use drugs (Van Etten et al., 1997; Van Etten and Anthony, 1999).

Of course, social factors may be associated with less drug use. The costs of use are higher for people who have greater stakes in conformity, who care about maintaining the respect of people to whom they are attached, and who care about the investments they have made in their futures. In control theory terminology, individuals with weak bonds to society are more likely to engage in risky, harmful, or criminal behaviors because they are not constrained by emotional ties to loved ones, commitments to conventional goals, or strong normative beliefs about what is right and wrong (Hirschi, 1969). Individuals who are strongly bonded to society are less likely to engage in risky behaviors. Individual decisions about their own use will depend on the strength of the social pressure to use relative to their perceptions of what is at stake if they do use, as well as their perceptions of what is normative behavior.

There is a growing body of evidence on processes of interplay between individual characteristics and social or contextual circumstances. This evidence has taken the field beyond overly simplistic "nature versus nurture" debates, in which an individual's genes have been advanced as the ultimate causes of drug dependence from one side and an individual's social circumstances have been advanced as the ultimate cause of drug dependence from the other side. Especially in research on the causal processes that lead toward drug dependence, there is compelling reason to recast this argument. In place of "nature versus nurture" is a conceptual model of "nature transacting with nurture" (e.g., see Collins et al., 2000). The transactions involve a dynamic interplay between the individual and the environment, social and otherwise.

For example, with respect to certain facets of early temperament and personality, such as extroversion and openness to experience (sometimes called novelty seeking), there is evidence of inheritance from one generation to the next, a set of heritability estimates from studies of monozygotic and dizygotic twins, and evidence on the importance of experiences after conception (e.g., see Rose et al., 1988; Eaves et al., 1999; True et al., 1999). Regarded as individual-level characteristics, these facets of temperament and personality help to determine an individual's repertoire of behavior, including social activities with peers and illegal drug use (e.g., see Kosten et al., 1994; True et al,. 1999; Kendler and Prescott, 1998a, 1998b). In turn, outgoing behavior and social activities may shape whether and when an individual participates in higher-risk social groups that ultimately may include opportunities to try illegal drugs such as cocaine. Nevertheless, it would be a mistake to assume that there is no reciprocal transaction, and there is evidence that the social interactions and circumstances of these environments also shape the individual's future behavior and activities, including the probability and frequency of future entry into higher-risk social groups, membership in these social groups, and socialization into the social roles of the groups. Hence, the individual-level characteristics and behaviors are involved in selection of environmental circumstances, and the environmental circumstances, in turn, shape the future individual-level characteristics and behaviors.

A similar theme of dynamic interplay and transaction has emerged in recent research on parental influences on adolescent and young adult socialization and behavior, including levels of youthful and young adult drug involvement. Recent observational studies provide suggestions of parental influence on drug involvement under some circumstances, even when affiliation with drug-using peers and variations attributable to different neighborhood environments are taken into account (e.g., see Chilcoat and Anthony, 1996; Brook et al., 2000). Nonetheless, there are contrary observations about the influence of parents (e.g., see Petraitis et al., 1998; Kendler et al., 2000; Collins et al., 2000) and an increased appreciation for the influence of adolescent children on the variations in parenting styles and practices they experience in individual household environments (e.g., see Daniels et al., 1985; Niederhiser et al., 1999). Future research may be expected to yield more integration of the individual-oriented and the environment-oriented models to account for development of drug involvement over the life span, with increasing attention to multilevel or contextual influences of family and neighborhood (e.g., see Kendler et al., 1997; Chilcoat et al., 1996; Duncan et al., 1997; Groenewegen et al., 1999; Petronis and Anthony, 2000).

Research on drug use is especially interesting in relation to these transactions because the pharmacological actions of drugs have been found to be of importance in several different ways. Behavioral science research provides a quite clear view of the reinforcing functions of drug use. From behavioral laboratory evidence on experienced cocaine users, it is clear that many of these users respond to the positively reinforcing functions of cocaine use in a predictable way: they work hard to secure more cocaine. One may infer that outside the laboratory, this behavioral response to the reinforcing functions of cocaine includes a willingness to enter into higher-risk social environments in which there are opportunities to use cocaine. In sequence, facets of the individual's personality are expressed in the behavior of entering higher-risk social environments in which cocaine is available. Once cocaine use begins, the cocaine-associated reinforcement may help draw the individual back to these environments, and the environmental circumstances again shape the probability and frequency of future return.

A more recent line of evidence from the neuroscience research on postsynaptic signaling mechanisms provides an additional example of the transactions between nature and nurture. As noted earlier, environmental exposure to cocaine actually produces a change in the expression of genes, with presumed impact on future sensitivity to the drug and the development of dependence. Here, there is a clear example of a feature of the environment (i.e., a drug) that does not change the genetic makeup of the individual, but rather alters the expression of the genes within the individual's genome. This altered gene expression, in turn, has implications for the future behavior of the drug-using individual, whether he or

she will seek out future opportunities to use cocaine, and whether ultimately he or she requires treatment for cocaine dependence.

Despite the many investigations that have shed light on the suspected
risk factors, there remains much to be learned about causal mechanisms
determining use, dependence and addiction. Difficult methodological and
data-related hurdles confront efforts to draw strong inferences about the
individual-level and social-level circumstances, conditions, and processes
that determine use.

For social scientists and policy analysts, the problem is especially
complicated (see Manski, 2000 and Musto, 1995). Even if credible empirical evidence for social interactions should emerge, such evidence is likely
to leave open basic questions about the processes at work. Does the stigma
associated with drug use fall as the prevalence of use in the peer group
rises? Do youth learn about the attractiveness of drug use by observing it
in their environment (Feldman, 1968)? Manski (2000:130) illustrates this
problem as follows:

> To see the importance of understanding endogenous interactions at a
> deeper level, consider the crack cocaine epidemic of the 1980s, which
> appears to have subsided during the 1990s. A plausible explanation of
> the course of the epidemic begins with positive expectations interactions
> as youth of the '80s may have observed some of their peers initiate crack
> usage and apparently enjoy it. There also may have been positive prefer-
> ence interactions of the stigma-reducing type. Eventually, however,
> youth of the '90s may have observed the devastating long-term out-
> comes experienced by addicts of the '80s, and subsequently may have
> chosen not to initiate crack use themselves. If this story of observational
> learning is correct, then an information campaign warning of the devas-
> tating effects of crack addiction might have been effective in the early
> stages of the epidemic, but superfluous later on.

Without better data, researchers will continue to be unable to evaluate risk factors associated with intensification, abuse, addiction, desistance, and relapse. In particular, there are no consumption data and no
longitudinal data available to the public. Lacking data on quantity, existing studies generally focus on prevalence of use within a specified time
period. Without longitudinal data, the problem of causal interpretation of
risk factors is likely to remain unresolved.

CONSEQUENCES OF DRUG USE

Concerns about the consequences of drug use for users and nonusers
are central to U.S. drug policy, as manifest by drug prevention curricula,
public service advertisements, and public statements by government officials. Yet much greater attention is given to statistical patterns of drug

prevalence—the number and percentage of people in various demographic groups that have recently or have ever used drugs—than to a careful description of the quantity and frequency and consequences of use, or to the causal relationships among these variables (see MacCoun, 1998; Reuter and Caulkins, 1995). The emphasis on prevalence is explicit in the National Drug Control Strategy (NDCS) reports published by the White House over the past decade, which provide an annual list of specific national goals for drug policy. For many years, the list consisted entirely or almost exclusively of goals pertaining to reductions in the prevalence of drug use. The 1998 document, *Performance Measures of Effectiveness*, was an important departure in this respect, offering a lengthy and detailed list of goals pertaining to reductions in various indices of the quantity of drug consumption and its health and behavioral consequences.

The long-time emphasis on prevalence is understandable. Logically, most (but not all) of the risks of drug use are borne only by those who decide to use drugs; if there were no drug users, there would be no drug-related harms. The threshold separating the nonuser and the user is viewed as a kind of irrevocable Rubicon in the formal perspective of criminal law, as well as the informal perspective of concerned parents, spouses, and teachers. Tracking trends in prevalence is and should be an essential metric for drug policy analysis, but it is a fairly limited one, based on a crude dichotomy between those who use and those who do not use drugs.

In this section, we argue that that there are compelling reasons to expand and improve the monitoring and analysis of the consequences of drug consumption. Such improvements would lay the foundation for analyzing the complex relationship between drug use patterns and their consequences. We then raise some largely unexplored conceptual and analytic issues involving the complex relationship between drug use patterns and their consequences. We end with a discussion of the effects of laws and their enforcement on the consequences of drug use.

Monitoring Consumption and Its Consequences

Box 2.2 provides a list of major categories of harmful consequences associated with drug use in contemporary American society; the list has several notable features. First, the categories of consequences are quite heterogeneous—medical, psychological, sociological, and economic. Second, the consequences vary with respect to their primary bearers—some are mostly borne by users themselves, others by their intimates and neighbors, others by society. Third, some flow primarily from the psychopharmacological properties of the drugs and their effects on user behaviors, while others are at least partly attributable to the acquisition and use of

BOX 2.2   Abbreviated List of Drug-Related Harms

Physical/mental illnesses
Diseases transmitted to others
Accident victimization
Health care costs (drug treatment)
Health care costs (drug-related illnesses, injuries)
Reduced performance in school
Reduced performance at workplace
Poor parenting, child abuse
Psychopharmacological crime and violence
Economically motivated crime and violence
Fear and disorder caused by users and dealers
Criminal justice costs
Corruption of legal authorities
Strain on source-country relations
Infringements on liberty and privacy
Violation of the law as an intrinsic harm

Source: Adapted from MacCoun et al. (1996).

drugs in the context of a particular form of legal prohibition and its enforcement—a point we address in greater detail later in this section.

In Table 2.2, we briefly list indicators and consequences of drug use as
reflected in some of the major federally funded data sources.[10] The National Household Survey of Drug Abuse and Monitoring the Future also
collect self-reported measures on the consequences of drug use. Some of
these measures are problematic because they require respondents to
draw potentially invalid causal attributions about the link between their
drug use and various conditions—e.g., attributing certain health states to
drug use as opposed to a co-occurring illness, or attributing antisocial
behaviors to drug use when they might have occurred in its absence.
Even when the items don't require such inferences, their placement in the

---

[10]Other federally funded sources not listed in the table provide additional data—the
emergency department and medical examiner data of the Drug Abuse Warning Network
(DAWN), the ADAM data on drug use by arrestees, reports of drug-related crime in the
Uniform Crime Reports (UCR), the Centers for Disease Control and Prevention's epidemiological tracking of HIV and AIDS among injecting drug users, and the annual counts of
drug-related deaths in vital statistics registers. To a large extent, many of these latter sources
have been used less as systems for analyzing drug-related harm than as proxy indicators
for hard or heavy drug use of the kind that is underestimated by the major self-report
surveys.

TABLE 2.2 Indicators of Drug Use Intensity and Consequences in Federally Funded Data Sources

Drug Use	Federally Funded Data Sources						
	DATOS	DC-MADS	MTF	NCS	NHSDA	NYS	TEDS
Amount	Yes	Yes	Yes	Yes	Yes	Yes	No
Frequency	Yes	Yes	Yes	Yes	Yes	Yes	Yes
Ever used	Yes	Yes	Yes	Yes	Yes	Yes	No
First use	Yes	Yes	Yes	Yes	Yes	No	Yes
Heaviest use	Yes	No	No	Yes	No	No	No
Last/recent use	Yes	Yes	Yes	Yes	Yes	Yes	No
Behavioral consequences	Yes	Yes	Yes	Yes	Yes	Yes	No
Health consequences	Yes	Yes	Yes	No	Yes	Yes	No
Perceived risks	Yes	Yes	Yes	No	Yes	No	No
Drug availability	No	No	Yes	No	Yes	No	No
Setting	No	Yes	Yes	No	No	No	No
Increased use for same effect	Yes	Yes	No	No	Yes	No	No
Withdrawal symptoms	Yes	Yes	No	Yes	No	No	No
Expected future use	Yes	No	Yes	No	No	No	No
Illegal activities	DATOS	DC-MADS	MTF	NCS	NHSDA	NYS	TEDS
Problems with police (gen.)	Yes	No	Yes	Yes	No	No	Yes
Illegal acts/violations	Yes	Yes	Yes	No	Yes	Yes	No
Arrests	Yes	Yes	No	No	Yes	Yes	No
Health and mental health	DATOS	DC-MADS	MTF	NCS	NHSDA	NYS	TEDS
Health status	Yes	Yes	Yes	Yes	Yes	Yes	No
Pregnancy status	Yes	Yes	No	Yes	Yes	Yes	Yes
Health statistics	No	No	No	No	Yes	Yes	No
HIV status	Yes	No	No	Yes	No	Yes	No
Mental health status	Yes	Yes	Yes	Yes	Yes	Yes	Yes
Emotional well-being/satisf.	Yes	No	Yes	Yes	Yes	Yes	No

continues

TABLE 2.2 Continued

Drug Use	Federally Funded Data Sources						
	DATOS	DC-MADS	MTF	NCS	NHSDA	NYS	TEDS
Social support	Yes	No	Yes	Yes	No	Yes	No
Stressful life events	Yes	No	No	Yes	No	Yes	No
Problems at work	Yes	Yes	No	Yes	No	Yes	No
Behavior risks	No	Yes	Yes	Yes	No	Yes	No
Victimization	Yes	No	Yes	Yes	No	Yes	No
Domestic violence	Yes	No	No	Yes	No	Yes	No
DSM codes/diagnosis	Yes	No	No	Yes	No	No	Yes
History/psych problems	Yes	Yes	No	Yes	No	Yes	No
Tx. History/psych problems	Yes	Yes	No	Yes	Yes	Yes	Yes
Family history/psych probs.	Yes	No	No	Yes	No	No	No
Family history/drug use	Yes	No	No	Yes	No	No	No
HIV risk behaviors	Yes	Yes	No	Yes	Yes	Yes	No
Social values and attitudes	No	No	Yes	No	No	Yes	No
Leisure activities	Yes	No	Yes	No	No	No	No

Note: DATOS = Drug Abuse Treatment Outcome Study; DC-MADS = (Washington) DC Metropolitan Area Drug Study; MTF = Monitoring the Future; NCS = National Comorbidity Survey; NHSDA = National Household Survey on Drug Abuse; NYS = National Youth Survey; TEDS = Treatment Episode Data Set

SOURCE: Excerpted and adapted from a larger table published by the Substance Abuse and Mental Health Data Archive at http://www.icpsr. umich.edu/SAMHDA/varmat.html, 3/19/00.

context of detailed questions about drug use may distort recall and re-porting.

Sources of data on drug use consequences are not well suited for supporting *causal* inferences. Indeed, the phrase "drug use consequences" is potentially misleading, as many apparent consequences may actually be spurious correlations. Relative to nonusers, heavy drug users are known to be disproportionately impulsive, less educated, less likely to be employed, more criminally involved, and less healthy. Drug use can cause or augment these characteristics, but it can also be a consequence of one or more of these characteristics. Isolating the causal role of drug use is a difficult challenge; there is a small body of laboratory experiments with adult volunteers, but this type of research is ethically and methodologi-cally constrained.

These limitations for drawing causal inferences mean that existing data provide a fragile and incomplete foundation for recent efforts to estimate the aggregate consequences of U.S. drug use (Harwood et al., 1998; Rice, 1999). The inadequacy of these estimates has been documented by Cohen (1999), Kleiman (1999) and Reuter (1999). Moreover, these ag-gregated estimates are of limited value for policy analysis. They may facilitate budgetary planning and serve a rhetorical role in mobilizing public support for drug policy, but they provide little insight into the dynamics of the drug problem or its responsiveness to alternative strate-gies and tactics of policy intervention.

Dose-Response Relationships

Some alternate methodologies for improving understanding of drug use consequences are available. One underutilized approach for under-standing the relationship between drug use and its consequences is dose-response analysis—a standard methodology in pharmacology (Julien, 1998), epidemiology (Lilienfeld and Stolley, 1994), and technological risk analysis (Morgan, 1981). In a simple dose-response analysis, the strength or intensity of a given type of response (e.g., a physical symptom) is plotted (on the vertical axis) as a function of increasing dose (on the horizontal axis). Alternatively, the vertical axis depicts the percentage of subjects (e.g., laboratory animals, human participants) displaying the re-sponse in question. Dose-response curves show that organismic responses to many biological or technological stimuli have an S-shape, with rela-tively little response at very low doses, a steep rise in response probability or intensity, and an eventual plateau. These S-shaped curves graphically depict three key concepts (Julien, 1998:33). The potency of the stimulus is shown by the location of the curve on the horizontal (dose) axis; more potent stimuli are shifted toward the left end of the axis, so that smaller doses are required to yield a given response. The maximum effect of the stimulus is shown by the peak of the curve on the vertical axis. Finally, the steepness of the slope of the curve depicts the difference between ineffective and effective doses with respect to producing the effect of interest.

Dose-response curves are routinely used to study some properties of psychoactive drugs (Gable, 1993; Julien, 1998)—in particular, the effective dose (ED), which is usually the dose needed to produce the drug's major psychopharmacological effect in 50 percent of respondents and the lethal dose, (LD), which is the dose sufficient to kill 50 percent of respondents. The ratio between the effective dose and the lethal dose is a common index of the drug's overdose potential, and common street drugs vary widely in their ED:LD ratios. These analyses are largely based on laboratory analyses, often using animal subjects. Much less common are dose-response analyses based on field research, examining psychoactive drug use by humans in naturalistic field settings. In contrast, such analyses are fairly common in the epidemiological literature on alcohol consumption. For example, we have fairly good epidemiological evidence on the dose-response relationships between alcohol consumption and road fatalities, stroke fatalities, breast cancer, and violent criminality (Corrao et al., 1999; Edwards et al., 1994).

Very little is known about the dose-response relationships for the consequences of drug use depicted in Box 2.2. Understanding those dose-relationships is an ambitious, but in our view a fruitful, research agenda. Among the questions that might be addressed:

1. What are the acute risks of a given incident of drug use? In other words, what is the dose-response relationship, for a given consequence, across the range of doses actually taken in street use of each drug?

2. What are the chronic risks of a career of drug use? In other words, what is the dose-response relationship if the horizontal axis is converted to cumulative dose over time? Chronic risks will vary with the user's experience with the drug (e.g., tolerance reduces overdose potential at any given dose, but the poor health consequences of prolonged use may leave experienced users more vulnerable in other ways). Cumulative risks are often difficult for casual users to observe; by definition, such evidence takes longer to accumulate, and heavy users are often socially isolated from casual users. Moreover, there is psychological evidence that people have difficulty appreciating that statistically small acute risks can accumulate to large probabilities with repeated exposure to a hazard (Doyle, 1997).

3. How does the cumulative dose-response relationship over a drug-using career vary according to rate and tempo at which that total dose is accumulated? Some risks may vary mostly as a function of the quantity

consumed per incident; possible examples include overdoses, domestic violence, and motor vehicle accidents. Other risks may vary mostly as a function of the frequency of consumption; possible examples include dependency, income-generating crime, lost productivity, and poor parenting.

4. Are there lagged or delayed effects of drug use? Examples of this would include AIDS deaths as a lagged consequence of injection drug use with contaminated needles, and liver cirrhosis as a lagged effect of alcohol consumption.

5. How do these dose-response parameters vary across types of drugs, types of users (age, gender, socioeconomic status, etc.), and geographic, temporal, and cultural variations in the purity and potency of the substance and the ways in which it is consumed (e.g., snorting versus smoking)?

6. How can we determine the causal direction of dose-response relationships? One approach is through laboratory experiments; for example, many studies have examined the effects of various drugs on cognitive or psychomotor functioning or on aggressive behavior. But these studies provide limited evidence on drug use in realistic social environments or on the aggregate contribution of drugs to various categories of harm. Correlational field studies are vulnerable to the possibility that individuals with a higher propensity for danger self-select higher consumption levels (Zuckerman, 1994). This will spuriously inflate the quantity-risk relationship.

A better understanding of this full range of dose-response relationships would be valuable for many reasons. First, this information might provide an important deterrent to initiation for nonusers and to escalation for casual users. Second, such information would provide a firmer foundation for estimates of the aggregate costs of drug use (Harwood et al., 1998; Rice, 1999). Third, it would facilitate longitudinal inferences regarding trends in drug use and its outcomes. For example, to the extent that morbidity and mortality are sometimes lagged consequences of drug use or consequences of cumulative rather than incidental use, data on emergency room visits and drug-related deaths are potentially misleading as proxies for otherwise underestimated hard drug prevalence. Fourth, a better understanding of dose-response relationships might support more effective decision making about the allocation and targeting of drug policy instruments and resources (e.g., arrests, prison space, treatment slots, prevention efforts) across types of users, drugs, and settings. Finally, this kind of information might facilitate the development of more sophisticated and credible analytical models of the drug problem, its trends over time and space, and its potential responsiveness to various policy initiatives.

Distribution of Drug Use and Its Consequences

Researchers have devoted considerable attention to the aggregate distribution of alcohol consumption and its changes over time and across settings and modalities of use (see Edwards et al., 1994; Skog, 1993). Like many human attributes, the frequency distribution of alcohol consumption has an asymmetric, positively skewed shape. This asymmetry partly reflects the fact that consumption is bounded on one end at zero, but only fuzzily bounded at the high end by human biological constraints. It may also reflect multiplicative relationships among the causes of consumption and, conceivably, the nature of addiction (c.f., Skog, in Edwards et al., 1994). There is good reason to expect a similar distributional form for many if not all of the illegal psychoactive drugs (Everingham and Rydell, 1994).

Whatever its causes, this skewed distribution may have important consequences for drug policy analysis and intervention. First, it implies that the harmful consequences of drug use are not evenly distributed across all users. Many harms are disproportionately concentrated among heavy users—sharing of infected needles, unsafe sexual behavior, and income-generating violent crime.

These observations enable better understanding of drug use and its consequences. Everingham and Rydell (1994) used an analysis of the statistical distribution of cocaine consumption in an attempt to understand two seemingly contradictory patterns in the early 1990s. On one hand, there was a fairly dramatic decline in the prevalence of cocaine use (i.e., the number of users) between 1983 and 1990. On the other hand, various indicators of the harmful health and crime consequences of cocaine remained fairly stable over the same period. Using a variety of indirect sources of evidence—since direct data was not available—and a simple epidemiological model of the flow of individuals between nonuse, casual use, and heavy use, Everingham and Rydell estimated that while cocaine prevalence declined between 1983 and 1990, the total quantity of cocaine consumption remained fairly stable. According to their estimates, 22 percent of the current users of cocaine accounted for 70 percent of the total cocaine consumed in 1990. Their conclusion was that the decline in cocaine prevalence was primarily due to the cessation of use by casual experimenters, leaving a hard core of heavy, persistent users (Figure 2.1).[11]

---

[11]This skew pattern is common in data on antisocial behavior; for example, roughly 5 percent of criminal offenders account for at least half of all crimes committed (see Moffitt, 1993).

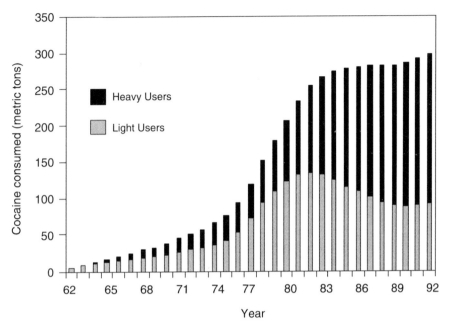

FIGURE 2.1 Change in statistical distribution of cocaine consumption over time. Source: Adapted from Everingham and Rydell (1994).

This type of systems research, better supported by data, has potential to provide a more complete picture of patterns and consequences of drug use.

Alcohol researchers have used the analysis of consumption distributions to conduct a fruitful—if still unresolved—debate about the relative efficacy of two alternative targeting strategies for drug policy (Edwards et al., 1994; MacCoun, 1998; Rose, 1992). One strategy is to disproportionately target the heaviest users, because they account for such a large share of total consumption and, as a consequence, are at higher risk of causing harm to themselves and others. Others argue that there may be greater aggregate benefit from reducing consumption among casual users; they pose fewer risks individually, but they typically outnumber heavy users by a wide margin.[12]

---

[12]In the public health literature, this latter notion is referred to as the "prevention paradox"; see Rose (1992). A strong version was proposed by Ledermann (1956), who hypothesized that there was a fixed relationship between the mean and variance of the alcohol distribution, so that reductions in the mean would bring about reductions at the extremes. This strong version has been rejected empirically (Skog, in Edwards et al., 1994)

Obviously, a comprehensive drug control program should target both typical users and hard-core users. The relative effectiveness of targeting typical versus hard-core users will probably vary according to several factors (MacCoun, 1998). Everything else being equal, it will be more effective to target typical users when the dose-response curve rises very quickly with small doses and when the statistical distribution of consumption is fairly symmetric. It should be added that reducing typical users can also be effective as an attempt to decrease the eventual number of hard-core users. It will be more effective to target heavy users when the dose-response curve rises slowly at low doses and when the statistical distribution of consumption is heavily skewed. Thus the ability to create accurate dose-response curves promises benefits for reduced consumption of illegal drugs.

Reciprocal Effects of Drug-Related Harms on Levels of Use

Complicating any analysis of the relationship between drug use patterns and drug-related harms is the possibility that the risks of drug use have a reciprocal causal influence on the prevalence, incidence, and quantity of drug use. The decision to use, or to escalate, illegal drug use may not reflect a purely rational risk calculation (see MacCoun, 1993), but it seems likely that both potential users and current users are influenced by their perceptions of the risks—health risks, legal risks, and social risks. Still, evidence on this point is surprisingly ambiguous. Analyses of Monitoring the Future data consistently show a negative correlation between the perceived riskiness of drugs and the likelihood of their use (Bachman et al., 1998), but the causal direction of this correlation is not clear.

Musto (1971, 1987) and Johnston (1991) have each proposed a "generational forgetting" account of drug epidemics, in which the risks and disorder associated with the use of a drug become increasingly visible, triggering a reduction in initiation. As the number and visibility of users declines over time, this risk information becomes less accessible, and initiation begins to rise again, renewing the cycle. This model is plausible but largely untested. There are simply too few cycles of data to test the model, much less establish the cyclical nature of drug epidemics. On the surface at least, the generational forgetting model also conflicts with another piece of conventional wisdom in drug policy circles—the contention that providing risk information is relatively ineffective as a strategy for discouraging drug use (discussed in Chapter 7). But it is possible that direct observation of hard-core users has a discouraging effect that is more powerful or more credible than classroom-based risk information (see Fazio et al., 1978; Feldman, 1968).

MacCoun (1997) notes that the total harm (of a given type, for a given drug) is the product of average harm (per incident of use) × total use (number of incidents of use). Thus, if reductions in average harm bring about increases in total use, there is no guarantee that a drop in average harm will produce a decline in total harm. Critics of harm reduction strategies (such as needle exchange) often contend that such approaches send the wrong message—potentially undermining attempts to discourage drug use. Although that claim is rarely articulated in any detail, MacCoun (1998) has examined several plausible interpretations. One is relevant to the present discussion: specifically, the notion that a reduction in the average harmfulness of an incident of drug use may make drugs more desirable. MacCoun (1998) cites evidence from other domains suggesting that interventions to reduce risk can have offsetting behavioral effects; for example, the presence of air bags tends to make people drive slightly faster, everything else being equal. Yet in the domains that have been studied, the safety interventions have been beneficial on the whole, despite these offsetting effects. MacCoun argues that the available evidence suggests that needle exchange programs reduce net harm in this same sense. But he argues that as a general principle, all drug interventions should be evaluated for their effects on several key dimensions: the likelihood of using a drug, the quantity and frequency of drug use, and the average harmfulness (by various criteria) of each incidence of use.

Separating the Effects of Drug Use from the Effects of Illegality of Use

No responsible analysis of the harmful consequences of drug use can ignore the possibility that many of the harms of drug use are either caused or augmented by the legal prohibition against these drugs and its enforcement. Drug prohibition is inevitably a source of government intrusion into citizens' lives. Many (but not all) overdoses occur due to the unknown purity and potency of illegally purchased drugs. The sharing of contaminated syringes is largely a consequence of the artificial scarcity created by their illegality. And much of the criminality and violence associated with drug use (but by no means all) is due to the high price of illegal drugs and the conditions of their sale in illegal markets.

Consider the drug-crime link. Goldstein (1985) has provided a useful distinction between three types of links between drugs and violence. First, psychopharmacological violence is attributable to the fact that the ingestion of some drugs (e.g., alcohol, stimulants, barbiturates, PCP) makes some individuals more excitable, irrational, or violent than they would be otherwise. Second, economically compulsive violence occurs when addicted users engage in economically motivated violent crime (e.g., robbery) in order to support an expensive habit of drug use. Finally, systemic violence occurs as a consequence of the nature of illegal drug trafficking—territorial disputes among dealers, conflicts with disgruntled customers and angry neighbors, intimidation to promote debt collection, and so on. Goldstein and colleagues (1992) estimate that in New York City in 1988, 74 percent of all drug- and alcohol-related homicides fell into the systemic category; of those, 61 percent involved crack cocaine and 27 percent involved powder cocaine. Another 4 percent of all drug- and alcohol-related homicides were primarily economically compulsive. Only 14 percent were primarily psychopharmacological in nature, and 68 percent of those involved alcohol—a legal drug. Two open questions are whether the relative frequencies of each type of homicide have changed over time, and whether nonhomicide drug crimes fit a similar profile.

But as several authors have argued in detail (Kleiman, 1992; MacCoun et al., 1996; MacCoun and Reuter, 2001), the premise that drug prohibition causes some drug-related harm does not necessarily imply that ending prohibition would, on net, reduce total drug-related harm. It is likely that many of the harmful consequences of drug use would be significantly reduced under a regulated policy of legal access to drugs—but not all harms. And even if average harm declined overall, there is no guarantee that net or total harm would decline as a result. Recall that *total harm = average harm per incident of use × total use*. If average harm declined under legalization, the effect on total harm would then depend on whether total use increased. If the average harmfulness of an incident of use (on any given dimension of harm) dropped but total use increased, the net effect on total harm is uncertain; it could fall, remain constant, or increase significantly (MacCoun and Reuter, 2001). Thus, legalization is an unproven and potentially risky strategy for reducing drug-related harms.

For these reasons, the observation that drug illegality contributes to drug harmfulness is by no means tantamount to endorsing drug legalization. In discussing this point, we acknowledge concerns about the fear of sending the wrong message about the harms of drugs. However, inadequate analysis of the consequences of drug use gives a rhetorical advantage to advocates of legalization without allowing a serious examination of the merits and weaknesses of their arguments. Moreover, the failure to address the full consequences of drug prohibition results in lost opportunities for reducing drug-related harm under a policy of prohibition.

REFERENCES

Adams, L.D., W. Gong, S.D. Vechia, R.G. Hunter, and M.J. Kuhar
1999 CART: From gene to function. *Brain Research* 848(1-2):137-40.

Anthony, J.C., and J.E. Helzer
1995 Epidemiology of drug dependence. In Ming T. Tsuang, Mauricio Tohen, and G. E.P. Zahner, eds., *Textbook in Psychiatric Epidemiology*. New York. John Wiley and Sons.

Argawal, D.P., and H.W.Goedde
1990 *Alcohol Metabolism, Alcohol Intolerance, and Alcoholism.* Berlin: Springer-Verlag.

Bachman, J.G., L.D. Johnston, and P.M. O'Malley
1998 Explaining recent increases in students' marijuana use: Impacts of perceived risks and disapproval, 1976 through 1996. *American Journal of Public Health* 88:887-892.

Becker, G.S., M. Grossman, and K.M. Murphy
1994 An empirical analysis of cigarette addiction. *American Economic Review* 84:396-418.

Becker, G.S., and K.M. Murphy
1988 A theory of rational addiction. *Journal of Political Economy* 96:675-700.

Brewer, D.D., R.F. Catalano, K. Haggerty, R.R. Gainey, and C.B. Fleming
1998 A meta-analysis of predictors of continued drug use during and after treatment for opiate addiction. *Addiction* 93(1):73-92.

Brook, J.S., M. Whiteman, S. Finch, and P. Cohen
2000 Longitudinally foretelling drug use in the late twenties: Adolescent personality and social-environmental antecedents. *Journal of Genetic Psychology* 161(1):37-51.

Bucholz, K.K., A.C. Heath, and P.A. Madden
2000 Transitions in drinking in adolescent females: Evidence from the Missouri adolescent female twin study. *Alcoholism—Clinical and Experimental Research* 24(6):914-23.

Buck, A.A., T.T. Sasaki, J.J. Hewitt, and A.A. Macrae
1968 Coca chewing and health. An epidemiologic study among residents of a Peruvian village. *American Journal of Epidemiology* 88(2):159-77.

Caulkins, J.P.
1995 Estimating Elasticities of Demand for Cocaine and Heroin with Data from the Drug Use Forecasting System. H. John Heinz III School of Public Policy and Management, Carnegie Mellon University.
1994 *Developing Price Series for Cocaine.* Drug Policy Research Center. Santa Monica, CA: RAND.

Caulkins, J.P., and P. Reuter
1998 What price data tell us about drug markets. *Journal of Drug Issues* 28:593-612.
1997 Setting goals for drug policy: Harm reduction or use reduction? *Addiction* 92:1143-1150.

Chaloupka, F.J.
1991 Rational addictive behavior and cigarette smoking, *Journal of Political Economy* 99:722-742.

Chaloupka, F.J., M. Grossman, and J.A. Tauras
1998 *The Demand for Cocaine and Marijuana by Youth.* Working paper 6411. Cambridge, MA: National Bureau of Economic Research.

Chaloupka, F.J., and H. Wechsler
    1997   Price, tobacco control policies and smoking among young adults. *Journal of Health Economics* 16:359-373.

Chilcoat, H.D., and J.C. Anthony
    1996   Impact of parent monitoring on initiation of drug use through late childhood. *Journal of the American Academy of Child and Adolescent Psychiatry* 35(1):91-100.

Chilcoat, H.D., N. Breslau, and J.C. Anthony
    1996   Potential barriers to parent monitoring: Social disadvantage, marital status, and maternal psychiatric disorder. *Journal of the American Academy of Child and Adolescent Psychiatry* 35(12):1673-82.

Childress, A.R., A.V. Hole, R.N. Ehrman, S.J. Robbins, A.T. McLellan, and C.P. O'Brien
    1993   Cue reactivity and cue reactivity interventions in drug dependence. *NIDA Research Monographs* 137:73-95.

Cohen, M.A.
    1999   Alcohol, drugs and crime: Is "crime" really one-third of the problem? *Addiction* 94:644-647.

Coie, J.D., N.F. Watt, S.G. West, J.D. Hawkins, J.R. Asarnow, H.J. Markman, S.L. Ramey, M.B. Shure, and B. Long.
    1993   The science of prevention: A conceptual framework and some directions for a national research program. *American Psychologist* 48:1013-1022.

Collins, W.A., E.E. Maccoby, L. Steinberg, E.M. Hetherington, and M.H. Bornstein
    2000   Contemporary research on parenting: The case for nature and nurture. *American Psychology* 55(2):218-32.

Cooper, J.R., F.E. Bloom, and R.H. Roth
    1996   Cellular foundation of neuropharmacology. Pp. 9-48 in *The Biochemical Basis of Neuropharmacology*, 7th Edition. New York: Oxford University Press.

Cornish, J.L., P. Duffy, and P.W. Kalivas
    1999   A role for nucleus accumbens glutamate transmission in the relapse to cocaine-seeking behavior. *Neuroscience* 93(4):1359-1367.

Cornish, J.L., and P.W. Kalivas
    2000   Glutamate transmission in the nucleus accumbens mediates relapse in cocaine addiction. *Journal of Neuroscience* (Online). 20(15):RC89.

Corrao, G., V. Bagnardi, A. Zambon, and S. Arico
    1999   Exploring the dose-response relationship between alcohol consumption and the risk of several alcohol-related conditions: A meta-analysis. *Addiction* 94:1551-1573.

Crane, B.D., A.R. Rivolo, and G.C. Comfort
    1997   *An Empirical Examination of Counterdrug Interdiction Program Effectiveness.* IDA paper, p. 3219. Alexandria, VA: Institute for Defense Analyses.

Crum, R.M., M. Lillie-Blanton, and J.C. Anthony
    1996   Neighborhood environment and opportunity to use cocaine and other drugs in late childhood and early adolescence. *Drug and Alcohol Dependence* 43(3):155-61.

Curtis, R., and T. Wendel
    2000   *Lockin' Niggas Up Like It's Goin' Out of Style: The Differing Consequences of Police Interventions in Three Brooklyn, New York, Drug Markets.* Conference on Drug Markets and Law Enforcement Strategies. Arlington, VA: National Institute of Justice.
    1999   *Toward the Development of a Typology of Illegal Drug Markets.* Unpublished paper prepared for Committee on Data and Research for Policy on Illegal Drugs.

Daniels, D., J. Dunn, F.F. Furstenberg, Jr., and R. Plomin
  1985 Environmental differences within the family and adjustment differences within pairs of adolescent siblings. *Child Development* 56(3):764-74.

DeSimone, J.
  1998 Is marijuana a gateway drug? *Eastern Economic Journal* 24:149-164.

Doyle, J. K.
  1997 Judging cumulative risk. *Journal of Applied Social Psychology* 27:500-524.

Duncan, T.E., S.C. Duncan, H. Hops, and A. Alpert
  1997 Multi-level covariance structure analysis of intra-familial substance use. *Drug and Alcohol Dependence* 46(3):167-80.

Eaves, L., A. Heath, N. Martin, H. Maes, M. Neale, K. Kendler, K. Kirk, and L. Corey
  1999 Comparing the biological and cultural inheritance of personality and social attitudes in the Virginia 30,000 study of twins and their relatives. *Twin Research* 2(2):62-80.

Edwards, G., P. Anderson, T.F. Babor, S. Casswell, R. Ferrence, N. Giesbrecht, C. Godfrey, H.D. Holder, P. Lemmens, K. Mäkelä, L.T. Midanik, T. Norström, E. Österberg, A. Romesljö, R. Room, J. Simpura, and O. Skog
  1994 *Alcohol Policy and the Public Good.* Oxford, England: Oxford University Press.

Everingham, S.S., and C.P. Rydell
  1994 *Modeling the Demand for Cocaine.* Prepared for the Office of National Drug Control Policy and the U.S. Army. Santa Monica, CA: RAND.

Everingham, S.M.S., C.P. Rydell, and J.P. Caulkins
  1995 Cocaine consumption in the United States: Estimating past trends and future scenarios. *Socio-Economic Planning Sciences* 29:305-314.

Fagan, J.
  1992 Drug selling and licit income in distressed neighborhoods: The economic lives of street-level drug users and dealers. In A.V. Harrell and G.E. Peterson, eds., *Drugs, Crime, and Social Isolation.* Washington, DC: Urban Institute Press.

Fazio, R.H., M.P. Zanna, and J. Cooper
  1978 Direct experience and attitude-behavior consistency: An information processing analysis. *Personality and Social Psychology Bulletin* 4:48-51.

Feldman, H.
  1968 Ideological supports to becoming and remaining a heroin addict. *Journal of Health and Social Behavior* 9(14):31-155.

Foroud, T., and T.K. Li
  1999 Genetics of alcoholism: a review of recent studies in human and animal models. *American Journal of Addictions* 8(4):261-278.

Gable, R.S.
  1993 Toward a comparative overview of dependence potential and acute toxicity of psychoactive substances used nonmedically. *American Journal of Drug and Alcohol Abuse* 19:263-281.

Garmezy, N.
  1983 Stressors of childhood. In N. Garmezy and N. Rutter, eds., *Stress, Coping and Development in Children.* New York: McGraw-Hill.

Goldstein, P.
  1985 The drug/violence nexus: A tripartite conceptual framework. *Journal of Drug Issues* 14:493-506.

Goldstein, P., H.H. Brownstein, and P.J. Ryan
   1992   Drug-related homicide in New York: 1984 and 1988. *Crime and Delinquency* 38:459-476.

Gossop, M., P. Griffiths, B. Powis, and J. Strang
   1994   Cocaine: Patterns of use, route of administration, and severity of dependence. *British Journal of Psychiatry* 164(5):660-664.

Gottfredson, D.C.
   2000   *Delinquency Prevention in Schools.* New York: Cambridge University Press.
          Gottfredson, D.C., M.A. Harmon, G.D. Gottfredson, E.M. Jones, and J.A. Celestin
   1996   *Compendium of Prevention Program Outcomes and Instrument Locator.* Ellicott City, MD: Gottfredson Associates, Inc.

Groenewegen, P.P., H.G. Leufkens, P. Spreeuwenberg, and W. Worm
   1999   Neighbourhood characteristics and use of benzodiazepines. *Netherlands Social Science Medicine* 48(12):1701-1711.

Grossman, M., F.J. Chaloupka, and C.C. Brown
   1996   *The Demand for Cocaine by Young Adults: A Rational Addiction Approach.* Working paper 5713. Cambridge, MA: National Bureau of Economic Research.

Hansen, W.B., and P.M. O'Malley
   1996   Drug use. In R.J. DiClemente, W.B. Hansen, and L.E. Ponton, eds. *Handbook of Adolescent Health Risk Behavior.* New York: Plenum Press.

Harwood, H.J., D. Fountain, and G. Livermore
   1998   *The Economic Costs of Alcohol and Drug Abuse in the United States, 1992.* Rockville, MD: National Institute on Drug Abuse.

Hatsukami, D.K., and M.W. Fischman.
   1996   Crack cocaine and cocaine hydrochloride. Are the differences myth or reality? *Journal of the American Medical Association* 276(19):1580-1588.

Hawkins, J.D., M.W. Arthur, and R.F. Catalano
   1995   *Building a Safer Society: Strategic Approaches to Crime Prevention: Preventing Substance Abuse.* Chicago: University of Chicago Press.

Hawkins, J.D., R.F. Catalano, and J.Y. Miller
   1992   Risk and protective factors for alcohol and other drug problems in adolescence and early adulthood: Implications for substance abuse prevention. *Psychological Bulletin* 112(1):64-105.

Hirschi, T.
   1969   *Causes of Delinquency.* Berkeley: University of California Press.

Hung, A.
   2000   A Behavioral Theory of Addiction. Working Paper, The Heinz School, Carnegie Mellon University.

Institute of Medicine
   1997   *Dispelling the Myths About Addiction: Strategies to Increase Understanding and Strengthen Research.* Washington, DC: National Academy Press.
   1996   *Pathways of Addiction: Opportunities in Drug Abuse Research.* Washington, DC: National Academy Press.
   1995   *The Development of Medications for the Treatment of Opiate and Cocaine Addictions: Issues for the Government and Private Sector.* Washington, DC: National Academy Press.
   1994   *Reducing Risks For Mental Disorders: Frontiers for Preventive Intervention Research.* Washington, DC: National Academy Press.

Johanson, C.E., F.F. Duffy, and J.C. Anthony
1996 Associations between drug use and behavioral repertoire in urban youths. *Addiction* 91(4):523-534.

Johnston, L.D.
1991 Toward a theory of drug epidemics. In L. Donohew and H.E. Sypher, eds., *Persuasive Communication and Drug Abuse Prevention*. Hillsdale, NJ: Lawrence Erlbaum Associates.

Julien, R.M.
1998 *A Primer of Drug Action*, 8th ed. New York: W.H. Freeman.

Kelz, M.B., J. Chen, W.A. Carlezon, Jr, K. Whisler, L. Gilden, A.M. Beckmann, C. Steffen, Y.J. Zhang, L. Marotti, D.W. Self, T. Tkatch, G. Baranauskas, D.J. Surmeier, R.L. Neve, R.S. Duman, M.R. Picciotto, and E.J. Nestler
1999 Expression of the transcription factor deltaFosB in the brain controls sensitivity to cocaine. *Nature* 16:401(6750):272-276.

Kendler, K.S., and C.O. Gardner, Jr.
1998 Twin studies of adult psychiatric and substance dependence disorders: Are they biased by differences in the environmental experiences of monozygotic and dizygotic twins in childhood and adolescence? *Psychological Medicine* 28(3):625-633.

Kendler, K.S., L. Karkowski, and C.A. Prescott
1999 Hallucinogen, opiate, sedative and stimulant use and abuse in a population-based sample of female twins. *Acta Psychiatrica Scandinavica* 99(5):368-376.

Kendler, K.S., J. Myers, and C.A. Prescott
2000 Parenting and adult mood, anxiety and substance use disorders in female twins: An epidemiological, multi-informant, retrospective study. *Psychological Medicine* 30(2):281-294.

Kendler, K.S., and C.A. Prescott
1998a Cocaine use, abuse and dependence in a population-based sample of female twins. *British Journal of Psychiatry* 173:345-350.
1998b Cannabis use, abuse, and dependence in a population-based sample of female twins. *American Journal of Psychiatry* 155(8):1016-1022.

Kendler, K.S., P.C. Sham, and C.J. MacLean
1997 The determinants of parenting: An epidemiological, multi-informant, retrospective study. *Psychological Medicine* 27(3):549-563.Kendler, K.S., L.M. Karkowski, L.A. Corey, C.A. Prescott, and M.C. Neale
1999 Genetic and environmental risk factors in the aetiology of illicit drug initiation and subsequent misuse in women. *British Journal of Psychiatry* 175:351-356.

Kessler, R.C., and R.H. Price
1993 Primary prevention of secondary disorders: A proposal and agenda. *American Journal of Community Psychology* 21(5):607-633.

Kleiman, M.A.R.
1999 "Economic cost" measurements, damage minimization and drug abuse control policy. *Addiction* 94:638-641.
1992 *Against Excess: Drug Policies for Results*. New York: Basic Books.

Koob, G.F.
2000 Neurobiology of addiction. Toward the development of new therapies. *Annals of the New York Academy of Science* 909:170-185.

Kosten, T.A., S.A. Ball, and B.J. Rounsaville
1994 A sibling study of sensation seeking and opiate addiction. *Journal of Nervour and Mental Disease* 182(5):284-289.

Ledermann, S.
1956   *Alcool, Alcoolisme, Alcoolisation*, Volume 1. Paris: Presses Universitaires de France.

Leshner, A.
1997   Addiction is brain disease, and it matters. *Science* 278.

Levitt, S.D., and S.A. Venkatesh
1998   *An Economic Analysis of a Drug-Selling Gang's Finances.* Working paper 6592. Cambridge, MA: National Bureau of Economic Research.

Lilienfeld, D.E., and P.D. Stolley
1994   *Foundations of Epidemiology*, 3rd ed. New York: Oxford University Press.

Luthar, S.S., and G. Cushing
1999   Neighborhood influences and child development: A prospective study of substance abusers' offspring. *Development and Psychopathology* 11(4):763-784.

MacCoun, R.
1993   Drugs and the law: A psychological analysis of drug prohibition. *Psychological Bulletin* 113:497-512.
1998   Toward a psychology of harm reduction. *American Psychologist* 53:1199-1208.

MacCoun, R., and P. Reuter
2001   *Drug War Heresies: Learning from Other Vices, Times, and Places.* New York: Cambridge University Press.

MacCoun, R., P. Reuter, and T. Schelling
1996   Assessing alternative drug control regimes. *Journal of Policy Analysis and Management* 15:1-23.

Maldonado, R., A. Saiardi, O. Valverde, T.A. Samad, B.P. Roques, and E. Borrelli
1997   Absence of opiate rewarding effects in mice lacking dopamine D2 receptors. *Nature* 388(6642):586-589.

Manski, C.F.
2000   Economic analysis of social interactions. *Journal of Economic Perspectives* 14:115-136.
1995   *Identification Problems in the Social Sciences.* Cambridge, MA: Harvard University Press.

Merikangas, K.R., R.L. Mehta, B.E. Molnar, E.E. Walters, J.D. Swendsen, S. Aguilar Gaziola, R. Bijl, G. Borges, J.J. Caraveo-Anduaga, D.J. DeWit, B. Kolody, W.A. Vega, H.U. Wittchen, and R.C. Kessler
1998a Comorbidity of substance use disorders with mood and anxiety disorders: Results of the International Consortium in Psychiatric Epidemiology. *Addictive Behavior* 23(6):893-907.

Merikangas, K.R., M. Stolar, D.E. Stevens, J. Goulet, M.A. Preisig, B. Fenton, H. Zhang, S.S. O'Malley, and B.J. Rounsaville
1998b Familial transmission of substance use disorders. *Archives of General Psychiatry* 55(11):973-979.

Moffitt, T.E.
1993   Adolescent-limited and life-course-persistent antisocial behavior: A developmental taxonomy. *Psychological Review* 100:674-701.

Morgan, M.G.
1981   Probing the question of technology-induced risk. *IEEE Spectrum* 18:58-64.

Musto, D.F.
1995   Perception and regulation of drug use: The rise and fall of the tide. *Annals of Internal Medicine* 15:123(6):468-469.

1971/ *The American Disease: Origins of Narcotic Control.* New York: Oxford University
1987   Press.

National Development and Research Institutes
   1997 *Natural History of Crack Distribution/Abuse.* Rockville, MD: National Institute on
        Drug Abuse.

Negrete, J.C.
   1992 Cocaine problems in the coca-growing countries of South America. *CIBA Founda-
        tion Symposium* 166:40-50.

Neiderhiser, J.M., D. Reiss, E.M. Hetherington, and R. Plomin
   1999 Relationships between parenting and adolescent adjustment over time: Genetic
        and environmental contributions. *Developmental Psychology* 35(3):680-692.

O'Brien, C.P.
   1995 Drug addiction and drug abuse. In *The Pharmacological Basis of Therapeutics*, 9th
        Edition, J.G. Hardman and L.E. Limbard, eds. New York: McGraw Hill.

O'Brien, C.P., and A.T. McLellan
   1996 Myths about the treatment of addiction. *Lancet* 347:237-240.

Office of National Drug Control Policy
   1999 *The Price of Illicit Drugs: 1981 through the Second Quarter of 1998.* Washington, DC:
        Abt Associates.
   1997 *What America's Users Spend on Illegal Drugs: 1988-1995.* Washington, DC: Abt As-
        sociates.

Olds, M.E., and P. Milner
   1954 Positive reinforcement produced by electrical stimulation of septal area and other
        regions of the rat brain. *Journal of Comparative and Physiological Psychology* 47:419-
        427.

Orphanides, A., and D. Zervos
   1995 Rational addiction with learning and regret. *Journal of Political Economy* 103(4):739-
        758.

Petronis, K.R., and J.C. Anthony
   2000 Perceived risk of cocaine use and experience with cocaine: Do they cluster within
        U.S. neighborhoods and cities? *Drug and Alcohol Dependence* 57(3):183-192.

Petraitis, J., B.R. Flay, T.Q. Miller, E.J. Torpy, and B. Greiner
   1998 Illicit substance use among adolescents: A matrix of prospective predictors. *Sub-
        stance Use and Misuse* 33(13):2561-2604.

Reuter, P., R. MacCoun, and P. Murphy
   1990 *Money from Crime: A Study of the Economics of Drug Dealing in Washington, D.C.*
        Report R-3894-RF. Santa Monica, CA: RAND.

Reuter, P.
   1999 Are calculations of the economic costs of drug abuse either possible or useful?
        Addiction 94:635-638.

Reuter, P., and J. Caulkins
   1995 Redefining the goals of national drug policy: Recommendations from a working
        group. *American Journal of Public Health* 85:1059-1064.

Rice, D.P.
   1999 Economic costs of substance abuse, 1995. *Proceedings of the Association of American
        Physicians* 111:119-125.

Riley, K.J.
   1997   Crack, Powder Cocaine, and Heroin: Drug Purchase and Use Patterns in Six U.S.
          Cities. Office of National Drug Control Policy and the National Institute of Jus-
          tice.

Ritz, M.C., R.J. Lamb, S.R. Goldberg, and M.J. Kuhar
   1988   Cocaine self-administration appears to be mediated by dopamine uptake inhibi-
          tion. *Progress In Neuro-Psychopharmacology and Biological Psychiatry* 12(2-3):233-9.6.
   1987   Cocaine receptors on dopamine transporters are related to self- administration of
          cocaine. *Science* 237(4819):1219-1223.

Robbins, S.J., R.N. Ehrman, A.R. Childress, J.W. Cornish, and C.P. O'Brien
   2000   Mood state and recent cocaine use are not associated with levels of cocaine cue
          reactivity. *Drug and Alcohol Dependence* 1:59(1):33-42.

Rose, G.
   1992   *The Strategy of Preventive Medicine.* New York: Oxford University Press.

Rose, R.J., M. Koskenvuo, J. Kaprio, S. Sarna, and H. Langinvainio.
   1988   Shared genes, shared experiences, and similarity of personality: Data from 14,288
          adult Finnish co-twins. *Journal of Perspectives in Social Psychology* 54(1):161-171.

Rydell, C.P., and S.S. Everingham
   1994   *Controlling Cocaine.* Report prepared for the Office of National Drug Control
          Policy and the U.S. Army. Santa Monica, CA: RAND.

Saffer, H., and F. Chaloupka
   1995   *The Demand for Illicit Drugs.* Working paper 5238. Cambridge, MA: National Bu-
          reau of Economic Research.

Self, D.W.
   1998   Neural substrates of drug craving and relapse in drug addiction. *Annals of Medi-
          cine* 30(4):379-389.

Sellers, E.M., and R.F. Tyndale
   2000   Mimicking gene defects to treat drug dependence. *Annals of the New York Acad-
          emy of Science* 909:233-246.

Siegel, R.K.
   1984   Cocaine aroma in the treatment of cocaine dependency. *Journal of Clinical Psy-
          chopharmacology* 4(1):61-62.

Simon, D., and E. Burns
   1997   *The Corner: A Year in the Life of an Inner City Neighborhood.* New York: Broadway
          Books.

Skog, O.J.
   1993   The tail of the alcohol consumption distribution. *Addiction* 88:601-610.

Stallings, M.C., J.K. Hewitt, T. Beresford, A.C. Heath, and L.J. Eaves
   1999   A twin study of drinking and smoking onset and latencies from first use to regu-
          lar use. *Behavioral Genetics* 29(6):409-421.

Tourangeau, R., L.J. Rips, and K. Rasinski
   2000   *The Psychology of Survey Response.* New York: Cambridge University Press.
True, W.R., A.C. Heath, J.F. Scherrer, H. Xian, N. Lin, S.A. Eisen, M.J. Lyons,

J. Goldberg, and M.T. Tsuang
   1999   Interrelationship of genetic and environmental influences on conduct disorder
          and alcohol and marijuana dependence symptoms. *American Journal of Educa-
          tional Genetics* 88(4):391-397.

Tsuang, M.T., M.J. Lyons, R.M. Harley, H. Xian, S. Eisen, J. Goldberg, W.R. True, and S.V. Farina
  1999 Genetic and environmental influences on transitions in drug use. *Behavioral Genetics* 29(6):473-479.

Tsuang, M.T., M.J. Lyons, J.M. Meyer, T. Doyle, S.A. Eisen, J. Goldberg, W. True, N. Lin, R. Toomey, and L. Eaves
  1998 Co-occurrence of abuse of different drugs in men: the role of drug-specific and shared vulnerabilities. *Archives of General Psychiatry* 55(11):967-972.

Uhl, G.R.
  1999 Molecular genetics of substance abuse vulnerability: A current approach. *Neuropsychopharmacology* 20(1):3-9.

Uhl, G.R., G.I. Elmer, M.C. LaBuda, R.W. Pickens. F.E. Bloom, and D.J. Kupfer, eds.
  1995 Genetic influences in drug abuse. In *Psychopharmacology: The Fourth Generation of Progress*. New York: Raven Press.

Van Etten, M.L., and J.C. Anthony.
  1999 Comparative epidemiology of initial drug opportunities and transitions to first use: Marijuana, cocaine, hallucinogens and heroin. *Drug and Alcohol Dependence* 54(2):117-125.

Van Etten, M.L., Y.D. Neumark, and J.C. Anthony.
  1997 Initial opportunity to use marijuana and the transition to first use: United States, 1979-1994. *Drug and Alcohol Dependence* 49(1):1-7.

Wise, R.A.
  1978 Catecholamine theories of reward: A critical review. *Brain Research* 152:215-247.

Yoshida, A., L. Hsu, and M. Yasunami
  1991 Genetic of human alcohol metabolizing enzymes. *Progress in Nucleic Acid Research and Molecular Biology* 40:235-287.

Yoshimoto, K., S. Ueda, M. Nishi, Y. Yang, H. Matsushita, Y. Takeuchi, B. Kato, Y. Kawai, K. Noritake, S. Kaneda, Y. Sorimachi, and M. Yasuhara
  2000 Changes in dopamine transporter and c-Fos expression in the nucleus accumbens of alcohol-tolerant rats. *Alcohol—Clinical and Experimental Research* 24(3):361-365.

Zuckerman, M.
  1994 *Behavioral Expressions and Biosocial Bases of Sensation Seeking*. New York: Cambridge University Press.

Part II

Data for Monitoring
the Nation's Drug Problems

Accurate description of trends and cross-sectional patterns in drug use, prices, and other relevant variables is essential to informed analysis and development of drug control policy. Theorizing and qualitative observation do not carry one very far toward the objective of assessing the effectiveness of alternative policies. Adequate data are necessary first to monitor the nation's drug problems and then to analyze policy impacts.

In Part II, we examine the data now regularly collected by the federal government and other agencies to monitor the nation's drug problems and consider how these data could be enhanced. Chapter 3 describes and evaluates these data. Chapter 4 examines principles for and the organization of such data collection in the federal statistical system.

The types of data discussed here are essential to inform drug control policy, but they do not suffice. Richer data aiming to shed light on specific aspects of drug use and detailed features of drug markets are needed to support research evaluating particular drug control instruments. However, such richer data may be collected as the need arises, rather than on the regular schedule that is basic to the monitoring function. Data needs for analysis of particular drug control instruments are discussed in Part III.[1]

---

[1]The committee invited officials at a number of public agencies and private organizations to comment on the accuracy of descriptions of their programs that are discussed in the rest of this report. These agencies and organizations include: the Office of National Drug Control Policy, the National Institute on Drug Abuse, the National Institute of Justice, the Bureau of Justice Statistics, the Substance Abuse and Mental Health Services Administration, the Centers for Disease Control and Prevention, and the Institute for Defense Analyses. The committee's written requests and the comments of those who replied to them can be found in the public access file for this study.

3

Data Needs for
Monitoring Drug Problems

This chapter examines several types of data that are or should be regularly collected and disseminated by the federal government and other agencies to monitor the nation's drug problems. We first describe and evaluate the main data systems providing information on drug use. We then discuss surveillance data that would be useful to provide early warnings of drug epidemics. Next we evaluate the System to Retrieve Information from Drug Evidence (STRIDE) data, the primary existing series on drug prices and purity. Finally, we discuss how aggregate statistics on drug production, consumption, and prices could be incorporated into the national macroeconomic accounts.

DATA ON DRUG USE

Four datasets are widely used to monitor trends and cross-sectional patterns in drug use in the United States. Two are nationwide population surveys: Monitoring the Future (MTF) surveys school students, and the National Household Survey of Drug Abuse (NHSDA) surveys the noninstitutionalized residential population age 12 and over. These surveys are based on probability samples of known populations. Hence these data can be used to draw conventional statistical inferences about the surveyed populations.

The other two data systems sample events rather than persons: the Arrestee Drug Abuse Monitoring (ADAM) surveys booked arrestees, and the Drug Abuse Warning Network (DAWN) provides information on drug-related episodes at emergency rooms and within the coroner's juris-diction. These "event-based" surveys have been used for operational pur-poses in the criminal justice and public health systems. They also are capable of providing evidence on emerging problems in high-risk popu-lations.

In this section we describe each of the four surveys, none of which provides information on drug consumption; we go on to recommend study of the feasibility of obtaining such information. Next we discuss issues of population coverage and sample size in the four surveys. We then investigate how nonresponse and inaccurate response may affect measurement of levels and trends in drug use.

Description of the Surveys

The four primary surveys used to monitor drug use in the United States collect information on whether the respondent used a wide range of illegal drugs (see Table 3.1). Specific questions are asked about alcohol, tobacco, marijuana, cocaine, hallucinogens, heroin, inhalants, and non-medical use of psychotherapeutics. The surveys also include various lev-els of detail on the respondent's demographics, health status, insurance, drug treatments, illegal activities, perceptions, and geographic location.

The *National Household Survey of Drug Abuse (NHSDA)* is a multi-stage probability sample providing annual self-report estimates of the number of drug users, their pattern of use, and their characteristics. The survey covers the U.S. civilian population age 12 and older. About 2 percent of the population is not covered, including persons who are in the military, in jail, in a long-term residential treatment regimen, and those who are homeless but not in shelters.

The National Commission on Marihuana and Drug Abuse conducted the first survey in 1972-1973. The National Institute on Drug Abuse (NIDA) then conducted surveys approximately every 2 to 3 years from 1973 to 1991. Since 1992, the Substance Abuse and Mental Health Service Administration (SAMHSA) has conducted the survey annually. Over the years, the sample size has been increased from 9,000 in 1988 to 26,000 in 1998 and 70,000 in 1999. The sample is now sufficiently large to enable estimation of the prevalence of illegal drug use in each of the 50 states. The sampling scheme is also stratified to ensure adequate representation by age, race, and ethnic background.

The instrument includes questions about the drug use of the respon-dent. For each drug and for combinations of drugs, the survey elicits information on the frequency of use within the respondent's lifetime, past year, and past 30 days. Respondents are asked the age when they were first exposed to and first used each drug, as well as when they last used it.

Questions are also asked about perceived risks associated with using illegal drugs, the actual health and behavioral consequences of use, and the availability of drugs. In early waves of the survey, respondents were asked to specify the amount and cost of marijuana and cocaine consumed within the past 30 days. However, these consumption and expenditure questions have not been asked since the early 1990s.

Given the sensitive nature of the questions posed, substantial resources are devoted to eliciting accurate responses. The surveys are conducted by face-to-face interviews in the home or at a private location, if possible. Various steps are taken to ensure confidentiality and anonymity, but frequently this is not possible for respondents ages 12-17 (U.S. General Accounting Office, 1993).[1]

Monitoring the Future (MTF) is an ongoing annual study of students in public and private schools in the United States based on a sample developed using a multistage random selection procedure. It assesses the prevalence of and trends in self-reported drug use among school students. It also asks questions concerning peer norms regarding drugs, beliefs about the dangers of illegal drugs, and perceived availability of drugs (Johnston et al., 1993, 1998). Illegal drugs, alcohol, tobacco, psychoactive pharmaceuticals (non-medical use), and inhalants are included. Students who have dropped out of high school (about 15 percent of those who enter) are not surveyed.

The University of Michigan's Institute for Social Research has conducted the survey each year since 1975. The survey initially focused on high school seniors but expanded to include 8th and 10th grade students in 1991. In 2000, 13,286 12th grade students were surveyed in 134 schools. Sample sizes for students in 8th and 10th grades were 17,311 (156 schools) and 14,576 (145 schools), respectively.

The MTF instrument includes questions about the drug use of student respondents. For each drug, the survey elicits information on the frequency of use within the respondent's lifetime, past year, and past 30

---

[1]Prior to the interview, respondents are repeatedly assured that their identities will be handled with utmost care in accordance with the federal law. During the interview, the respondent responds to sensitive questions, including those on drug use. The interviewer neither sees nor reviews the answers to those questions. After the answer sheet is complete, the respondent places them in an envelope that is then sealed and mailed, with no personal identifying information attached, to the Research Triangle Institute. Interviews are designed to be conducted in private settings, with only the interviewer and respondent present. Often, however, the interview is not completely private—especially for respondents ages 12 to 17. According the Office of Applied Statistics of the Substance Abuse and Mental Health Services Administration, at least 40 percent of the interviews with respondents in this age group are not completely private.

TABLE 3.1 Characteristics of Major Drug Data Collection Systems

Survey/Data Collection System	Sample	Data Collection	Sampling
National Household Survey of Drug Abuse (NHSDA)	18,000 interviews per survey (calendar) year during 1994-96; 25,000 per year in 1997-98; 70,000 per year starting in 1999	Personal Interview at home using Audio-CASI	Nationally representative multistage sample of the general population
Monitoring the Future (MTF)	Approx. 50,000 8th 10th, and 12th graders surveyed each year.	In-class questionnaire and follow-up survey	Nationally representative sample of students in school
Arrestee Drug Abuse Monitoring (ADAM) Program	Adult males and females arrested and booked during the data collection period. Generally each site collects quarterly data from 200-250 adult male arrestees, 100-150 adult female arrestees, 100-150 juvenile male arrestees (at 12 sites) and a small sample of female juvenile arrestees (at 8 sites).	Personal interview and urinalysis	Sample of arrests in selected booking facilities
Drug Abuse Warning Network (DAWN)	National representative sample of more than 600 nonfederal, short-stay emergency department visits per year. Data are also collected from approximately 146 medical examiners and coroners in 41 metropolitan areas.	Medical record abstraction	Probability sample of emergency department presentations; census of selected medical examiner facilities

Frequency of Data Collection	Geographic Coverage	Prevalence Estimates	Purpose
Throughout the calendar year	National	Lifetime; past 12 months; past 30 days	To track use of illegal drugs and other addictive substances and to collect related information from among the general population.
Throughout the calendar year with longitudinal follow-up of 12th graders once every 2 years	National	Lifetime, past 12 months; past 30 days	To track use of illegal drugs and other addictive substances among students registered for school.
Quarterly: data are collected for a two-week period, four times a year	23 cities	None	To track the illegal drug use among arrests.
Throughout the year	National	None	To track emergency department cases and medical examiner deaths caused by the use of illegal drugs or the abuse of prescription and over-the-counter drugs.

days. Respondents are asked when they first used the drug. Questions are also asked about perceived risks associated with using drugs, about the actual health, social, and behavioral consequences of use, about the availability of drugs, about the setting in which the student consumes drugs, and about expected future use.

Given the sensitive nature of the questionnaire, major efforts are made to obtain valid responses and to ensure confidentiality. For 8th and 10th graders, the survey is anonymous. Seniors (12th grade) are asked to provide identifying information so that follow-up surveys can be conducted. This tracking information is administered separately from the questionnaire and kept apart from it to protect privacy. Nonetheless, the degree to which the loss of anonymity has compromised the validity of self-reports is uncertain (General Accounting Office, 1993).

Beginning with the graduating class of 1976, follow-up surveys have been administered biannually by mail to representative subsamples of respondents up to age 32, and then again at age 35 and 40. The resulting panels provide the only detailed, ongoing source of longitudinal data on drug use in the United States.[2] In principle, these panel data would permit researchers to address pressing questions regarding the effects of policies on drug use and the effects of drug use on behavior, as well as basic epidemiological questions regarding duration of drug use episodes. However, citing concern for the confidentiality of respondents' identities, the Institute for Social Research has not made the MTF longitudinal data available to external researchers.

The lack of access to the longitudinal data from Monitoring the Future has been a major concern among researchers, and the committee shares this concern. Without effective research access, the quality of the MTF data can not be assessed objectively, nor can judgments be made about whether to collect additional longitudinal data. While MTF cross-sectional data are made available in public-use format via the Inter-university Consortium for Political and Social Research (ICPSR) archive, the critical longitudinal data are not available to researchers outside the MTF team. These data are important for answering questions related to the continued pattern of drug use, which is key to policy decisions regarding the efficacy of alternative drug policies. These data in particular, and longitudinal data on drug consumption in general, may provide essential information for evaluating the efficacy of alternative drug policies. Two features about illegal drug control policy make longitudinal data uniquely important. First, illegal drug consumption and markets are complex and involve many confounding factors. Second, drugs are addictive; that is,

---

[2]The National Longitudinal Survey of Youth has from time to time asked a few questions about drug use of the members of its sample, who were ages 14 to 21 in 1979.

consumption today influences consumption tomorrow. Longitudinal data are at least very valuable and perhaps essential to disentangle the many confounding factors and understand the addictive process. As discussed throughout this report, analysis of the dynamic process of drug use, evaluation of causal risk and protective factors, the relationship between prices, enforcement, and demand, and the effect of socioeconomic conditions on the illegal drug market all benefit from valid longitudinal data.

Recently, the MTF staff announced the availability of Internet-based access to its full dataset for cross-sectional studies. These data go beyond the public-use datasets and allow for more detailed and specific analyses. However, requests to use these datasets are mediated by MTF staff, who must execute the computer programs to extract the results, review them for privacy protection, and forward them to the requesters.

The committee is concerned that even this limited kind of access is not provided for the longitudinal datasets. The committee notes that the National Center for Education Statistics has developed a system for handling sensitive school-based surveys, including its longitudinal surveys. This system allows researchers and the public online access to public-use versions of these datasets. It also extends researchers access to the full datasets upon their agreement to abide by a privacy agreement.

The committee emphasizes its serious concern for the lack of research access to the MTF panel data. Providing access to the underlying data, while ensuring appropriate protections for confidentiality, is an important objective of statistical policy. Wide access to datasets encourages use of the data and enlists the broad community of researchers in the task of analyzing and understanding current trends. Equally important is that external analysis provides the critical function of reviewing the data and the methods of those who gather the data and helps inform the research community and policy makers about the usefulness and limitations of the data. At the same time, it alerts policy makers to the need for improvements and the best applications of the results.

In our view, it is in the public interest to have full access to all data of MTF, with appropriate protection for confidentiality. **The committee recommends that the Office of National Drug Control Policy and the granting agency (currently the National Institute on Drug Abuse) establish an oversight committee of statisticians and other experts, knowledgeable in procedures for balancing the needs for public access with the goal of confidentiality, to establish guidelines for providing access and for monitoring whether access to the data is quickly and easily provided.**

There are a number of possible approaches that the oversight committee could recommend. One is that the National Institute on Drug Abuse undertake an agreement with the National Center for Education Statistics to deposit the MTF files in its archives so that they can be made available to researchers on the same basis as other sensitive school-based surveys. Other approaches may be even more effective. **In any case, the committee recommends that the granting agency require that the contractors who gather data for Monitoring the Future move immediately to provide appropriate access to the longitudinal data. Finally, the committee recommends that if access is not provided in accordance with the guidelines of the oversight committee, the Office of National Drug Control Policy and the granting agency consider whether the public interest requires relocating the grant in another organization that will provide the level of access necessary for the data to be most useful for purposes of informing public policy on illegal drugs.**

The **Arrestee Drug Abuse Monitoring Program (ADAM)** is a redesign of the Drug Use Forecasting program (DUF), which operated first in 13 sites and later in 23 sites from 1987 to 1996. As a precursor to ADAM, a history of the development of the DUF program is important. DUF was designed to capture information about illegal drug use among persons arrested and held in booking facilities (usually jails). Active criminal offenders are a population found by research to be at extremely high risk for drug use (Hser et al., 1998; Wish and Gropper, 1990). They also constitute a population of special concern because of the social harm caused by their drug use. It is well documented that offenders who use illegal drugs commit crimes at higher rates and over longer periods of time than other offenders, and that predatory offenders commit fewer crimes during periods when they use no hard drugs (Chaiken and Chaiken, 1990).

The DUF program had two components which have been continued in the ADAM program. The first was a structured questionnaire administered by a trained interviewer to an arrested person who had been in a booking facility for not more than 48 hours. Second, a biological assay was included in the form of a urine specimen collected from the respondent to corroborate self-reported claims of drug use (National Institute of Justice, 1992, 1994, 1998). DUF/ADAM is the only national drug use survey that regularly utilizes drug testing. Data were collected each quarter on approximately 225 males in each site. Later, adult females and juvenile males and females were added to some but not all site samples. By 1992, as virtually the only source of continuous information on drug use within an offender population, DUF had come to be thought of as one of the major indicators of illegal drug use (U.S. General Accounting Office, 1993).

The U.S. General Accounting Office found that although DUF had a variety of uses and benefits, there were serious problems associated with its sampling methods. Some of these shortcomings are remedied in the new ADAM design (National Institute of Justice, 1998; 1994; U.S. General Accounting Office, 1993). The ADAM program was implemented in 1997 in the 23 DUF sites and 12 new sites to improve estimates of drug use among booked arrestees. The new ADAM methodology carefully defines the population being sampled in each site (typically all arrests at the county level). A goal of ADAM, according to the National Institute of Justice, is to provide estimates that are equally precise in each site. The new methodology therefore tailors case production to such factors as site size and the rates at which booked arrestees test positive in different jails (National Institute of Justice, 1998).

ADAM has also initiated a probability-based sample of arrests in each site, involving the random selection of a sample from a roster of all booked arrestees who were eligible to be interviewed during the referent data collection period. Selection intervals are based on the case flow in each site, so that interviewing is conducted when the greatest volume of arrests occurs.

The new design facilitates better individual site estimates and also supports important research on within-city and city-to-city variations in the nature of drug markets and in patterns of use among arrestees. Available resources do not permit the implementation of ADAM in a representative sample of jurisdictions across the country.

The *Drug Abuse Warning Network (DAWN)* compiles data on hospital emergency department episodes that medical staff conclude were the result of the abuse of legal and illegal drugs. The survey is administered in an ongoing national probability sample of general-purpose, nonfederal, short-stay hospitals with at least one 24-hour emergency department. The current sample design, which has been employed since 1988, is based on the survey of hospitals conducted by the American Hospital Association. The sample is updated once each year as new survey information is released. Hospitals are compensated for the time expended by the staff in preparing the DAWN records. Emergency department estimates are produced for 21 metropolitan statistical areas and for the nation. Hospitals outside these 21 areas are sampled to allow for national estimates based on a probability sample.

The survey covers episodes involving persons age 6 and older who were treated in the hospital's emergency department with a presenting problem that medical staff decide was induced by or related to the nonmedical use of a legal drug or any use of an illegal drug. The DAWN report records a limited set of information about the patient and the drug use that caused the emergency department episode. DAWN classifies the motive for drug abuse as dependence, suicide attempt or gesture, or to achieve psychic effects. DAWN data elements are abstracted retrospectively from medical documentation produced during the patient's treatment in the Emergency Department.

DAWN also collects information on drug-related deaths from selected medical examiner offices. In 1999, 139 medical examiners and coroners in 41 metropolitan areas reported to DAWN. However, this component is not based on a probability sample. As a result, drug-related deaths from DAWN cannot be extrapolated to the nation as a whole or to individual metropolitan areas in which medical examiner participation is incomplete. Also, medical examiners review only a limited number of the deaths occurring in their jurisdiction, and the types of cases under medical examiner review varies across jurisdictions. There is no linkage between the medical examiner and emergency department components of DAWN.

Consumption Data

Existing surveys of drug use collect information on frequencies of use but not on the quantity of drugs that users consume. The absence of information on drug consumption leaves a major gap in the nation's ability to monitor the dimensions of drug problems. Data on drug consumption are essential for understanding the operation of drug markets; the dynamics of initiation, intensification, and desistance; the response of drug use to changes in prices; and the public health and economic consequences of drug use. **The committee recommends that work be started to develop methods for acquiring consumption data.**

The committee acknowledges that obtaining accurate consumption data may present problems that cannot be easily solved. Accurate quantity information cannot be elicited directly if drug consumers do not have quantitative knowledge of the weight and purity of the drugs bought on any given purchase occasion. The committee could not find systematic research on the subject, but discussions with the Drug Enforcement Administration staff and ethnographers suggest that drug users commonly describe the purchased material in informal terms (e.g., bags, vials, rocks, lines) that do not translate into precise measures of weight and purity.

Even if drug users cannot provide precise information on the weight and purity of their drug purchases, they may be able report valuable data related to consumption. In particular, they may be able to report their expenditures on drugs and to give informal descriptions of the quantity consumed (see the section below on drug prices).[3] Whether or not consumers can or will provide accurate information about these details of drug purchases warrants investigation.

Consumers' lack of quantitative knowledge of what they have bought is also a source of serious difficulty in acquiring data on drug prices. This is because the price is the cost of a specified quantity of a drug with a

---

[3]Earlier waves of the NHSDA asked these types of quantity questions about cocaine and marijuana consumption.

specified purity. Because quantity and purity information are needed to estimate both prices and consumption, the committee has concluded that the acquisition of price and consumption data is usefully thought of as different aspects of the same problem. A method for acquiring information on the price, quantity, and purity of retail drug purchases is outlined in the section below on drug prices.

Population Coverage and Sample Size Issues

What the NHSDA and MTF Can and Cannot Reveal About Drug Use

The NHSDA and MTF are national probability surveys of particular segments of the U.S. population. Setting aside the response problems discussed later in this chapter, the sample data can be used to draw inferences about the surveyed populations. MTF does not survey high school dropouts. The NHSDA excludes about 2 percent of the population age 12 and older, including active military personnel, persons living in institutional group quarters (e.g., prisons and residential drug treatment centers) and homeless people not living in shelters.

Incomplete coverage is a problem if one wants to draw inferences for the general population or the excluded subpopulations, rather than the surveyed subpopulations. The groups not covered by the NHSDA and MTF sample designs may be particularly important for monitoring drug use in the United States. High school dropouts, homeless people, and people in institutions may exhibit substantially higher rates of drug use than the general population.[4] These high-risk "hidden populations" may contribute disproportionately to drug use in general and the use of more stigmatized drugs in particular (U.S. General Accounting Office, 1993).

The NHSDA and MTF data alone cannot be used to draw inferences about groups that are not surveyed. Similarly, the data cannot provide reliable estimates for subpopulations that are surveyed but for whom the effective sample sizes are small.[5] Thus, these surveys cannot be used to draw precise inferences about variation in drug use across important

---

[4]Also excluded are active military personnel who are less likely to use drugs. The Worldwide Survey of Substance Abuse and Health Behaviors among Military Personnel covers active military personnel (see, for example, Bray et al., 1995; Bachman et al., 1999; Mehay and Pacula, 1999). Chapter 7 provides further discussion.

[5]As in many large-scale national surveys, the NHSDA and MTF use complex sample designs that first sample clusters and then respondents within clusters. In clustered samples, the number of observations is not tantamount to the effective sample size. These survey design effects should be accounted for when evaluating the precision of an estimator. For further details of the effective sample sizes in the national drug use surveys, see Gfroerer et al. (1997b).

demographic and geographic groups. For example, the MTF sample cannot be used to accurately estimate prevalence rates by race or by state. The NHSDA, which has recently been redesigned to provide adequate representative subsamples for each of the 50 states, cannot reasonably be used to draw conclusions about local drug use. Many important drug control policies, however, occur within local boundaries.

These surveys may also be ineffective at describing the characteristics of illegal drug users, or at least users of more stigmatized drugs. Consider heroin. With only 63 past-year heroin users in the 1998 NHSDA survey, little can be learned about the demographic or socioeconomic characteristics of this group.

The committee recommends that methods be developed to supplement the data collected in the National Household Survey of Drug Abuse and Monitoring the Future in order to obtain adequate coverage of subpopulations with high rates of drug use. One possibility is to broaden the sampling frames of the existing surveys. MTF might be redesigned to cover teenagers rather than just students. The NHSDA might be expanded to cover institutionalized populations. Redesigning MTF and expanding the NHSDA pose challenging tasks, but the committee does not see insurmountable scientific problems given sufficient will and resources. Another possibility is to combine data from the NHSDA and MTF with other sources of information. In the next section, we discuss some of the data sources that could be linked.

What the ADAM and DAWN Can and Cannot Reveal About Drug Use

ADAM and DAWN are samples of particular events in the United States. These surveys can be used to draw inferences about the population of users identified through these events. ADAM is designed to provide estimates of the frequency and characteristics of arrests in which the arrested person has used drugs. DAWN can be used to estimate the number of person-visits to emergency departments for problems related to illegal drugs. Tracking drug use through arrest and emergency department events could serve to detect emerging problems in high-risk populations. ADAM and DAWN could also be used to evaluate the burden placed on the criminal justice system and hospitals by drug-related episodes. It remains the case, however, that ADAM and DAWN provide information on events, rather than people. These data cannot be used to infer drug use in general populations.[6]

---

[6]As noted by the Substance Abuse and Mental Health Administration with regard to DAWN, "The survey is designed to capture data on [emergency department] episodes that

Linking Data Systems

It is too much to expect that any single omnibus sample design should be able to serve all needs effectively. It has often been suggested, in other settings, that data systems designed for specific purposes could be linked (National Research Council, 1995; Charles, 2000). In fact, federal agencies responsible for gathering data to monitor trends in drug use demonstrate a clear appreciation of the importance of linking data samples collected at different times. Careful linkage of data from one reporting period to the next promotes ready interpretation of upward or downward trends when warranted by the validity and precision of the data (e.g., see Substance Abuse and Mental Health Administration, 1999; National Household Survey on Drug Abuse Series: H-11; Tables 2.2-2.10).

There has been less attention to linkages of drug data across different reporting systems in a manner that discloses systematic jurisdictional or geographical variation. That is, the samples for each data system often have been defined and made operational quite independently, without a plan for linking the data across systems. Each data system offers its own annual or more frequent reports, but there is little integration of the evidence from multiple data sources, even when the sources serendipitously have included the same jurisdictions or geographical areas within their samples.

Table 3.2 illustrates the nature of an overlap in recent samples for a selection of federal drug use monitoring systems. Atlanta, for example, has been included at the "primary sampling unit" level in recent samples of all five of the listed activities: NHSDA, DUF/ADAM, DAWN, the Community Epidemiology Work Group, and Pulse Check (the latter two are explained below in the section on data for early warning of drug epidemics). Baltimore has been included in all but one of the samples.

A table of this type demonstrates an opportunity for linking data sources in a manner that could promote the study of local area variation in drug use and drug policy. A synthetic analysis of data from multiple drug use monitoring systems within single jurisdictions, over time, would have certain value for local planning efforts. To some extent, the Community Epidemiology Work Group and Pulse Check activities provide for a synthesis of information from these multiple sources, as well as from state or locally sponsored monitoring activities that augment the federal data systems (e.g., see Sloboda and Kozel, 1999). This synthesis is informal and qualitative in nature rather than formal and quantitative.

---

are induced by or related to the use of an illegal drug or the nonmedical use of a legal drug. Therefore, DAWN data do not measure prevalence of drug use in the population." (Office of Applied Studies, 1999:1)

TABLE 3.2   A Selection of Metropolitan Statistical Areas Represented in Two or More Samples Used For Federal Drug Surveillance Initiatives

Metropolitan Statistical Areas	NHSDA	DUF-ADAM	DAWN	CEWG	PULSE CHECK
Atlanta, GA	x	x	x	x	x
Baltimore, MD	x	x	x	x	
Boston, MA	x	x	x	x	
Chicago, IL	x	x	x	x	x
Dallas, TX	x	x	x	x	
Denver, CO	x	x	x	x	x
Detroit, MI	x	x	x	x	
Houston, TX	x	x			
Los Angeles, CA	x	x	x	x	x
Miami-Hialeah, FL	x	x	x	x	x
Minneapolis-St. Paul, MN	x	x	x		
New York, NY	x	x	x	x	x
Newark, NJ	x	x			
Philadelphia, PA-NJ	x	x	x	x	
Phoenix, AZ	x	x	x	x	
San Antonio, TX	x	x	x		
San Diego, CA	x	x	x	x	x
St. Louis, MO-IL	x	x	x	x	
Washington, DC	x	x	x	x	x

Note: NHSDA = National Household Survey on Drug Abuse; DUF/ADAM = Drug Use Forecast/Arrestee Drug Abuse Monitoring Program; DAWN = Drug Abuse Warning Network; CEWG = Community Epidemiology Work Group; Pulse Check = key informant surveillance.

To be sure, there are isolated examples of integration across multiple drug data sources to characterize individual metropolitan areas. There has also been creative use of census data, treatment admissions data, and mortality data in an attempt to apply NHSDA results to a "small area estimation" task (e.g., see Substance Abuse and Mental Health Administration, 1997). There is, however, no systematic and continuing effort to perform data syntheses in a manner that could help the sum of the parts supply more information than can be extracted from each data source analyzed independently.

The committee does not take a position on the many complex and difficult issues that would almost certainly be involved in effectively linking different datasets on illegal drugs. While we do not make formal recommendations, in our judgment the feasibility of linking the national drug use surveys with other databases warrants serious investigation. With respect to analyses of already-gathered data, a mechanism could be created to allow investigators to discover the serendipitous overlap in these samples and to make the required linkages across datasets. With respect to the planning of future samples, a mechanism could be created to promote more deliberate linkages of data sources, rather than leave this linkage up to chance. Three possibilities are outlined below.

Linking Federal, State, and Local Data Systems. In its 1993 evaluation of drug use surveys, the U.S. General Accounting Office weighed how to effectively measure use at the state and local level, concluding that there are no obvious solutions. Its report found that the NHSDA would be "an expensive tool and would not constitute a useful indicator of some of the more serious drug use problems" and recommended that it should continue to be used to provide national prevalence estimates but not state-level estimates. This recommendation notwithstanding, the NHSDA sample size was subsequently increased in an effort to produce reliable state-level estimates.

There are in place several federally coordinated systems of state-administered data on illegal drugs that might usefully be studied as models.[7] The Drug and Alcohol Services Information System of the Substance Abuse and Mental Health Administration is compiled from information provided by state substance abuse agencies. The Center for Substance Abuse Treatment sponsors State Needs Assessment Studies, conducted by selected state substance abuse agencies. The Centers for Disease Control and Prevention collaborates with state health agencies to collect sensitive data in the Behavioral Risk Factor Surveillance System. The National Drug Intelligence Center links law enforcement intelligence data on drugs, gangs, and violence from nearly 15 federal agencies, and the Regional Information Sharing System integrates data from state and local law enforcement agencies (see Charles, 2000, for further details). In addition to these federally coordinated efforts, there are several states that have developed their own systems of linking data from multiple in-state sources. For example, California and Washington have such systems.

Linking NHSDA with Offender Databases. It has sometimes been suggested that the NHSDA data be linked with ADAM and with surveys of prison populations by the Bureau of Justice Statistics (BJS) in an effort to produce national estimates that appropriately cover the high-risk subpopulation of offenders. The feasibility of such linkages is not yet clear and should be investigated. ADAM, after all, is a survey of events (ar-

---

[7]There is a long list of studies that include state or local data. A partial list of over 50 studies with state-specific information can be found using a searchable database: http://neds.calib.com/datalocator/search.cfm.

rests) rather than of persons. The BJS prisoner surveys do cover the institutionalized offender population that the NHSDA misses, but they are at present performed only once every five years or more. There are three relevant BJS surveys:

• The Survey of Inmates in State Correctional Facilities, conducted every five years, provides information on individual characteristics of prison inmates. In addition to standard elements, such as current offenses and sentences, criminal histories, family background, and education level, data are collected on prior drug and alcohol abuse and on exposure to treatment and other in-prison services. Data for this survey are collected through personal interviews with a nationally representative sample of 14,000 inmates in about 300 state prisons and exist for 1974, 1979, 1986, 1991, and 1997.

• The Survey of Inmates in Federal Correctional Facilities, first conducted in 1991 and again in 1997, collects data on the same variables used in the Survey of Inmates in State Correctional Facilities. These are also self-report data, elicited through personal interviews with a probability-based sample of 4,041 federal inmates. Based on the completed interviews, estimates for the entire correctional population are developed. Data from the combined inmate surveys are reported as the Survey of Inmates in State and Federal Correctional Facilities. The interview completion rate exceeds 90 percent for both the federal and state surveys.

• The Survey of Inmates in Local Jails is periodically administered to collect data on the family background and personal characteristics of jail inmates. It includes detailed data on past drug and alcohol use and history of contact with the criminal justice system. The survey relies on personal interviews with a nationally representative sample of almost 6,000 jail inmates. Data are available from this series for years 1978, 1983, 1989, and 1996.

For a more complete description of these BJS Surveys, see Appendix B.

Linking NHSDA with Treatment Databases. It has also been suggested that the NHSDA data be linked with DAWN and with surveys of populations receiving treatment in an effort to produce national estimates of the high-risk subpopulation in need of and who receive treatment.[8] The feasi-

---

[8]Many of these people are included in the universe covered by general population surveys, such as the NHSDA, which includes treatment clients who are in ambulatory settings or those who receive short detoxification in a clinic or hospital setting. Excluded are clients who are receiving long-term residential drug treatment.

bility of such linkages is not yet clear. DAWN, after all, is a survey of events (emergency department drug-related cases) rather than of persons. The Substance Abuse and Mental Health Administration, working cooperatively with state substance abuse agencies, compiles lists of treatment facilities and periodically collects information about the number and characteristics of persons receiving treatment. There are three relevant treatment data sets:

• The Drug and Alcohol Services Information System includes a national roster of treatment facilities, a census of these facilities and information about clients.
• The Uniform Facility Data Set is an annual census of clients in treatment. It tracks the number and characteristics of clients in treatment as of a reference date each fall.
• The Treatment Episode Data Set uses admissions records to compile information about patients in facilities receiving public funding.

These surveys, however, are primarily designed to describe the characteristics and efficacy of treatment programs. They do not include persons needing treatment who do not get it. Furthermore, they are not designed as samples of people receiving treatment, but rather provide samples of treatment episodes.

Implications of Response Problems
for Analysis of Levels and Trends in Drug Use

Whether the subject of interest is prevalence, frequency, or quantity consumed, questions about the quality of self-reports of drug use are inevitable. The usefulness of the data obtained from a survey is reduced if some sampled individuals fail to answer one or more questions on the survey (nonresponse) or give incorrect answers (inaccurate response). In particular, nonresponse and inaccurate response may lead investigators to draw incorrect conclusions from the data provided by a survey. Response problems occur to some degree in nearly all surveys but are arguably more severe in surveys of illegal activities. For example, some individuals may be reluctant to admit that they engage in illegal behavior, whereas others may brag about such behavior and exaggerate it.

It is widely thought that nonresponse and inaccurate response may cause surveys such as the NHSDA and MTF to underestimate the prevalence of drug use in the surveyed populations (Caspar, 1992). It is often assumed, however, that these surveys provide accurate information about trends. For example, the principal investigators of MTF state that "biases in the [MTF] survey will tend to be consistent from one year to another, which means that our measurement of trends should be affected very little by such biases" (Johnston et al., 1998:47-48). Similarly, Anglin et al. (1993) state that "it is easier to generate trend information . . . than to determine absolute level."[9]

Consider, for instance, drawing inferences on the levels and trends in annual prevalence of use rates for adolescents during the 1990s.[10] Data from MTF imply that annual prevalence rates for students in 12th grade increased from 29 percent in 1991 to 42 percent in 1997. Data from the NHSDA indicate that the annual prevalence rates of use for adolescents ages 12 to 17 increased from 13 percent in 1991 to 19 percent in 1997.[11] Both series suggest that from 1991 to 1997, the fraction of teenagers using drugs increased by nearly 50 percent. Does the congruence in the NHSDA and MTF series for adolescents imply that both surveys identify the trends, if not the levels, or does it merely indicate that both surveys are affected by response problems in the same way?

This section discusses the effects of nonresponse and inaccurate response in the NHSDA and MTF on estimates of levels and trends in the prevalence of drug use. The conclusions vary by response problem. If nonresponse is the only significant problem (that is, incorrect responses do not occur), then the data provided by the NHSDA and MTF provide bounds on prevalence levels and identify the directions of sufficiently large changes in prevalence. If inaccurate responses are also present, then the data alone may not identify levels, trends, or even the directions of large changes in prevalence. With certain assumptions, both the levels and trends can be identified. In a paper prepared for the committee, Pepper provides a more detailed discussion (see Appendix D).

The committee concludes that these response problems, although not

---

[9]These same ideas are expressed in the popular press as well. Joseph Califano, Jr., the former secretary of health, education and welfare, summarizes this widely accepted view about the existing prevalence measures: "These numbers understated drug use, alcohol and smoking, but statisticians will say that you get the same level of disassembling every year. As a trend, it's probably valid" (Molotsky, 1999).

[10]Annual prevalence measures indicate use of marijuana, cocaine, inhalants, hallucinogens, heroin, or nonmedical use of psychotherapeutics at least once during the year. Different conclusions about trends and levels might be drawn for other outcome indicators.

[11]Similar qualitative differences in levels are generally found if one compares same-age individuals, although the magnitudes are much less extreme. Gfroerer et al. (1997b) reports that the age-adjusted prevalence rates from MTF are between 0.92 to 2.24 times the NHSDA rates. In all but one case (8th graders consuming cocaine), these ratios are over 1 with many reaching at least 1.4. The remaining differences may be due to variation in the survey methodologies as well as in the surveyed populations. MTF excludes dropouts, whereas the NHSDA surveys all adolescents living in noninstitutionalized quarters. In the NHSDA, adolescents may complete the questionnaire in the presence of their guardians. In MTF, guardians are not present, but peers are.

unique to drug use surveys, do hinder inferences on the levels and trends in the proportions of people who are consuming illegal drugs in the United States. These problems, however, do not imply that the data are uninformative or that the surveys should be discontinued. Rather, researchers using these data must either tolerate a certain degree of ambiguity or must be willing to impose strong assumptions. The problem, of course, is that ambiguous findings may lead to indeterminate conclusions, whereas strong assumptions may be inaccurate and yield flawed conclusions (Manski, 1995; Manski et al., 2000).

There are practical solutions to this quandary. If stronger assumptions are not imposed, then the way to resolve an indeterminate finding is to collect richer data. Data on the nature of the nonresponse problem (e.g., the prevalence rate of nonrespondents) and on the nature and extent of invalid response in the national surveys might be used to both supplement the existing data and to impose more credible assumptions. A sure remedy is to increase the frequencies of correct responses in surveys.

Nonresponse. Nonresponse is an endemic problem in survey sampling. Approximately 15 percent of the students surveyed by MTF fail to respond to the questionnaire and approximately 25 percent fail to respond to the NHSDA.[12] These nonresponse rates are similar to those achieved by the National Survey of Family Growth, which also asks for sensitive information, and not much higher than those of the Current Population Survey, which is used to measure the unemployment rate. **The committee recommends a systematic and rigorous research program (1) to understand and monitor nonresponse and (2) to develop methods to reduce nonresponse to the extent possible.** The inferential problems that may arise in the absence of a better understanding of nonresponse are elaborated below.

The MTF and NHSDA data are uninformative about the behavior of nonrespondents. Thus, these data do not identify prevalence unless one makes untestable assumptions about the responses that nonrespondents would have given if they had responded. A simple example illustrates the problem. Suppose that 100 individuals are asked whether they used illegal drugs during the past year. Suppose that 25 do not respond, so the nonresponse rate is 25 percent. Suppose that 19 of the 75 respondents used illegal drugs during the past year and that the others did not. Then the reported prevalence of illegal drug use is 19/75 = 25.3 percent. How-

---

[12]The 25 percent nonresponse rate for the NHSDA includes both unit (household) and element (person) nonresponse. The 15 percent nonresponse rate cited for MTF includes student nonresponse only. Schools that refuse to participate in the MTF survey are replaced by similar schools. School nonresponse and replacement are addressed later in the chapter.

ever, true prevalence among the 100 surveyed individuals depends on how many of the nonrespondents used illegal drugs. If none did, then true prevalence is 19/100 = 19 percent. If all did, then true prevalence is [(19 + 25)/100] = 44 percent. If between 0 and 25 nonrespondents used illegal drugs, then true prevalence is between 19 and 44 percent. Thus, in this example, nonresponse causes true prevalence to be uncertain within a range of 25 percent.

Prevalence rates and trends can be identified if one makes sufficiently strong assumptions about the behavior of nonrespondents. The most common assumption is that nonresponse is random conditional on a set of observed covariates. It implies that prevalence among nonrespondents is the same as prevalence among respondents with the same values of the covariates. The NHSDA, for example, provides sampling weights that can be used to correct for nonresponse under the assumption the fraction of drug users is identical for respondents and nonrespondents within observed subgroups (e.g., age, sex and race groups).

The committee is not aware of empirical evidence that supports the view that nonresponse is random. In fact, there is limited empirical evidence to the contrary.[13] Caspar (1992) used a shortened questionnaire and monetary incentives to elicit responses from 40 percent of the nonrespondents to the 1990 NHSDA in the Washington, D.C., area. He found that nonrespondents have higher prevalence rates than do respondents. It is not known whether this finding applies to all nonrespondents or only those who responded to Caspar's survey.

Rather than impose the missing-at-random assumption, it might be sensible to assume that the prevalence rate of nonrespondents is no less than the observed rate for respondents.[14] Maintaining this assumption,

---

[13]Reporting on a study in which nonrespondents in the NHSDA were matched to their 1990 census questionnaires, Gfroerer et al. (1997a) conclude that "the Census Match Study demonstrates that response rates are not constant across various interviewer, respondent, household, and neighborhood characteristics. To the extent that rates of drug use vary by these same characteristics, bias due to nonresponse may be a problem. However, it is not always the case that low response rates occur in conjunction with high drug use prevalence. Some populations with low response rates (e.g., older adults and high income populations) tend to have low rates of drug use. On the other hand, some populations (e.g., large metro residents and men) have low response rates and high drug use rates" (p. 292). The Census Match Study demonstrates that there are observed differences between respondents and nonrespondents. In principle, these differences could be accounted for using sampling weights if the missing-at-random assumption holds. The census does not reveal the drug use behavior of nonrespondents.

[14]While this appears to be a credible assumption, there are alternative views. In particular, if persons inclined to give false negative reports decline to fill out the questionnaire while persons inclined to give false positive accounts participate in the survey, the observed rates would be upward biased. Still, even if the maintained assumption does not warrant unquestioned acceptance, it certainly merits serious consideration.

Pepper obtained bounds on prevalence (Appendix D). The lower bound results if prevalence among nonrespondents equals that among respondents. The upper bound results if all nonrespondents use illegal drugs. True prevalence is within these bounds. Using data from MTF, Pepper found that annual prevalence for 12th graders lies between 29 and 40 percent in 1991 and between 42 and 51 percent in 1997. Thus, the data place prevalence within about a 10 percentage point range. The estimates imply that prevalence increased in the 1990s, although the magnitude of the increase is not revealed. In particular, from 1991 to 1997, prevalence increased by at least 2 percentage points (from 40 to 42 percent) and may have increased by as much as 22 points (from 29 to 51 percent).

Using data from the NHSDA, Pepper found that annual prevalence for adolescents ages 12 to 17 was between 13 and 35 percent in 1991 and between 19 and 39 percent 1997. Thus, the data restrict the prevalence rate to a 20 percentage point range. The direction of any trend is not revealed. Prevalence might have fallen by 16 percentage points (from 35 to 19 percent) or increased by 26 percentage points (from 13 to 39 percent). Thus, in the absence of additional information, the NHSDA data are uninformative about the direction of even large changes over this period.

The direction and magnitude of the change in prevalence can be identified if one makes sufficiently strong assumptions about drug use among nonrespondents. The magnitude is identified if one assumes that prevalence is the same among respondents and nonrespondents. The direction is identified if one assumes that prevalence among nonrespondents did not decrease by too much. In the NHSDA data on 12- to 17-year-olds, Pepper found that true prevalence increased from 1991 to 1997 under the assumption that prevalence among nonrespondents did not decrease by more than 18 percentage points during this period. This assumption may be acceptable to many observers, but it cannot be verified or refuted empirically using any data of which the committee is aware. Thus, potentially strong though possibly plausible assumptions are required to estimate the direction of the trend of prevalence, whereas weaker assumptions suffice to bound prevalence levels.

School Nonresponse and Replacement in MTF. School nonresponse is a particularly troubling source of uncertainty in estimates obtained from MTF data. MTF asks schools to participate in its study, and students are sampled from the participating schools. Each year, between 30 and 50 percent of the selected schools decline to participate, in which case a similar school (in terms of size, geographic area, and other characteristics) is recruited as a replacement. If a 30 to 50 percent nonresponse rate were incorporated into the bounds described earlier, then the MTF data would not identify the direction of even the largest changes in prevalence. This problem does not arise if the decision of a school to participate in MTF is unrelated to illegal drug use among its students. The principal investigators of MTF argue that this is the case (Johnston et al., 1998), but there is little empirical evidence to support (or refute) their claim. Perhaps the investigators are right, in which case school nonresponse does not affect identification of trends from MTF data. Alternatively, nonrespondent schools may have very different prevalence levels and trends, in which case MTF cannot be used to identify trends. We simply do not know.

Also troubling is the method of replacing nonrespondent schools. The replacement schools are not found using the original sampling scheme, but instead are purposefully selected to be "similar" to schools that decline to participate. If there are unobserved differences between the replacement and the dropout schools, the sampling properties are compromised. Replacing schools does not solve the nonresponse problem.

In the committee's judgment, alternatives to the current MTF sample design warrant serious consideration as means to more effectively collect information on teenage drug use. A household survey of teenagers similar in design to the National Longitudinal Survey of Youth or the NHSDA would almost certainly achieve higher response rates and would, moreover, cover school dropouts. Or the present school-based design of MTF might be retained, but the manner of selecting respondent schools changed to enhance response rates. At a minimum, the survey design should explicitly account for school nonresponse, with any replacement schemes formally considered to be part of the sample design.

Inaccurate Response. Self-report surveys on deviant behavior invariably yield some false reports. Respondents concerned about the legality of their behavior may falsely deny consuming illegal drugs. Desires to fit into a deviant culture may lead some respondents to falsely claim to consume illegal drugs. Thus, despite considerable resources devoted to reducing misreporting in the national drug use surveys, invalid response remains an inherent concern.

This measurement problem is conceptually different from the nonresponse problem. The fraction of nonrespondents is known, but the fraction of respondents who give invalid responses is not. Thus, the methods used to investigate the effects of nonresponse are not applicable to incorrect response. Rather, one must obtain information or make assumptions about self-reporting errors.

There is a large literature that provides evidence on the magnitude of misreporting in some self-reported drug use surveys. Validation studies have been conducted on arrestees (Harrison 1992, 1997; Mieczkowski, 1990), addicts in treatment programs (Darke, 1998; Magura et al., 1987, 1992; Morral et al., 2000; Kilpatrick et al., 2000), employees (Cook et al.,

1997), people in high-risk neighborhoods (Fendrich et al., 1999), and other settings. See Harrison and Hughes (1997) for a review of the literature.

Despite this literature, little is known about misreporting in the NHSDA and MTF. Existing validation studies have largely been conducted on samples of people who have much higher rates of drug use than the general population. Respondents are usually not randomly sampled from some known population. The response rates to these surveys are often quite low.

A few studies have attempted to evaluate misreporting in broad-based representative samples. However, lacking direct evidence on misreporting in the national probability surveys, these studies make strong, unverifiable assumptions to infer validity rates. Biemer and Witt (1996) analyzed misreporting in the NHSDA under the assumption that smoking tobacco is positively related to illegal drug use and independent of valid reporting. They found false negative rates (that is, the fraction of users who claim to have abstained) in the NHSDA that vary between 0 and 9 percent. Fendrich and Vaughn (1994) evaluated denial rates using panel data on illegal drug use from the National Longitudinal Survey of Youth (NLSY), a nationally representative sample of individuals who were ages 14 to 21 in the base year of 1979. Of the respondents to the 1984 survey who claimed to have ever used cocaine, nearly 20 percent denied use and 40 percent reported less frequent lifetime use in the 1988 follow-up. Of those claiming to have ever used marijuana in 1984, 12 percent later denied use and just over 30 percent report less lifetime use. These logical inconsistencies in the data are informative about validity only under the assumption that the original 1984 responses are correct.

Both of these studies require unsubstantiated assumptions to draw conclusions about validity. Arguably, smokers and nonsmokers may have different reactions to stigma and thus may respond differently to questions about illegal behavior. Arguably, the self-reports in the 1984 National Longitudinal Survey of Youth are not all valid. Thus, neither study can be used to draw strong conclusions about validity rates.

Still, several broad conclusions about misreporting have been drawn. At the most basic level, there appears to be consistent evidence that some respondents misreport their drug use behavior. More specifically, valid self-reporting of drug use appears to depend on the timing of the event and the social desirability of the drug. Recent use may be subject to higher rates of bias. Misreporting rates may be higher for stigmatized drugs, such as cocaine, than for marijuana. False negative reports seem to increase as drug use becomes increasingly stigmatized. The fraction of false negative reports appears to exceed the fraction of false positive reports, although these differences vary by cohorts. Finally, the validity rates can be affected by the data collection methodology. Surveys that can effectively ensure confidentiality and anonymity and that are conducted in noncoerced settings will tend to have relatively low misreporting rates.

Without knowledge of the fraction of respondents who misreport their drug use, it is not possible to identify either prevalence levels or trends. Johnston et al. (1998) argue that invalid reporting rates in the national surveys are low and vary little from year to year so that the data can be used to infer trends. Pepper discusses some potentially plausible assumptions about incorrect response that make it possible to bound prevalence level (Appendix D). It is not known, however, whether either Johnston's or Pepper's assumptions are correct.

Concerns about inaccurate response in the NHSDA and MTF are not new. In fact, in a new effort to learn more about the validity of self-reports, SAMHSA is undertaking a project that works with a subsample of about 2,000 people from the 1999 NHSDA panel. The study will administer the questionnaire following normal procedures, then will hold debriefing sessions in which respondents will be encouraged to give true answers to the questions, on the grounds that the results are important because policy will be based on them. Respondents will then be offered $25 for a urine sample and $25 for a hair sample. This effort went into the field in September 1999. The sample is limited to those ages 12 to 25, the age group that has the highest rates of drug use. Data collection will continue for one year. The questions cover use of tobacco, marijuana, opiates, and amphetamines. The committee is encouraged by the recent initiation of a project to evaluate inaccurate response in the NHSDA, but this project should be considered as only the first step.

Without consistent and reliable information on inaccurate response in the national surveys, researchers will be forced to make unsubstantiated assumptions about the validity of responses. **Thus, the committee strongly recommends a systematic and rigorous research program (1) to understand and monitor inaccurate response in the national use surveys and (2) to develop methods to reduce reporting errors to the extent possible.**

DATA FOR EARLY WARNING OF DRUG EPIDEMICS

The U.S. government, in partnership with the individual states, has created a remarkable source of surveillance information that provides timely early warning about infectious disease outbreaks in essentially all local area jurisdictions, and the spread of epidemics across the nation. On occasion, this surveillance network also has functioned quite well to detect and to disrupt epidemics of noninfectious origin, but not for such drugs as cocaine, crack, MDMA ("ecstasy"), or other illegal drugs.

Several definitions may help to clarify this discussion. First, an "epidemic" refers to an unusual occurrence of disease or a health-related condition or event (e.g., drug-taking) in a specified place, time, and population; in this case, "unusual" means more than expected for that place, time, and population. Epidemics are defined by their unexpected or unusual character rather than by magnitude; in order to promote early response to threats that might grow exponentially if left unattended, there is a quite low quantitative threshold for declaring that an epidemic might be starting.

Second, early in the epidemic process, as a disease, health-related condition, or event begins to mount within a specified place, time, and population, the term "outbreak" sometimes is used. As a term, "outbreak" is less exact than "epidemic," and some epidemiologists say "outbreak" where others say "epidemic," but most would agree that outbreak is what we call an epidemic in its earliest stages, and that many outbreaks do not progress to become epidemics. In many ways, an outbreak is like an epidemic's embryo, and the embryo may not hatch.

Third, in the context of public health work, "surveillance" refers to the intelligence activities: deliberate efforts to detect unusual occurrence of disease, health-related conditions or events, in a manner that can be distinguished by its practicality, completeness of coverage of local area populations, and timeliness, rather than by its accuracy or scientific validity and precision. If it is to be successful, surveillance must occasionally result in a falsely positive warning—that is, an outbreak that remains in embryonic form and does not become an epidemic. In light of the catastrophes that can occur when disease epidemics are not detected until very late stages, the occasional falsely positive warning is the penalty paid in order to escape warnings about public health disasters of major significance that come too late.

This overview of basic public health concepts may come as a surprise to readers who are accustomed to thinking about drug abuse surveillance in terms of the data collection systems discussed in this chapter. None of these data systems is especially timely, and none has a fine-grained coverage of local areas within the nation. If they were refined to give detailed coverage of all local areas, they would be so costly as to be completely impractical.

Nevertheless, a cursory reading of the background history of these data systems reveals that they were intended to provide surveillance information concerning the drug use of the U.S. population (NHSDA, MTF, DUF/ADAM), as well as overdoses and other hazards associated with drug use (DAWN). The questions raised about the suitability of these data to measure drug use must be held in check when this intention is brought into focus. A surveillance system generally is designed to value falsely positive warnings about outbreaks and epidemics at the level of local areas more than falsely negative warnings, and to provide information that will help public health officials responsible for local, state, and national emergency responses to mobilize early against emerging threats. As such, the principles guiding construction of surveillance systems are not necessarily the same as the principles that guide the construction of survey instruments for policy evaluation.

Nonetheless, we also can see that these survey data systems often fall short in terms of the principles of surveillance. It is difficult to characterize reports from these systems as timely, although it is clear that available resources are not sufficient or are not deployed in a manner that allows more timely reporting. It also is difficult to characterize the systems as being useful for local responses to drug problems. It is feasible for MTF to provide reports on local areas, by aggregating information across schools, but the MTF staff has not produced reports of this type, reportedly because of concern about violation of the confidentiality and privacy of schools and students participating in the MTF assessments each year.

Partly in response to a recognition that the nation's large data systems lack the timeliness and local area coverage of standard public health surveillance systems, the National Institute on Drug Abuse has fostered development of a Community Epidemiology Work Group (CEWG) initiative, and the Office of National Drug Control Policy has fostered development of Pulse Check. For the limited number of local areas that are included within their catchment boundaries, CEWG and Pulse Check provide a periodic check on local area conditions. For example, CEWG reports in the early 1980s represent one of the earliest sources of information about displacement of the use of powder cocaine by the freebase forms of cocaine, such as crack, which became more widely available during the later 1980s. CEWG reports also have provided one track of the epidemic spread of methamphetamine ("ice") smoking from the West to the East, often along major interstate highways. NIDA has produced instructional manuals and guidelines for community groups and leaders who may wish to organize local area community epidemiology work groups, although CEWG participation continues to provide coverage of no more than a small fraction of local areas in the country.

It may be useful to consider the approaches that infectious disease epidemiologists have taken when they have faced the task of designing and maintaining surveillance for the U.S. population. Whereas a complete history and review of these approaches is beyond the scope of this report, a useful example is the National Notifiable Disease Surveillance System, which captures reports of cases of specific diseases of public health importance (mainly diseases of infectious origin). The reports themselves originate with practitioners and are published on a weekly basis in a periodical, *Morbidity and Mortality Weekly Reports,* and in electronic form on the Internet. As described in one report, "State and local public health officials rely on health-care providers, laboratories, and other public health personnel to report the occurrence of notifiable diseases to state and local health departments. Without such data, trends cannot be accurately monitored, unusual occurrences of diseases might not be detected" (*Morbidity and Mortality Weekly Reports,* 1997).

One might ask what motivates the practitioners to provide the case reports for processing and tabulation. The answer is, in part, the existence of state laws and regulations, which mandate reporting of specified "notifiable" diseases and conditions. The mandated list of notifiable diseases differs across the states, as do the requirements for information to accompany each report. The Centers for Disease Control and Prevention (CDC) has become a partner with the states in this process, first by offering technical assistance, and more recently by establishing policies that regularize reporting of cases and a set of uniform criteria for public health surveillance. For example, the CDC definitions provide for distinctions between laboratory-confirmed cases, epidemiologically linked cases (e.g., in which the patient had contact with one or more infected or exposed other), probable and suspected cases (e.g., classified as "probable" or "suspected" for reporting purposes on the basis of clinical features but not confirmed by laboratory tests). In addition to receiving weekly reports, the CDC collates the reports and publishes them weekly in the *Morbidity and Mortality Weekly Reports,* with a level of detail for states, cities, and counties that has never been seen in national surveillance of drug use or drug-associated problems.

About five years ago, a CDC steering committee was convened to help create integrated public health information and surveillance systems for the United States. The final report of the steering committee provides a comprehensive overview of the CDC's notifiable disease reporting system, as well as supplemental sources of public health information and surveillance. The report is remarkable for its scope and depth, but it is striking that it does not discuss the integration of surveillance activities or information on the use of illegal drugs, one of the foremost public health challenges that faces the nation.

At first, one might ask whether this omission is due to the highly sensitive and confidential nature of information about an individual's drug use. After all, a physician or other health care provider might hesitate to provide a report about an illegal activity. In counterpoint, it is possible to reply that the same types of consideration come into play with respect to other notifiable diseases, including sexually transmitted diseases such as syphilis and gonorrhea, and one imagines that the confidentiality of notifiable information about HIV and AIDS cases is as sensitive or more sensitive than the confidentiality of information about an individual's past use of a specific drug.

It also is instructive to note that, in a particular episode, the CDC's surveillance systems were capable of identifying a drug-related toxicity very early in the course of an epidemic, and they also were successful in mounting a public health intervention campaign that ended the epidemic within 12 months of its detection. The story of this late 20th century public health success has been told by Anthony and Van Etten (1999), who stress that the credit for reporting the first cases belongs to a single physician health care provider who noticed a possible connection between an idiopathic syndrome of eosinophilia myalgia and his patients' extramedical use of nutritional supplements. These nutritional supplements were being taken by the patients, without medical prescription, for some of the reasons illegal drug users give for their use of such drugs as marijuana (e.g., to relieve tension, for calming purposes, to aid sleep). The consequences of consuming apparently contaminated supplies of the nutritional supplement (l-tryptophan) included the serious and potentially fatal eosinophilia myalgia syndrome. CDC officials recognized the similarities in clinical and epidemiological features of the reported cases with the clinical features reported for fatalities in a rapeseed oil epidemic in Spain some years before. The federal officials' recognition of these similarities led them to increase their efforts to identify possible cases and to launch small clinical case-control studies to test alternative causal hypotheses. Within nine months of the first case report, the several small case-control studies allowed tracing of the etiologic agent back to contaminated batches of l-tryptophan imported from Japan; manufacturers and sellers complied with a voluntary ban on sales of the product, and the epidemic stopped. Follow-up laboratory investigation traced the contamination to a change in production methods used in some factories in Japan.

Hence, the CDC's method of surveillance by collecting and collating reports of notifiable diseases and other health-related conditions and events provides a model that might be emulated in the nation's efforts to gain a capacity for more timely and locally targeted drug intervention efforts. These methods are not necessarily suitable for evaluation of national policy or even local area policies. Nonetheless, they may prove to be an important element in a national plan for gathering of data about drug-taking, and the consequences of drug-taking in the U.S. population.

Against this background, the committee makes the following conclusions and recommendations:

The nation's capacity for early warning of drug epidemics is quite limited, except perhaps in the areas already covered by the Community Epidemiology Work Group and Pulse Check techniques, or in the local areas surveyed for DUF/ADAM and MTF. Even when these surveys have sufficiently large samples to answer questions about variation from place to place or from time to time, the data for local areas generally are not collated and reported for use by public health authorities in the local areas, at the state level, or nationally. The exceptions are to be found in occasional local area reports in the Community Epidemiology Work Group publications.

In contrast, the nation has developed a quite refined capacity for early warning of infectious disease epidemics and health-related conditions and events captured by the CDC's routine surveillance networks. To some extent, the success of these surveillance networks and their provision of information that is useful in guidance of public health action rests on state-level regulations and laws about notifiable diseases and conditions, including sensitive conditions such as syphilis, gonorrhea, and HIV/AIDS, with due attention to confidentiality and privacy of the case reports. Nonetheless, even when the conditions are not mandated as notifiable conditions, the CDC surveillance network has demonstrated its capacity to detect and to disrupt epidemics as they occur.

Development of the nation's capacity to detect outbreaks and epidemics of drug-taking at an early stage can have the benefit of careful study of the surveillance systems developed for other health-related conditions. The report of the CDC steering committee provides an overview of principles and procedures for creation of an integrated public health information and surveillance system. Illegal drug use and its associated hazards do not appear to have been considered explicitly by the CDC steering committee. **The committee recommends that the Office for National Drug Control Policy and the Centers for Disease Control and Prevention undertake to develop principles and procedures for information and surveillance systems on illegal drug-taking and its associated hazards.**

DATA ON DRUG PRICES

Data on prices of illegal drugs are important for many drug policy studies. Analyses of price levels and price changes provide information about the effects of policy interventions and market forces that influence the supply of and demand for drugs. For example, a policy action that increases the price of an illegal drug (possibly an increase in legal penalties for selling it) may greatly reduce use of the drug if the demand for it is sensitive to price (highly elastic) but not if the demand is insensitive to price (inelastic). Consequently, estimates of price elasticities of demand and of price changes in response to policy interventions are important components of cost-effectiveness analyses of alternative approaches to reducing drug use. Price data are also used in studies of the effectiveness of enforcement and interdiction activities. In these studies, the increase (if any) in the price of an illegal drug following a major enforcement or interdiction action has been used to indicate the effectiveness of the action (see, for example, Yuan and Caulkins, 1998; Crane et al., 1997; DiNardo, 1993). Agencies of the federal government use price data to estimate quantities of illegal drugs consumed in the United States. Consumption is not measured directly, but estimates of expenditures on illegal drugs are available from surveys. Consumption is estimated by dividing expenditures by a price estimate (National Research Council, 1999). Caulkins and Reuter (1996) provide further discussion of the uses of price data in drug policy analysis.

The most widely used source of data on prices of illegal drugs is the System to Retrieve Information from Drug Evidence (STRIDE). STRIDE contains records of acquisitions of cocaine, heroin, and other illegal drugs by undercover agents and informants of the Drug Enforcement Administration (DEA) and the Metropolitan Police of the District of Columbia (MPDC). The data include the type of drug acquired, the amount acquired, its purity, the date of the acquisition, and the city in which the acquisition took place. If the acquisition was a purchase (as opposed to a seizure, for example), the data include the price paid. Several features of these data make them unique among drug price datasets. Specifically, the STRIDE data:

- Are records of individual purchases,
- Include the quantity and purity of each purchase,
- Have wide geographical coverage and span a time period from the late 1970s to the present, and
- Are readily available to analysts.

These features make the STRIDE data highly attractive to policy analysts who study factors that affect or are affected by the prices of illegal drugs.

Policy analyses involving drug prices often begin by using STRIDE or, occasionally, other data to construct a *price index* (see, for example, Abt Associates, 1999; Grossman et al., 1996; Crane et al., 1997; Chaloupka et al., 1998; Saffer and Chaloupka, 1995; Caulkins, 1994; Rhodes et al., 1994; DiNardo, 1993). The price index provides the indicator of price levels and movements in the subsequent analysis. For example, Yuan and Caulkins (1998), Crane et al. (1997), and DiNardo (1993) use movements in price indices as indicators of the effectiveness of enforcement or interdiction actions. Grossman et al. (1996), Chaloupka et al. (1998), and Saffer and Chaloupka (1995) use price indices to estimate models of the demand for illegal drugs.

This section provides an evaluation of the suitability of the STRIDE price data for use in drug policy analyses. It also evaluates the methods that have typically been used to construct drug price indices. It concludes with suggestions for developing improved price indices for illegal drugs. The major conclusions of this section are:

1. The STRIDE price data have been collected for administrative purposes and not with an eye to producing reliable data on the prices of illegal drugs. The procedures used to collect the price data do not conform to standard methods that have been developed by statistical agencies for estimating wholesale or retail prices.

2. Comparing the price data on illegal drugs collected by different agencies indicates that there are major inconsistencies among datasets. As a result, the committee concludes that the STRIDE price data are unlikely to be representative of the prices for illegal drugs paid by most users of these substances.

3. The committee concludes that a major effort is needed to improve the quality and reliability of the price data. Such an effort will require a further assessment of the reliability of the STRIDE data along with an investigation into alternative methods for collecting improved price data.

Given the techniques that underlie the collection of the STRIDE price data, it is not surprising that they contain significant problems of reliability and interpretation. The data are mainly records of drug acquisitions made to support criminal investigations and prosecutions. The decision of the DEA to buy drugs is based on criteria that aim at serving this objective. The criteria were not designed with policy analysis in mind and are almost certainly not the ones that would be used if the objective were to develop price indices or to support policy analyses of markets for illegal drugs. In particular, as we explain below, the STRIDE data are not a random sample of an identifiable population and are not designed to be representative of the population of drug transactions in any city or the nation.

The STRIDE data are widely used by those who study price trends and construct total expenditure estimates. They are also used in analytical studies, such as ones that estimate the impact of price on consumption or of interdiction efforts on prices. While it is sometimes recognized that the STRIDE price data are not accurate measures of the prices paid by consumers of and traffickers in illegal drugs, their use is often defended as being "realistic" or at least reasonably accurate, perhaps containing a small and hopefully constant multiplicative error. This view is based on the assumption that prices paid by Drug Enforcement Administration and other law enforcement agents must be realistic. If the prices were not realistic, then dealers would become suspicious, and agents might be endangered or unable to buy drugs.

This argument misses an important distinction between realistic and representative prices. In any given market, there is not a single price for a specified quantity and purity of an illegal drug. There is a distribution of prices. To be useful for policy analysis, price data must be representative of this distribution. The distribution of prices paid by law enforcement agents need not be representative of the distribution of prices in the market even if the price paid in each transaction is realistic. The price paid by a law enforcement agent is likely to be realistic if it is within the range of the distribution of market prices. There are infinitely many distributions of prices that are realistic by this definition, but there is only one true market distribution. Figure 3.1 illustrates this point. The solid line shows a possible distribution of market prices. The dashed line shows a hypothetical distribution of "realistic" prices. The two distributions are very different. The realistic prices in the figure tend to be higher than the market prices but are well within the range of the market price.

STRIDE Data

STRIDE records drug acquisitions made in support of criminal investigations by the Drug Enforcement Administration and the Metropolitan Police of the District of Columbia. A criminal investigation by the Drug Enforcement Administration begins when the staff of a DEA field office learn of a drug shipment or marketing operation. This information is usually received from an informant or a wiretap. Officials in the field office must decide whether to initiate their own investigation based on this information or turn the information over to state or local law enforcement agencies for further investigation. If the investigation is turned over to a state or local agency, then there is no record of it in STRIDE unless the local agency is the Metropolitan Police of the District of Columbia. Records of MPDC acquisitions of illegal drugs are included in STRIDE because chemical analyses of drugs acquired by the Metropolitan Police of the District of Columbia are carried out in a DEA laboratory.

There are over 160 DEA field offices. DEA officials told members of the committee that the criteria for deciding whether to initiate a criminal investigation are locally determined. The criteria vary among field offices and over time within field offices. For example, New York and Miami are major ports of entry for cocaine. Consequently, the DEA field offices in those cities tend to focus on seizing shipments that arrive at international airports and other international points of entry in the New York and Miami areas. The DEA offices in New York and Miami devote relatively

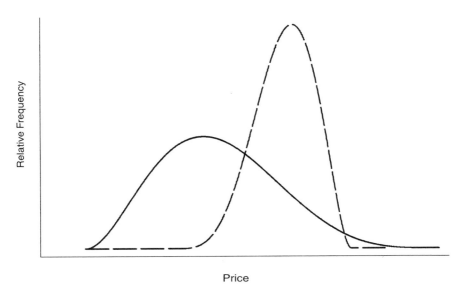

Price

FIGURE 3.1   A possible distribution of market prices (solid line) and a hypothetical distribution of "realistic" prices that differs from the market distribution (dashed line).

little attention to retail and wholesale dealers, leaving responsibility for them to local authorities. A DEA agent who had experience in the New York and the Phoenix field offices reported that a sales operation that would generate great excitement in Phoenix might attract no interest in New York. Chicago has become a major cocaine transshipment point in recent years, and the Chicago field office is increasingly focused on seizing large shipments. It tends to take an interest in retail or wholesale dealers only if they are associated with especially violent street gangs that are unusually dangerous to the community. Moreover, because the Drug Enforcement Administration is primarily oriented toward disrupting and dismantling large distribution and sales organizations rather than individual retail dealers, it tends to focus on wholesale and higher level operations, leaving most retail-level enforcement to state and local authorities. Thus, most purchases of drugs by DEA agents and informants are of larger-than-retail quantities.

In summary, the STRIDE data are gathered according to criteria that serve the law enforcement objectives of DEA field offices. The data acquisition procedures are not designed to provide representative samples of price distributions in drug markets. Assessing the reliability of the STRIDE data is therefore an important issue for researchers in this field.

Appendix A explores some of the implications of the data acquisition process for the usefulness of the STRIDE data for policy analysis. The appendix describes two models of the relation among the price, quantity, and purity of cocaine base purchased in the Washington, D.C., area during 1990-1998. One model was developed by using STRIDE records of purchases by agents and informants of the Drug Enforcement Administration. The other model was developed by using STRIDE records of purchases by agents and informants of the Metropolitan Police of the District of Columbia. If the price data in STRIDE were representative of true market conditions in the Washington area, then estimates of price distribution obtained from the DEA and MPDC models would be identical up to the effects of random sampling errors. The results presented in the appendix, however, show that there are large, systematic differences between price distributions estimated from the two datasets. There are also large differences between estimates of price changes over time.

The finding that the DEA and the MPDC data lead to different price estimates and trends implies that the two datasets on prices of cocaine base cannot both be representative of actual market conditions in the Washington area. The data do not indicate the accuracy with which either dataset approximates true market conditions. It is possible that one of the datasets gives a good approximation and the other does not. It is also possible that neither dataset gives a good approximation. Similar comparisons cannot be made using data for other cities because records of purchases of illegal drugs by the local police of other cities are not available. Nonetheless, the results obtained with the Washington data and examination of the data acquisition criteria on which STRIDE is based persuade the committee that the STRIDE data has serious methodological shortcomings and is likely to contain major and at present unknown errors.

The data presumably capture shifts in the location of the distribution of prices that are large compared with the width of the distribution and to the effects of variations in data-acquisition criteria. The large reductions in cocaine and heroin prices that apparently occurred during the 1980s (Rhodes et al., 1994) may be examples of such location shifts. However, in the absence of independent evidence on the extent to which the STRIDE price data are accurate indices of the prices of illegal drugs at either the wholesale or retail level, the committee concludes that the STRIDE price data are of questionable reliability for use in estimating demand functions, in estimating the effects of policy interventions that may cause modest price changes, and in carrying out other economic and policy analyses that require accurate measures of price variations.

The inadequacy of the existing STRIDE price data is a major impediment to reliable assessments and research on illegal drugs. The committee is unaware of any effort that is under way in the federal government or elsewhere to develop methods for collecting price data on illegal drugs.[15] **The committee recommends that work be started to develop methods for improving existing data and acquiring more reliable drug price data.**

The committee has not attempted to design a method for gathering price data. However, we do offer a suggestion as a starting point for further investigation of the best way to acquire price data that would be suitable for economic and other policy analyses.

1. It may be possible to carry out a survey in which randomly sampled individuals in one or more cities are asked the price of their last drug purchase (if any), the date of the purchase, the name of the drug, and the quantity purchased. As in ADAM, the quantity would be specified in informal terms such as bags, vials, lines, etc. Alternatively, randomly sampled individuals could be asked to keep diary records of their purchases over some period of time. The survey would be designed to reach high-risk groups, such as homeless people as well as those currently reached by surveys such as the NHSDA. Respondents would be assured of confidentiality and that their responses will not put them in legal jeopardy.

2. In addition, arrangements would be made for professional buyers to make purchases of drugs. The prices paid would be recorded and the purchased material sent to a laboratory for determination of the quantity (in grams) and purity of the purchased material. The professional buyers would be provided with immunity from arrest while making purchases. The information thus acquired would make it possible to estimate quantity and purity conditional on the informal description of quantity purchased (bag, vials, lines, etc.), the price paid, and the city in which the purchase was made.

The committee notes that providing professional buyers with immunity from arrest requires significant changes in existing policies of law

---

[15]Some surveys of drug users include questions about recent expenditures on drugs. The survey of the Arrestee Drug Abuse Monitoring Program (ADAM) is an example. The information obtained in such surveys cannot be used to estimate drug prices, however. The most important reason is that the surveys of which the committee is aware do not provide quantitative information on the quantity and purity of the purchased drug. ADAM, for example, asks no questions about purity. Although respondents have the option of providing quantitative information on the quantity purchased, they are also permitted to use informal terms such as "bag," "balloon," "foil packet," "rock," and "line" that do not have precise quantitative equivalents. In addition, ADAM surveys only arrestees, who are not necessarily representative of the entire population of drug users in the cities that participate in the ADAM program. The National Household Survey of Drug Abuse does not ask questions about expenditures on drugs.

enforcement organizations. This may prevent implementation of Step 2 in the short run. However, records of drug purchases in STRIDE include informal descriptions of the quantities that were bought. Accordingly, a short-run alternative approach of limited usefulness that is easier to implement is to use STRIDE's informal descriptions. The committee stresses that this is a short-run, temporary alternative and not a long-run substitute for developing a reliable technique for price measurement.

3. The information acquired in steps 1 and 2 could be combined to yield an estimate of the distribution of prices in individual transactions in the area and for the time period in which the data were gathered. The information could also be used to estimate the distribution of quantities purchased and purity.

Another approach, which might be taken in parallel with the approach just described, would be for the Drug Enforcement Administration to establish a small pilot study to develop procedures for well-designed and routinized collection of price data on illegal drugs. This approach would involve the DEA's setting up a small statistical unit with the responsibility of designing experiments to collect more reliable price data and of working with field offices to implement the plan. This approach is an example of the usefulness, described in detail in Chapter 4, of upgrading the statistical expertise in agencies. The price collection effort could be undertaken collaboratively with other government statistical agencies who have experience in collecting price data and doing surveys on illegal drugs.

Price Indices

A price index is an indicator of the price of a unit of a commodity or of a group of commodities. For example, if the commodity of interest is retail quantities and purities of cocaine base, the index might be the price of one gram of 75 percent pure cocaine base. If retail quantities and purities of cocaine base and powder cocaine are both of interest, then the price index might be a weighted average of the prices of 1 gm of 75 percent pure cocaine base and 1 gm of 50 percent pure powder cocaine.

The construction of a price index is relatively simple if one observes a random sample of purchase prices of the commodity or commodities of interest (e.g., a random sample of purchases of 1 gm of 75 percent pure cocaine base). The index is then the average of the observed prices. However, a dataset on prices of illegal drugs is unlikely to contain multiple records of purchases of, say, 1 gm of 75 percent pure cocaine base. For example, for the period January 1984 to June 1998, the STRIDE data that were made available to the committee contain no records in which exactly

1 gm of 75 percent pure cocaine base was purchased. Therefore, the price index for an illegal drug must be inferred from prices of purchases of a range of quantities and purities. This is done by using statistical methods to estimate the relation between the mean (or median) price of the drug, the quantity and purity of the material purchased, and any other relevant variables (e.g., the calendar year or city in which the purchase was made). Abt Associates (1999), Crane et al. (1997), Caulkins (1994), Rhodes et al. (1994), and DiNardo (1993), among others, have constructed price indices for cocaine this way.

An important problem in the construction of a price index for an illegal drug is that the available data may record only a small number of purchases in a given city and time period. This is the case in STRIDE, for example (see Appendix A). Therefore, analysts have typically pooled data from different cities and different forms of cocaine to obtain samples that are large enough to permit precise inference. Such pooling presents no special difficulties if the dependence of the mean (or median) price on quantity and purity (called the price function) is the same in all cities and for all commodities (e.g., for powder cocaine and cocaine base).

There are, however, good reasons for expecting the price function to be different in different cities and for different forms of cocaine. Retail markets in different cities may be supplied by different distribution networks and may interact only weakly if at all. For example, a cocaine user in Washington, D.C., is unlikely to buy cocaine in Chicago or to know the price of cocaine there. Thus, the mechanisms that tend to equalize the prices of many legal products in different cities are weak in markets for illegal drugs. In addition to being influenced by different distribution networks, prices in different cities may be influenced by differences in the aggressiveness of law enforcement, income levels, and poverty rates, among other factors. Similar reasoning applies to the prices of different forms of cocaine. Converting one form to another requires skills that many cocaine users and dealers do not possess. The cost of conversion tends to separate the markets for the two forms of cocaine. Appendix A and Caulkins (1997) show that the STRIDE data produce different price functions for powder cocaine and cocaine base in the same city and that price functions that are estimated from the STRIDE data are different in different cities.

When different cities and commodities have different price functions, then a price index that is estimated from pooled data can exhibit fluctuations and trends that do not exist in any of the markets whose data were pooled. In other words, the price index can exhibit fluctuations and trends that are artifacts of the pooling procedure and do not reflect true market conditions. The occurrence of such artifacts is especially likely when, as happens in STRIDE, the relative numbers of observations from different cities or for different forms of cocaine vary from year to year (Appendix A). However, variations in relative numbers of observations are not the only possible source of misleading price fluctuations and trends. Variations over time in the shapes of the distributions of prices are another. The STRIDE data exhibit variations over time in the distributions of prices.

Figures 3.2 and 3.3 present a simple example that illustrates this problem. In this example, the price of cocaine depends only on the quantity purchased; large quantities cost less per gram than small ones. Figure 3.2 shows hypothetical price functions in two cities. These functions give the average price of cocaine according to quantity purchased. Suppose that the price functions do not change over time. Then the price of 1 gm of cocaine is $80 in city 1 and $120 in city 2. The prices do not vary over time, so true market prices show no trends or fluctuations over time.

Suppose, now, that the available data consist of the following numbers of observations of price and quantity in each of 10 years:

Year	Number of Observations from City 1	Number of Observations from City 2
1	20	40
2	25	35
3	30	30
4	35	30
5	20	25
6	45	30
7	50	25
8	55	35
9	50	30
10	55	40

The number of observations in city 1 tends to increase over time (possibly due to increasing aggressiveness of law enforcement), but year 5 is an exception to this trend. The number of observations in city 2 varies from year to year but shows no upward or downward trend. Assume that the purchased quantities of cocaine are in the range 0-2 gm in both cities. The purchase price of a given quantity varies randomly around the price function for the city in which the purchase is made. In this example, the range of variation is approximately ±$20.[16]

Suppose that a price index series is constructed by pooling the data from the two cities. In each year, the data from the two cities are combined and a price function is estimated from the combined data. The price index for that year is the price of 1 gm of cocaine according to the esti-

---

[16]Specifically, the variation of price at a given quantity is normally distributed with a mean of zero and a standard deviation of 10.

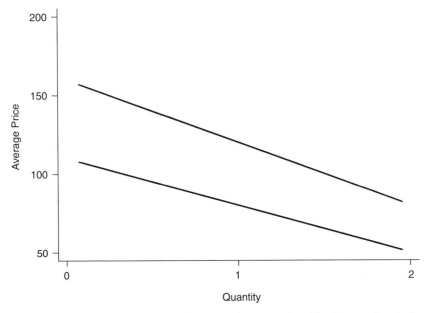

FIGURE 3.2   Hypothetical price functions for two cities. The bottom line is for city 1, and the top line is for city 2.

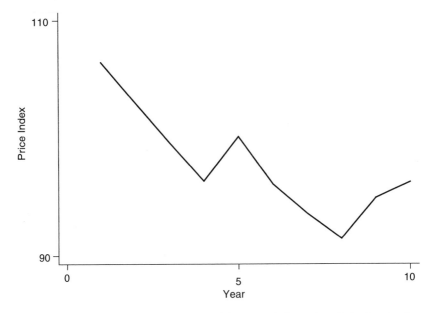

FIGURE 3.3   Price index series obtained from pooled city 1 and city 2 price data.

mated price function. Figure 3.3 shows the resulting price index series. The price index tends to decrease from years 1 to 8, but there is an upward fluctuation in year 5. The index increases from years 8 to 10. However, the trend and fluctuations shown in Figure 3.3 are artifacts of the pooling of the data from cities 1 and 2. The true average price of 1 gm of cocaine does not vary over time in either city. Thus, the price index obtained from the pooled data is highly misleading. Pooling has given rise to the appearance of price trends and fluctuations that do not exist in the markets in which the data were collected.

Misleading results such as those illustrated in Figure 3.3 can be avoided by estimating separate price functions for each time period (e.g., year), market (e.g., city in the example), and commodity of interest. The price function for a given time period, market, and commodity is used to estimate the price of one unit of the commodity in that time period and market. A combined price index is constructed as a weighted average of the prices obtained for all commodities and markets in the given time period. If there are several different amounts or purities of interest, then the estimated price of each can be included in the weighted average. The weight assigned to a particular market and commodity is proportional to the quantity of the commodity that is sold in that market. The weights can be based on quantities sold in a base year or they can be based on yearly sales volumes. In the former case, the price index varies over time only if market prices vary. In the latter case, the price index also reflects variations in the relative sales volumes of different commodities and in different markets. The relative merits of different weighting schemes are discussed in economics textbooks and depend to some extent on the intended use of the price index. The committee does not take a position on which weighting scheme is best for drug policy analysis.

To date, most of the research constructing or using prices on illegal drugs has not relied on the extensive research and practical experience on price indices that exists in the federal government and in the academic community. The committee notes that the principles underlying the construction of price indices are well established in the official national statistical community. For example, the Bureau of Labor Statistics uses standard and well-tested procedures to construct retail and wholesale price indices, taking into account regional differences, seasonal variation, and other factors.

The committee recommends that a major effort be devoted to "importing" standard procedures on constructing price indices into the development of price indices for illegal drugs. This effort should take place in collaboration with federal statistical agencies that specialize in this area, particularly the Bureau of Labor Statistics. Appropriate techniques would address a number of important issues. Aggregating across different prices in different regions, which was discussed above, is one issue that must be confronted. Future price indices developed from the STRIDE data should take account of differences between the prices of cocaine base and powder cocaine and the dependence of price on quantity (such as on the number of packages purchased). The use of appropriate methods would minimize spurious price movements caused, for example, by variations over time in the numbers of observations in different cities and variations in the relative numbers of observations of transactions of cocaine base and powder cocaine.

Improving existing price data and developing new methods for collecting more accurate price data are among the highest priorities for improving data on illegal drugs. Until accurate price data are constructed, the nation will remain poorly informed about the trends in prices of illegal drugs, about short-run movements, about the efficacy of short-term interventions, and about the trends or levels of total expenditures on illegal drugs. Improving price data requires immediate and high-level attention from the agencies involved in producing accurate and timely information on illegal drugs.

DEVELOPMENT OF A SET OF NATIONAL DRUG ACCOUNTS

One of the major shortcomings of current information systems on illegal drugs is the lack of a systematic set of accounts that track the dollar flows in this sector. The current national income and product accounts focus on market transactions in the legal sector of the economy. Two major omissions are nonmarket activities (such as the value of work at home or the environment) and illegal market activities. The latter include not only production and expenditures on illegal drugs but prostitution, illegal gambling, money laundering, bribes, and smuggling.

The committee recommends that consideration be given to constructing a set of satellite accounts that track the flows in sectors comprising legal and illegal drugs. This set of accounts would be called the National Drug Accounts. These satellite accounts would not enter into the current core national income and product accounts.

Purpose

National drug accounts would serve several purposes. First, they would help track the drug economy. They would provide information on its importance to the total economy, its size relative to the sizes of relevant sectors of the legal economy (e.g., tobacco, pharmaceuticals), and whether it is growing or shrinking. Information on total consumption and production could be used to develop improved estimates of the social costs of illegal drugs.

Second, national drug accounts would provide data for aggregate studies of the drug economy, or parts of it, such as the cocaine segment. For example, the study by RAND of the cost-effectiveness of alternative approaches to controlling cocaine was handicapped by the lack of reliable data on the major segments of the cocaine market (Rydell and Everinghom, 1994). A set of National Drug Accounts could provide the necessary data. Indeed, it seems unlikely that empirical economic analyses of the illegal drug industry can be carried out without moving toward a rudimentary set of national illegal accounts.

Third, a set of National Drug Accounts, together with existing data and accounts on other addictive substances, could help researchers better understand a number of major policy issues in the drug market. Some examples of issues that would be aided by improved data are the substitution and complementarity patterns with other goods and services, the impact of drugs on the overall economy, and the impact on international trade flows.

Finally, because such accounts would ideally include both financial flows as well as physical flows, they would help with tracking money laundering and the drug and drug-financed linkages between the United States and other countries.

Elements of National Drug Accounts

The structure of National Drug Accounts would be similar to that of existing accounts for the legitimate economy. The important components would be:

- A set of expenditure accounts, in current and constant prices, for major illegal and legal drugs.
- A set of production accounts for the production of each of the major sector.
- A set of income accounts breaking down the incomes earned in this sector into the major components (wages, profits, cost of goods sold, etc.).
- A set of import and export accounts that estimate the trade flows between the United States and other countries.
- A set of flow-of-funds accounts that track the monetary component of the "circular flow" of sales and purchases.
- A set of regional accounts focusing on production, expenditures, and income by state.

These accounts could be constructed independently as they would rely on different surveys or estimates. Although it would be ideal to have each of the six components, construction of even one or two would be helpful.

Feasibility

The federal government and statistical agencies in other countries currently prepare a wide variety of supplemental accounts of the kind proposed here. For example, the U.S. Bureau of Economic Analysis, which is responsible for constructing the National Income and Product Accounts, has prepared environmental and natural resource accounts, accounts for research and development, transportation satellite accounts, and proto-type accounts for unpaid household work. While the committee has not investigated the practices in other countries, there have apparently been attempts to build a set of drug accounts for Colombia and some consideration of integrating accounts for drugs has been given in The Netherlands.

The accounts could be readily constructed for legal drugs. Moreover, there are rough estimates of many of the components for illegal drugs. However, it must be emphasized that constructing a full and accurate set of accounts would be difficult because of the problems with obtaining the data on many prices and quantities. There is likely to be strong synergy between the data needed to construct the National Drug Accounts and the data needs discussed elsewhere in this report (see particularly the discussion of the utility of better data on prices and on total consumption).

One of the advantages of using the methodology of the National Income and Product Accounts is that uncertainties are retained as statistical discrepancies rather than being swept under the rug.

REFERENCES

Abt Associates
    1999   The Price of Illicit Drugs: 1981 through the Second Quarter of 1998. Report prepared for the Office of National Drug Control Policy.
Anglin, M.D., J.P. Caulkins, and Y.I. Hser
    1993   Prevalence estimation: Policy needs, current status, and future potential. *Journal of Drug Issues* 345-361.
Anthony, J.C., and M. Van Etten
    1999   Epidemiology and its rubrics. In *Comprehensive Clinical Psychology*, Bellack and Hersen, eds. Amsterdam: Pergamon.
Bachman, J.G., P. Freedman-Doan, and P.M. O'Malley
    1999   Changing patterns of drug use among U.S. military recruits before and after enlistment. *American Journal of Public Health* 89:672-677.

Bray, R.M., L.A. Kroutil, S.C. Whelless, M.E. Marsden, S.L. Bailey, J.A. Fairbanks, and T.C. Hartford
    1995   *Department of Defense Survey of Health Related Behaviors Among Military Personnel.* Research Triangle Park, NC: Research Triangle Institute.

Biemer, P., and M. Witt
    1996   Estimation of measurement bias in self-reports of drug use with applications to the national household survey on drug abuse. *Journal of Official Statistics* 12(3):275-300.

Caspar, R.
    1992   Followup of nonrespondents in 1990. In C.F. Turner, J.T. Lessler, and J.C. Gfroerer, eds., *Survey Measurement of Drug Use: Methodological Studies.* DHHS Pub. No (ADM) 92-1929. Washington, DC: U.S. Department of Health and Human Services.

Caulkins, J.P.
    1994   *Developing Price Series for Cocaine.* Santa Monica, CA: RAND.
    1997   Is crack cheaper than (powder) cocaine? *Addiction* 92:1437-1443.

Caulkins, J.P., and R. Padman
    1993   Quantity discounts and quality premia for illicit drugs. *Journal of the American Statistical Association* 88:748-757.

Caulkins, J., and P. Reuter
    1996   The meaning and utility of drug prices. *Addiction* 91:1261-1264.

Chaloupka, F.J., M. Grossman, and J.A. Tauras
    1998   *The Demand for Cocaine and Marijuana by Youth.* Working paper 6411. Cambridge, MA: National Bureau of Economic Research.

Chaiken, J.M., and M. Chaiken
    1990   Drugs and predatory crime. *Drugs and Crime*, Michael Tonry and James Q. Wilson, eds. Vol. 13 of *Crime and Justice: A Review of Research.* Chicago: University of Chicago Press.

Charles, B.
    2000   Successful Database Integration Models and Prospects for Cross-Application to Drug Prevention Database Integration. Unpublished paper presented at a meeting of the Committee on Data and Research for Policy on Illegal Drugs, Washington, DC.

Cook, R.F., A.D. Bernstein, and C.M. Andrews
    1997   Assessing drug use in the workplace: A comparison of self-report, urinalysis, and hair analysis. In L. Harrison and Hughes, eds., *The Validity of Self-Reported Drug Use: Improving the Accuracy of Survey Estimates.* NIDA Research Monograph, Number 167. Washington, DC: U.S. Department of Health and Human Services.

Crane, B.D., A.R. Rivolo, and G.C. Comfort
    1997   *An Empirical Examination of Counterdrug Interdiction Program Effectiveness.* IDA paper P-3219. Alexandria, VA: Institute for Defense Analyses.

Darke, S.
    1998   Self report among injecting drug users: A review. *Drug Alcohol Dependence* 51:253-263.

DiNardo, J.
    1993   Law enforcement, the price of cocaine, and cocaine use. *Mathematical and Computer Modeling* 17:53-64.

Grossman, M., F.J. Chaloupka, and C.C. Brown
   1996   *The Demand for Cocaine by Young Adults: A Rational Addiction Approach.* Working paper 5713. Cambridge, MA: National Bureau of Economic Research.

Fendrich, M., T.P. Johnson, S. Sudman, J.S. Wislar, and V. Spiehler
   1999   Validity of drug use reporting in a high risk community sample: A comparison of cocaine and heroin survey reports with hair tests. *American Journal of Epidemiology* 149(10):955-962.

Fendrich, M., and C.M. Vaughn
   1994   Diminished lifetime substance use over time: An inquiry into differential underreporting. *Public Opinion Quarterly* 58(1):96-123.

Gfroerer, J., J. Lessler, and T. Parsley
   1997a Studies of nonresponse and measurement error in the national household survey on drug abuse. In L. Harrison and Hughes, eds., *The Validity of Self-Reported Drug Use: Improving the Accuracy of Survey Estimates.* NIDA Research Monograph 167: 273-295. Washington, DC: U.S. Department of Health and Human Services.

Gfroerer, J., D. Wright, and A. Kopstein
   1997b Prevalence of youth substance use: The impact of methodological differences between two national surveys. *Drug and Alcohol Dependence* 47:19-30.

Harrison, L.D.
   1992   Trends in illicit drug use in the United States: Conflicting results from national surveys. *International Journal of the Addictions* 27(7):917-947.
   1997   The Validity of Self-Reported Drug Use in Survey Research: An Overview and critique of research methods. In L. Harrison and A. Hughes, eds., *The Validity of Self-Reported Drug Use: Improving the Accuracy of Survey Estimates.* NIDA Research Monograph 167: 17-36. Washington, DC: U.S. Department of Health and Human Services.

Harrison, L., and A. Hughes, eds.
   1997   *The Validity of Self-Reported Drug Use: Improving the Accuracy of Survey Estimates.* NIDA Research Monograph 167. Washington, DC: U.S. Department of Health and Human Services.

Horowitz, J., and C.F. Manski
   1998   Censoring of outcomes and regressors due to survey nonresponse: Identification and estimation using weights and imputations. *Journal of Econometrics* 84:37-58.

Hser, Y.I.
   1992   Prevalence estimation: Summary of common problems and practical solutions. *Journal of Drug Issues* 23(2):335-343.

Hser, Y.I., K. Boyle, and M.D. Anglin
   1998   Drug use and correlates among sexually transmitted disease patients, emergency room patients, and arrestees. *Journal of Drug Issues* 28(2):437-454.

Johnston, L.D., P.M. O'Malley, and J.G. Bachman
   1998   *National Survey Results on Drug Use from the Monitoring the Future Study, 1975-1997*, Vol. I. Rockville, MD: National Institute on Drug Abuse.
   1993   *National Survey Results on Drug Use from the Monitoring the Future Study, 1975-1992.* Vols. I and II. Rockville, MD: National Institute on Drug Abuse.

Kilpatrick, K., M. Howlett, P. Dedwick, and A.H. Ghodse
   2000   Drug use self-report and urinalysis. *Drug and Alcohol Dependence* 58(1-2):111-116.

Magura. S., D. Goldsmith, C. Casriel, P.J. Goldstein, and D.S. Linton
   1987   The validity of methadone clients' self-reported drug use. *International Journal of Addiction* 22(8):727-749.

Magura. S., Freeman, Q. Siddiqi, and D.S. Lipton
    1992   The validity of hair analysis for detecting cocaine and heroin use among addicts. *International Journal of Addictions* 27:54-69.

Manski, C.F.
    1995   *Identification Problems in the Social Sciences.* Cambridge, MA: Harvard University Press.

Manski, C.F., J. Newman, and J.V. Pepper
    2000   *Using Performance Standards to Evaluate Social Programs with Incomplete Outcome Data: General Issues and Application to a Higher Education Block Grant Program.* Thomas Jefferson Center Discussion, paper 312.

Mehay, S.L., and R.L. Pacula
    1999   The Effectiveness of Workplace Drug Prevention Policies: Does 'Zero Tolerance' Work? October. NBER Working Paper No. W7383

Mieczkowski, T.M.
    1996   The prevalence of drug use in the United States. In M. Tonry, ed., *Crime and Justice: A Review of Research* 20:347-414.
    1990   The accuracy of self-reported drug use: An evaluation and analysis of new data. In R. Weisheit, ed., *Drugs, Crime and the Criminal Justice System.*

Molotsky, I.
    1999   Agency survey shows decline last year in drug use by young. *New York Times,* August 19.

Morbidity and Mortality Weekly Reports
    1997   <http://epbiwww.cwru.edu/mmwr/vol46/web site> (accessed February 27, 2001).

Morral, A.R., D. McCaffrey, and M.Y. Iguchi
    2000   Hardcore drug users claim to be occasional users: Drug use frequency underreporting. *Drug and Alcohol Dependence* 57(3):193-202.

National Institute of Justice
    1998   *Annual Report on Drug Use Among Adult and Juvenile Arrestees.* A Research Report. Washington, DC: U.S. Department of Justice.
    1994   *Drug Use Forecasting: Annual Report on Adult & Juvenile Arrestees.* Washington, DC: U.S. Department of Justice.
    1992   *Drug Use Forecasting: Annual Report on Adult & Juvenile Arrestees.* Washington, DC: U.S. Department of Justice.

National Research Council
    1999   *Transnational Organized Crime: Summary of a Workshop.* Committee on Law and Justice. P. Reuter and C. Petrie, eds. Washington, DC: National Academy Press.

National Research Council and Institute of Medicine
    1994   *Integrating Federal Statistics on Children: Report of a Workshop.* Committee on National Statistics and Board on Children, Youth, and Families. R. Hauser and M. Straf, eds. Washington, DC: National Academy Press.

Office of Applied Studies
    1997   Substance Abuse in States and Metropolitan Areas: Model Based Estimates from the 1991-1993 National Household Surveys on Drug Abuse Summary Report. Washington, DC: U.S. Department of Health and Human Services.

Office of National Drug Control Policy
    1997a   *Report of the Drug Control Research, Data, and Evaluation Committee.* Washington, DC: U.S. Government Printing Office.

1997b *What America's Users Spend on Illegal Drugs, 1988-1995.* Washington, DC: U.S. Government Printing Office.

Reuter, P.
  1997 Drug use measures: What are they really telling us? *National Institute of Justice Journal,* April 1999.
  1993 Prevalence estimation and policy formulation. *Journal of Drug Issues* 23(2):167-184.

Rhodes, W., R. Hyatt, and P. Scheiman
  1994 The price of cocaine, heroin and marijuana 1981-1993. *Journal of Drug Issues* 24:383-402.

Rydell, C.P., and S.S. Everingham
  1994 *Controlling Cocaine: Report prepared for the Office of National Drug Control Policy and the U.S. Army.* Santa Monica, CA: RAND.

Saffer, H., and Chaloupka, F.
  1995 *The Demand for Illicit Drugs.* Working paper 5238. Cambridge, MA: National Bureau of Economic Research.

Sloboda, Z., and N. Kozel
  1999 Frontline Surveillance: The Community Epidemiology Work Group on Drug Abuse. In *Drug Abuse: Origins & Interventions,* M. Glantz and C. Hartel, editors. Washington, DC: American Psychological Association Press.

Steel, E., and H.W. Haverkos
  1992 Epidemiologic studies of HIV/AIDS and drug abuse. *American Journal of Drug Alcohol Abuse* 18(2):167-175.

Substance Abuse and Mental Health Services Administration
  1999 Year-*End 1998 Emergency Department Data from the Drug Abuse Warning Network.* Washington, DC: U.S. Department of Health and Human Services.
  1997 *Substance Abuse in State and Metropolitan Areas: Model Based Estimates from the 1991-1993 National Household Surveys on Drug Abuse Summary Report.* Washington, U.S. DC: Department of Health and Human Services.

U.S. General Accounting Office
  1993 Drug Use Measurement: Strengths, Limitations, and Recommendations for Improvement. GAO/PEMD-93-18. Washington, DC: U.S. General Accounting Office.

Wish, E.D., and B.A. Gropper
  1990 Drug testing by the criminal justice system: Method, research, and applications. Pp. 321-339 in J.Q. Wilson and M. Tonry, editors, *Drugs and Crime:.* Chicago: University of Chicago Press.

Yuan, Y., and J.P. Caulkins
  1998 The effects of variation in high-level domestic drug enforcement on variation in drug prices. *Socio-Economic Planning Sciences* 32:265-276.

4

Drug Data Organization

C hapter 3 focused on the substantive innovations necessary to improve the quality, range, reliability, and usefulness of data on illegal drugs. Improving the data requires more than gifted survey researchers or fine questionnaires, however. The history of data collection indicates that the organizational structure of data collection is a critical feature of the overall system. This chapter briefly reviews the current organizational environment and makes recommendations on how the federal government can strengthen and advance the effort.

Effective policies to reduce the costs and damages associated with illegal drugs require accurate and timely data on all aspects of drug markets, consumption, prevention, and impacts. As this report documents, at present the quality of some data is poor, often data are simply unavailable, and policies in many areas are therefore poorly informed. Improving policies and introducing fruitful innovations will require a quantum improvement in the nation's statistical efforts in this area.

The Office of National Drug Control Policy has reported that data on illegal drugs are collected by 18 federal agencies. In fact, the bulk of the data are collected by a much smaller number of agencies: the National Institute of Justice, the Drug Enforcement Administration, the National Institute on Drug Abuse, and Substance Abuse and Mental Health Service Administration. The Bureau of Justice Statistics and the National Center for Health Statistics have also collected some drug-related data in connection with their broader statistical responsibilities.

Each of the data collections is built on an infrastructure consisting of its professional staff, survey researchers (who in this area are mostly contractors or grantees), and analysts. They rely on the cooperation of respondents, schools, hospitals, treatment facilities, medical examiners, and the criminal justice system. In the committee's judgment, regular professional and impartial reporting would greatly increase the cooperation of these key participants in the statistical processes that provide key indicators.

The ultimate goal of the recommendations in this chapter is to improve the quality and usefulness of the data so that they can better serve public understanding and policy making on illegal drugs. The central point of this chapter is that the substantive recommendations in this report cannot be implemented without improvements in the practices of statistical agencies and a consolidation of the federal effort along with determined leadership to implement these organizational improvements.

The scope of this chapter is limited to a review of the adequacy of the organizational structures for the collection, analysis, and reporting of statistical data on illegal drugs. This means that we are considering how to improve the quality and timeliness of data, for example, on the price or total consumption of cocaine, heroin, and marijuana. We do not consider the organizational issues involved in research on illegal drugs, such as how to best determine the relationship between interdiction and use or between crime and drug laws. Producing high-quality statistical data is a prerequisite for empirically informed research, but only data needs are considered here.

UPGRADING INDEPENDENCE AND PROFESSIONALISM

Regardless of the organizational structure of data collection on illegal drugs, it is essential that the federal government set a goal of protecting and strengthening the statistical reporting practices, independence, and scientific integrity of organizations charged with collecting the data. This section presents some principles that can serve as guidelines for ensuring that the institutional structure of agencies that collect and report drug data reflects the best practices for statistical agencies and is conducive to the collection of high-quality data. They apply both to existing agencies and to any new or consolidated agencies that might be created in the future.

A critical part of the process of improving the value of data and research on illegal drugs for policy purposes is to ensure that the agencies that collect the data have the resources, independence, and professional staff to engage in the range of activities necessary for producing high-quality data collection and statistical reports. The federal government has considerable experience in this area. A 1992 report of the Committee on National Statistics of the National Academies has examined these issues (National Research Council, 1992), and we draw in part on that effort in setting out the following principles for agencies collecting statistical data on illegal drugs.

Improving the quality and usefulness of drug statistics requires that statistical data collection and reporting are assigned to agencies or offices within agencies that have statistical reporting as their major focus. High-quality statistical data collection cannot be an accident of activities carried out in support of some other mission—such as providing treatment or apprehending violators. It is essential that statistical organizations report results regardless of their programmatic impact, and their work not be subject to review by agencies or officials whose success will be judged based on the actual outcome of the data collection.

We divide the principles for strengthening statistical agencies into two components. First is a commitment to quality and professional standards. The following are guidelines for professionalism that should be maintained and strengthened in agencies providing data on illegal drugs:

1. To maintain a commitment to high standards, the agency head needs a strong professional background and reputation. The relevant skills would be either in survey research and statistics or in the subject field of the agency.

2. To encourage the highest standards of professionalism and adherence to providing independent and high-quality data, agency heads must be insulated from policy direction regarding the content of reported results. This can be enhanced when agency heads have fixed terms or are appointed as career members of the Senior Executive Service, so that they are not subject to political removal.

3. Adequate resources are needed to build up a professional staff that is knowledgeable and skilled in regular statistical reporting and in the design and implementation of surveys.

4. Improving the professionalism of an agency's work requires that the staff and methodological research of the agency be integrated with the broader professional community and can draw on the full science base in the relevant field.

The second component is sufficient independence so that the statistical agency can provide credible and useful data to the government and to the public. Independence from policy direction regarding the issuance of reported results is particularly important when the data and subject are controversial and when data collection is plagued by methodological difficulties—both of which apply to the nth power to data on illegal drugs.

The following are guidelines for maintaining and strengthening independence for agencies providing data on illegal drugs:

1. When appropriate, consideration should be given to upgrading the status of statistical agencies within departments, including direct reporting to departmental secretaries, so that their personnel and results gain credibility. This will also serve to focus their mission on statistical reporting and distinguish it from research, service delivery, and policy analysis. This is particularly important if statistical data collection is consolidated into one or two lead agencies, as recommended in the section on consolidation below.

2. Statistical results should be released without prior political or administrative review. For certain key data, it may be useful to have data released on a predetermined schedule and to institute the practice (used for key economic data) of prohibiting comment by administration officials until one hour after the official release. It may also be useful to limit prior access to the statistical reports to the President and his or her immediate staff. All these steps would help to reduce or eliminate departmental and White House "spin" of data releases.

3. It may be useful for Congress to set up its own parallel analysis based on professional expertise to be released at the same time as the executive branch release, as is currently the case when the Joint Economic Committee analyzes key economic data.

In well-run statistical agencies, a most important principle governs the respective roles of policy makers and the statisticians who provide information. Policy makers articulate the need for information, and statisticians respond with answers based on best professional practices. In such agencies, the reports issued by statisticians are not subject to the kind of policy review that might alter their content or emphasis. Compared with other statistical efforts in the federal government (such as the economic agencies), the collection and reporting of statistical data on illegal drugs are not always free from such policy review. In fact, the release of major data series—such as results from the Monitoring the Future survey and the National Household Survey on Drug Abuse—has been the occasion for high-level press conferences and detailed prior review by policy makers. The following new standards should guide the release of these reports:

1. It is essential that statistical agencies have clearly defined and well-accepted missions. The mission is often defined by legislation or regulation and evolves over time. A clear mission is critical for planning the program of a statistical agency and for evaluating its performance.

2. Once it is assigned to produce high-quality statistical data in a given area, an agency should be able to issue statistical reports based on professionally designed methods. As is the practice at the Bureau of Labor Statistics and the Bureau of the Census, for example, these reports should be issued without intervening policy review. Direct reporting of results by expert statisticians is a key marker of professional integrity. Policy direction regarding data collection procedures or reporting of data reduces the credibility of reporting, slows down the release of the data, and reduces the usefulness of the data for policy and research. It also limits the research on statistical techniques and methods that is vital to improve the reliability, validity, and relevance of key statistical indicators.

3. Putting this principle in yet another way, there should be clear separation of the purposes of data collection—which should be decided by policy makers—from how the questions are to be asked and the final content of the report—which are best decided by the statisticians and other relevant specialists.

Many of the guidelines listed above for increasing the professionalism of agencies will also help ensure independence. For example, enhancing the professional qualifications for the heads of statistical agencies will help ensure that the direction of data collection has a professional rather than a political motivation. In addition, many of the guidelines on independence will reinforce the professionalism of agencies.

The usefulness and integrity of these statistical efforts would be greatly enhanced by improving the dissemination of data and results. There are many approaches available to make the results and data more widely available. Some agencies use data archives to release public-use files containing the original data from surveys or data compilations. Others provide this material to researchers upon request. In some cases, to protect the confidentiality of sensitive material, statistical agencies have established special procedures to give researchers access while requiring confidentiality agreements that ensure the privacy of respondents.

The committee emphasizes that open access to the original material (while always using practices consistent with protecting individual privacy) encourages use of the data and enlists the broad community of researchers in the task of analyzing and understanding current trends. Just as important is that external analysis provides the critical function of reviewing the data and methods of the agency and helps inform the research community and policy makers about the usefulness and limitations of the data. At the same time, it alerts policy makers to the need for improvements and the best applications of the results.

Several agencies currently make some or all of their material available in this way. However, making data and research widely available is not universal practice. All drug-related agencies need to improve access to and encourage widespread analysis and reporting of their data. When access is not currently provided, steps need to be taken to provide it.

The committee recommends that public-use files of all major statistical series should be deposited in a data library. On a broader level, every agency sponsoring the collection of population-based data related to illegal drugs should require in their contracts and grants the timely deposit of public-use files in an appropriate data library or its dissemination in other ways.

In connection with this recommendation, see the committee's recommendation in Chapter 3 specifically regarding the longitudinal file of data from the Monitoring the Future survey. Finally, we recognize the importance of ensuring that confidentiality be preserved. In the committee view, it is sponsors rather than data collectors who should make decisions regarding the level of detail released.

IMPROVING ECONOMIC DATA ON ILLEGAL DRUGS

One of the major messages of this report is that economic data relating to illegal drugs need to be substantially improved. Major gaps have been identified in the collection and reporting of reliable data about the prices, total consumption, and expenditure on illegal drugs. The deficiency in this area arises in part because economic data for the most part have been ancillary to law enforcement efforts. In addition, efforts to collect reliable economic data have been hampered by a lack of accepted procedures for collecting economic information about illegal activities. In the committee's view, major efforts are needed to improve such data.

The methodologies for collecting economic data on illegal drugs are at present insufficiently developed to begin regular collection of statistical data. The first stage in improved collection of economic data would be to improve the methodologies in this area.

One approach would be to assign the tasks of designing, collecting, reporting, and validating statistical series on economic data, such as prices, expenditures, and consumption, to a newly constituted economic working group. This group would consist of professional statisticians located in economic statistics agencies, such as the Bureau of Labor Statistics and the Bureau of Economic Analysis, as well as economists and statisticians with expertise in these methods who are working in an existing statistical unit of an agency focused on illegal drugs.

The first assignment of the economic working group would be to develop, test, and validate methods and procedures to report on prices, expenditures, and total consumption. The working group would need sufficient funds and independence to sponsor broadly based research activities. Its research would begin with thorough analysis of existing information and methodologies. The results of these efforts could be widely reported in the professional literature and subject to careful review and analysis before full-scale data collection begins.

It is likely that the data collection efforts for economic data will need to be separated from law enforcement activities. To accomplish this, after a review of the relevant law, either the executive branch would issue rules or the Congress would enact legislation to provide legal protection to researchers collecting economic data so that they can proceed without having to become a part of a law enforcement effort.

The committee recommends the formation of an executive branch board to review proposed data collection protocols that might be used as a part of a research effort to design, collect, report, and validate statistical series on economic data, such as prices, expenditures, and consumption. It may be necessary to have rules or legislation enabling the board to exercise its functions in a manner that clearly separates law enforcement from this research enterprise.

IMPROVING COORDINATION

It is important to consider the coordination of statistical data collection related to illegal drugs in the broader context of such coordination across the entire federal government. One of the recurrent issues in the decentralized U.S. federal statistical system is how best to coordinate data collection by different agencies.

At a workshop held on February 17-18, 2000, the committee heard from representatives of the Office of Management and Budget (OMB), agencies that collect drug statistics, and other experts. The presentations, including comments from the chief statistician of the United States and from officials charged with reviewing data collection activities proposed by health and justice agencies, illuminated the roles of both OMB and the Office of National Drug Control Policy in overseeing data collection related to illegal drugs.

The presenters noted that the decentralization of the federal statistical system is reflected in the many agencies that report statistics relevant to illegal drugs. Since the 1930s, OMB and its predecessor agencies have been charged with reviewing agency proposals to collect statistical data from the public. The Federal Reports Act of 1940 provided that agencies were required to seek budget office review of all forms used to collect information from 10 or more persons. Subsequent legislation—in particular the Paperwork Reduction Act of 1980—defined and broadened OMB's authority in this area to include the coordination of all federal agency statistical data collection.

OMB can and does use its authority to encourage agencies to coordinate their data collection so as to improve the quality of the information collected and limit the burden on the public. In particular, it uses the authority of the Paperwork Reduction Act to encourage common terminology, constructs, and definitions in the data collected across the statistical system.

OMB has a very small staff available for review of statistical surveys. Its activities are limited to coordination and review of proposals to collect data. The OMB staff does not issue statistics or review results before they are issued. It frequently charters interagency groups to improve coordination of data collection among agencies. It also works to identify budget gaps and help to find ways to fill them.

Current legislation places responsibility for some coordination at the departmental level. For example, the Department of Health and Human Services Data Council has been examining ways of consolidating and improving statistical reporting and data collection concerning illegal drugs.

The Office of National Drug Control Policy (ONDCP) has authority to facilitate and coordinate data collection concerning illegal drugs. For example, it was at ONDCP's suggestion that the National Household Survey of Drug Abuse was carried out each year rather than every 3 years, and its size markedly increased. Likewise ONDCP suggested that Monitoring the Future include 8th and 10th graders rather than just 12th graders. Its authority stems from several of its functions.

First, ONDCP is called on to certify the compliance of agency budgets with the President's drug strategy. When agencies submit their budgets to OMB, the budgets go to ONDCP for certification that they comply with the drug strategy. Only the President can overrule ONDCP. In practice this procedure means that ONDCP is an influential part of the budget review process and can therefore require agencies to show how their budgets provide for the collection of needed statistical data. Alternatively, ONDCP can use this process to raise questions about the propriety of proposed data collection or its location. ONDCP uses the certification process to influence agency decisions regarding the initiation and maintenance of data collection efforts.

Second, OMB consults ONDCP during its review of the data collection proposals of the different agencies. ONDCP can use these occasions to review these proposals and suggest the inclusion of data items relevant to drug control policy.

Third, the ONDCP has chaired a Drug Control, Research Data and

Evaluation Advisory Committee since 1994. The committee has chartered a subcommittee on data, research, and interagency coordination, which has representatives from the major drug control program agencies. The subcommittee's 1999 report on drug control research data and evaluation contains a useful inventory of federal data collection projects that contain information relevant to drug control policy (Executive Office of the President, 1999).

ONDCP currently is the lead agency for coordinating data collection on illegal substances and drug control in the federal government. In this role, ONDCP and its data subcommittee have analyzed the current structure of data collection, have identified some of the weaknesses in the current data system and have discussed design of survey instruments (Executive Office of the President, 1999). However, it has not seen a need to take any major initiatives to reorganize data collection efforts, nor is that the role of the data subcommittee.

At present, reporting, compilation, and analysis of the voluminous data on illegal drugs are largely spread through the many agencies that collect the data. While ONDCP does issue annual reports, they are largely concerned with setting policy and describing the results of federal activities. Many of the annual reports focus on policy goals and implementation strategies, and there is relatively little analysis of the underlying trends and data issues.

It would be useful to have an annual report on illegal drugs in the United States that presents and assesses the most important statistical series. Such a report would collect in one place the major data on the health, law enforcement, international, and economic facets of illegal drugs and related issues along with an appropriate commentary. Such a report could be modeled after similar reports in other areas, such as the Annual Energy Outlook of the Energy Information Administration and the Economic Report of the President prepared by the Council of Economic Advisers; these documents present the data in a scholarly fashion that can survive changing perspectives, policy approaches, and administrations. For this purpose, it would be important to have the report issued by an agency with an adequate staff of professional analysts and researchers.

CONSOLIDATING DATA COLLECTION

The 18 agencies that collect and report a wide variety of statistical indicators related to illegal (and closely related legal) drugs are currently located in the Department of Justice, the Department of State, Department of Defense, the Department of Labor, the Department of Housing and Urban Development, and several organizations within the Department of

Health and Human Services. In addition, the Office of National Drug Control Policy directly sponsors data collection. In many cases, these agencies collect statistics on illegal drugs as a part of a broader survey or data collection. For example, the National Center for Health Statistics has collected information relating to illegal drugs as a part of its National Health Interview Survey and the Bureau of Justice Statistics has collected such data as a part of the Census of Jails. Other systems are more targeted to illegal drug-related issues, such as the Arrestee Drug Abuse Monitoring Program of the National Institute of Justice and the National Household Survey on Drug Abuse of the Substance Abuse and Mental Health Services Administration.

In the long run, the quality of the statistical data on illegal drugs will be enhanced if data collection efforts are consolidated into a smaller number of agencies that either conduct or sponsor the major data collection. In the committee's view, there are many different routes to consolidate data collection, and we recognize that the final form will depend on the focus of the effort and the evolution of capabilities among different agencies. The major point is not that there is a single right way to consolidate efforts. Rather, when decisions are made about the structure of data collection, a decision that over the long run furthers consolidation is preferable to one that further fragments or reinforces the existing fragmentation of data collection efforts.

The committee reviewed a number of different possible models for consolidation of data collection. One that appears attractive would organize the major current data collections into two lead statistical agencies: one for health-related data and one for justice-related data. For example, the health-related data might be consolidated in the National Center for Health Statistics, while data related to law enforcement might be collected primarily by the Bureau of Justice Statistics. These two agencies are identified because they have evolved into full-line statistical agencies with professional statistical staffs and a considerable degree of independence.

If data collection efforts are consolidated in a smaller number of agencies, it will be important to retain the expertise and continuity of effort of existing agencies. There are a number of ways to ensure that the transitional costs are minimized:

1. Statistical agencies could improve the quality of the data by placing actual data collection in agencies with the greatest expertise in the collection of data in particular formats. For example, school-based surveys could draw on the expertise of the National Center for Education Statistics, hospital-based surveys could draw on the expertise of the National Center for Health Statistics, and justice-based surveys could draw on the expertise of the Bureau of Justice Statistics.

2. One area of particular concern is producing price indices and other economic data on illegal drugs. To date, the efforts to construct these data have proceeded without drawing on the expertise of agencies that specialize in price and other economic data, such as the Bureau of Labor Statistics. The procedure described above for developing economic statistics will improve work in this area.

3. Consideration should be given to using interagency transfer of funds to obtain the services of professional statistical organizations so as to strengthen and extend the professional expertise pool for data collection, review, and analysis.

4. To maintain adequate resources for the collection of statistics on illegal drugs, policy, research, and operating agencies (such as the Substance Abuse and Mental Health Services Administration, the National Institute on Drug Abuse, the National Institute of Justice, and the Drug Enforcement Administration) could retain a role in funding (much as the National Institutes of Health does with the National Center for Health Statistics) and thereby ensure that the capacity to compile data on illegal drugs is maintained. Block grant money and other needed funds should be transferred to the lead statistical agencies using interagency transfers to ensure continuity of funding.

5. The lead statistical agencies should foster collaboration with drug policy and research agencies to ensure that their work is relevant to clinical and law enforcement needs. Such arrangements are currently in place in other fields. For example National Institute on Child Health and Human Development funds the National Survey of Family Growth. The staff of the National Institutes of Health plays a large role in shaping the survey, yet the statistical lead is assumed by the National Center for Health Statistics.

6. It is important to maintain the continuity of the professional staffs that currently work on surveys while their work is integrated into the work of the statistical agencies. Alternatively, they could continue to collect data under delegated authority from the statistical agencies, but operating within a framework that emphasizes the independence of statistical operations.

Consolidating the authority to collect and report statistical data on illegal drugs in a very small number of statistical agencies is a long-term goal. It should not be undertaken until these agencies acquire adequate financial resources as well as the requisite professional and technical expertise and staff. In the interim, the committee recommends strengthening the existing organizations for data collection, analysis, and reporting so that they would adhere more closely to appropriate professional standards for statistical units.

CONCLUSION

In summary, the quality, range, reliability, and utility of statistical data on illegal drugs can be improved by undertaking several measures to improve the institutional structure at the federal level. Two key steps are necessary for improving the quality of data on illegal drugs:

1. Efforts should be taken to strengthen the professional staffs and capabilities of the organizations responsible for data collection and analysis and to increase the independence of their operations.

2. Data collection should over the long run be consolidated into a small number of statistical agencies, perhaps two, which would take a leadership role in organizing and collecting statistical data at the federal level.

Upgrading collection efforts in existing agencies and consolidation of data collection are essential tasks for improving the scope and quality of data on illegal drugs. Unless these organizational goals are achieved, the nation will continue to be poorly informed and policies on illegal drugs will be operating largely in the dark. But these steps require determined and effective leadership. Our final recommendation therefore concerns the need for leadership in organizational improvements and reorganization.

The committee recommends that the Office of National Drug Control Policy place organizational improvements for data high on its agenda in the immediate future. If it does not move quickly to implement the changes required to improve statistical data the President and Congress should find other ways to ensure that the substantive and organizational changes are swiftly and effectively achieved.

REFERENCES

Executive Office of the President
    1999   *Report of the Drug Control Research, Data, and Evaluation Committee.* Washington, DC: Office of National Drug Control Policy.

National Research Council
    1992   *Principles and Practices for a Federal Statistical Agency.* Committee on National Statistics. Washington, DC: National Academy Press.
    2001   *Principles and Practices for a Federal Statistical Agency, Second Edition.* Committee on National Statistics. Washington, DC: National Academy Press.

Part III

Research for Drug Policy

The final part of this report examines the research now available to inform drug control policy, identifies important gaps in knowledge, and makes commensurate recommendations. Current policy instruments include an array of activities related to enforcement—domestic enforcement, interdiction, crop eradication, and administrative and informal sanctions—and a wide range of prevention and treatment programs being implemented throughout the country.

It is inevitably difficult to assess the effects of the diverse activities that, taken together, comprise the nation's effort to diminish illegal drug trafficking and use. The present state of knowledge varies considerably across the different policy instruments, with a considerable amount known about some instruments and little at all about others. In part, the state of knowledge reflects the differential investments that the nation has made in research and data collection. Research on enforcement has received very little support; as a consequence, we know very little about the effectiveness of the many dimensions of enforcement policy. Drug treatment research has been supported in a sustained, serious manner; as a consequence, a significant body of work exists. Prevention research has focused almost entirely on school-based programs, virtually ignoring the many other community-based efforts under way. The specificity of the committee's recommendations varies across areas, reflecting variation in the state of knowledge.

We begin our review in Chapter 5 with supply-reduction policy. This chapter and Chapter 6 contain the recommendations regarding the agenda of principal concern to this committee: strengthening research and data on enforcement strategies. The discussion in Chapter 5 stresses the need for research on how drug suppliers respond to enforcement policy and, more broadly, the need for research on the operation of drug markets. The discussion in Chapter 6 pays particular attention to both the declarative and deterrent effects of sanctions against use of illegal drugs. Given the high rate of incarceration under current drug sentencing and its financial and human costs, such research is imperative.

In Chapter 7 the discussion turns to research on programs aimed at preventing or delaying drug use among children and youth. The widespread adoption of many prevention programs whose effects—beneficial or harmful—are unknown requires urgent research attention. Chapter 8 examines the use of randomized clinical trials to test the effectiveness of new treatment protocols in different settings, with diverse clients and for different types of drugs. Special attention is paid to the potential benefits and ethical problems of including no-treatment control groups in clinical trials.

Choosing the right mix of instruments to control the sale of illegal drugs and reduce their use presents complex policy problems: there are many different lines of attack. The committee believes that sustained and systematic research efforts such as those recommended here are essential if the nation is to have any hope of improving the quality of its decision making.

5

Supply-Reduction Policy

To many, it seems obvious that reducing the supply of drugs offers an important way to control the drug problem. If there were no drugs to use, there would be no problem. If lesser quantities of drugs reached consumers in the United States, the problem would be diminished. If drugs were harder to find, or riskier to obtain, or simply more expensive, some potential users might be discouraged from starting, and some current users might seek treatment or abandon their use.

In this chapter, we concentrate on enforcement and other policy instruments that aim to reduce drug supply. We discuss the problems of measuring or otherwise estimating the effectiveness of supply-reduction efforts, assess current knowledge of retail drug markets, explain why an understanding of these markets is important for supply-reduction policy, and assess knowledge of the extent to which arrested drug dealers may be replaced by others. Enforcement efforts directed at drug users are examined in Chapter 6.

DIMENSIONS OF SUPPLY-REDUCTION POLICY

Efficacy and Justice as Evaluative Criteria

The belief that reducing the supply of drugs can help to control the drug problem is but one concern that drives the public commitment to enforcing the drug laws. In addition, the public enthusiasm for enforcement, including imprisonment of offenders, is supported by the view that it is morally wrong to produce and sell drugs, and that those who do so despite laws prohibiting this activity ought to be punished. In short, many people believe not only that enforcement of drug laws helps to solve the problem of drug use, but also that enforcement advances the cause of justice. Of course, a countervailing libertarian view argues that government enforcement of drug laws intrudes on individual freedoms and hence should be minimized to the extent possible.

For a committee of the National Research Council, the fact that some of the enthusiasm for enforcement derives from a moral view of what is right and wrong, as well as from a practical, empirical claim that such policies will succeed in controlling the drug problem creates a difficulty. Scientists know how to measure things and how to reach conclusions about whether a particular intervention works to solve a particular problem or achieve a specified goal. With respect to the question of what sorts of acts are good or bad, and what constitutes a good versus a bad effect, scientists have no special expertise to offer. In a democratic society, that is a job for all citizens, and their representatives, not for scientists alone. What scientists can do is to help citizens judge whether the practical reasoning that links drug enforcement and supply-reduction efforts to the severity of the drug problem is sound, and what the available empirical evidence seems to say about the efficacy of these efforts. That is what we aim to do in this chapter and the next.

We note, however, that findings of either efficacy or inefficacy cannot determine whether the nation should enhance, reduce, or abandon efforts to reduce drug supply and to enforce drug laws. Such efforts could be supported even if ineffective if they were considered a just response to people who produce or sell drugs. And they could be abandoned even if considered effective if they came to be regarded as sufficiently unjust. The worst of all worlds would be one in which the nation supported drug enforcement efforts that were both ineffective and unjust. The best of all worlds would be one in which the policies used were both just and effective. The point is that supply-reduction and drug law enforcement efforts have to be evaluated in terms of their justice as well as their practical effect. It is important to think about whether it is bad to produce and sell prohibited drugs as well as whether it is effective in discouraging people from doing so by threatening to punish them. It is important to think about whether the laws that are enforced are fair, and whether they can be enforced fairly as well as whether the laws can help protect children from having early experiences with drug use that bode poorly for their future. In this discussion, we on occasion note issues of justice as well as efficacy, but it is important to emphasize that the committee's expertise lies in judgments about impact and efficacy against agreed-on objectives, not in our views of justice or social value.

Supply-Reduction Policy and Drug Law Enforcement

Supply-reduction policy is often treated as identical with drug law enforcement. While there is a substantial overlap among the interventions that belong in each category, there is an important conceptual difference between these ideas, and there are some policy interventions that belong in one category but not the other. Supply-reduction efforts include all those interventions that are made to reduce the availability of drugs to unauthorized users. This category includes many things that are not ordinarily thought of as drug law enforcement. For example, it includes efforts to persuade farmers in foreign countries to substitute legitimate crops for illegal drugs. It also includes efforts to police the regulatory boundary between drugs prescribed for legitimate users and those who would like to abuse them. Some activities, such as crop replacement, are supply-reduction efforts but are not law enforcement efforts.

By the same token, drug law enforcement includes many interventions that do not aim to reduce the supply of drugs. For example, it is a crime in all states to possess and use certain drugs as well as to sell them. Nearly 1 million people a year are arrested for personal possession or use of small amounts of drugs (Office of National Drug Control Policy, 1999a).[1] Enforcement of laws prohibiting personal possession or use is properly seen as operating on the demand side rather than the supply side of the drug problem. Such enforcement adds the threat of arrest to all the other reasons that already exist to avoid using illegal drugs and brings current drug users into the criminal justice system, where they can be sent to jail or sent to drug treatment alternatives to jail.

Plausible Efficacy: Reasoning About Supply-Reduction Efforts

To begin our analysis of supply-reduction instruments, it is useful to lay out the logic that links supply-reduction policy to drug use. Many common errors of reasoning show up in policy debates about supply-reduction policy.

Some drug policy analysts appear to believe that supply-reduction efforts fail to deter drug use because most drug users are addicted and

---

[1]It was sale of alcohol, not possession for home use, that was prohibited during Prohibition. Except in a few states, individuals were always allowed to manufacture and use alcohol for their own use, yet the policy was viewed as prohibition. It is clear that the nation's drug policy is much more prohibitive than Prohibition was (Bonnie and Whitebread, 1974).

compulsive in their use; they will "do anything" and "pay anything" to consume drugs.[2] If this is true, then supply-reduction efforts can have very little effect on the quantity of drugs consumed. Rather, such efforts simply act to increase the profits of illegal dealers by enabling them to raise the prices of drugs. This argument ignores the possibility that users and potential users who are not yet addicted to drugs could be dissuaded from experimenting with them by high prices or by the inconvenience and danger of buying drugs. It also ignores the possibility that increases in the price and inconvenience of buying drugs may cause older users who are tired of "the life" to make serious efforts to quit their use. Effects such as these appear to occur with changes in price for legal addictive commodities, such as alcohol, tobacco, and caffeine. Why shouldn't they occur for heroin, cocaine, marijuana, and amphetamines? Indeed, the best current estimates of the elasticity of cocaine consumption with respect to price is that it lies between -0.59 and -2.5: if accurate, this means that a 10 percent increase in the price of the illegal drugs will lead to at least a 5.9 percent reduction in overall levels of use. Apparently it is not true that all drug users will do anything or pay any price (although some of them will do a lot and pay a lot) for drugs. If drug users can be discouraged from using drugs by high prices, unavailability, or risks associated with buying and using drugs, and if enforcement and supply-reduction efforts can raise the price and risks, then these efforts may succeed in dissuading new users from starting, experimental users from advancing to higher levels of use, and advanced users from continuing to use drugs even when treatment is available to them.

Other researchers suggest that drug enforcement and supply-reduction efforts will fail because they cannot succeed in meaningfully raising the price or reducing the availability of drugs. In this view, there is a plentiful supply of people willing to run the moral, economic, and physical risks of dealing drugs for the profit that can be earned. One can agree that there are many people in sufficiently desperate circumstances that dealing in drugs represents a relatively attractive income earning opportunity. But there are many things about dealing in drugs that are unattractive and are made unattractive by its illegal status. In thinking about how drug enforcement affects opportunities for drug dealing, one begins with the idea that each dealer is threatened with the prospect of arrest and

---

[2]Researchers have debated the effect of price increases in light of drug addiction; see Barthold and Hochman (1988), Chaloupka (1991), Warner (1991), Pollak (1976, 1970), and Winston (1980). Research that reports findings of low sensitivity to price in the short run includes Becker, Grossman, and Murphy (1991), Becker and Murphy (1988), and Chaloupka (1991).

imprisonment. But the greater risk may come not from the police, but from other dealers and criminals. Indeed, from the point of view of a drug dealer, one of the worst consequences of the illegality of drugs is that the police and courts do not assist in enforcing contracts and providing security. A drug dealer must absorb all the costs of contract enforcement and security, possibly to the point of being willing to use violence.

Dealing drugs is an economically and physically risky business. That fact dissuades some people from entering the business. It also motivates those people who enter to demand compensation for their risks by increasing the price. In addition, dealers must manage their inventories and transactions so as to minimize the risks of theft and arrest. This means that drugs flow through the supply system less openly and more expensively than would be true if drugs were legal. Indeed, current estimates indicate that the price of illegal drugs is much above the price that would obtain if they were sold in legitimate markets (discussed below). This is a combined effect of both the illegal status of the drugs (which expose drug dealers to attacks from other criminals even if the police do nothing) and of enforcement efforts (which expose drug dealers to the specific threat of arrest by government agents). It is difficult to know what portion of that price increase should be attributed to what effect, but it does suggest that making drugs illegal does increase their price.

Economic theory is unequivocal about the direction of the effect of drug law enforcement on total supply. Enforcement tends to reduce the supply of drugs because it makes drug dealing more risky, demanding, and unpleasant than it would be if drugs were legal. Therefore, at any given price, smaller quantities of drugs come into the market than would be the case in the absence of antidrug laws and law enforcement. How big this effect is and how much it matters in reducing drug use and the adverse consequences of drug use are empirical questions. As we discuss in the remainder of this chapter, the answers to these questions are unknown at present.

A main concern of this chapter is the quality of available empirical evidence on the effectiveness of supply-reduction efforts. Economic or other theory does not provide a basis for making confident or quantitative judgments about the effectiveness of these efforts. Empirical evidence of efficacy is needed to evaluate the benefits and costs of the substantial investments that the nation has made in supply reduction. The required evidence is largely nonexistent. The problem is not just that the relevant studies have not been done. Systems for acquiring the needed data are inadequate or nonexistent. Moreover, the analytic problems of inferring efficacy would be highly complex even if good data were available. The committee makes several recommendations about what can be done to improve evidence on the effectiveness (or lack thereof) of supply-reduction efforts. Developing this evidence is an urgent matter, for the nation's investment in supply reduction, in terms of both money and the exercise of state authority, is very large.

The next two sections introduce the two main modes of research that have been used to evaluate supply-reduction policy. Impulse-response analysis seeks to draw causal inferences directly from temporal sequences of events without specifying the mechanism leading from the hypothesized cause (the impulse) to the suspected effect (the response).[3] Systems research refers to the development of formal models of the behavior of agents who interact in a social system and the use of such models to predict system outcomes as policy varies.

IMPULSE-RESPONSE ANALYSIS

The principle of impulse response analysis is remarkably simple: interventions take place and one observes the consequences. Impulse-response analysis has much appeal when an intervention of interest is the only notable event occurring in a time period under study. Laboratory experiments conducted in tightly controlled environments aim to achieve this ideal. When it is not possible to ensure that the intervention of interest is the only notable event, researchers often recommend performance of multiple independent experiments with randomized assignment of interventions. Randomized assignment enables a probabilistic form of impulse-response analysis from which one may learn the distribution of responses following an intervention of interest. On occasion, natural experiments in uncontrolled environments may approximate the conditions of laboratory or randomized experiments.

Supply-reduction interventions are neither performed in the controlled environments of laboratories nor randomized in the field. Measurements of the response variable of most direct interest, namely the supply of drugs, are not readily available. For these reasons, impulse-response analysis of supply-reduction policy poses a formidable challenge.

In the absence of data on drug supply, impulse-response analysis of supply-reduction policy has mainly sought to connect policy to domestic drug prices. Standard economic analysis predicts that if interdiction and domestic enforcement succeed in reducing the supply of drugs, then the price of drugs will rise, and consumption of drugs will fall, everything

---

[3]Macro economists studying how an outcome (e.g., gross domestic product) responds to some factor (e.g., a percentage change in interest rate) coined the term "impulse response" analysis (see Frisch, 1933). Another term commonly used to describe the same basic methodology is "stimulus-response analysis."

else being equal. This motivates analysis that attempts to relate enforcement activities to domestic drug prices.[4]

Figure 5.1 portrays the standard economic reasoning. The curve labeled "Demand" shows the quantity of a drug that consumers wish to purchase at any given price, and the curve labeled "$Supply_0$" shows the quantity that producers are willing to sell at any given price. The intersection of the supply and demand curves is the market equilibrium: the price P_0 at which the quantities demanded and supply are equal, so that the market is in balance. If the government were to intensify interdiction, domestic enforcement, and other supply-reduction activities, the cost of production would rise and thus shift the supply curve up. The result, everything else being equal, would be a new equilibrium with a higher price (P_1) and lower consumption (Q_1). This is the classic view of the effect of supply-reduction policy on the market.

A formal impulse-response analysis of supply reduction policy was performed in the Institute for Defense Analyses (IDA) study (Crane et al., 1997) assessed by the committee in its Phase I report. This research sought to connect specific interdiction activities (what we refer to as the impulse) to particular subsequent domestic drug price fluctuations (what we refer to as the response). It also sought to connect aggregate spending on interdiction (the impulse) to long-term trends in domestic drug prices (the response). Informal use of impulse-response analysis is common in public discussions of supply-reduction policy. Time-series data describing spending on enforcement are often juxtaposed with data on drug prices, the idea being that the effects of enforcement should be seen in the price data.

We first examine issues that arise in impulse-response analysis relating specific enforcement activities to particular fluctuations in domestic drug prices. We then consider in some depth the use of long-term trends in domestic drug prices to assess the effectiveness of supply-reduction policy writ large.

---

[4]Public officials sometimes call attention to the magnitude of drug seizures and suggest that seizures show the success of enforcement. However, there is no clear way to relate seizures to drug supply. Seizures may induce traffickers to initiate new shipments to replace goods captured in transit, in which case the quantities of drugs entering the United States and reaching local markets may fall by much less than the amount seized, perhaps not at all. Or seizures may increase traffickers' perceptions of the riskiness of the drug trade, and so deter them from initiating new shipments. If so, drug quantities may fall by more than the amount seized. We do not know the extent to which replacement occurs or the magnitude of the deterrent effects of enforcement. Hence data on seizures alone should not be used to judge the effectiveness of enforcement.

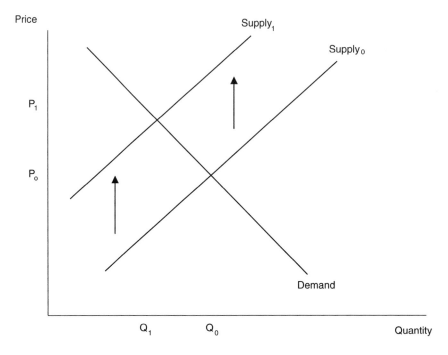

FIGURE 5.1   Supply and demand for illicit drugs

As noted earlier, measurement of the time-series variation in drug prices is problematic at present. There are also difficulties in characterizing the timing and character of enforcement activities. The discussion below focuses on issues that would arise even if satisfactory data were available.

Enforcement Activities and Domestic Drug Price Fluctuations

Efforts to connect specific enforcement activities to particular price fluctuations must inevitably confront the basic fact that enforcement activities are not the only notable events that may affect drug prices. It is unreasonable to suppose that, except for enforcement activities, the supply and demand forces that determine drug prices are stable over time. One obvious source of price fluctuations is time-series variation in drug demand. For example, the demand for cocaine may fluctuate as a result of changing attitudes toward cocaine consumption, a changing mix of light and heavy users, and changing patterns of enforcement and penalties for cocaine possession. Another source of price fluctuations may be variation in the supply of drugs due to changing source country conditions, from weather to political stability.

Even if all determinants of drug prices except enforcement were time-invariant, the dynamics that connect enforcement to domestic drug prices would be complex. An enforcement activity undertaken in a specific place and time presumably does not generate an instant response in drug prices. Does the response in drug prices begin to appear a week, month, or year following the enforcement activity? Does the response persist for a week, month, year, or longer before dissipating? The time path of the response in drug prices presumably depends on the nature of the enforcement activity, on the inventories of drugs held by traffickers in domestic and foreign locations, on the speed with which new drug production can replace seizures, and on the deterrent effect of the enforcement activity on trafficking. Moreover, the time path of the response may vary geographically, depending on the nature of the drug distribution networks and enforcement activities in different locales.

If a single enforcement activity could be undertaken in isolation, as in a laboratory experiment, it would be relatively straightforward to track the time path of the response in drug prices. However, what we actually observe results from the conjunction of numerous enforcement activities undertaken in different times and places, as well as of the many other forces operating on the demand and supply of drugs. This considerably complicates analysis.

The difficulty of carrying out impulse-response analysis is well illustrated by the large upward fluctuation in cocaine prices that the STRIDE data (described in Chapter 3) show to have occurred in 1990. Accepting the STRIDE data as valid, for purposes of the present discussion, the price of domestic cocaine increased sharply between mid-1989 and mid-1990. It returned to its early 1989 level between mid-1990 and late 1991. The price increase occurred shortly after the Bush administration's war on drugs began, suggesting that the war may have contributed to the increase. The war on drugs included a variety of enforcement activities. It is not possible to determine through impulse-response analysis the separate effects of these actions. Moreover, the war on drugs and the 1990 price increase also roughly coincided with the dismantling of the Medellin cartel in Colombia, which may have caused a temporary increase in the price of cocaine by temporarily disrupting production and distribution operations. If one had independent evidence on the magnitude of the response to the collapse of the Medellin cartel, then it might be possible to infer the combined effects of the various actions undertaken during the war on drugs, but no such evidence is available. Thus, considerable uncertainty exists as to the cause of the largest upward fluctuation in domestic cocaine prices in the past 15 to 20 years.

Despite the difficulties, there may be situations in which impulse-response analysis of domestic price fluctuations can yield useful findings. Consider, for example, the effect of an unusually large interdiction action on cocaine prices in a single city. Suppose that, for relatively long periods before and after the interdiction event, records were available of all inter-diction activities, domestic enforcement actions, gang wars, and other events that might affect price. Suppose further that the interdiction action of interest did not occur contemporaneously with other unusually large interdiction or enforcement actions. Then it might be possible to use the records of normal enforcement activities together with data on prices to infer the price response to normal events. If so, then any abnormal price response following the interdiction event of interest might reasonably be interpreted as a consequence of this event. This interpretation would not be unambiguous, because one can never be sure that one has taken into account all possible confounding events. However, such analysis might at least be suggestive.

The committee is not aware of impulse-response analyses of supply-reduction policy performed in the manner just described. Indeed, as dis-cussed in Chapter 3, the existing price data are unlikely to be accurate enough to support such an analysis. This form of impulse-response analy-sis would require not only improved price data but also extensive data on interdiction, domestic enforcement, and other factors that may affect prices. Although such data are currently unavailable, it is conceivable that they might be assembled over time. This warrants further investiga-tion.

In addition to impulse-response studies of price movements, it may be possible to evaluate experiments in police departments. For the last 30 years or so, several departments have conducted experiments in which a particular law enforcement strategy has been tried in certain police dis-tricts or precincts, but not in others. The districts are sometimes selected randomly or after an effort to match experimental and control units. Such work has been done, for example, to evaluate the effect of foot patrol officers and intensified patrol in unmarked patrol cars. Although all such experiments must deal with the likelihood that some criminal activities will be displaced to neighboring areas, this problem can be partially ad-dressed by gathering crime data and interviewing citizens in these adjoin-ing locations as well as in the experimental and control areas.

Enforcement and Long-Term Price Trends

Impulse-response thinking has often been used to infer the broad effectiveness of interdiction and domestic enforcement policy from long-term trends in drug prices. The Institute for Defense Analyses (IDA) study contained an analysis in which aggregate spending on interdiction was taken to be the impulse and the long-term trend in the domestic price of cocaine was taken to be the response. To infer the effect of interdiction spending on the price trend, the IDA report put forward two assumptions about what the time-series path of cocaine prices would have been in the absence of interdiction activities. One is that, in the absence of interdiction in the source zone, price would have remained constant over time. The other is that, in the absence of both source and transit zone interdiction, price would have decreased on an exponential curve over time. These counterfactual price paths both lay below the observed time series of domestic cocaine price. The IDA report concluded that the positive differences between observed cocaine prices and the counterfactual price paths measure the effect of source and transit zone interdiction on price.

Whereas the IDA report used particular counterfactual assumptions, informal impulse-response arguments not invoking explicit counterfactuals have been common in public discussions of enforcement policy. Notwithstanding the measurement problems discussed in Chapter 3, there is widespread agreement about two basic features of drug prices during the past 20 years:

• *Price Decline in the 1980s:* During the 1980s, domestic prices of illegal cocaine and heroin fell very substantially. Since then, prices may have fluctuated over short periods of time but have been relatively stable over the longer term.

• *Prices Remain High:* Throughout the 1980s and 1990s, the prices of illegal cocaine and heroin remained much higher than prices in the small legal markets for pharmaceutical drug use and also much higher than prices of broadly comparable licit agricultural commodities.

The question is: What should be made of these features of drug prices? It has been particularly common to observe that in the 1980s, sharp increases in spending on domestic enforcement and interdiction coincided with sharp decreases in the domestic prices of cocaine and heroin. Juxtaposition of these two trends, shown in Figure 5.2, has led many to conclude that supply-reduction policy has been ineffective.

For example, a recent essay in the *New Yorker* states (Hertzberg, February 7, 2000:31-32):

> At the level of national government, discussion of drug policy has been dormant since the nineteen-eighties ushered in the crack epidemic, just say no, three strikes and you're out, and the prison boom. . . .Yet the failure of the twenty-year "drug war" has never been more apparent. The most damning evidence can be found in the most recent "Fact Sheet" handed out by the White House Office of National Drug Control Policy.

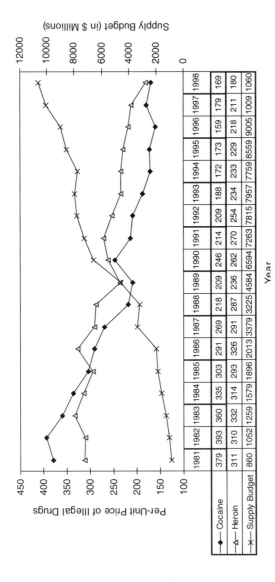

	1981	1982	1983	1984	1985	1986	1987	1988	1989	1990	1991	1992	1993	1994	1995	1996	1997	1998
Cocaine	379	393	360	335	303	291	269	218	209	246	214	209	188	172	173	159	179	169
Heroin	311	310	332	314	293	326	291	287	236	262	270	254	234	233	229	218	211	180
Supply Budget	860	1052	1259	1579	1896	2013	3379	3225	4584	6594	7263	7815	7957	7759	8559	9005	1009	1060

FIGURE 5.2 Enforcement spending and drug prices over time.

Sources: The cocaine and heroin prices are based on the STRIDE data, as reported in Office of National Drug Control Policy (2000, Table 42). These prices reflect retail purchases of less than 1 gram for cocaine, and of less than 0.1 gram for heroin. The cocaine estimates are for the price of a pure gram. The heroin estimates are the price per pure 0.1 gram. The supply budget is from Office of National Drug Control Policy (1997, 1998). The budget figures include domestic law enforcement, international enforcement, and interdiction.

... The surest measure of the success of drug interdiction and enforce-ment is price: if drugs are made harder to come by, the price must in-crease. According to the "Fact Sheet," however, the average price of a gram of pure cocaine dropped from around $300 in 1981 to around $100 in 1997; for heroin the price fell from $3,500 to $1,100.

Much the same reasoning appears in recent testimony of Eric Sterling (2000) to the House Committee on Appropriations:

> In the streets, our policy is a failure. As best we can reckon, the street prices of heroin and cocaine are near historic lows. A pure gram of co-caine was $44 in 1998, down from $191 in 1981. Heroin prices have fallen from $1200 per gram to $318 per gram over the same period. This means traffickers are discounting the risks they face. This means the traffickers are finding it easier to get drugs to our streets, not harder.

Analysts cognizant of the many forces acting on the drug market are aware that juxtaposition of spending and price trends does not suffice to evaluate supply-reduction policy. Clearly interdiction and domestic en-forcement have not made cocaine and heroin prohibitively expensive. At the same time, the fact that the prices of illegal drugs have remained well above the prices of similar legal commodities suggests that policies seek-ing to reduce drug supply have had some effect on prices. It is difficult to go beyond these broad statements in the absence of a deeper understand-ing of the manner in which drug markets have operated in the past 20 years.

Moreover, it is essential to keep in mind that the only meaningful conclusions about the effectiveness of past drug policy are ones that com-pare this policy with some well-defined alternative. When considering the effect of supply-reduction policy on drug prices, one needs to specify an alternative policy and predict the counterfactual path that prices would have taken under this alternative. Any conclusion about the effectiveness of recent policy necessarily depends on what alternative policies one en-tertains and what one predicts the counterfactual price paths would have been.

Suppose, for example, that spending on domestic enforcement and interdiction had been much below its 1980s level. Would the 1998 price of a pure gram of cocaine have remained at its 1981 level of nearly $400, would the price have fallen to its observed level of around $200, or would it have fallen further? Research to date on supply-reduction policy does not provide a basis for answering this basic counterfactual question.

What Explains the 1980s Price Drop?

The sharp fall in illegal drug prices during the 1980s has long per-plexed analysts of drug policy, and this committee as well. It is easy to cite multiple factors that may have contributed to the phenomenon, but it is very difficult to determine their respective roles. Caulkins and Reuter (1998:602-603) offer these possible explanations for the price drop:

> [I]t is possible for overall price to decline even as enforcement stringency increases if the declines in the other cost-components more than offset the increase in enforcement's component. For example, import costs might decline as smugglers acquire experience (Cave and Reuter, 1988). Labor costs might decline if the industry shifted to less skilled labor (e.g. from pilots to small boat crew members) or if there was a decline in the prevailing wage for the current dealer (e.g. aging dealer/users whose legitimate labor force opportunities weaken as their drug-using careers lengthen). Risk compensation for the physical risks of selling drugs could decline if the markets stabilized and the risk of being killed declined. Stares (1996) argues that the trend toward globalization, improved communication and transportation networks, and the persistence of poverty in source countries are enhancing the ability to bring drugs to market cheaply.

As Caulkins and Reuter suggest, there are many ways in which the costs of drug production and distribution may have fallen during the 1980s, shifting the supply curve downward and thus implying lower equilibrium prices, everything else being equal. Production efficiencies may have stemmed from new higher-yielding crops or from economies of scale as the industry adjusted to the heightened demand associated with the emergence of crack. The drug industry may have experienced the learning-curve effect often associated with new industries as they find ways to be more efficient in their operations.[5] The cost of marketing drugs may have fallen as retail selling was taken over by juveniles willing to work for low wages. High profits may have attracted new producers and dealers into the market and may have led existing dealers to expand their transaction volumes (Kleiman, 1992).

At the same time, the demand for drugs may have changed during the 1980s. The usual presumption has been that demand for cocaine increased until the mid-1980s as the crack epidemic took hold. However, at least two countervailing forces were at work as well. First, the federal government substantially increased spending on prevention and treatment programs. The Office of National Drug Control Policy estimates that from fiscal year 1981 to 1989, federal spending on treatment doubled and spending on prevention increased by a factor of 8 (Office of National Drug Control Policy, 1999b). An increase in spending on mass media prevention campaigns should, if effective, unambiguously shift the de-

---

[5]Learning by doing has a long history in studies of industrial organization, productivity, and growth. Arrow (1962) provides a seminal theoretical treatment of the subject.

mand function for drugs downward. An increase in spending on treatment is more difficult to assess. To the extent that treatment is effective and the increased spending makes treatment more available, the demand for drugs should shift downward. However, it may be that the spending increase reflects increases in the cost of treatment or increases in the number of persons requiring treatment as drug consumption rose.

Second, the intensity of domestic enforcement increased substantially during the 1980s. Whereas enforcement directed at dealers aims to reduce the supply of drugs, enforcement directed at users aims to reduce the demand for drugs. To the extent that increased enforcement directed at users deterred drug purchases or incapacitated users, the demand for drugs should have shifted downward during the 1980s. See Chapter 6 for further discussion.

It is unclear how much of the 1980s price fall was due to production and distribution innovations, how much to changes in demand-side forces, how much to changes in enforcement that may have affected both the supply and demand for drugs, and how much to the insensitivity of supply or demand to the increased enforcement that occurred during that time. Sorting out this matter is of more than historical interest. Understanding what happened in the 1980s would help in the design of drug policy today.

Prices of Illegal Drugs and Comparable Legal Commodities

There appears to be nearly unanimous support for the idea that the current policy enforcing prohibition of drug use substantially raises the prices of illegal drugs relative to what they would be otherwise.[6] The basic economic argument underlying the near consensus is that enforcement of prohibition raises the costs of drug production and distribution. The basic empirical finding is that prices of illegal drugs as measured by STRIDE are substantially higher than the retail prices of comparable legal commodities.[7]

---

[6]See, for example, Caulkins and Reuter (1998), Koper and Reuter (1996), Moore (1990), Morgan, (1991), Nadelmann (1991), Reuter and Kleiman (1986). Miron (1999) draws a somewhat more ambivalent conclusion. Contrasting the price effects of enforcement against the tax and regulatory costs imposed on legal markets, Miron (1999) argues that the illegal price of cocaine may not be inflated at all and is at most two to three times higher than the legal price.

[7]This empirical finding should be tempered by two caveats. First, as we discussed in Chapter 3, the STRIDE data do not constitute a representative sample of retail prices. Second, even if the price data were valid, price measures only the pecuniary cost of buying illegal drugs. Enforcement of prohibition presumably raises the nonpecuniary costs of buying drugs as well—time costs, threat of robbery and physical harm, and the threat of arrest. These costs may be substantial.

Comparison of the illegal price of cocaine to the legal pharmaceutical price reveals that the illegal price substantially exceeds the legal price. In 1981 the illegal price exceeded the legal price by a multiplicative factor of almost 50, in 1998 by a factor of nearly 2.5. Pharmaceutical prices are not likely to be valid as measures of the prices of recreational drugs in a hypothetical regime of regulated use, but the large pre-1990 markups are nonetheless suggestive. Moore (1990), citing similar figures, concludes "these data make it clear that prohibition and supply-reduction efforts can increase the price of psychoactive drugs well above levels that would obtain in a legal market."[8] Nadelmann (1991), Morgan (1991), and Kleiman (1992) draw similar conclusions. Miron (1999), focusing on data from the late 1990s, finds the evidence less persuasive.[9]

Price markups along the production and distribution process have also been used as suggestive evidence of the effects of enforcement. Reuter and Kleiman (1986: Table 1) displays interval price estimates at various stages of the process for a pure kilogram of heroin, cocaine, and marijuana. Many of the intervals are wide, reflecting the limitations of existing data. Nevertheless, two general conclusions may be drawn. First, the markups from the farm to retail distribution are substantial. The retail price may be 100 times the farmgate price for cocaine and marijuana and perhaps 1,000 times for heroin. Second, a substantial portion of the final price is added in the final stages of distribution. For heroin and cocaine, prices increase between 7 and 13 times in the transition from import to retail; for marijuana, prices increase 2 to 6 times.[10]

---

[8]Moore, focusing on data from the mid-1980s, found that heroin prices were inflated by a factor of 70, cocaine by 8, and marijuana by 15.

[9]The markups in the later 1990s appear to be much less than those in the 1980s. Some of the change is due to the large drop in the retail price of cocaine that occurred in the 1980s. The major change, however, appears to be a rise in the price of legal cocaine, which increased by a factor of 3.6 since 1990 and 8.5 since 1981. There is some evidence that the rise in the pharmaceutical price resulted in part from supply shortages in the late 1980s and "inadequate competition among the domestic manufactures of bulk cocaine" (U.S. Department of Justice, 1998). Some of the increase might also be an artifact of the price series, which is based on prices from two different distributors, one covering the late 1990s and one covering 1981-1991.

[10]A number of other researchers have estimated similar markups. For cocaine, the retail price is generally reported to be around 200 times larger than the farmgate price, and 70 times larger than the price in Colombia (Caulkins and Reuter, 1998, and Miron, 1999). Reuter (1988) reports the Colombia retail markup to be substantially less and Reuter and Kleiman (1986) bound the markup between 65 and 267. Finally, the border to retail markup is reported by the Office of National Drug Control Policy (1997b) and Caulkins and Reuter (1998) to be about 6 to 7 times, whereas Reuter and Kleiman (1986) find the factor to be between 13 and 16.

These data have been used to evaluate the price effects of the current prohibition environment. Only part of the price markup from farmgate to retail can be attributed to enforcement of prohibition; after all, bringing drugs to market incurs real resource costs. The question is: How much?

Several researchers have used aggregate data on seizures (both drugs and other assets), incarceration rates, and estimated wage rates to make educated guesses on the part of the markup that is due to enforcement of prohibition. Caulkins and Reuter (1998) argue that risk compensation accounts for over half of the total cost of production, while seizures and money laundering fees account for another 10-15 percent of production costs. Thus, they estimate that enforcement accounts for about 60-70 percent of the retail price of cocaine. Miron (1999) finds that arrests and seizures account for as much as half the illegal price, but that these costs are nearly offset by tax and regulatory costs incurred in legal markets. Any markup, Miron argues, must be due to "secrecy cost" (i.e., nontrivial actions taken to avoid detection) that he does not evaluate.

Other analyses compare the price markups in the production process for cocaine with markups for agricultural commodities that may be comparable to cocaine. Caulkins and Reuter (1998) suggest substantial price markups similar to those observed for cocaine are consistent with some goods (e.g., the farmgate value of wheat in a box of shredded wheat is about 2.5 percent of the retail price) but not others (e.g., the border value of a pound of sugar is about 50 percent of the retail value). Miron (1999) claims that all kinds of common agricultural products (e.g., cocoa, coffee, tea, beer) have farmgate-to-retail markups comparable to that of cocaine. For example, the price of raw coffee beans in Colombia is $0.75 per pound, while the per-pound price of espresso at Espresso Royale in Boston is $111.30.

Of course, Miron's conclusion rests on his assumption that the Espresso Royale retail price is the relevant measure. The per-pound price of a cup of coffee at Dunkin Donuts is $25.43, and the retail price of Roaster Whole supermarket beans is $6.36 per pound. Whether one should measure the retail price at Espresso Royale, Dunkin Donuts, or the supermarket is an open question. If restricted to supermarket prices, beer is the only good for which Miron finds markups similar to cocaine, and for it taxes are usually a big component of the markup.

In any case, the relevance of these comparisons between cocaine and legal agricultural commodities is not clear. The reasons for the coffee markup and the cocaine markup are likely to be very different. For illegal drugs, a relatively substantial fraction of the costs may be due to risk and asset seizures. For legal agricultural commodities, a relatively large fraction of costs are associated with marketing (e.g., packaging and advertising), taxes, and regulations.

To summarize, basic economic thinking combined with comparisons of the prices of illegal drugs to pharmaceutical drug prices and to prices of legal agricultural commodities have led to the consensus view that illegal drug prices are raised by the existing prohibition policy. Thus, enforcement of prohibition through interdiction and domestic enforcement do appear to affect the market. However, the marginal effect of enforcement spending remains uncertain. As Caulkins and Reuter (1998:603) state, "it is not clear how much enforcement is 'enough' to keep prices high." Nor is it known which specific enforcement measures contribute to price increases, which do not, and by how much specific effective measures increase prices.

SYSTEMS RESEARCH

Economists have long developed highly sophisticated systems models to explain markets for goods and services. Systems research, which consists of formal efforts to model behavior of actors or agents in a social system, was used to evaluate supply-reduction policy in the RAND study (Rydell and Everingham, 1994) assessed in the committee's Phase I report, as well as in several other recent analyses. A Simulation of Adaptive Response (SOAR) model was developed by Caulkins et al. (1993) to simulate the effects of enforcement activities on the route and mode choices of smugglers. Economic models of the cocaine trade have been developed by Kennedy et al. (1993) and Riley (1993) and used to simulate the impacts of voluntary crop substitution programs and forced crop eradication, among other enforcement activities.

Even in the absence of empirical analysis, systems research can play a useful role in evaluating supply-reduction policy. Thoughtful development of formal behavioral models encourages coherent thinking about the technology of drug production, transport, and distribution. It forces one to make explicit judgments about the manner in which enforcement activities may affect the behavior of producers and traffickers. Simulation exercises can show how assumptions translate into predictions of policy impacts. The performance of sensitivity analyses can clarify the critical empirical questions that must be answered to credibly predict the consequences of enforcement policy.

Systems research can do much more to inform supply-reduction policy if a model's assumptions and parameter values have firm foundations. The central requirement is empirical research illuminating how drug production, transport, and distribution respond to interdiction and domestic enforcement activities. In the absence of empirical research, analysts can argue endlessly about the realism of any systems model that may be proposed. With it, analysts may be able to develop models whose predictions of policy impacts are widely accepted.

To date, systems research on supply-reduction policy has had to rest on weak empirical foundations. In part because the data available to support empirical study of interdiction and domestic enforcement are so limited, analysts have not been able to provide strong grounding for the assumptions about the behavior of drug producers and traffickers that are embedded in systems models. There is uncertainty about how consumers respond to variation in prices (see Chapter 2). Current knowledge about the structure of retail drug markets is largely based on qualitative ethnographic and journalistic research, as this chapter notes. Current knowledge about how the production process responds to supply-reduction policies is very limited.

Substitution, Deterrence, and Adaptation

In the committee's view, systems research has much potential to inform supply-reduction policy and drug control policy more generally. However, this potential cannot be realized quickly or easily. **The committee recommends that the Office of National Drug Control Policy and other agencies support a sustained program of data collection and empirical research aiming to discover how drug production, transport, and distribution respond to interdiction and domestic enforcement activities. The committee strongly recommends that empirical research address three critical issues: geographic substitution, deterrence, and adaptation:**

• *Geographic substitution:* interdiction and domestic enforcement activities commonly target drug production, transport, and distribution in specific geographic areas. To what extent can producers and traffickers thwart geographically delimited operations by shifting their activities elsewhere?

• *Deterrence:* interdiction and domestic enforcement activities may reduce existing drug supply through seizures and eradication, and they may reduce future supply through deterrence of new drug production and trafficking. Seizures and eradication are directly observable in principle, but deterrence is not. How can the deterrent effects of supply-reduction activities be measured? How large are they?

• *Adaptation:* drug production and trafficking may respond to supply-reduction activities by drawing on inventories, by increasing production, by initiating cultivation in new territories, or by altering geographic routes of distribution. How quickly can such adaptation occur, and what happens to supply and price during the period of adaptation? To the extent that supply-reduction operations deter new drug supply, how long do the deterrent effects last before new supply sources emerge?

With such a program in place, we envision a gradual process of model improvement as new findings on the nature of production, transport, and distribution accumulate.

Assessing Crop-Reduction Policy

Assessment of crop-reduction policy provides a ready illustration of the importance of substitution, deterrence, and adaptation. As this report was being written, an ongoing debate about the effectiveness of crop-reduction policy continued to evolve. The immediate issue was the wisdom of the Clinton administration's request to Congress in spring 2000 for emergency funding to support Colombia in its efforts to suppress production of cocaine and heroin in southern Colombia. This emergency funding request followed the large increase in coca and poppy cultivation that appears to have occurred in Colombia in the latter 1990s.

Geographic substitution of cultivation looms large as an issue in assessing crop-reduction policy. The recent dramatic rise in coca cultivation in Colombia has coincided with equally dramatic falls in coca cultivation in Peru and Bolivia. These events have become inextricably linked in public discussions of crop-reduction policy as the "balloon effect," described in a recent *New York Times* special report on "Cocaine War" (Larry Rohter, April 21, 2000):[11]

> The rapid expansion of coca production in Colombia is in large part a consequence of two developments. One is what is known as the "balloon effect"—the reappearance of a problem in a new place after it has been squeezed in another—which followed successful American-led campaigns against coca growers in Peru and Bolivia.

The geographic substitution suggested by the balloon effect has potentially strong implications for the effectiveness of crop-reduction policy. The *New York Times* article contains this passage: "One additional concern, both in Andean capitals and in Washington, is that any success against coca cultivation in Colombia will inevitably lead to a resurgence of coca growing in Peru or Bolivia." The article does not offer an explicit argument for this prediction, but the basis appears to be static competitive economic theory. This theory predicts that, in the absence of resource

---

[11]The second development cited is miscalculations by Colombian President Pastrana in his efforts to negotiate with the F.A.R.C. guerillas.

constraints, an exogenous event removing one farm from production should generate an increase in product price that induces another farm to enter, restoring the original status quo. If cocaine production fits this simple competitive story, then geographic substitution of cultivation may even be one-for-one, entirely negating the effectiveness of crop-reduction efforts in Colombia.

Committee discussions with government analysts of drug production suggest that cocaine production may fit the simple competitive story in some important respects. First, resource constraints do not prevent substitution from occurring. A variety of current and potential source countries appear to have plentiful land suitable for growing coca, as well as the requisite labor supply. Second, there are no obvious barriers to the entry of new farms to replace those in which production ceases.

However, open empirical questions regarding deterrence and adaptation suggest that cocaine production may not fit the story in other important respects. Deterrence occurs if potential growers in country A, observing the success of U.S.-led crop-reduction efforts in country B, decide not to initiate production because they anticipate that the U.S. government will lead successful crop-reduction efforts against them as well. [12] In the context of the current policy debate, deterrence can counter the prediction of the *New York Times* article that success against coca cultivation in Colombia will inevitably lead to a resurgence of coca growing in Peru or Bolivia.

Static competitive theory abstracts from the adaptation by growers and governments, which may be an important consideration in evaluation of crop-reduction policy. Static theory contemplates a single enforcement action by government followed by an immediate response by growers. The reality, however, is a dynamic of action and reaction as envisioned in the theory of sequential games. In the absence of deterrent effects, the effectiveness of crop-reduction policy depends on (1) how quickly potential growers commence new planting following the disruption of production elsewhere and (2) how quickly governments become aware of new planting and act to suppress it. In the presence of deterrent effects, adaptation issues become more subtle as responses (1) and (2) become linked together.

In summary, land on which cocaine can be grown is plentiful. There is evidence that past campaigns against coca growers have caused produc-

---

[12]Viewed from the perspective of economic theory, deterrence departs from the simple competitive story told above in that the success of crop-reduction policy in country B now does more than raise the price of cocaine; it also changes the expectations of potential growers in country A.

tion to shift to other geographical areas. Such shifting significantly decreases and may entirely vitiate the effect of crop suppression on the supply of cocaine. It is unknown whether deterrence measures can be developed that would diminish or prevent geographical shifting of production in response to suppression of coca cultivation in limited areas.

Issues of substitution, deterrence, and adaptation have arisen repeatedly in the committee's deliberations on supply-reduction policy as well as in presentations made to the committee in public workshops. These issues arise as much in discussion of domestic law enforcement as in discussion of interdiction policy. The remainder of this chapter examines questions related to domestic enforcement, beginning with the structure of retail drug markets.

RETAIL DRUG MARKETS

A retail drug market is the set of people, facilities, and procedures through which a drug such as cocaine is transferred from suppliers to users. Users and suppliers interact through retail markets. Much law enforcement activity is aimed at disrupting this interaction by increasing the price that users must pay, decreasing the quality (purity) of the drugs that are sold, making it more difficult for users and sellers to find each other, or increasing the risks of buying and selling drugs. Other actions to reduce drug use also operate, at least in part, through their effects on retail markets. For example, a successful treatment or prevention program is likely to reduce the demand for drugs and therefore the earnings of individuals who sell them. This in turn may reduce the number of drug sellers. A program that improves legitimate employment for youths may also reduce the number of individuals who sell drugs, thereby increasing the difficulty that users encounter in finding drugs for sale and perhaps increasing the price that users must pay.

There are many questions about retail drug markets whose answers, were they available, would be useful to policy makers. For example:

1. What is the price elasticity of the demand for powder cocaine? For cocaine base (crack)? Other drugs? That is, by how much does the quantity consumed decrease (increase) in when the retail price increases (decreases)? If the price increases, to what extent is the reduction in consumption caused by cessation of use by casual users? By heavy users? To what extent is the reduction in consumption caused by decreased use but not cessation by casual users? By heavy users? To what extent does a price increase limit initiation of new users? To what extent does the demand for one drug depend on the price of other drugs? What are the dynamics of the response of demand to price changes?

2. How do changes in the costs of production or in wholesale prices affect retail prices? For example, suppose that the wholesale price of cocaine in Colombia increases from $1.00 to $1.50 per pure gram (an increase of 50 percent) at a time when the retail price in the United States is $100. Does the price change in Colombia cause the U.S. retail price to increase by $0.50? By $50? By an amount between these extremes? What are the dynamics of the response? The answers are unknown but have obvious implications for the effectiveness of actions that increase the price of cocaine in Colombia.[13]

3. Analyses of the STRIDE price data have shown that there is little relation between the retail price of cocaine and its purity. The same is true for heroin. Why is there no relation between price and purity? For example, why don't sellers of higher-quality cocaine either charge higher prices or cut their product so that they are able to make more sales at the existing price?[14] More generally, how do market conditions and other variables influence the purity of drugs that are sold at retail? Kleiman (1992) wrote that "no student of the drug markets has ever produced anything like a convincing theory to explain how changes in market conditions cause changes in average purities over time or from market to market." Kleiman's statement remains true today.

4. By how much (if at all) do policy interventions that increase the risks of selling cocaine or other illegal drugs (for example, an aggressive program of seeking out and arresting drug dealers) deter persons from dealing illegal drugs? Increase the price of cocaine? Increase the difficulty that consumers experience in finding sellers?

5. To what extent is employment in the retail drug trade affected by

---

[13]Several investigators (Caulkins, 1994; Crane et al., 1997; Abt Associates, 1999) have attempted to use STRIDE price data to analyze the relation between retail prices and prices at higher levels of the production and distribution chain. As discussed in Chapter 3, the committee concludes that STRIDE data do not provide reliable indicators of retail price movements in actual drug markets. Moreover, for the reasons that are explained earlier in this chapter, existing data do not permit firm conclusions to be reached about the causes of price changes.

[14]Some observers have suggested that the answer to this question is that buyers and sellers of cocaine do not have information about purity. Although it is true they do not have the quantitatively precise information that a laboratory analysis would provide, there are many ways for them to obtain approximate information. For example, dealers often distribute free samples to enable consumers to assess purity (Simon and Burns, 1997). Indeed, STRIDE contains over 4,000 records of cocaine acquisitions through free samples. In addition, impure crack cocaine can have a distinctive texture and leave a residue when smoked. Powder cocaine is soluble in alcoholic beverages such as vodka, but many of its impurities are not.

the availability of legitimate employment opportunities? For example, to what extent do increases in legitimate employment opportunities or wages for unskilled labor draw individuals away from drug dealing?

Interest in such questions is not restricted to markets for illegal drugs. Similar questions are routinely asked and answered in economic analyses of markets for legitimate products and labor markets. Indeed, economists have developed theoretical models and statistical methods for studying retail markets and labor markets. There is little doubt that these models and methods can be adapted for application to markets for illegal drugs. The main obstacle to doing so is lack of the required data. The economic analysis of legal markets uses data on prices, purchase frequencies, quantities bought and sold, employment levels, and wages, among other variables. Reliable data of these kinds on markets for illegal drugs do not exist.

And because they do not exist, current knowledge of these markets is based largely on investigations by ethnographers and journalists. Ethnographic and journalistic research has provided invaluable information about the organization of drug markets, their effects on neighborhoods, and the behavior of market participants. The results of this research provide essential inputs to any economic analyses that may be undertaken in the future, but ethnographic and journalistic research is largely descriptive and case-specific. As a result, it has only a limited ability to provide quantitative answers to questions such as the ones listed above. It is the committee's view that until data required for economic analyses of retail drug markets become available, policy interventions aimed at influencing these markets will be largely shots in the dark, and estimates of the effectiveness of these interventions will be largely speculative.

We summarize below current knowledge and significant outstanding questions about aspects of retail drug markets that are especially important for policy analysis. The topics discussed are the social organization of retail drug markets, price determination in retail markets, issues of labor supply, and the problem of estimating demand functions and price elasticities of demand for illegal drugs.

Social Organization of Retail Markets

The social organization of retail drug markets has been investigated in ethnographic studies. Curtis and Wendel (1999, 2000) have identified three forms of retail organizations in the New York City area: freelance dealers, corporate-style organizations, and socially bonded organizations. The National Development and Research Institutes (1998) have also documented the existence of such organizations in the crack cocaine trade in New York.

Freelancing tends to be the most visible, disruptive, and violent form of market organization. Socially bonded organizations are based on social ties, such as kinship, ethnicity, and neighborhood. They are held together by personal relationships, are often discreet about their sales practices (for example, they tend not to advertise drugs openly in the street), and are often less violent and disruptive to their communities than are other types of drug-dealing organizations. Some socially bonded organizations provide substantial financial support to the neighborhoods in which they operate. Thus, these organizations are more likely to be tolerated or even supported by neighborhood residents (Curtis and Wendel, 1999). According to Curtis and Wendel (1999, 2000), corporate-style businesses tend to be more visible, violent, and disruptive than are socially bonded ones. Corporate-style organizations are large and hierarchical, often with few opportunities for advancement for street-level employees. The separation of ownership and labor in corporate-style organizations can create serious tensions among employees (Curtis and Wendel, 1999). In discussing implications of different forms of social organization for the effectiveness of efforts by local police to disrupt retail markets and arrest their participants, Curtis and Wendel (2000) conclude that police operations against corporate-style businesses are most likely to succeed. Operations against socially bonded businesses are least likely to succeed.

The implications of different forms of social organization for economic analysis have not been investigated and are uncertain. It is possible though unverified that members of socially bonded organizations are less likely than are freelancers or lower-level corporate employees to respond to legitimate employment opportunities. It is also possible that differently organized businesses have different policies on drug prices and purity. For example, a socially bonded business that sells mainly to residents of the neighborhood in which its members live may charge less or provide higher-quality drugs than does a corporate-style business that is selling to strangers and feels no special ties to the communities in which it operates. However, the committee is unaware of the existence of any research on the relations, if any, among social organization, prices, and purity.

Two studies describe ways that drug markets have changed in response to increased police pressure (National Development and Research Institutes, 1998; Curtis and Wendel, 1999). In New York, there appears to be evidence of geographic substitution. For example, some drug sellers now operate delivery services that take orders by telephone and deliver drugs to customers' homes or offices. Other businesses allow customers to contact sellers by beeper and then arrange discreet meetings over the telephone. Delivery and beeper services operate out of sight and reduce the risks of detection by police relative to sales in streets or known drug-dealing locations.

Curtis and Wendel (1999) describe considerable fragmentation of the retail market for drugs in New York City. They report that even within a relatively small geographical area, there are many different markets rather than a single one. For example, some markets exist in bars and sell a highly adulterated form of cocaine to occasional sniffers. Cocaine injectors and freebasers do not purchase such material. Moreover, sellers of highly adulterated powder cocaine in bars do not want to service injectors and freebasers, because doing so would attract unwanted attention.

In an interview with two committee members, Richard Curtis of the John Jay College of Criminal Justice described a situation in which a classical musician in New York sold cocaine to midtown clients, many of whom were in the fashion industry. This seller knew the purity level desired by each client and prepared cocaine accordingly. He sold purer cocaine to freebasing customers than to sniffers. He also charged different customers different prices for the same material, possibly depending on his familiarity with the customer or the customer's familiarity with market prices.

Curtis also described geographical fragmentation of the market. Customers in midtown or lower Manhattan tend not to travel to Harlem or Washington Heights to buy drugs, although doing so would save them money.

In addition, the risk of detection by undercover police has increased the difficulty that a new customer has in finding a dealer. Curtis reported that it is easy to find low-purity powder cocaine in a bar, but a first-time buyer of purer powder cocaine or of cocaine base is likely to have to operate through a broker. The broker may buy the drug and deliver it to the customer, or he may introduce the customer to the seller. Either way, selling through a broker reduces the risks to the seller and increases the customer's monetary and search costs. National Development and Research Institutes (1998) has also reported increased use of brokers and middlemen in the retail crack trade in New York.

It is unknown whether market fragmentation like that in New York exists in other cities. If so, then fragmentation undoubtedly explains part of the considerable dispersion of prices that is present in the STRIDE data. (For example, Appendix Figure A.6 shows that agents of the Drug Enforcement Administration pay considerably more for cocaine base in Washington, D.C., than do agents of the Metropolitan Police of the District of Columbia.) Regardless of its geographical extent, the causes of market fragmentation are poorly understood. Moreover, different customer needs, price discrimination by sellers, and geographical separation do not explain all of the variation in cocaine prices. In the interview with committee members, Curtis reported that cocaine prices in New York can vary greatly over distances of a few blocks. The cause of such variation is not known but seems not to be sellers' ignorance of the prices that their competitors charge. Sellers, according to Curtis, are well informed about the prices that other sellers charge. Similarly, buyers apparently know many dealers. For example, Riley (1997) reports the results of a survey of drug-using arrestees in six cities. He found that cocaine-using arrestees knew on average between 7 and 26 dealers, depending on the city and the form of cocaine. He does not report whether buyers know the prices that various dealers charge.

Price Determination

The forces that determine the retail prices of illegal drugs are not well understood. It is clear that prices are highly dispersed. That is, there is not a single price of, say, cocaine base in a given market but, rather, a distribution of prices that may be very wide. In Washington, D.C., for example, the retail price of cocaine base can vary among purchase occasions by a factor of two or more (see Appendix Figure A.6). The relation between retail prices and prices at wholesale and other levels is also not well understood. As mentioned earlier, analysts have proposed a variety of models of the relation between retail prices of cocaine in the United States and prices in, say, Colombia, but data that would support a persuasive analysis are not available.

There is some evidence that drug dealers charge different prices to different customers and that prices can be substantially above marginal costs. In a competitive market with fully informed consumers, the price of a good equals the marginal cost of supplying it. No seller can charge more than the market price, and a seller who charges less than the market price will lose money. Price discrimination among buyers is impossible in such a competitive market. However, as noted earlier, drug markets are highly fragmented (at least in New York), and prices vary widely among dealers and among the customers of a given dealer.

Levitt and Venkatesh (1998) provide further evidence on these matters. They analyzed the financial records of a drug-dealing street gang in a large American city.[15] They report that gang members attempted to charge buyers whom they thought were naïve higher prices. If price differences among customers do not reflect different costs of serving them,

---

[15]Levitt and Ventakesh (1998) do not identify the city or time period of study in order to preserve confidentiality.

including costs such as the risk of being arrested or robbed, then price discrimination is being practiced. Although there are many dealers in a large city, the fragmentation of the market may enable them to have local market power (for example, if it is costly for customers to search for another dealer). Levitt and Venkatesh also report that during the 4-year period they studied, the retail price of crack sold by the gang exceeded marginal costs by 25 to 150 percent.[16] Their measure of marginal cost captures financial costs but not nonfinancial ones such as the risk of arrest and imprisonment. Nonetheless, the presence of large markups and the existence of price discrimination are consistent with local market power and noncompetitiveness in the market studied by Levitt and Venkatesh (1998).

The causes of market fragmentation and noncompetitiveness are not clear. For example, if dealers know the prices that are charged by their competitors, why is it that low-price dealers do not raise their prices to levels comparable to those of high-price dealers? If buyers know many sellers, why do they not seek a seller with a low price? Do prices vary systematically according to the social organization of the seller's operation (e.g., corporate style, socially bonded, etc.)? How important are search costs and nonprice factors to buyers? Does the extent of market fragmentation vary with the level and type of law enforcement? The answers to these questions are unknown.

The committee recommends research on how illegal drug prices are determined. Much law enforcement activity is aimed, at least in part, at increasing the price of drugs. Without reliable knowledge of how retail prices are determined, one can only speculate about the effectiveness of such programs.

Ethnographers who study drug dealers and consumers can carry out some of the needed research. For example, an ethnographer could ask sellers for information about their prices and could ask consumers about their knowledge of prices charged by different sellers. An ethnographer might also be able to monitor price levels in a neighborhood and ask dealers about the causes of any large price changes that occur. The resulting information would not necessarily have the theoretical and statistical validity of the results that economists obtain with formal models and large survey datasets, but it has the potential to provide increased understanding of important but poorly understood aspects of retail drug mar-

---

[16]Levitt and Venkatesh also report that markups of price over marginal cost were not necessarily positive during gang wars, when entering the gang's territory to buy drugs was more than usually dangerous. During some periods of gang war, the price of drugs sold by the gang was below the estimated marginal cost.

kets. Other research issues are more difficult to address. For example, persuasive research on the relation between retail and wholesale prices will not be possible unless and until improved price data become available.

Labor Supply Issues

It is likely that the prices of illegal drugs and the difficulty of obtaining them would increase if substantial numbers of retail dealers could be induced to accept legitimate employment in place of drug dealing. Higher prices and search costs, in turn, would tend to decrease drug consumption. Thus, it is useful to investigate the extent to which drug dealers respond to changes in legitimate employment opportunities. The central issue is the extent to which drug dealers move between illegal and legal employment in response to changes in employment opportunities, relative wages, and relative risks.

Labor economists have developed sophisticated models and statistical techniques for investigating individuals' decisions to participate in the labor force or not, the process of searching for employment, and the means by which employees are matched to employers. However, empirical investigations of these topics rely on large cross-sectional and longitudinal datasets that provide detailed information about the employment status and history, earnings, education, and personal characteristics of probability samples of individuals. Similar data pertaining to actual and potential drug dealers do not exist. Therefore, it has not been possible to use the methods of labor economics to study labor supply in markets for illegal drugs.

There have, however, been several ethnographic and other less formal studies of labor supply in retail drug markets. These have taken place in several different cities, have gathered information from nonrandom and arguably nonrepresentative samples of individuals, and have reached conflicting conclusions.[17] Simon and Burns (1997) studied a drug-dealing neighborhood in Baltimore, MD. They report that many of the drug dealers they encountered lacked the skills, self-confidence, and motivation needed to obtain and hold legitimate jobs. Richard Curtis (in an interview with committee members) reported that most of the dealers he knows in New York hold legitimate jobs and sell drugs on the side. He said that he had not seen dealers move in and out of the legitimate labor market.

---

[17]Most existing studies are based on interviews of arrested drug dealers, records of a single drug-dealing organization, or observations of dealers in a single neighborhood. It is arguable that none of these is representative of dealers and potential dealers in a city.

MacCoun and Reuter (1992: 477) studied arrested drug dealers in Washington, D.C., during the mid 1980s. They report that most members of their sample had legitimate employment in addition to drug selling, concluding that "drug selling seemed to be a complement to, rather than a substitute for, legitimate employment."

Fagan (1992), who studied labor force participation by drug dealers in the Washington Heights and Central Harlem sections of New York during the mid-1980s, reached a different conclusion. Fagan estimated an econometric model of the relation between participation in the legitimate labor force, drug-dealing activities, and indicators of skills, such as education levels. He found that increased drug market participation was associated with decreased participation in the legitimate labor force. Thus, drug selling and legitimate employment were substitutes. Fagan also found that increased education was associated with increased participation in legitimate labor. Fagan does not report how relative opportunities for legitimate and illegitimate employment may have changed over time or how individuals' employment arrangements (legal versus illegal) may have changed. Fagan's findings are suggestive but do not necessarily imply that increased opportunities or wages in the legitimate labor force attract drug dealers away from dealing. It is possible, for example, that, as in the Baltimore neighborhood studied by Simon and Burns (1997), the skills and motivation of those who sell drugs are so poorly matched to the needs of legitimate employers that no realistic change in relative employment opportunities would move them from drug dealing to legitimate jobs. Indeed, Fagan (1992:129) concluded that "in Central Harlem drug sellers are recruited largely from a universe of nonworkers who otherwise might not be in the labor force at all or would be engaged in other types of crime." Similarly, he concluded that drug selling in Washington Heights "apparently attracts workers with less human capital, people who might not otherwise fare particularly well in the formal economy."

Levitt and Venkatesh (1998) provide limited evidence for movement of drug dealers between legitimate and illicit employment. They quote one member of the gang they studied as saying that he quit his job at a fast food restaurant when he started earning a relatively high income by selling drugs but returned to the restaurant job when his drug-related earnings decreased. Levitt and Venkatesh also report that in the last year of their study, gang members' wages from selling drugs increased substantially and their participation in the legitimate labor market decreased.

In summary, the available evidence is incomplete and conflicting on the extent to which drug dealing is a substitute for legitimate employment. A much better understanding of labor force participation and supply by drug dealers and potential drug dealers could be obtained if the data needed to apply the methods of labor economics were available. **The committee recommends survey research on the labor supply of illegal drug dealers.** The Current Population Survey and the National Longitudinal Surveys, among others, routinely gather data on the supply of legitimate labor. Surveys using questions similar to those in the Current Population Survey and National Longitudinal Surveys could be carried out in drug-dealing neighborhoods of a few large cities. The surveys could be carried out over a period of years, and it is likely that many of the same individuals could be reinterviewed periodically, thereby providing longitudinal data. Methods such as those developed by the National Household Survey of Drug Abuse could be used to maintain confidentiality of responses and to ensure that respondents are not put in legal jeopardy by their answers to questions.

Estimating Demand Models and Price Elasticities

In economic systems, the price at which goods are transacted and the quantity of goods consumed are determined by the interaction between suppliers and consumers. Our focus here has been primarily on factors influencing the supply of illegal drugs to the retail market. Systems research on economic markets, however, must ultimately link the behavior of suppliers and consumers. Policies aimed at reducing the supply of drugs work via the market equilibrium.

The state of knowledge of demand functions and price elasticities of demand for illegal drugs is discussed in detail in Chapter 2. As we explain there, the estimation of demand functions for illegal drugs presents severe conceptual and data-related problems that have not yet been solved. Existing estimates of demand functions and price elasticities should be treated as suggestive first steps that are not conclusive.

LAW ENFORCEMENT AND RETAIL MARKETS

Two main objectives of law enforcement operations against retail drug markets are to reduce the number of drug dealers that operate in a city (or other geographical area) and to reduce the quantity of drugs that individual dealers sell. A third objective is to reduce the violence and community disruption that is associated with drug markets. Measures aimed at achieving the first two objectives are not necessarily consistent with achieving the third and vice-versa. For example, the committee has received anecdotal information indicating that in some large cities, police have negotiated agreements with drug dealers according to which the police agree to reduce their efforts to arrest dealers and the dealers agree to avoid violence. These agreements have apparently resulted in substantially reduced levels of violence in the neighborhoods to which they apply but not in reduced levels of drug sales.

Efforts to disrupt and reduce drug dealing have led to large increases in arrests, convictions, and incarcerations for drug law violations. State and local arrests for drug law violations rose from 676,000 in 1982 to 1,559,100 in 1998, an increase of 131 percent (Bureau of Justice Statistics, 2000). State and local arrests for the manufacture or sale of illegal drugs increased from 135,200 in 1982 to 330,500 in 1998, an increase of 144 percent. The number of convictions in state courts for felony drug trafficking increased from 165,430 to 212,504, or by 28 percent, between 1994 and 1996 (Bureau of Justice Statistics, 2000). During the same period, the number of traffickers sentenced to incarceration increased from 116,938 to 154,977, or by 33 percent. Incarcerations for drug law violations have increased more rapidly than incarcerations for other offenses. Between 1980 and 1996, the number of persons incarcerated in state facilities for drug law violations increased by a factor of 12.3. By contrast, the numbers of persons incarcerated for violent crimes, property crimes, and public order offenses (e.g., weapons, vice, and drunk-driving offenses) increased by factors of 2.8, 2.7, and 5.7, respectively (Bureau of Justice Statistics, 2000). In addition to arrests and incarceration, police have used civil remedies to disrupt drug markets (Davis and Lurigio, 1996; Green, 1996). For example, police may pressure landlords to evict drug-dealing tenants or may use increased enforcement of housing codes, fire codes, and nuisance abatement laws to disrupt indoor drug markets without necessarily arresting their participants.

A reduction in the number of drug dealers presumably reduces drug consumption by making drugs more expensive and more difficult to obtain. The state of knowledge of the relations among drug prices, search costs, drug-use prevalence, and drug consumption is discussed in Chapter 2. This section discusses what is known about the effectiveness of law enforcement operations in reducing the number of retail drug dealers in a city. The key issues concern the incremental effects of a change in the level of enforcement or of specific law enforcement actions. In other words, one would like to know the answers to such questions as:

1. By how much would a specified increase in the aggressiveness of police activity (e.g., more stopping and searching of violators of antiloitering laws, more vigorous enforcement of housing codes, more undercover operations against retail drug markets) reduce the number of drug dealers in a city? Increase the difficulty (search cost) of finding drugs? Increase the price of drugs? Decrease drug consumption?

2. Would a substantial reduction in the current level of enforcement activity lead to a substantial increase in the number of drug dealers? Decrease in search costs or the price of drugs? Increase in drug consumption?

3. To what extent does the drug market adapt to enforcement efforts by recruiting replacement dealers, finding more surreptitious ways of selling, or developing other distribution modes and routes?

There are serious obstacles to achieving even rough answers to these questions. One of the most important is that there is no statistically valid procedure in place for measuring the number of drug dealers that operate in any specified geographical area. Thus, it is not known how many dealers operate in a city or other area at any given time and, consequently, there is no reliable way of knowing whether the number of dealers has increased or decreased from one time period to another. Similarly, data on the quantity of drugs sold or consumed in a city are nonexistent, and existing data on drug prices are highly inadequate. The lack of data on the relevant outcome variables (numbers of drug dealers, search costs, prices, consumption) is a major obstacle to estimating the effectiveness of law enforcement operations against retail drug dealers.

Achieving an understanding of the effectiveness of law enforcement operations is further complicated by the many possible outcomes of such operations. Some of the consequences are consistent with the objectives of reducing the number of drug dealers and increasing search costs. For example:

1. The threat of arrest and incarceration may deter some individuals from becoming drug dealers, thereby reducing the number of dealers who operate in a city.

2. Arrest and incarceration prevent a dealer from selling drugs at least temporarily. If enough dealers are incapacitated in this way, then the total number of dealers in a city may be significantly reduced.

Other consequences tend to diminish the intended effects. For example:

3. Arrested drug dealers may be replaced by others. Replacement may occur through increased activity of existing dealers or by entry into the market of individuals who previously were not drug dealers.

4. Dealers may modify their behavior to make it less visible to police or to avoid encounters with the police. For example, drug sales operations may move from the street to indoor locations or operate as delivery ser-

vices. In addition, they may move to areas of a city where police activity is relatively low, or they may time their operations to coincide with periods of minimal police activity.

It may seem to some that a policy of "the more law enforcement, the better" is the safest way to proceed in the absence of knowledge of the effectiveness of any given level of enforcement. It may seem to others that the absence of such knowledge justifies a reduction in the level of enforcement. Neither view is supported by existing evidence. Aggressive law enforcement is costly to society. Some costs are pecuniary and must be paid through taxes: the costs of personnel, equipment, and facilities for the police, courts, and prisons. There are also substantial nonpecuniary costs of aggressive law enforcement: the physical danger to police, inconvenience to and possibly violation of the civil rights of law-abiding citizens, increased violence associated with drug markets, and disruption of communities in which police operations occur. Thus, it cannot be concluded that more law enforcement is necessarily better. More is better only if the benefits of additional enforcement exceed its costs. It is conceivable that the costs of the existing level of enforcement exceed its benefits, in which case less enforcement activity would be better. Conversely, less law enforcement may reduce the pecuniary and nonpecuniary costs of law enforcement but may increase drug dealing, drug consumption, and the social costs associated with drug dealing and consumption. Less law enforcement is better only if the reductions in pecuniary and nonpecuniary costs of enforcement exceed the social costs associated with increased drug dealing and consumption. In summary, there is no reason to believe that the current level of law enforcement is socially optimal, but it is unknown whether optimality lies in the direction of increased or decreased enforcement.

The sections that follow summarize current knowledge of deterrence and adaptive behavior and replacement and incapacitation of dealers. The committee concludes that very little is known about the effectiveness of law enforcement operations against retail drug dealers. Substantial data-acquisition and other efforts will be needed to remedy this situation.

Deterrence and Adaptive Behavior

Deterrence theory is based on the notion that increases in the certainty, speed, and severity of punishment result in declines in criminal behavior. Empirical research on deterrence typically seeks to relate time-series or cross-sectional variation in crime rates to variations in the intensity of enforcement. Some of this research takes the form of impulse-response analyses of police crackdowns on drug markets and drunk driving (Nagin, 1998). The next section describes serious difficulties that are involved in relating enforcement actions to changes in drug activity. A principal problem here is the lack of any direct measures of the number of drug dealers or of the level of drug dealing in a place.

Many studies use number or rate of arrests as a proxy for the level of drug dealing activity. See, for example, Braga et al. (1999), Green (1996), and Worden et al. (1993). Arrests, however, are still an inaccurate measure of drug dealing activity (Weisburd and Green, 1994, Worden et al. 1993). Arrests reflect both the level of drug-dealing activity and the skill or intensity of police activity in arresting drug dealers. Thus, an absolute increase in the level of arrests could reflect some mixture of an increase in the level of drug dealing, a change in the mode of drug dealing that increases the probability that dealing will lead to arrest (e.g., moving an indoor market into the street), or a change in police policy encouraging arrest when a drug deal is detected. Thus, arrest levels depend on the extent and effectiveness of police surveillance as well as the skill of dealers at concealing their operations (e.g., by moving them indoors or by operating delivery services). If, however, arrests occur primarily when drug dealing is highly visible and disruptive to the community, then measures of arrests could well be useful as indicators of the visibility of drug markets and the disruption that they cause. Also, shifts in the level of arrests without some indication of changes in arrest policy, or shifts in arrest of one subgroup without shifts in others, could serve as an indicator of changing participation in the market. In summary, because of the uncertainty about what factors cause any particular change in arrests, a reliable measure of the effectiveness of local law enforcement in deterring individuals from engaging in drug dealing cannot be generated.

Refraining from illegal acts is only one possible response of drug dealers or potential dealers to pressure from law enforcement authorities. There are many ways in which drug dealers can adapt to law enforcement in order to continue their sales operations with minimal disruption. One is by forming delivery or beeper services, eliminating the need for meetings between dealers and customers and thereby greatly reducing the visibility of a drug sales operation to the police. Similarly, the use of brokers or other intermediaries makes it harder for law enforcement officials to identify and locate dealers. Other forms of adaptation include changing the locations of drug-dealing operations or the hours of the day that they operate. The police cannot be active everywhere all the time. Thus, a crackdown at one location may lead to increased activities at another. Similarly, dealers may know the patrolling routines of police and arrange not to be visible during hours of police presence.

There is little evidence on the extent to which these adaptations take place and their consequences for the effectiveness of law enforcement. It is clear, however, that some level of adaptation occurs. Curtis and Wendel (1999) and National Development and Research Institutes (1998) have documented the development of delivery and beeper services in New York. National Development and Research Institutes (1998) and Richard Curtis (interview with committee members) have described the use of brokers and other intermediaries. Williams et al. (1989) have documented adaptation through shifting the hours in which drug selling occurs.

Green (1996) studied the extent of geographic displacement of drug dealing in response to the SMART program in Oakland, CA. This program combined increased enforcement of housing and fire codes with traditional tactics, such as arrests and stops at high-activity drug sites. Green found that police contacts with drug dealers decreased within two blocks of 40 percent of the sites and increased within two blocks of only 6 percent of the sites. It is not clear, however, whether this indicates a net decrease in drug dealing activity as a result of the SMART program. It is possible that police contacts decreased because dealers took actions to hide their operations from police while SMART was being carried out. It is also possible that drug sales increased at locations that were separated from the SMART sites by more than two blocks.

In summary, it is clear that drug dealers engage in various forms of adaptive behavior. It is not clear how important this behavior is in counteracting the effects of law enforcement operations. Nor is it clear what, if anything, the police can or should do in response if adaptive behavior does significantly impair the effectiveness of law enforcement.

Incapacitation and Replacement of Dealers

The basic principle of incapacitation (Blumstein et al., 1978:65) is that if an offender who commits crime at an annual rate of λ is removed from the streets for S years, $\lambda \times S$ crimes are averted. So, for example, if an offender who averages 100 crimes per year is incarcerated for 2 years, one can expect 200 crimes to be averted over the period. Incarceration may also have the added effect of deterring current and potential offenders from committing future crimes.

Of course, no such reductions in crime can be expected if the offender's crimes are replaced. The likelihood that an imprisoned (or deterred) offender's crimes will be replaced varies by type of offense. A serial rapist's crimes almost certainly are not replaced on the street, so one can expect his full array of crimes to be incapacitated. The situation might be quite different for a drug dealer. When drug dealers are imprisoned, their drug transactions may be effectively replaced by some combination of recruiting new sellers or by increasing the rate of activity of sellers already active in the market. To the extent that replacement occurs in drug markets, the major increase in the number of drug dealers incapacitated over the last 20 years may not have significantly diminished the viability of drug markets.

To illustrate how replacement in drug markets works, it may be helpful to focus on the short-run response of a single local retail crack selling operation, as described by Curtis. In New York City, Curtis observed crews consisting of a crew boss or owner and his sellers or slingers. An owner or crew boss could start a crack selling business by buying a kilogram of cocaine for $20,000. Once the boss or owner had enough cocaine, he could then hire a crew of sellers or slingers to sell it for him. Curtis described one crew that was headed by two cousins who were crew bosses. They hired a crew of 12 sellers to sell their drugs. The sellers in this crew ranged in age from 15 to 38. The owners bought bundles of prepackaged crack with each bundle containing 24 vials. The crack was then sold for $5 per vial. The owner typically gave a seller five bundles to sell and the seller would make 20 percent on each vial he sold.

If a crew member were arrested, some of the remaining 11 members of the crew would simply replace him by selling drugs during the times previously allotted to the arrested crew member. In the low-income neighborhood where this crew operated, many of these sellers worked only part-time at legitimate jobs and were usually trying to get more crack to sell and more hours to sell it. As they were employed only part-time, they had the extra time needed to step up their own drug selling activity in the event a fellow crew member was arrested. Hence the arrest of one seller seems to have led to increased activity among the remaining members of the crew.

The short-run response differed when the boss was arrested. In this case, some of the members tried to join other drug businesses in the neighborhood. In their search for alternative drug businesses, these sellers typically limited their search to a local operation in which they were more likely to know other crew bosses and the customers. Not knowing the customers would make them more likely to get arrested and not knowing the crew bosses could mean that they got a lower percentage cut for the drugs they sold. In the long run, the market is likely to adapt by replacing, in part, the local operation disrupted when a crew boss is arrested.

All of this suggests that the extent to which drug-selling activity is replaced in the event of an arrest may depend on the arrestee's placement in the drug-selling hierarchy. The arrest of an individual seller may imply total replacement. In the event a crew is "decapitated" by the arrest of the crew boss, replacement of drug transactions may be only partial. The local market may be substantially diminished if an entire crew is arrested, although in the longer run there is likely to be some degree of adaptation and replacement. Even in the short run, access to drugs may change little if buyers purchase drugs from several local crews simultaneously.

Focusing on the replacement of local crews provides an incomplete picture of whether recent increases in the incapacitation of drug dealers have resulted in significant reductions in local drug markets. The capacity to disrupt illegal drug markets will also depend on whether large numbers of the drug market's most powerful operatives have been incapacitated. Traffickers, who typically transport drugs from the source countries and arrange to have them smuggled into the United States, handle large volumes of drugs and operate within wide geographic ranges—at the international and interstate level (U.S . Sentencing Commission, 1995; Cooper, 1990; Wisotsky, 1986; Natarajan and Belanger, 1998). Similarly, wholesalers, who supply mid-level dealers, who in turn supply retail sellers, likewise buy and sell drugs in volume. By contrast, local crews such as those described above operate within the limited scope of a single neighborhood and handle much smaller volumes of drugs.

Incapacitating these high-level participants in the drug trade could have a substantial impact on shrinking drug markets, because in many ways they are likely to be the most difficult to replace. High-level traffickers and importers require contacts in both producer and transport nations or in different states in order to operate. They also require large sums of money to funnel into bribes, transport equipment (planes, boats, etc.) and personnel (e.g., couriers). Because these resources are required for high-level distribution, there is a limit on the size of the labor pool with the necessary contacts and capital to operate at this level (Moore, 1990; Covington, 2000b). There are likely to be fewer substitutes for persons at the top of the pyramid.

Certainly, the effects of incarceration on the retail drug market depend on whether the incapacitated offender can be replaced. They also depend, of course, on how long the replacement process takes. Even if there eventually is full replacement, supply may be driven down temporarily if the replacement process takes time. With some dealers being incarcerated and new ones taking their place, the key question is whether enforcement removes people at a faster rate than the market adapts to their absence.

The effect of incarceration may also vary by the type of drug. Covington (2000b) highlights two features of the market for crack cocaine. First, since crack is often "manufactured" using powder cocaine, the retail supply of crack depends on the amount of powder cocaine imported and sold at wholesale. Thus, incarcerating powder cocaine dealers may affect the market for both crack and powder cocaine.

Second, current law focuses much more on incapacitating dealers of crack than of powder cocaine. Sale of 5 gm of crack cocaine triggers a mandatory minimum sentence of 5 years in a federal prison, whereas it takes 500 gm of powder cocaine to trigger the same minimum 5-year sentence. This 100:1 ratio in the amount of powder cocaine required to trigger the same penalties as crack suggests that local crack dealers are receiving the same penalties as powder cocaine wholesalers and importers. The current penalty for sale of small amounts of crack cocaine has certainly imposed large costs of incarceration on society, as well as obvious costs on the individuals imprisoned (see Covington, 2000b). The value of the law depends on the degree to which it disrupts drug markets and on the extent to which incarcerated street level dealers are replaced.

How much have the recent increases in incarceration thinned the ranks of major traffickers, importers, and local distributors? To what extent is there replacement and how rapidly does it occur? Do the social costs of current rates of incarceration outweigh the benefits? In particular, with the growth of the population incarcerated for drug offenses, a critical question that must be addressed is the impact of imprisonment and sentence length on post-release consequences. Does the prison experience inhibit (through individual deterrence) or promote (through criminalization), further drug offending or other criminal activity, particularly by ex-offenders who participate in the drug markets as an economic activity? The committee would like to be able to answer these pressing questions, but the answers are elusive.

Blumstein (1993) has argued that replacement of dealers largely negates any incapacitative effects of incarceration. He highlights the large growth in the drug arrests of non-white juveniles after 1985, well after the growth in arrest of non-white adults began in 1980. Their arrest rate for drug offenses almost tripled between 1985 and 1989, a time when the nation's incarceration rate for drug offenses also almost tripled (Blumstein and Beck, 1999). He associates the recruitment of juveniles as a supply-side response to the growth in demand and as replacements for the incarcerated adults (Blumstein, 1995).

Conclusions and Recommendations

The committee concludes that little is known about the effectiveness of law enforcement operations against retail drug markets. In particular, the consequences of increasing or decreasing current levels of enforcement are not known. It is not known whether a significant decrease in law enforcement activity would lead to a significant increase in drug dealing and use. Nor is it known whether a significant increase in law enforcement would have the opposite effect.

There is little likelihood of learning more about the effectiveness of law enforcement in the near future. Answering important questions about the effectiveness of law enforcement requires reliable data on drug consumption, drug prices, the numbers of drug dealers that operate in cities, and the responses of dealers to law enforcement operations and opportunities in the legitimate labor market. As discussed in Chapter 3 and this chapter, such data are nonexistent at present. The committee has made recommendations about how this situation might be remedied. Carrying out these recommendations is a prerequisite to acquiring a better understanding of the effectiveness of law enforcement actions against retail drug markets.

In addition, it is necessary to explore alternative approaches to law enforcement. This should include investigating the effects of decreases as well as increases in law enforcement activity. Changes in drug enforcement policy should be designed so that their consequences can be measured and separated from the effects of other factors that influence drug markets. Arrangements must be made to acquire the data needed to evaluate the consequences of the actions that are taken. Such data is best acquired from state and local governments, supported with funding from the federal government. Agencies responsible for providing assistance to state and local jurisdictions should provide financial incentives for collecting data and for creating partnerships with researchers to evaluate outcomes.

The committee recommends that state and local governments be encouraged to explore and assess alternative approaches to law enforcement, including decreases as well as increases in the intensity of enforcement. Organizational arrangements should be made to ensure that the resulting changes in law enforcement measures and policy are well designed and that the data needed to evaluate their consequences are acquired and analyzed.

Under some circumstances, it may be ethical and appropriate to carry out randomized-design experiments in which different neighborhoods in a city are assigned randomly to increased or decreased enforcement regimes. For example, if the police do not have the resources needed to maintain equally high levels of enforcement in all drug-dealing neighborhoods, then some neighborhoods necessarily will receive less enforcement than others. It may then be appropriate to randomly assign varying levels of enforcement among neighborhoods.

Regardless of the designs of alternative approaches to enforcement, evaluation criteria should include levels of crime, violence, and community disruption as well as levels of drug consumption and numbers of drug dealers. Evaluation criteria may also include measures of the fairness with which different population segments are treated by law enforcement agents. The committee emphasizes that an improved understanding of the effectiveness of local law enforcement can be achieved only through such exploration combined with acquisition of data on drug consumption, prices, and labor market variables.

FINAL NOTE: EVENHANDEDNESS IN ENFORCEMENT

The nation has long maintained the expectation that law enforcement should be fair as well as effective. In particular, Americans expect that enforcement efforts will not target members of specific socioeconomic or demographic groups. As the Supreme Court stated in *Yick Wo v. Hopkins* in 1886, law enforcement officials violate the Constitution if they apply an otherwise valid law "with an evil eye and an unequal hand so as practically to make unjust discriminations between persons in similar circumstances." While society's concern for evenhandedness in enforcement is a normative matter, this concern generates empirical questions on which data and research can shed light: How evenhanded is enforcement policy today? What would alternative policies achieve?

A flash point of recent public discussions of evenhandedness in drug law enforcement has been the striking disparities between the racial or ethnic composition of the U.S. population and the racial or ethnic distribution of persons arrested, convicted, and imprisoned for drug offenses. In the year 1997, the U.S. population was estimated to be 82.7 percent white, 10.9 percent Hispanic, and 12.7 percent black. In the same year, those arrested for state drug offenses were estimated to be 62 percent white (the FBI's arrest data do not differentiate between non-Hispanic and Hispanic whites) and 36.8 percent black (Bureau of Justice Statistics, 1999:342). Among persons convicted for felony drug offenses in state courts in 1996, 45 percent were white and 53 percent were black (Bureau of Justice Statistics, 1999:432; note that there are no comparable data for 1997). Among state prisoners serving time for drug offenses in 1997, 41.5 percent were white (22.5 percent Hispanic and 19 percent non-Hispanic white) and 56.1 percent were black (Bureau of Justice Statistics, 1999—Prisoners in 1998, page 10, table 16).

While the existence of these disparities is widely acknowledged, there is no consensus about their interpretation. Some argue that the large disparity in arrest (37 percent black compared to 12 percent black in the population, or an arrest rate of blacks that is three times that of whites) is an indication of disproportionate surveillance in black neighborhoods and/or bias in arresting black users and sellers. They argue that NHSDA data show little difference between the races in their use of drugs (see below). Others argue that most drug arrests are not only in response to drug use, per se, but also to other types of illegal drug-related activity and that these arrests generate a large proportion of drug possession arrests. They also argue that blacks selling drugs tend more often to operate in street markets, whereas whites tend to operate more surreptitiously; hence the difference in arrest rates may be attributable to different vulnerability to arrest rather than to racial bias in the arrest process.

A similar argument arises over the difference between the black arrest percentage (37 percent) and the black prison percentage (56 percent). Some argue that these data show that the post-arrest operation of the criminal justice system is biased against blacks. They cite the 100:1 disparity in the federal sentencing rules for crack (predominantly sold by blacks) compared to powder cocaine (much more often sold by whites) as an indication of that bias. A counter-argument is that crack use and crack markets are much more often accompanied by violence, which warrants more severe treatment in the criminal justice system. In addition, it has been argued that the race of convicted drug offenders may be correlated with other factors, such as prior record, that can account for the differences in sentence severity.

These polar views, as well as intermediate hypotheses, can co-exist because we lack the data and research necessary to resolve the controversy. Perhaps the most basic problem is that we lack data on offense rates by racial/ethnic groups. It is clear that use prevalence rates do not vary substantially among racial and ethnic groups. Based on the 1998 NHSDA data, it has been estimated that 74.3 percent of all current (past 30 day) illegal drug users are white, 15.4 percent are black, and 10.3 percent are Hispanic, substantially equivalent to their proportions of the adult population. For cocaine, in particular, 64.8 percent of 30-day users were white, 18 percent were black and 16.9 percent were Hispanic. However, these basic prevalence figures do not tell the whole story because frequency of use (and therefore the real rate of offending) among various population groups is unknown. Most importantly, household surveys miss the heaviest users. Finally, rates of trafficking are unknown. In the absence of data about rates of offending, the available information on contacts with the criminal justice systems is consistent with multiple interpretations.

These issues are clearly complicated, and a simple comparison of race-specific ratios at different parts of the criminal justice system cannot prove bias, although they do prompt a search for a clearer explanation of the reasons for the difference. Until those explanations arrive, it is likely that concern about the possibility of bias will continue. Thus, it is important that research be directed at the factors that can explain the significant shift in the prevalence of blacks from use to arrest to conviction to imprisonment.

The committee has recommended better data on frequency and amount of consumption, as well as initiation of survey research on the labor supply of illegal drug dealers. These data are needed to better understand the impact of interventions on intensity of consumption and the operation of retail drug markets. The same survey research would enable the nation to make progress in determining how well enforcement meets the normative expectation of evenhandedness.

Research is also needed to determine the degree to which demonstrated racial differences in contact with the criminal justice system reflect enforcement policies that are racially neutral in intent but nevertheless yield disparate outcomes. For example, most drug arrests are produced by so-called street enforcement in urban areas, rather than by searches of private residences, bars, or clubs. To some, this may be an adequate explanation of the racial composition of arrests; to others, it may suggest that law enforcement agencies should change their priorities in order to erase the appearance of unfairness (Stuntz, 1998; Covington, forthcoming). What it suggests to the committee is the urgent need for research on drug law enforcement practices, such as street sweeps and vehicle stops, that have been shown to produce racially and ethnically disparate outcomes.

REFERENCES

Arrow, K.J.
  1962 The economic implications of learning by doing. _Review of Economic Studies_ 29(3):155-173.
Barthold, T.A., and H.M. Hochman
  1988 Addiction as extreme-seeking. _Economic Inquiry_ 26:89-106.
Beck, Allen J., M. Tonry, and J. Petersilia, eds.
  1999 _Crime and Justice: A Review of Research_ 26:17-61.
Becker, G.S., M. Grossman, and K.M. Murphy
  1994 An empirical analysis of cigarette addiction. _American Economic Review_ 84:396-418.
  1991 Rational addiction and the effect of price on consumption. _American Economic Review_ 81: 237-241.
Becker, G.S., and K.M. Murphy
  1988 A theory of rational addiction. _Journal of Political Economy_ 96:675-700.
Blumstein, A.
  2000 The Replacement of Drug Offenders to Diminish the Effects of Incarceration. Unpublished paper prepared for the Committee on Data and Research for Policy on Illegal Drugs.
  1995 Youth violence, guns, and the illicit-drug industry. _Journal of Criminal Law and Criminology_ 86(4):10-36.

1993   Making rationality relevant—The American Society of Criminology presidential address. *Criminology* 31(1):1-16.

Blumstein, Alfred, and Allen J. Beck

1999   Population growth in U.S. prisons. 1980-1996. In *Prisons*, Michael Tonry and Joan Petersilia, eds. In *Crime and Justice: A Review of Research*, Vol. 26, Michael Tonry, ed. Chicago: University of Chicago Press.

Bonnie, R., and C. Whitebread

1974   *The Marihuana Conviction: A History of Marihuana Prohibition in the United States.* Charlottesville: University Press of Virginia.

Braga, A., D. Weisburd, E. Waring, L.G. Mazerolle, W. Spelman, and F. Gajewski

1999   Problem-oriented policing in violent crime places: A randomized controlled experiment. *Criminology* 37:541-580.

Bureau of Justice Statistics

2000   *Drugs and Crime Facts*, report 165148. Available at http://www.ojp.usdoj.gov/bjs/pub/pdf/dcf.pdf.

1999   *Sourcebook of Criminal Justice Statistics—1998.* Washington, DC: U.S. Department of Justice.

Caulkins, J., and P. Reuter

1998   What price data tell us about drug markets. *Journal of Drug Issues* 28(3):593-612.

Caulkins, J.P.

1995   Estimating Elasticities of Demand for Cocaine and Heroin with Data from the Drug Use Forecasting System. Unpublished manuscript, H. John Heinz III School of Public Policy and Management, Carnegie Mellon University.

1994   *Developing Price Series for Cocaine.* Santa Monica, CA: RAND.

Caulkins, J., G. Crawford, and P. Reuter

1993   Simulation of adaptive response: A model of drug interdiction. *Mathematical and Computer Modeling* 17:37-52.

Cave, J., and P. Reuter

1988   *The Interdictor's Lot.* Department of Justice: Drug Enforcement Administration (DEA), [Docket No. 95-47], Roxane Laboratories, Inc.; Intent To Allow the Importation of a Schedule II Substance, Grant of Registration To Import a Schedule II Substance, Monday, October 19, 1998, *Federal Register* 63(201). Santa Monica, CA: RAND.

Chaloupka, F.

1991   Rational addictive behavior and cigarette smoking. *Journal of Political Economy* 99:722-742.

Chaloupka, F.J., M. Grossman, and J.A. Tauras

1998   *The Demand for Cocaine and Marijuana by Youth.* Working paper 6411. Cambridge, MA: National Bureau of Economic Research.

Cooper, M.H.

1990   *The Business of Drugs.* Washington, DC: Congressional Quarterly.

Covington, J.

2000a   Drug Treatment in Captive Populations. Unpublished paper prepared for the Committee on Data and Research for Policy on Illegal Drugs.

2000b   Incapacitating Drug Offenders. Unpublished paper prepared for the Committee on Data and Research for Policy on Illegal Drugs.

forth-   Round up the usual suspects: Racial profiling and the war on drugs. In D.
coming   Milovanovic and K. Russell, eds., *Petit Apartheid in Criminal Justice.*

Crane, B.D., A.R. Rivolo, and G.C. Comfort

1997 *An Empirical Examination of Counterdrug Interdiction Program Effectiveness*, IDA paper P-3219. Alexandria, VA: Institute for Defense Analyses.

Curtis, R., and T. Wendel

2000 *Lockin' Niggas Up Like It's Goin' Out of Style: The Differing Consequences of Police Interventions in Three Brooklyn, New York, Drug Markets.* Paper presented to the Conference on Drug Markets and Law Enforcement Strategies. Arlington, VA: National Institute of Justice.

1999 Toward the Development of a Typology of Illegal Drug Markets. Unpublished paper presented to the Committee on Data and Research for Policy on Illegal Drugs, National Research Council, Washington, D.C., May 1999.

Davis, R.C., and A. Lurigio

1996 *Fighting Back: Neighborhood Antidrug Strategies.* Thousand Oaks, CA: Sage.

DeSimone, J.

1998 Is marijuana a gateway drug? *Eastern Economic Journal* 24:149-164.

Everingham, S.S., and C.P. Rydell

1993 *Modeling the Demand for Cocaine.* Report prepared for the Office of National Drug Control Policy and the U.S. Army. Santa Monica, CA: RAND.

Everingham, S.M.S., C.P. Rydell, and J.P. Caulkins

1995 Cocaine consumption in the United States: Estimating past trends and future scenarios. *Socio-Economic Planning Sciences* 29:305-314.

Fagan, J.

1992 Drug selling and licit income in distressed neighborhoods: The economic lives of street-level drug users and dealers. In A.V. Harrell and G.E. Peterson, eds., *Drugs, Crime, and Social Isolation.* Washington, DC: Urban Institute Press.

Frisch, Ragnar

1933 Propagation and impulse problems in dynamic economics. *Economic Essays in Honor of Gustav Cassel.*

Ghemawat, P.

1985 Building strategy on the experience curve. *Harvard Business Review* 63(2):143-149.

Green, L.

1996 *Policing Places with Drug Problems.* Thousand Oaks, CA: Sage.

Grossman, M., F.J. Chaloupka, and C.C. Brown

1996 *The Demand for Cocaine by Young Adults: A Rational Addiction Approach.* Working paper 5713. Cambridge, MA: National Bureau of Economic Research.

Kennedy, M., P. Reuter, and K. Riley

1993 A simple economic model of cocaine production. *Mathematical and Computer Modeling* 17.

Kleiman, M.A.R.

1992 *Against Excess: Drug Policy for Results.* New York: Basic Books.

Koper, C.S., and P. Reuter

1996 Suppressing illegal gun markets: Lessons from drug enforcement. *Law and Contemporary Problems* 59(1):119-146.

Levitt, S.D., and S.A. Venkatesh

1998 *An Economic Analysis of a Drug-Selling Gang's Finances.* Working paper 6592. Cambridge, MA: National Bureau of Economic Research.

MacCoun, R.J., and P. Reuter
    1992   Are the wages of sin $30 an hour? Economic aspects of street-level drug dealing. *Crime and Delinquency* 38:477-491.

Miron, J.A.
    1999   Do Prohibitions Raise Prices? Evidence from the Market for Cocaine. Working paper, Boston University.

Moore, M.
    1990   Supply Reduction and Drug Law Enforcement. In M. Tonry and J.Q. Wilson, eds., *Drugs and Crime.* Chicago: University of Chicago Press.

Morgan, J.P.
    1991   Prohibition is perverse policy: What was true in 1922 is true now. In M.P. Krauss and E.P. Lazear, *Searching for Alternatives.* Stanford, CA: Hoover Institution Press.

Nadelmann, E.A.
    1991   Drug prohibition in the United States: Costs, consequences, and alternatives. *Science* 245:939-47.

Nagin, D.S.
    1998   Criminal deterrence research at the outset of the twenty-first century. *Crime and Justice: A Review of Research* 23:1-42. Chicago: University of Chicago Press.

Natarajan, M., and M. Belanger
    1998   Varieties of drug trafficking organization: A typology of cases prosecuted in New York City. *Journal of Drug Issues* 28(4).

National Development and Research Institutes
    1998   Natural History of Crack Distribution/Abuse. Report prepared for the National Institute on Drug Abuse.

National Research Council
    1999   *Assessment of Two Cost-Effectiveness Studies on Cocaine Control Policy.* Committee on Data and Research for Policy on Illegal Drugs. C.F. Manski, J.V. Pepper, and Y.F. Thomas, eds. Washington, DC: National Academy Press.
    1978   *Deterrence and Incapacitation: Estimating the Effects of Criminal Sanctions on Crime Rates.* Committee on Law Enforcement and the Administration of Justice. Blumstein, A., J. Cohen, and D. Nagin, eds. Washington, DC: National Academy Press.

Office of National Drug Control Policy, Executive Office of the President
    2000   *The National Drug Control Strategy: 2000 Annual Report.* Washington, DC: U.S. Government Printing Office.
    1999a *Drug Data Summary.* Washington, DC: U.S. Government Printing Office.
    1999b *The Price of Illicit Drugs: 1981 Through the Second Quarter of 1998.* Washington DC: Abt Associates.
    1998   *FY 1999 Budget Highlights: Federal Drug Control Programs.* Washington, DC: U.S. Government Printing Office.
    1997a The National Drug Control Strategy. Washington, DC: U.S. Government Printing Office.
    1997b *What America's Users Spend on Illegal Drugs, 1988-1995.* Washington DC: Abt Associates.

Pollak, R.A.
    1970   Habit formation and dynamic demand functions. *Journal of Political Economy* 78:745-763.
    1976   Habit formation and long-run utility functions. *Journal of Economic Theory* 13: 272-297.

Reuter, P.
  1988   Quantity illusions and paradoxes of drug interdiction: Federal intervention into vice policy. *Law and Contemporary Problems* 51:233-252.
Reuter, P., and M. Kleiman
  1986   Risks and prices: An economic analysis of drug enforcement. In M. Tonry and M. Norris, eds., *Crime and Justice: An Annual Review of Research*, Vol. 7. Chicago: University of Chicago Press.
Reuter, P., R. MacCoun, and P. Murphy
  1990   *Money from Crime: A Study of the Economics of Drug Dealing in Washington, DC.* Report R-3894-RF. Santa Monica, CA: RAND.
Riley, K.J.
  1997   Crack, Powder Cocaine, and Heroin: Drug Purchase and Use Patterns in Six U.S. Cities. Report prepared for the Office of National Drug Control Policy and the National Institute of Justice.
  1993   *Snow Job? The Efficacy of Source Country Cocaine Policies.* RAND Graduate School dissertation. Santa Monica, CA: RAND.
Rydell, C.P., and S.S. Everingham
  1994   *Controlling Cocaine.* Report prepared for the Office of National Drug Control Policy and the U.S. Army. Santa Monica, CA: RAND.
Saffer, H., and F. Chaloupka
  1995   *The Demand for Illicit Drugs.* Working paper 5238. Cambridge, MA: National Bureau of Economic Research.
Simon, D., and E. Burns
  1997   *The Corner: A Year in the Life of an Inner City Neighborhood.* New York: Broadway Books.
Stares, P.B.
  1996   *Global Habit: The Drug Problem in a Borderless World.* Washington, DC: Brookings Institution.
Sterling, E.E.
  2000   Testimony to the U.S. House of Representatives, Committee on Appropriations, March 23, quoted: *Can't Sweep This Under the Rug,* National Review Online, http://www.nationalreview.com/document/document041200.html.
Stuntz, W.
  1998   Race, class, drugs. *Columbia Law Review* 98:1795-1842.
U.S. Department of Justice
  1998   *The Supply of Illicit Drugs into the United States.* National Narcotics Intelligence Consumers Committee. (November). Washington, DC: Drug Enforcement Administration.
U.S. Sentencing Commission
  1995   *Cocaine and Federal Sentencing Policy.* Special Report to Congress.
Warner, R.E.
  1991   Legalizing drugs: Lesson from (and about) economics. *The Milbank Quarterly* 4(69):641-661.
Weisburd, D., and L. Green
  1994   Defining the street-level drug market In *Drugs and Crime: Evaluating Public Policy Initiatives.* D. MacKenzie and C. Uchida, eds. Thousand Oaks, CA: Sage.
Williams, T.
  1991   *Crackhouse.* Reading, MA: Addison-Wesley.

    1989   *The Cocaine Kids*. New York: Addison-Wesley.
Winston, G.C.
    1980   Addiction and backsliding: A theory of compulsive consumption. *Journal of Economic and Organization* 1:295-324.
Wisotsky, S.
    1986   *Breaking the Impasse in the War on Drugs*. New York: Greenwood.
Worden, R., T. Bynum, and J. Frank
    1994   Police crackdowns on drug abuse and trafficking. In D. MacKenzie and C. Uchida, eds., *Drugs and Crime: Evaluating Public Policy Initiatives*. Thousand Oaks, CA: Sage.

6

Sanctions Against
Users of Illegal Drugs

As traditionally conceptualized, the two prongs of drug control policy are supply reduction and demand reduction. Supply reduction is usually understood to be synonymous with enforcement of drug law prohibitions and international interdiction activities, whereas demand reduction is usually thought to encompass clinical treatment of drug abuse and addiction as well as the spectrum of activities aiming to prevent youths from using drugs (e.g., media campaigns, school-based education programs). This conceptualization is imperfect for two reasons. First, a large component of drug law enforcement focuses directly on reducing demand (e.g., apprehending and punishing users for possessing drugs). Second, the standard menu of demand-reduction activities tends to overlook (or take as given) the rich fabric of deeply ingrained social controls against illicit drug use, including legal controls.

LEGAL SANCTIONS AND SOCIAL CONTROL

In this chapter, the committee addresses sanctions against using drugs within the broad framework of social control. In people's daily lives, almost all of their behavior is shaped, channeled and controlled by the expectations and norms embedded in their relationships with their families, friends, teachers, employers and various social groups and organizations, and these norms and expectations vary substantially over the life course. Informal social controls may discourage drug use or, conversely, may encourage and reinforce it, depending on the social and developmental context. Some norms and expectations discouraging drug use (including alcohol and tobacco use) are formalized and "enforced" in social groups and organizational settings through various mechanisms of social discipline; sometimes such "private" sanctions are explicitly permitted and enforced by law (e.g., dismissals for using illegal drugs or alcohol on the job or for testing positive for illegal drugs).

A central point of dispute in the drug policy debate is the nature of the link between the drug laws and other forms of social control against drug use. On one side, defenders of strong prohibitions and severe penalties argue that these laws are needed to express, symbolize, and undergird social norms against drug use (DuPont, 1996). On the other side, critics of harsh penalties and zero-tolerance policies argue that over-reliance on formal controls can displace or weaken informal controls, especially when the intrusiveness and severity of the laws generate social alienation and discord (National Commission on Marihuana and Drug Abuse, 1973; Erickson, 1993). Despite its importance, the relationship between law and other forms of social control is poorly understood (Black, 1976; Ellickson, 1987), although the "expressive" function of law, and its relation to social norms, are receiving increasing attention in the legal literature (Lessig, 1995; Sunstein, 1996).

Sanctions against drug use are a preeminent feature of policy on illegal drugs, yet very little is known about the actual effects of these sanctions on drug use (independent of the effects of other social controls). Some observers have argued that enforcement of sanctions against users imposes substantial costs on individuals and on society without a demonstrable preventive effect beyond that achieved by the underlying illegality of the drug and strong social disapproval (New York County Lawyers' Association, 1996). Supporters of these sanctions argue that strong penalties against use, including criminal punishment, are necessary to deter drug use, to facilitate treatment of drug users, and to register social disapproval in the strongest possible terms—often called "zero tolerance" (DuPont, 1996). These arguments raise important empirical issues regarding the declarative, deterrent, and therapeutic effects of criminal punishment and other sanctions. This chapter addresses these issues.

PROHIBITIONS AND PUNISHMENT

A comprehensive regime of state and federal laws proscribes production and distribution of illegal drugs for nonmedical, nonscientific purposes. Standing alone, these prohibitions vividly express the society's opposition to nonmedical use of these drugs, while curtailing legitimate access and confining the drugs to an illicit market. Chapter 5 addresses what is known about the preventive effects of various methods of enforcing prohibitions against trafficking in illegal drugs. The question of interest in this section is what is known about the added preventive effects achieved by prescribing and enforcing sanctions against users.

Possession of any amount of illegal drugs is a crime under both federal and state law, typically punishable by incarceration. (The only exception is possession of small amounts of marijuana, which, in a handful of states, is punishable only by a fine.) Although possession offenses are typically prosecuted as misdemeanors, punishable by up to a year in the local jail, about 30 states classify possession of opiates or cocaine as a felony, punishable by a prison term and all the collateral consequences that accompany a felony conviction, such as loss of occupational licenses and the right to vote. In addition, all states punish possession of drug paraphernalia, including syringes, and other consumption-related behavior.

Enforcement

The federal government concentrates its enforcement effort on trafficking offenses—only 2 percent of the 27,000 federal drug arrests in fiscal year 1998 were for possession, and most of these were misdemeanor arrests in the District of Columbia. By contrast, 80 percent of the drug arrests made by state and local law enforcement agencies are for simple possession (i.e., possession of small amounts without evidence of intent to distribute).[1] More than 1.2 million arrests were made for drug possession offenses in 1998, and half of these were for possession of marijuana (Bureau of Justice Statistics, Drug and Crime Facts). The proportion of these arrests resulting in criminal convictions is unknown. Most people convicted of simple possession are sentenced as misdemeanants to probation or, in cases involving repeat offenders, short terms in local jails. (In 1996, for example, 11.3 percent of all jail inmates were incarcerated for a drug violation as their most serious offense.) However, more than 135,000 persons were convicted of felony possession charges in 1996, representing about 14 percent of all state felony convictions (Brown and Langan, 1999). And 70 percent of these offenders were sentenced to prison (29 percent) or local jail (41 percent). The mean maximum sentence length for felony drug possession offenders serving prison time was 42 months; for those sentenced to local jails, the mean maximum sentence was 5 months.

One of every seven drug arrestees in 1997 was a juvenile (Snyder, 1998). The number of juveniles arrested for drug offenses has increased

---

[1]Simple possession excludes possession with intent to sell drugs. Although some traffickers are convicted of simple possession as a result of plea agreements, most possession offenders are users, not dealers.

markedly since the 1980s. More than 220,000 juveniles were arrested for drug offenses in 1997, representing an 82 percent increase since 1993. In about 15 percent of all juvenile arrests in 1997, the most serious charge was a drug abuse violation, a liquor law violation, drunkenness, or driving under the influence. Between 1993 and 1997, the juvenile arrest rate for drug abuse violations (arrests per 100,000 juveniles ages 10-17) increased more than 70 percent. A similar pattern can be seen for curfew and loitering violations.

Most juvenile drug arrestees are processed in juvenile court (Stahl, 1999). Drug delinquency arrests processed in juvenile court (176,300) rose 143 percent between 1992 and 1996. Of these cases, delinquency petitions were filed in 109,500 (62 percent). About 60 percent of these drug delinquency petitions resulted in findings of delinquency (the juvenile-court equivalent of a "conviction") and about 25 percent of the delinquent offenders were placed in a residential facility.

The enforcement of sanctions against juveniles merits special attention for several reasons. First, preventing youths from initiating drug use or becoming regular users is one of the central goals of national drug policy. Second, youths are subject to a stronger and more diverse array of antidrug sanctions and controls than any other group in the population. The key policy question is whether the incremental preventive effect of enforcing these sanctions is sufficient to offset the costs of imposing them, including their counterproductive effects on the life prospects of young offenders (National Research Council, 2001).

Effects on Drug Use

In Chapter 8, the committee addresses the effects of enforcing sanctions against apprehended users on their subsequent drug use, concentrating particularly on the utility of intervention as an instrument of therapeutic leverage. In this section, however, we are interested in how prescribing and enforcing sanctions against drug users may function, at the population level, as an instrument of primary prevention. Sanctions against users may depress prevalence in two ways: by expressing social norms against drug use (declarative effects) and by dissuading people from using drugs due to fear of being apprehended and punished (deterrent effects).

Declarative Effects

Laws against drug use may generate declarative effects by expressing social disapproval of drug use and thereby symbolizing and reinforcing social norms against drug use and helping to shape individual beliefs and attitudes (Bonnie, 1981a). To the extent that these norms are rooted in moral antipathy toward drug use, strong sanctions against the behavior may also generate moralizing effects. (Andenaes, 1974; Zimring and Hawkins, 1973). It should also be noted, however, that under conditions of normative ambiguity or discord, punitive sanctions may also generate "reactance" in an alienated population and might actually provide an inducement for violation through a "forbidden fruit" effect. It is often suggested that laws against use of illegal drugs and underage use of alcohol and tobacco have such effects, although there is little direct evidence of this (MacCoun, 1993).

The empirical literature bearing on the declarative effects of legal sanctions is scant, mainly because it is so difficult to distinguish these effects from deterrent effects or to disentangle the effects of preexisting social norms and informal controls from the declarative effects of formally prescribed sanctions. In one of a series of studies investigating this issue, Grasmick et al. (1991) showed that an antilittering campaign increased the likelihood of compliance because people felt that violating the norm would be an occasion for shame or embarrassment. Similarly, substantial increases in seat belt use and child restraint after enactment of mandatory legal requirements appear to be attributable primarily to declarative effects (in this case, probably a pedagogical effect) rather than deterrence (Institute of Medicine, 1999). (Interestingly, proponents of so-called primary enforcement of seat belt laws—allowing a penalty for failing to wear a seat belt even if the driver has committed no other violation—argue that an increase in the deterrent threat is now needed to increase the rate of seat belt wearing beyond current levels.) No studies have successfully isolated the declarative effects of sanctions against use of illegal drugs from their deterrent effects.

General Deterrence

It is generally assumed that sanctions against drug use also depress the prevalence of drug use through deterrence—i.e., potential users refrain from initiating or continuing use due to fear of being punished. According to the basic postulates of deterrence theory, persons considering using drugs will weigh the expected utility of the behavior against the subjectively perceived risk of punishment. The deterrent effect of a legal threat is thought to be a function of the severity of the threatened sanction, the probability that it will be imposed and, under some circumstances, the swiftness with which it is applied.

In general, research on the relation between perceived risk of detection and punishment and self-reported drug use tends to show that perceived legal risk explains very little of the variance in drug use (MacCoun,

1993). Similarly, studies of the relation between prevalence of drug use and variations in legal penalties for drug use tend to find no relationship. For example, Chaloupka et al. (1998) found, using the Monitoring the Future survey data from 1982 and 1989, that variations in length of prison terms prescribed by state law were unrelated to prevalence or frequency of cocaine or marijuana use by high school seniors. They also found that substantial increases in prescribed fines would have little or no effect. These findings are unsurprising because, under present enforcement conditions, the deterrent effect of criminal sanctions against drug use is attenuated significantly by the low probability of detection for any given violation and even for repeated violations. Other factors, including the perceived benefits of drug use, fear of health-related risks, and informal social controls, may have a more significant influence on decisions about using drugs than legal deterrence. As in the case of underage alcohol and tobacco use, current enforcement may have a stronger effect on where people carry or use drugs, rather than on whether they do so.

The issue most extensively studied has been the impact of decriminalization on the prevalence of marijuana use among youths and adults. Penalties for possession of small amounts of marijuana for personal use were significantly reduced in 11 states in the 1970s (Bonnie, 1981b). All of these laws preclude incarceration for consumption-related marijuana offenses, making the offense punishable only by a fine, and most also classify the offense in a category (typically a civil infraction) that does not carry the stigmatizing consequence of having been convicted of a crime—hence the term "decriminalization."[2]

Most cross-state comparisons in the United States (as well as in Australia; see McGeorge and Aitken, 1997) have found no significant differences in the prevalence of marijuana use in decriminalized and nondecriminalized states (e.g., Johnston et al., 1981; Single, 1989; DiNardo and Lemieux, 1992; Thies and Register, 1993). Even in the few studies that find an effect on prevalence, it is a weak one. For example, using pooled data from the National Household Survey of Drug Abuse for 1988, 1990 and 1991, Saffer and Chaloupka (1995) found that marijuana decriminalization increased past-year marijuana use by 6 to 7 percent and past-

---

[2]The term "decriminalization" has sometimes been misunderstood to refer to "legalization" (i.e., making drugs legally available for nonmedical uses, as in the case of alcohol). However, as used by experts in criminal law and popularized by the National Commission on Marihuana and Drug Abuse in 1972, "decriminalization" refers to the repeal of criminal sanctions against possession for personal use, even though the drugs remain contraband and commercial access remains prohibited. The erroneous association between decriminalization and legalization has led some commentators to abandon the term in favor of "depenalization" to refer to these more lenient marijuana laws.

month use by 4 to 5 percent. Using Monitoring the Future survey data for 1982 and 1989, Chaloupka et al. (1998) estimated that decriminalizing marijuana in all states would raise the number of youths using marijuana in a given year by 4 to 5 percent compared with the number using it when marijuana use is criminalized in all states; however, they also found no relationship between decriminalization and past-month use or frequency of use.

It is worth emphasizing that any prediction of increased use after a reduction or elimination of penalties against users depends on awareness of the decriminalized status of the behavior. Although laws decriminalizing marijuana use typically received a great deal of publicity when they were adopted, it appears that most people in these states no longer have the impression that marijuana penalties in their states are distinctively different from marijuana penalties in other states (MacCoun and Reuter, 2001). In the absence of a salient and persistent impression that penalties for marijuana use are distinctly more lenient than penalties in other states, one would not expect prevalence of marijuana use to differ significantly in the decriminalized jurisdiction when compared with neighboring jurisdictions.

In summary, existing research seems to indicate that there is little apparent relationship between severity of sanctions prescribed for drug use and prevalence or frequency of use, and that perceived legal risk explains very little in the variance of individual drug use. However, there are many gaps in current knowledge concerning the declarative and deterrent effects of prescribing and enforcing penalties for drug possession. Studies thus far conducted have been limited in several ways.

First, existing research uniformly focuses on the effect of prescribed penalties. However, sanctions prescribed by statute do no more than set the outer boundary within which highly selective judgments are made by police, prosecutors, and judges. Virtually nothing is known about the deterrent impact of variations in enforcement on drug use or about the conditions under which deterrence can be increased. Second, deterrence studies typically rely on general population surveys to provide measures of undeterred drug use. However, the actual probability that sanctions will be imposed on violators differs widely across demographic groups, and it has been repeatedly demonstrated that persons arrested and punished for using drugs differ significantly from the population of users (Husak, 1992; Kleiman and Smith, 1992; Zimring and Hawkins, 1992; Tonry, 1995).

Third, very few studies have included the use of opiates or cocaine as the dependent variable. Most have tested the deterrent effects of punishment and social control on alcohol or marijuana use, drunk driving, or other crimes that have higher base rates (e.g., Meier and Johnson, 1977;

Ross, 1984). Since both social and legal sanctions for these crimes are relatively less severe than the penalties for opiate or cocaine offenses, the findings have limited generalizability. Deterrence research on opiate and cocaine offenses must also take account of the significant overlap between use offenses and distribution offenses. Most users are not dealers, but some become involved in dealing to support their habit.

Finally, most empirical studies on the general deterrent effects of law and social control have proceeded on a separate track from studies on the specific deterrent effects of punishment. This bifurcation of the empirical literature has led some researchers to suggest a revised, "perceptual deterrence" framework that incorporates both direct (arrests, incarceration) and indirect (friends' and acquaintances' experiences) punishment experiences in the conceptual model (Stafford and Warr, 1993).

As recommended by a study by the Institute of Medicine (1996), a new generation of research on the deterrence of drug use should be based on a model that integrates legal deterrence into a social control framework. This model would encompass a broad range of elements relating to the perceived costs and benefits of drug use. Such elements include economic costs (e.g., money and search time), personal costs (e.g., risks of dependence, disease, and violence); social, physiological, and psychological returns (e.g., pleasures, status, lifestyle); actual and perceived direct costs of punishment (e.g., arrest, incarceration, loss of income or drugs); social costs of punishment (e.g., job or relationship loss; see Williams and Hawkins, 1989); and motivational components (e.g., risk taking and sensation seeking).

A research agenda on deterrence should also recognize the distinctions in deterrent effects across populations of drug users and in different sectors of society. Research should also take adequate account of the balance of motivations and restraints on drug use, including both external restraints from threatened legal sanctions and internal restraints reflecting social and moral inhibitions. The threat of punishment carries different weight for different people, depending on their personal circumstances.

Differences in the effects of legal controls on illegal behaviors may reflect not only individual factors, but also the effects of contextual variables that either strengthen or neutralize the effects of legal controls—for example, by increasing the returns from drug use (or drug dealing) or by discounting the social costs of arrest and punishment. Many of these factors reflect the structure of opportunities and controls at the neighborhood or community level. In some cases, neighborhood effects powerfully reinforce legal deterrents to drug use. In other cases, neighborhood effects can delegitimize law and reinforce involvement with drugs (Tonry, 1995).

Other Considerations

Prescribing and enforcing punishments for drug use potentially contribute to the instrumental goals of drug control policy mainly by depressing the incidence, prevalence, and frequency of consumption. However, enforcing these laws can also facilitate treatment of arrested users (see Chapter 8). Rational drug control policy must also take into account the costs of enforcing sanctions against users in order to address the cost-effectiveness of different enforcement strategies, or to assess whether the benefits of a given approach bear a reasonable relationship to the costs, thereby confronting one of the critical issues in the drug policy debate. These costs include expenditure of resources for policing and for processing these cases; the losses attributable to stigmatization and imprisonment (see Demleitner, 1999; Erickson, 1993); and the negative impact on perceived legitimacy of the drug laws and on respect for the legal system, an effect that can also undermine the moral basis of obedience (Tyler, 1990).

The committee recommends that the National Institute of Justice and the National Institute on Drug Abuse collaboratively undertake research on the declarative and deterrent effects, costs, and cost-effectiveness of sanctions against the use of illegal drugs. Particular attention should be paid to the relation between severity of prescribed sanctions and conditions of enforcement and the rates of initiation and termination of illegal drug use among different segments of the population.

LOSS OF BENEFITS AND PRIVILEGES

In the Anti-Drug Abuse Act of 1988, Congress invoked a new category of sanctions for drug offenders to augment the criminal sanctions imposed by state and federal law. Under the act, federal and state judges are authorized to deny 460 types of federal benefits to persons convicted of any drug offenses, including simple possession. Benefits that may be denied or revoked include student loans and small business loans (Sullivan, 1989). In 1990, Congress directed the secretary of transportation to withhold a portion of a state's highway funds (beginning in 1993) unless it enacted laws mandating suspension of driving licenses for at least six months for all drug offenders, regardless of age (or unless the governor or legislature explicitly refused to do so). About twenty states have adopted such provisions, which typically apply to both drug and alcohol offenses. (Some state courts have struck down these statutes as applied to cases in which the predicate drug offense is unrelated to the operation of a motor vehicle.)

The Anti-Drug Abuse Act, as amended in 1990, requires public housing authorities to include lease provisions providing that drug-related activity on or near the premises is cause for termination of the lease, even in the absence of arrest or conviction for a drug offense, and also made lease holders subject to forfeiture for drug-related activity. In 1997, the Department of Housing and Urban Development promulgated a "one-strike" regulation empowering public housing authorities to terminate a resident's tenancy for "any drug-related activity on or near the premises," including activity by "a tenant, any member of the household, a guest or another person under the tenant's control." Application of this policy to persons other than tenants, including guests or adult children who do not live in the covered housing, and eviction of entire households because of a violation by one of its members, have been challenged in court, largely unsuccessfully (see Weil, 1991; Yoskowitz, 1992; Mock, 1998). The impact of this policy on drug-related activity does not appear to have been evaluated, either as a deterrent or as a mechanism to enable willing communities to root out local drug markets.

The precedent established by the 1988 act was extended in 1996 to welfare benefits. Section 115 of the Personal Responsibility and Work Opportunity Reconciliation Act of 1996 permanently denies food stamps or cash assistance to persons convicted of a drug felony. Although the federal law allows states to opt out of the ban, only eight have done so, and some states have gone further, excluding drug felons from state assistance programs as well as the federal program. A few states modified the ban to apply only to persons whose convictions were for drug trafficking (rather than possession), or to exempt persons who are enrolled in or who have successfully completed drug treatment (National Governor's Association, 1997). Although it has been estimated that Section 115 permanently denies welfare eligibility to as many as 200,000 people per year (*Harvard Law Review*, 1997), data regarding its application are not available.

The ban on welfare benefits is under constitutional challenge. Its defenders rely on both the declarative effects (emphasizing the need to promote personal accountability) and the deterrent effects. Critics of the welfare ban argue that it has a disproportionate impact on minority women, that loss of economic support increases the already heightened risk of abuse and neglect in families without stable income and housing, and that loss of support will also increase foster care costs. Insofar as the committee can ascertain, the welfare ban has not been evaluated.

These practices raise two important questions regarding the premises and consequences of current policy on illegal drug use. First, and most important, what is the added value of benefit deprivation in deterring drug use or registering social disapproval? These laws add drug-specific deprivations to the criminal sanctions for drug offenses (e.g., confinement, fines) and the typical collateral consequences of all criminal convictions (including loss of the right to vote if the conviction is for a felony). For some, these supplemental sanctions may be justified simply because people who use illegal drugs are not deserving of assistance by the state. However, in the absence of such an independent moral justification, the instrumental argument for these sanctions would appear to be that threatened loss of student loans, driver's licenses, and welfare benefits augments deterrence, promotes user accountability and suppresses the demand for drugs. At the present time, however, there is no evidence one way or the other regarding whether these added noncriminal sanctions (denial or revocation of privilege or benefits) exert any additional deterrent effect.

Second, what are the costs or side-effects of these practices? In some ways, this is a subset of more general questions now being raised about the costs of stigmatization associated with criminalization of drug offenders, including the consequences of imprisoning, as felons, such a large proportion of the nation's young black male population (Nagin, 1998). However, the specificity of the supplemental sanctions for drug offenders (denial of housing and welfare benefits) raises further questions about the desirability of further stigmatizing people who have used illegal drugs.

Denial of benefits and privileges implicates a key ethical issue in drug abuse prevention. Sanctions and punishments, of whatever kind, exert their preventive effects at the population level—by symbolizing strong social disapproval and thereby reinforcing drug-free social norms, by deterring initiation by youths, and by encouraging recreational users to terminate use as they move into traditional social roles. However, denial of benefits and privileges intended to maintain normative disapproval and credible deterrent threats, tend to fall largely on the most disadvantaged part of the population.

The committee recommends that the National Institute of Justice and the National Institute on Drug Abuse collaborate in stimulating research on the effects of supplemental sanctions, including loss of welfare benefits, driver's licenses, and public housing, on the use of illegal drugs.

EMPLOYMENT SANCTIONS

In 1986, President Ronald Reagan issued an executive order directing federal agencies to establish a comprehensive employee drug testing program, setting the stage for adoption of drug testing policies throughout the workforce. In 1989, the National Drug Control Strategy, predicted that workplace drug testing would prove to be a powerful deterrent to drug use (1989:57): "Because anyone using drugs stands a very good chance of being discovered, with disqualifications from employment as a possible consequence, many will decide that the price of using drugs is just too high."

The American Management Association reports that the proportion of its 700,000 members operating drug testing programs rose from 21 percent in 1987 to 81 percent by 1996 (American Management Association, 1999). Similar trends are reported by the nation's largest companies. The percentage of medium-to-large firms using some form of drug testing nearly doubled from 32 percent in 1988 to 62 percent in 1993 (Hartwell et al., 1996). However, despite these trends among larger firms, small businesses do not require drug testing.

According to the National Household Survey of Drug Abuse in 1994, one third of adults in the workforce reported that their employers operate a drug testing program. About 14 percent of the employed respondents reported that their employers tested *only* at hiring, whereas the remainder (18 percent) reported that their firms conducted random postemployment testing (Hoffman and Lavison, 1999). Under a random testing protocol, employees are automatically selected for periodic testing in the absence of any dangerous incident or individualized suspicion. Some employers limit the classes of employees subject to random testing to "safety-sensitive" positions, requiring only "for-cause" testing for other employees. Presumably, a large proportion of employers conduct for-cause testing on the basis of an injury or suspicion of intoxication or impairment. For-cause testing is uncontroversial because it is generally perceived as fair and most likely helps to deter workers from becoming intoxicated on the job. Because random testing is the only policy likely to exert a significant deterrent effect on whether workers continue to use drugs at all, this discussion focuses exclusively on this practice.

In the public sector, drug testing practices are circumscribed by the Fourth Amendment's ban against unreasonable searches. In general, random testing of public employees is permissible if the program applies only to employees holding safety-sensitive positions or perhaps to positions implicating the integrity of the agency's mission. Otherwise, the courts have ruled that random testing constitutes an unreasonable invasion of employee privacy (*Harmon v. Thornburgh*, 878 F 2d 484 (D.C. Cir. 1989) cert. denied 493 U.S. 1056, (1990)).

In the private sector, the law generally leaves employers free to adopt whatever testing policy they choose. Federal law encourages drug-free workplaces, and drug testing is explicitly authorized under the Americans with Disabilities Act. (This act prohibits disability-based discrimination against persons with histories of drug addiction as long as they are not currently using illegal drugs.) The practice of drug testing is unregulated by most states. However, at least eight state legislatures have prohibited random testing of employees in positions that are not safety-sensitive, and a few state supreme courts have embraced a similar approach in the absence of legislative action. As indicated, however, the law in most states leaves employers free to adopt a random testing program for all employees, and it appears that many employers have done so.

The question of interest is whether the expanding practice of workplace drug testing deters drug use by employees.[3] In 1994, the National Academies' Committee on Drug Use in the Workplace concluded that the preventive effects of drug testing have never been adequately demonstrated and that there existed no conclusive "scientific evidence from properly controlled studies" that employment drug testing programs widely discourage drug use or encourage rehabilitation. Subsequent research has provided some additional evidence bearing on the deterrent effect of drug testing in the military, but this evidence does not cast much light on the effect of testing in civilian employment.

Testing in the Military

In the U.S. military services, random testing is required of the entire workforce and, since 1995, all services have automatically imposed a severe sanction (discharge) on all violators. Two recent studies yield some evidence that the military's zero-tolerance drug policies, including routine drug testing (adopted in 1980), have deterred illegal drug use among enlistees. One study, by Bachman et al. (1999), based on the longitudinal panel data from the Monitoring the Future survey, tracked cohorts of seniors (classes of 1976 to 1995) for two years after graduation, and compared active-duty recruits with nonmilitary classmates who entered college and civilian employment.

The study found that the prevalence of marijuana or cocaine use before graduation was about the same among seniors who chose to enlist in the military as it was among those who chose to go to college or enter the civilian workforce. However, during the follow-up interview two years

---

[3]There are other goals that could be served by employee drug testing, including screening employees to identify applicants or employees at high risk for impaired performance or reduced productivity. However, a 1994 National Academies report found that "clear evidence of the deleterious effects of drugs other than alcohol on safety and other job performance indicators" is lacking (National Research Council, 1994:107). Random testing is a costly and imperfect method of identifying poorly performing employees (Rothstein, 1991). Direct testing of performance, for-cause testing of apparently intoxicated workers, or—possibly—random testing of employees in safety-sensitive positions would be much more cost-effective.

later, the prevalence of marijuana use and cocaine among people on active duty was substantially lower than it was among their classmates. Although it is possible that the self-reports by active-duty personnel are less trustworthy than those of other respondents, the data are suggestive of a deterrent effect and also tend to show, somewhat surprisingly, that there was no substantial self-selection (i.e., high school drug users were no less likely than their peers to enlist in the military), even though such a self-selection effect was evident for smokers after the military toughened its smoking policies in the late 1980s.

The second study, conducted by Mehay and Pacula (1999), used data from the National Household Survey of Drug Abuse and the Department of Defense's Worldwide Survey of Health Related Behaviors to compare military and civilian populations before and after adoption of the military's zero-tolerance policy in 1981. They concluded that, in 1995, military employees were about 16 percent less likely to report using drugs during the past year as their civilian counterparts, and that very little of this difference appears to be attributable to self-selection bias. Noting, however, that selection bias might more heavily influence younger age groups, they estimated that the deterrent effect might be as low as 4 percent.

Testing in the Civilian Workforce

Mehay and Pecula observed that a zero-tolerance, frequent testing protocol, similar to the military approach, probably would not be cost-effective in the civilian sector, but they suggest that a less frequent testing policy, with a more lenient second-chance sanction, might yield a 10 percent deterrent and "can be expected to reduce drug use in a cost-effective manner." In the committee's view, however, extrapolating in this way from the military experience to the civilian sector is questionable. Even if the prospect of being subjected to drug testing does not affect drug users' initial decisions to seek employment with a particular firm, employees have an opportunity for exit not available to people on active duty in the military when they find out about a firm's testing program. As a result, self-selection is likely to be a much more substantial factor in civilian employment than in the military setting, especially when employment opportunities without drug testing are plentiful.

Until recently, nationally representative data that could be used to examine the association between drug use and drug testing outside the military have not been collected (National Research Council, 1994). However, the 1994 National Household Survey of Drug Abuse included a special workplace module that contained a series of questions about workplace drug testing programs. It therefore became possible to ascertain the relationship between employee drug use and the characteristics of workplace drug testing. Hoffman and Lavison (1999) found that adults who use marijuana or cocaine at least weekly are more likely than other employed adults to work for companies with no testing program and less likely to work for companies with preemployment testing or a random postemployment program. For example, compared with persons who never used marijuana or who used it more than three years earlier, people who used marijuana at least weekly within the year prior to the survey were about one-third as likely to work for employers with postemployment drug testing. However, because the study is cross-sectional, it cannot shed any light on whether this association is attributable to self-selection (drug testing deters current drug users from working for firms with testing programs) or to deterrence (the threat of drug testing leads drug users to terminate or reduce their drug use).

Some proponents of employment drug testing point to the fact that the percentage of employees who test positive has declined significantly (from 18 percent in 1987 to 5 percent in 1997) in tandem with a significant increase in the proportion of large employers requiring drug testing (from 21 percent in 1987 to 81 percent in 1997). It is clear, however, that there need be no causal link between these two trends. First, the decline in percentage of positive tests reflects the overall decline in prevalence of drug use in the young adult population, which began in the early 1980s and extended into the 1990s. Second, a greater proportion of drug tests are based on random selection and therefore the pool of employees being tested has been expanded to include more nonusers.

The committee recommends that the Bureau of Labor Statistics monitor the measures taken by employers to discourage use of illegal drugs by their employees, including drug testing, and that the National Institute on Drug Abuse support rigorous research on the preventive effects and cost-effectiveness of workplace drug testing.

SCHOOL SANCTIONS

School Discipline

There is very little systematic evidence regarding the application of school disciplinary sanctions to student use of illegal drugs (or alcohol or tobacco). Two recent surveys shed some light on the subject. In 1997 the Department of Education commissioned a survey of school principals in a nationally representative sample of regular public elementary, middle and secondary schools in the United States (National Center for Education Statistics, 1998). According to their reports, a substantial majority of schools purport to have a zero-tolerance policy toward student use of alcohol (87 percent), tobacco (79 percent) or illegal drugs (88 percent). (Zero tolerance in this context refers to a school or district policy mandating predetermined punishments for specific offenses.) High schools were slightly less likely to have zero-tolerance policies for tobacco use (72 percent) than for alcohol (86 percent) or illegal drug use (89 percent). One-fourth of the principals (27 percent), representing about 21,000 schools nationwide, reported having taken significant disciplinary action against student use of alcohol, tobacco, or illegal drugs during 1996-1997. These actions included expulsion (18 percent), transfers to alternative schools or programs (20 percent), and suspension for periods of five days or more (62 percent). About half of high schools (45 percent) and a third of middle schools (36 percent) reported conducting occasional "drug sweeps" (locker searches or dog searches) during 1996-1997.

Additional data can be gleaned from the National Study of Delinquency Prevention in Schools, a national study of schools conducted during spring 1997 and the 1997-1998 school year, which included principal reports of school sanctions (Gottfredson et al., 2000). The survey found that almost all schools have written policies about drugs, and almost all schools report that they usually expel or suspend students for possession of alcohol or illegal drugs. A substantial majority of schools report that they impose these sanctions automatically for possession of illegal drugs (77 percent) or alcohol (67 percent). The study also revealed that 46 percent of high schools conducted routine locker searches and 31 percent of high schools used dogs to sniff for drugs, guns, or bombs. No evaluative data on the effectiveness of these practices is available.

Drug Testing in High Schools

Drug testing programs have become well established in professional and college sports. Notwithstanding occasional highly publicized violations, it is generally agreed that drug testing in this setting, for both deterrent and declarative purposes, is both legitimate and effective.[4]

In contrast, the legitimacy (and value) of mandatory drug testing of

---

[4]Drug testing for professional athletes is on strong ethical footing because an opportunity to participate in professional sports, and to reap the rewards of doing so, is a "pure" privilege, and athletes who want to reap those rewards can fairly be expected to submit to drug testing as a condition of participation. Such contractual arrangements are wholly devoid of coercive elements. These observations are generally applicable to college athletics as well, although a connection between tuition and athletic scholarships for many athletes does introduce a slightly coercive element.

high school athletes is much more controversial. On one hand, widespread implementation of mandatory drug testing programs for high school athletes could deter use among students who want to participate in athletics and could also help to establish a drug-free culture in the schools when combined with other norm-setting activities. On the other hand, such programs involve a significant coercive element, because testing is linked to participation in an activity that might be regarded as a core educational and developmental opportunity for many students. Although the constitutionality of mandatory drug testing for high school athletes has been affirmed by the U.S. Supreme Court (515 U.S. 646, 1995), many students and parents are strongly opposed to these programs.

Although no systematic survey of drug testing has yet been conducted, the study by Gottfredson et al. (2000) reveals that approximately 9 percent of secondary schools conduct some sort of testing program, presumably focused on athletes. Newspaper and litigation reports indicate that some school districts are requiring testing as a condition for participation in all extracurricular activities. At the present time, however, there is no scientific evidence regarding the effects of these programs, either on drug use or on the learning environment. The National Institute on Drug Abuse has recently funded a three-year randomized controlled trial of drug testing in 18 schools, to be conducted by the Oregon Health Sciences University (Linn Goldberg, personal communication). Data from a pilot study conducted by these investigators suggests that testing of athletes does have a significant deterrent effect—a noteworthy and intriguing finding in light of the fact that the testing protocol being implemented in this study has been designed to eliminate any risk to the students that positive tests could be disclosed to law enforcement authorities or lead to any form of school discipline beyond suspension of athletic participation.

The committee recommends that the National Institute on Drug Abuse and the Office of Educational Research and Improvement support rigorous research on the preventive effects, costs, and cost-effectiveness of drug testing in high schools, with a particular emphasis on the relationship between drug testing and other formal and informal mechanisms of social control.

REFERENCES

American Management Association
  1999 About AMA. [Online]. Available: http://www.amanet.org/aboutama/.
Andenaes, J.
  1974 *Punishment and Deterrence.* Ann Arbor: University of Michigan Press.

Bachman, J.G., P. Freedman-Doan, P.M. O'Malley, L.D. Johnston, and D.R. Segal
1999 Changing patterns of drug use among U.S. military recruits before and after enlistment. *American Journal of Public Health* 89(5):672-677.

Beyth-Marom, R., and B. Fischhoff
1997 Adolescents' decisions about risks: A cognitive perspective. In *Health Risks and Developmental Transaction During Adolescence*, J. Shulenber, J. Maggs, and K. Hurnelmans, eds. New York: Cambridge University Press.

Black, D.
1976 *The Behavior of Law.* New York: Academic Press.

Bonnie, R.J.
1981a The meaning of decriminalization: A review of the law. *Contemporary Drug Problems* 10:277-99.
1981b Discouraging the use of alcohol, tobacco and other drugs: The effects of legal controls and restrictions. *Advances in Substance Abuse* 2:145-184.

Brown, J.M., and P.A. Langan
1999 *Felony Sentences in the United States, 1996.* NCJ 175045. Bureau of Justice Statistics. Washington, DC: U.S. Department of Justice.

Chaloupka, F.J., M. Grossman, and J.A. Tauras
1998 *The Demand for Cocaine and Marijuana on Youth.* Working Paper No. 6411. Cambridge, MA: National Bureau of Economic Research.

Demleitner, N.V.
1999 Preventing internal exile: The need for restrictions on collateral sentencing consequences. *Stanford Law and Policy Review* 11(Winter):153-163.

DiNardo, J., and T. Lemieux
1992 *Alcohol, Marijuana, and American Youth: The Unintended Effects of Government Regulation.* Working Paper No. 4212. Cambridge, MA: National Bureau of Economic Research.

DuPont, R.
1996 Harm reduction and decriminalization in the United States: A personal perspective. *Substance Use and Misuse* 31:1929-1945.

Ellickson, R.
1987 A critique of economics and sociological theories of social control. *Journal of Legal Studies* 16:67-99.

Erickson, P.G.
1993 The law, social control, and drug policy: Models, factors, and processes. *International Journal of Addictions* 28(12):1155-1176.

Gottfredson, G.D., D.C. Gottfredson, D. Cantor, S. Crosse, and I. Hartman
2000 *The National Study of Delinquency Prevention in Schools.* Ellicott City, MD: Gottfredson Associates, Inc.

Grasmick, H.G., R.J. Bursik, Jr., and K.A. Kinsey
1991 Shame and embarrassment as deterrents to noncompliance with the law. *Environment and Behavior* 23:223-251.

Hartwell, T.D., P.D. Steele, M.T. French, and N.F. Rodman
1996 Prevalence of drug testing in the workplace. *Monthly Labor Review* 119:35-42.

Harvard Law Review
  1997 Welfare reform—Punishment of drug offenders—Congress denies cash assistance and food stamps to drug felons—Personal Responsibility and Work Opportunity Reconciliation Act of 1996, Pub. L. No. 104-193, S 115, 110 Stat. 2105 (To be codified at 42 U.S. S 862A). *Harvard Law Review* 110(February):983-988.
Hoffman, J.P., and C.L. Lavison
  1999 Worker drug use and workplace drug-testing programs: Results from the 1994 National Household Survey on Drug Abuse. *Contemporary Drug Problems* 26(Summer):331-354.
Husak, D.
  1992 *Drugs and Rights.* New York: Cambridge University Press.
Institute of Medicine
  1999 *Reducing the Burden of Injury: Advancing Prevention and Treatment.* R. Bonnie, C. Fulco, and C. Liverman, eds. Washington, DC: National Academy Press.
  1996 *Pathways of Addiction.* Washington, DC: National Academy Press.
Johnston, L.D., P.M. O'Malley, and J.D. Bachman
  1981 Marijuana Decriminalization: The Impact on Youth, 1975-80. Monitoring the Future Occasional Paper No. 13, Institute for Social Research, University of Michigan.
Kellam, S.G., C.H. Brown, and J.P. Fleming
  1982 Developmental epidemiological studies of substance abuse in Woodlawn: Implications for prevention research strategy. In *Problems of Drug Dependence*, L. Harris, ed. National Institute on Drug Abuse Research Monograph 41. Washington, DC: U.S. Department of Health and Human Services.
Kleiman, M.R., and K.D. Smith
  1992 *Against Excess: Drug Policy for Results.* New York: Basic Books.
Lessig, L.
  1995 The regulation of social meaning. *University of Chicago Law Review* 62(3):943-1045.
MacCoun, R.J., and P. Reuter
  2001 *Drug War Heresies: Learning from Other Vices, Times, and Places.* New York: Cambridge University Press.
MacCoun, R.J.
  1993 Drugs and the law: A psychological analysis of drug prohibition. *Psychological Bulletin* 113(3):497-512.
McGeorge, J., and C.K. Aitken
  1997 Effects of cannabis decriminalization in the Australian Capital Territory on university students' patterns of use. *Journal of Drug Issues* 27(4):785-793.
Mehay, S.L., and R.L. Pacula
  1999 *The Effectiveness of Workplace Drug Prevention Policies: Does "Zero Tolerance" Work?* National Bureau of Economic Research, Working Paper No. 7383. [Online]. Available: http://www.nber.org/papers/w7383.
Meier, R., and W. Johnson
  1977 Deterrence as social control: The legal and extralegal production of conformity. *American Sociological Review* 42:292-304.
Mock, N.H.
  1998 Punishing the innocent: No-fault eviction of public housing tenants for the actions of third parties. *Texas Law Review* 76:1495-1531.

Nagin, D.
　1998　Deterrence and incapacitation. In *The Oxford Handbook of Crime and Punishment*, Michael Tonry, ed. New York: Oxford University Press.

National Center for Education Statistics
　1998　*Violence and Discipline Problems in the U.S. Public Schools: 1996-97.* Statistical Analysis Report, March 1998, NCES 98-030. Washington, DC: U.S. Department of Education.

National Commission on Marihuana and Drug Abuse
　1973　*Drug Use in America: Problem in Prospective.* Washington, DC: U.S. Government Printing Office.

National Governor's Association
　1997　*Summary of Selected Elements of State Plans for Temporary Assistance for Needy Families.* Washington, DC: NGA Center for Best Practices.

National Research Council
　2001　*Juvenile Crime, Juvenile Justice.* Washington, D.C.: National Academy Press.
　1994　*Under the Influence: Drugs and the American Workforce.* Washington, DC: National Academy Press.
　1993　*Preventing Drug Abuse: What Do We Know?* Committee on Substance Abuse Prevention Research. D.R. Gerstein and L.W. Green, eds. Washington, DC; National Academy Press.
　1978　*Deterrence and Incapacitation: Estimating the Effects of Criminal Sanctions on Crime Rates.* Committee on Law Enforcement and the Administration of Justice. Blumstein, A., D. Nagin, and J. Cohen, eds. Washington, DC: National Academy Press.

New York County Lawyers' Association
　1996. Report and recommendation of the drug policy task force. [Online] http://www.druglibrary.org/schaffer/library/studies/nycla/nycla.html

Office of National Drug Control Policy, Executive Office of the President
　1989　*The National Drug Control Strategy: 1989 Report.* Washington DC: U.S. Government Printing Office.

Quadrel, M.J., B. Fischhoff, and W. Davis
　1993　Adolescent (in)vulnerability. *American Psychology* 48(2):102-116.

Ross, H.L.
　1984　Social control through deterrence: Drinking and driving laws. *Annual Review of Sociology* 10:21-35.

Rothstein, M.A.
　1991　Workplace drug testing: A case study in the misapplication of technology. *Harvard Journal of Law and Technology* 5:65-93.

Saffer, H., and F. Chaloupka
　1995　*The Demand for Illicit Drugs.* Working Paper No. 5238. Cambridge, MA: National Bureau of Economic Research.

Single, E.W.
　1989　The impact of marijuana decriminalization: An update. *Public Health Policy* 10:456-466.

Snyder, H.N.
　1998　Juvenile arrests 1997. NCJ 173938. Office of Juvenile Justice and Delinquency Prevention. Washington, DC: U.S. Department of Justice.

Stafford, M., and M. Warr
   1993   A reconceptualization of general and specific deterrence. *Journal of Research in Crime and Delinquency* 30(2):123-135.

Stahl, A.L.
   1999   *Juvenile Court Processing of Delinquency Cases, 1987-1996.* FS-99104. Office of Juvenile Justice and Delinquency Prevention. Washington, DC: U.S. Department of Justice.

Sullivan, C.D.
   1989   User-accountability provisions in the Anti-Drug Abuse Act of 1988: Assaulting civil liberties in the war on drugs. *Hastings Law Journal* 40:1223-1251.

Sunstein, C.R.
   1996   On the expressive function of law. *University of Pennsylvania Law Review* 144:2021-2053.

Thies, C.F., and C.A. Register
   1993   Decriminalization of marijuana and the demand for alcohol, marijuana and cocaine. *Social Science Journal* 30:385-399.

Tonry, M.
   1995   *Malign Neglect: Race, Crime and Punishment in America.* New York: Oxford University Press.

Tyler, T.
   1990   *Why People Obey the Law.* New Haven: Yale University Press.

U.S. Department of Justice
   1999   Bureau of Justice Statistics. Available on-line at: http://www.ojp.usdoj.gov/bjs/dcf/enforce.htm [Accessed April 6, 2001]

Wagner, F., and J.C. Anthony
   1999   Tobacco smoking as a gateway to the world of illicit drug use. *Abstracts of the 61st Annual Scientific Meeting of the College on Problems of Drug Dependence.* Philadelphia: Temple School of Medicine.

Weil, L.
   1991   Drug-related evictions in public housing: Congress' addiction to a quick fix. *Yale Law and Policy Review* 9:61-189.

Williams, K., and R. Hawkins
   1989   Controlling male aggression in intimate relationships. *Law & Society Review* 23:591-612.

Yoskowitz, J.
   1992   The war on the poor: Civil forfeiture of public housing. *Columbia Journal of Law and Social Problems* 25:567-600.

Zimring, F.E., and G. Hawkins
   1992   *The Search for Rational Drug Control.* Cambridge, England: Cambridge University Press.
   1973   *Deterrence: The Legal Threat in Crime Control.* Chicago: University of Chicago Press.

7

Preventing Drug Use

P revention can be broadly defined to encompass an array of noncoercive activities intended to prevent, reduce, or delay the occurrence of drug-taking or associated complications, such as clinical syndromes of drug dependence and threats to public safety. This chapter emphasizes nonlegal, noncoercive approaches to reducing drug use in populations that are not yet seriously involved with drugs. They include efforts to educate people about the consequences of substance use, to change their beliefs about the acceptability or utility of substance use, and to increase or make more salient the costs of substance use. We address what is known, what is not known, and what data and research are needed to increase useable knowledge about the effectiveness of a wide range of approaches.

It is important to note at the outset that although this report concerns itself with illegal drug use, the notion that the use of tobacco, alcohol, and marijuana increases the probability of later illegal drug use, which is generally accepted in the prevention field, requires that these other substances be considered in this chapter. It is also the case that almost all of the available research in this area deals with what are called "gateway" substances, rather then cocaine, crack, heroin, and the other illegal drugs that are the focus of the other chapters of this report.

PREVENTION STRATEGIES

There are a number of possible factors that might be manipulated to reduce substance use, as suggested in Chapter 2. Many deliberate prevention activities are based on the expectation that altering one or more of these factors will result in reduced substance use (Center for Substance Abuse Prevention, 1999; U.S. Department of Education, 1999). A wide assortment of modalities, delivery schedules, and targeting mechanisms are used to alter these factors. The following paragraphs describe some of the more common prevention modalities in use today. Based on a taxonomy for a recent national study of delinquency prevention in schools (Gottfredson et al., 2000), these modalities are neither exhaustive nor evaluative, but instead are intended to provide a sense for the variety of different activities that can be and are undertaken for the purpose of preventing subsequent substance use.

Mass media campaigns. These efforts are most often aimed at changing norms regarding drug use by demonstrating negative consequences for use, positive consequences for nonuse, changing opinions about the prevalence of use or the types of people who use, and increasing skills for resisting drugs. Media avenues might include the use of billboards, newspapers, radio, and television, as well as collaborations with the entertainment industry, music videos, and interactive media. The ongoing National Youth Anti-Drug Campaign of the Office of National Drug Control Policy is an example of such a media campaign implemented at the national level. Reducing pro-drug media messages is also included in this category of prevention activity.

Community organizing and coalitions. These efforts require collaboration among several community entities to develop community-wide strategies for reducing substance use. They generally involve representatives from community agencies working together to specify goals for reducing substance use, develop collaborative strategies for reaching those goals, and implement those strategies over a period of several years. Often, these community planning groups are more grassroots in nature, involving and empowering community residents in addition to professional staff. Well-known examples of this type of strategy include Project STAR (Pentz et al., 1989) and Project Northland (Perry et al., 1996).

Family training, counseling, and case management. This category includes efforts to alter family management practices or to build parenting skills in general through instruction or training. These activities often teach parents skills for monitoring or supervising their children, increasing emotional attachments, helping their children succeed in school, or otherwise assisting their children in the development of skills and competencies that will be needed to avoid substance use. An example is the Strengthening Families Program (Kumpfer et al., 1996). Family therapy often focuses on building the same skills, but it is generally more intensive than parent training activities and usually involves high-risk adolescents and their families. Family case management includes a variety of monitoring and intervention activities to assist families who are in need of services. Drug-involved families may be encouraged to seek treatment, and conditions that might facilitate relapse are addressed.

Classroom instruction. This is the most common strategy used in schools. The content of these interventions varies, but they can be grouped into three main classes: Information-only interventions teach students factual information about drugs and the consequences of use. Skill-building interventions increase students' awareness of social influences to engage in misbehavior and expand their repertoires for recognizing and appropriately responding to risky or potentially harmful situations. Normative education interventions change perceptions of the norms related to substance use. Many instructional programs contain different mixes of these three types. Two well-known examples are the Drug Abuse Resistance Education (D.A.R.E.) program and Life Skills Training. The most effective of these instructional programs use what are called cognitive-behavioral or behavioral instructional methods, which rely on modeling, providing rehearsal, and coaching in the display of new skills (Gottfredson, 2001).

Cognitive behavioral, behavioral modeling, and behavior modification strategies. Behavior modification strategies focus directly on changing behaviors. They involve timely tracking of specific behaviors over time and behavioral goals, using feedback and positive or negative reinforcement to change behavior. These strategies rely on reinforcers external to the student to shape behavior; an example of their use is the Good Behavior Game (Dolan et al., 1993; Kellam et al., 1994; Kellam and Anthony, 1998). Larger or more robust effects on behavior are obtained by teaching students to modify their own behavior using a range of cognitive strategies. Efforts to teach students cognitive-behavioral strategies involve modeling or demonstrating behaviors and providing rehearsal and coaching in the display of new skills. Students are taught, for example, to recognize the physiological cues experienced in risky situations. They rehearse this skill and practice stopping rather than acting impulsively in such situations. Students are taught and rehearsed in such skills as suggesting alternative activities when friends propose engaging in a risky activity. And they are taught to use prompts or cues to remember to engage in behavior. Lochman's (1992) Anger Coping Training is an example of this type of preventive intervention.

Other counseling, social work, psychological, and therapeutic strategies. Family prevention and cognitive-behavioral approaches often involve counseling specifically targeted at certain behaviors or cognitions. Prevention can also consist of more generic individual counseling, case management, or similar group-based interventions other than those described above. Student assistance and peer counseling programs, popular in many schools, are included in this category.

Mentoring, tutoring, and work study strategies. These efforts primar-ily aim to increase the stakes in conformity and reduce individuals' predis-positions to use drugs. Mentoring is distinguished from counseling be-cause it is generally provided by a lay person rather than a trained coun-selor and is not necessarily guided by a structured approach. Tutoring includes individualized assistance with academic tasks.

Recreational, community service, enrichment, and leisure activities. These are activities intended to provide constructive and fun alternatives to drug use. Drop-in recreation centers, after-school and weekend programs, dances, community service activities, and other events are offered in these programs as alternatives to more dangerous activities. The popular Mid-night Basketball is included in this category.

School and discipline management. This category includes interventions to change the decision-making processes or authority structures to en-hance the general capacity of the school. These activities parallel those described under community organizing above, but they are contained within a school building or a school system. These interventions often involve teams of staff and (sometimes) parents, students, and community members engaged in planning and carrying out activities to improve the school. They often diagnose school problems, formulate school goals and objectives, design potential solutions, monitor progress, and evaluate their efforts. Activities aimed at enhancing the administrative capability of the school by increasing communication and cooperation among members of the school community are also included. Examples include Project PATHE (Gottfredson, 1986) and Comer's School Development Process (Comer, 1985; Cook et al., 1998). Often these interventions also include efforts to establish or clarify school rules or discipline codes and mechanisms for the enforcement of school rules—strategies discussed in more detail in Chapter 6.

Establishment of norms and expectations for behavior. These activities in-clude school-wide or community-wide efforts to redefine norms for be-havior and signal appropriate behavior. Activities include newsletters, posters, ceremonies during which students declare their intention to re-main drug-free, and displaying symbols of appropriate behavior. Some well-known interventions in this category are Red Ribbon Week, spon-sored through the Department of Education's Safe and Drug-Free Schools and Communities program.

Classroom and instructional management. Aside from teaching specific content intended to reduce the probability that students will use drugs, teachers can also use instructional methods designed to increase student engagement in the learning process and hence increase their academic performance and bonding to the school (e.g., cooperative learning techniques and "experiential learning" strategies) and classroom organization and management strategies. The latter include activities to establish and enforce classroom rules, uses of rewards and punishments, time management to reduce down-time, strategies for grouping students within the class, and the use of external resources, such as parent volunteers, police officers, and professional consultants as instructors or aides. The Seattle Social Development Project (Hawkins et al., 1992) relied in large part on such classroom and instructional management strategies.

Regrouping students. Schools can reorganize classes or grades to create smaller units, continuing interaction, or different mixes of students or to provide greater flexibility in instruction. This category includes changes in the school schedule (e.g., block scheduling, scheduling more periods in the day, changes in the lengths of instructional periods); adoption of schools-within-schools or similar arrangements; tracking into classes by ability, achievement, effort, or conduct; formation of grade-level "houses" or "teams"; and decreasing class size. These changes are often intended to increase sources of social control for students.

Exclusion of intruders and contraband. These interventions are designed to prevent intruders (who might be drug dealers) from entering the school. They include the use of identification badges, visitor's passes, security personnel posted at school entrances, locks, cameras, and other surveillance methods. They also include efforts to prevent contraband from entering the school, such as locker searches and drug-sniffing dogs. These strategies are discussed in greater detail in Chapter 6.

Manipulation of school composition. These interventions determine who will be enrolled in the school and include such strategies as the use of selective admissions practices, assignment of students with problem behavior to "alternative schools," and other exclusionary or inclusionary practices. Zero-tolerance policies, which automatically expel students who bring drugs to school, are an example of such a strategy. These sanction-related policies are discussed at greater length in Chapter 6.

Although little is known about the extent to which these different prevention strategies are used in local communities, a recent national study of school-based prevention attempted to describe the prevalence of prevention strategies used in schools (Gottfredson et al., 2000). The investigators asked school principals to report which of 14 types of discretionary prevention activities—instruction, counseling, norm change, recreation, etc.—were currently in place in their schools, and to name each specific activity currently under way in each of the 14 categories. On average, principals reported 9 of the 14 types of prevention activities under way in their schools. The median number of different specific prevention activities named was 14—and this underestimates the total number of activities because principals were asked to name only their discretionary activities rather than all activities. Prevention curricula were the most popular modality, used in 76 percent of the nation's schools. Every type of prevention activity included in the survey was used in at least 40 percent of the schools. Clearly, a wide variety of prevention strategies is currently in use in U.S. schools.

LIMITED EVIDENCE OF EFFECTIVENESS

What is known about the effectiveness of prevention is limited by the types of prevention that have been studied. Although a wide variety of prevention strategies are in use, most studies of effectiveness are of classroom instructional strategies. For example, in a recent meta-analysis of school-based programs (Gottfredson et al., forthcoming), 78 percent of the treatment-control comparisons of program effectiveness involve instructional programs, such as ALERT (Ellikson and Bell, 1990; Ellickson et al., 1993) and Life Skills Training (Botvin et al., 1984a, 1984b). It comes as no surprise, then, that most reviews of substance abuse prevention have focused on distinctions among types of instructional programs rather than on the broader array of strategies which have not been well studied.

At least 20 reviews and meta-analyses of drug prevention programs were published during the 1980s and 1990s. The most recent of these generally conclude that substance abuse prevention efforts are "effective" for preventing substance use, in the sense that the studies reviewed report statistically significant differences between subjects receiving and not receiving the preventive intervention on some measure of substance use, at least immediately following the termination of the prevention activity, and in rare cases months or years beyond that point (Botvin, 1990; Botvin et al., 1995; Dryfoos, 1990; Durlak, 1995; Ennett et al., 1994a, 1994b; Gerstein and Green, 1993; Gorman, 1995; Gottfredson, 1997; Gottfredson et al., forthcoming; Hansen, 1992; Hansen and O'Malley, 1996; Hawkins et al., 1995; Institute of Medicine, 1993, 1994; Norman and Turner, 1993; Tobler, 1992; Tobler and Stratton, 1997). (One study—Gorman, 1995—a review limited to the effects of one type of program on one specific substance, is the only exception.) However, certain practices in the reporting of original research and in the summaries of these findings have tended to overstate the effectiveness of prevention activities.

For example, there is an "availability" bias in the published literature. Studies showing limited effectiveness often are difficult to publish and may remain unpublished technical reports available only in the original investigator's office. Lipsey and Wilson (1993) summarized the results of 302 reviews of psychological, behavioral, and educational interventions and found that effect sizes in published studies were 0.14 standard deviations larger than in unpublished studies. They also noted, however, that this bias could not completely account for the positive findings found in the studies.

Effects are also sometimes exaggerated when either the original research or subsequent summaries highlight only the few statistically significant findings among the many nonsignificant ones, a subsample for which results are significant, or results for a "high-fidelity" sample. These are all examples of selective attention to positive findings that operate similarly to the availability bias mentioned above. Often studies measure substance use or a related outcome using multiple measures, and only one of the several measures may show a statistically significant positive effect. Summaries of this research will almost always omit the information about the null findings. Of course, this practice increases the likelihood of false positives because each test involves a 5 percent chance of a false positive, and this probability cumulates over multiple tests. This same type of bias is evident in some federal activities to identify effective programs. Criteria for effectiveness require only a single positive finding, rather than a preponderance of positive findings (e.g., U.S. Department of Education, 1999). More careful research identifies the primary outcome of interest at the outset and limits the hypothesis testing to that outcome, or uses one composite of multiple outcomes of interest to avoid increasing the risk of false positives.

The practice of reporting results for high-fidelity samples is also often misleading because it confounds other factors with the success of the program. For example, a study that randomly assigns schools to treatment and control conditions may find that only half of the schools assigned to the treatment condition faithfully implemented the program. Yet outcomes for only this high-fidelity sample often are presented instead of, or in addition to, the comparisons of the treatment and control schools as they were actually assigned. Investigators argue that the comparison of the original groups underestimates the actual program effect, because it includes schools that did not actually carry out the program. What they fail to point out is that in selecting the high-fidelity sample, they are also likely to be selecting on unmeasured extraneous factors that may also be related to the outcome of interest, including high teacher morale, effective school leadership, and favorable school-community relations. This selection renders the groups nonequivalent in ways that have not been measured and cannot be controlled.

Most reviews of drug prevention programs have also focused on statistical significance rather than the magnitude of effects as the sole criterion for determining effectiveness. Because significance levels depend in part on the number of cases included in the study, and because statistical significance does not necessarily map into practical significance, the policy relevance of this information is questionable.

A handful of reviews go a step farther by providing a measure of the magnitude of the effect of different types of prevention strategies, irrespective of statistical significance. The magnitude of the program effect is often expressed as a standardized mean difference effect size (ES), a measure of the difference between the program and comparison groups relative to the standard deviation of each measure employed. The use of the ES allows for the direct comparison of effects across studies and outcomes. ESs typically range from −1.0, indicating that the treatment group performed one standard deviation lower than the comparison group, to +1.0, indicating that the treatment group performed one standard deviation higher than the comparison group (although larger absolute values do occur).

Rosenthal and Rubin (1982) showed that the ES can be translated into differentials in success rates between the program and comparison groups, greatly facilitating the interpretation of the ES. For example, assuming an overall success rate of 50 percent, an ES of 0.50 translates into a success rate of 62.5 percent for the program group and 37.5 percent for the comparison group—a success rate differential of 25.[1] The practical significance of an effect size depends largely on the seriousness of the outcome for the population and the effort needed to produce the effect. Lipsey (1992) argues that even a small effect (e.g., an ES of 0.10) for serious criminal behavior has practical significance. A small percentage difference between treated and untreated subjects on a prevalence measure in a high-frequency offending population could represent a large volume of crime. Likewise, small effect sizes on measures of very serious crimes are worthy of note because preventing even a small number of such crimes is important.

Only a handful of reviews of prevention programs have reported ESs. One of the earliest was Tobler (1986), who reported ESs derived from 98 research studies. These studies yielded 159 different measures of program effectiveness on some measure of substance use (including cigarette use).

---

[1]To see the algebra for this translation, let y indicate success so that $y = 1$ if successful and 0 otherwise, and let $z = 1$ if a respondent is assigned to the program and 0 to the comparison. In this example, we observe $P[y = 1] = 0.5$ and that $ES = \{ P[y = 1 \mid z = 1] - P[y = 1 \mid z = 0] \} / \sqrt{V(y)} = 0.5$. Thus,

$$P[y = 1 \mid z = 1] - P[y = 1 \mid z = 0] = 0.25 \qquad (1)$$

and, assuming that half of subjects are assigned to the program,

$$P[y = 1 \mid z = 1] + P[y = 1 \mid z = 0] = 1. \qquad (2)$$

Solving these two equations implies $P[y = 1 \mid z = 1] = 0.625$ and $P[y = 1 \mid z = 0] = 0.375$.

The mean effect size across all of these measures was 0.24. Tobler's most recent analysis examined 120 programs of school-based drug prevention programs between 1978 and 1990 (Tobler and Stratton, 1997). This study showed median effect size of 0.14 on measures of tobacco, alcohol, and other drug use across all programs.

Results from the most recent meta-analysis of school-based drug prevention programs (Gottfredson et al., forthcoming) documents effect sizes slightly smaller than those from previous meta-analyses.[2] This study found that across 88 relevant published treatment-control comparisons, the mean effect size for school-based prevention activities on measures of alcohol and other drug use (but not tobacco use) is statistically significantly different from zero. The mean effect size was 0.054, which (assuming a control group prevalence rate of 50 percent) translates into about a 2.7 point difference between the prevention and control groups in the percentage of students who report using a substance. Although the average effect size across all studies is small, the range of average effect sizes observed from study to study is broad (–.44 to .54) and varies by type of prevention program.

In contrast to these small effects of substance abuse prevention programs are the larger effects found on a wider array of outcomes of psychological, behavioral, and educational interventions. Lipsey and Wilson (1993), summarizing effect sizes from 302 reviews of such studies, reported an average of the average effect sizes across these reviews of 0.50 with a standard deviation of 0.29. Thus, relative to a much broader set of social and behavioral outcomes, substance use is more difficult to alter, at least through the types of prevention strategies that have been studied.

GAPS IN THE EXISTING KNOWLEDGE BASE

The limited evidence available suggests that some forms of prevention activities are effective for reducing some measures of substance use. Some studies produce a substantial effect, and others no effect or negative effects. This section takes a closer look at the available evidence in order to highlight its limitations as a basis for policy decisions.

---

[2]Gottfredson et al. (forthcoming) recalculated effect sizes based on the entire population that received any of the program whenever possible. Also, if multiple effect sizes were available for different measures of substance use, these multiple measures were averaged to obtain one effect size per study. These practices, as well as the exclusion of effects on tobacco use, may explain the slightly lower estimates of the magnitude of effects found in this study.

For Whom Does Prevention Work?

Universal Programs

Most of what we know about the effectiveness of prevention comes from studies of "universal" programs, which target the general population. These universal approaches, which often focus on incipient or "gateway" drug use, are based on the assumption that early experimentation with tobacco, alcohol, and marijuana can lead to more frequent use of these substances and progression into the use of other more dangerous substances. This gateway notion is rooted in early conceptions of marijuana as a stepping-stone to more serious drug involvement (Wagner and Anthony, 1999) as well as research evidence of a statistical link between age at first use of drugs and later more frequent or problematic use (Brunswick and Boyle, 1979; O'Donnell and Clayton, 1979; Robins and Przybeck, 1985; Anthony and Petronis, 1991)

Findings such as these and subsequent analyses of sequences of drug use patterns over time led to a developmental stage theory of adolescent involvement in legal and illegal drugs (Kandel, 1975; Kandel and Faust, 1975). According to this perspective, use of alcohol and tobacco precedes the use of illegal drugs, and the use of marijuana precedes the use of other illegal drugs. Early descriptions of this developmental process (e.g., Kandel, 1982) were careful to point out that most individuals who reach a given stage of substance use discontinue it for one reason or another, and that only a small subgroup of users at earlier stages actually progress to the next stage of use.

Although sophisticated research demonstrated that the use of legal drugs is associated with increased probability of marijuana use, and the use of marijuana is associated with increased probability of other illegal drug use (Yamaguchi and Kandel, 1984), the authors stress the limitations on the inferences about the link between use of one drug and use of another. They point out (p. 679) that personality and lifestyle variables, as well as environmental factors such as availability and supply, also explain the transition from one drug to another and from one level of use to another. In particular, they pointed out the need to control for individual propensity variables prior to the time of initiation into legal drug use. These effects due to heterogeneity in population characteristics are confounded with the early use of gateway substances.

The models do not rule out the alternative interpretation that some individuals are more likely to use more drugs, to use more dangerous drugs, to persist in their use for a longer period of time, and to begin their use earlier than others. This idea is consistent with the well-established findings in the criminological literature (Moffitt, 1993) that the offending population consists of two distinct groups: a large group of individuals who experiment with illegal activities for a relatively short time during adolescence and then desist, and a small group of offenders who begin their criminal careers earlier, end them later, and offend at higher rates during their criminal careers. The latter group is responsible for the majority of the crime that occurs.

MacCoun (1998) also notes that there are several plausible causal interpretations of the basic findings that tobacco, alcohol, marijuana, and hard drug use are associated and tend to occur in a particular sequence. One interpretation suggests that the association is spurious or noncausal—specifically, the notion (discussed earlier) that the use of the early and late drugs in the sequence reflects some common risk factors, with timing determined by price and availability. Other interpretations are causal—for example, experiences with the early substances in the sequence might: (a) stimulate one's interest or appetite for the later substances, (b) change one's beliefs about the severity of health, legal, or social risks of drug use, (c) bring one into contact with a subculture of hard drug users, or (d) bring one into contact with hard drug sellers. Interestingly, the first causal interpretation is widely cited in the United States as a basis for stringent sanctions against marijuana; the latter three interpretations were influential in the development of Dutch drug policy, which seeks to separate "soft" and "hard" drug markets and cultures (see MacCoun and Reuter, 1997).

Few actual data are available to direct policy decisions about the targeting of prevention activities, but debates over appropriate targeting have appeared at the margins of the prevention literature. Although the field continues to be predominated by the gateway ideas, a few commentators have questioned this approach (Brown and Kreft, 1998; Gilham et al., 1997; Gilchrist, 1991). Brown and Kreft (1998) argue that the "no use" messages typically conveyed in universal prevention programs actually increase use among those most at risk for using. These youths are more knowledgeable about drugs and their effects than prevention curricula assume, and the naive messages conveyed in the programs serve to create cognitive dissonance in the minds of these youths.

Gilham et al. (1997) argue that the results of research on these universal prevention programs is misleading because the programs have no effect on the large proportion of the population that is not likely to use drugs even without benefit of prevention programming, but they may have large effects on the smaller population that is at risk. They argue that the more substantial effects on potential users are diluted in studies that report findings for the entire population.

For example, suppose that 98 percent of a population targeted for universal prevention programming will never use heroin, and that the program is effective for preventing use among 1 percent of the remaining population. Should the results indicate that the program was effective for preventing heroin use among 1 percent of the population, or among 50 percent of those at risk for using heroin?

This illustrates the point that the small effects observed in studies of prevention programs may mask larger effects—both negative and positive—for different user groups. If this is true, it is important to understand the heterogeneity in the population and target prevention activities accordingly. However, only scant evidence is available on differential effects for different user groups (e.g., nonusers, casual or experimental users, users).

Reviews and meta-analyses of prevention effectiveness fail to differentiate among programs that target at-risk and universal populations. Relatively few effectiveness studies conducted on at-risk populations have reported effects on substance use outcomes. In an ongoing meta-analysis of school-based prevention (Gottfredson et al., forthcoming), only 7 of the 88 studies for which effect sizes could be computed targeted populations that were at elevated risk for developing problem use.

A handful of studies have compared the effectiveness of universal prevention activities for groups that differed according to their level of use at baseline. In one of these studies (Hansen et al., 1988), the researchers compared students who had received a 12-session resistance skills program with a control group. Results were reported separately for students who reported no marijuana use at baseline and for the entire population. Statistically significant program effects were found only for baseline nonusers of marijuana. When these students were combined with those who had already initiated marijuana use at baseline, no effects were found.

Studies of the ALERT program provide another example of differential effectiveness for groups differing in level of baseline use (Bell et al., 1993; Ellickson and Bell, 1990, Ellickson et al., 1993). ALERT is a universal social resistance-skill curriculum consisting of eight lessons taught a week apart in the 7th grade, followed by three 8th grade booster lessons. The researchers reported the results from this program separately for baseline nonusers, baseline "experimenters," and baseline "users," and also separately for cigarette use, alcohol use, and marijuana use and by follow-up period.

The program's most consistent effects were found for marijuana use. Statistically it significantly reduced the use of marijuana among students at each risk level, but the strongest effects were for the lowest risk group: those students who had not initiated either cigarette or marijuana use at the time of the baseline measurement. For all groups, small positive program effects were initially observed for alcohol use, but they too eroded by 8th grade, by which time the higher-risk participants actually reported more statistically significant alcohol use than the control group. The follow-up studies showed that once the lessons stop, so did the program's effects on drug use.

Programs for High-Risk Populations

These examples suggest (but by no means are sufficient to establish) that universal prevention programs designed to prevent initiation in the general population may either increase use or have no effect on use for the most at-risk segment of the population. In contrast are programs that are specifically designed for high-risk populations. Relatively few studies have assessed the effects of such programs on substance use, but Lochman's anger-coping program is one example.

This program targets boys in 4th through 6th grades who are identified as highly aggressive and disruptive by their teachers; these are risk factors for later serious and chronic substance use. In this intervention, a school counselor and a mental health professional provide intensive training and coaching in behavioral and cognitive skills necessary for self-control. The intervention is delivered to small groups of boys over a 12- to 18-week period.

The effectiveness of this intervention was investigated in a series of studies that systematically varied features of the program to learn more about its essential elements. These studies in general found that the intervention was effective for reducing disruptive behavior in the short run. A three-year follow-up study, conducted when boys from several of the studies were 15 years old, found that the intervention had a statistically significant effect on self-reported alcohol and substance abuse (Lochman, 1992).

This study suggests that programs carefully designed to reduce known risk factors for use in high-risk populations may be effective for reducing drug use, even if they are not about drugs per se. No research has examined potential diffusion effects of prevention efforts. It is well known that peer groups have large effects on individual substance use; it stands to reason that if members of one's peer group are positively affected by a preventive intervention, this effect will spread to the "untreated" members of the peer group.

To the extent that such diffusion of effects occurs, prevention effects are underestimated. This may be an important side-effect of prevention, and it may be that the diffusion effect obtained from an intensive preventive intervention targeting a small group of high-risk youths is larger than the effect that would be obtained by targeting all youths with a universal program. Nothing is known about these possible trade-offs.[3] The pieces of evidence available are insufficient to support a conclusion about the optimal targeting strategy for prevention efforts. Clearly, additional research is needed.

For example, it would be useful to identify a subpopulation at elevated risk for serious and chronic drug use, randomly assign this population to receive prevention as usual, high-quality universal prevention programming, or intensive targeted high-quality programming. The study would follow these subjects for several years, measuring drug use initiation, frequency and quantity of use, age at cessation of use from each category of drug, and problems related to use. Such a study would provide invaluable evidence about the relative merits of targeted versus universal prevention for high-risk populations. Even more informative would be a study that, in addition to the above, applied the same conditions to a general population of youths not at elevated risk for drug problems.

The targeting issue is closely related to the issue of how best to measure the effectiveness of prevention programs. The success of universal programs is most often measured by reductions in the prevalence of use in the general population. The success of programs targeting higher-risk populations could focus on the quantity of use or the problems related to use. This issue is discussed next.

What Outcomes Can Prevention Programs Expect to Alter?

This report is about data and research needs for policy on illegal drug use. The committee has chosen to focus its attention primarily on illegal drugs, whose use is very costly to both individuals and society. Studies of the effectiveness of prevention programs generally do not measure the effects of use of illegal drugs, such as cocaine and heroin, primarily because such use has not been frequent in the school-attending populations and school districts where most of this research has been conducted. This disconnect is not troublesome for most prevention researchers and policy makers because, as noted earlier, a major assumption in this field is that early use of cigarettes, alcohol, and marijuana lead to later use of more harmful substances.

---

[3]It may be possible to infer something about the size of the diffusion effect by comparing the effect sizes of studies that randomly assign subjects within a social unit, such as a school, with studies that randomly assign the social units. Diffusion effects should weaken the effect in the within-unit design more than in the between-unit design. Everything else being equal, the magnitude of the difference in effects for these two designs would be a measure of diffusion effects.

This assumption is made explicit in a recent cost-effectiveness study of school-based drug prevention programs for reducing cocaine consumption (Caulkins et al., 1999). The authors found no studies that provided an estimate of the direct effect of prevention programs on later cocaine use. They had to estimate this effect indirectly in a two-stage process (from the National Household Survey of Drug Abuse), by combining estimates from evaluations of prevention program effects on the age of marijuana initiation and the correlation between the age of marijuana initiation and the quantity of cocaine later consumed. By combining these two estimates and making different assumptions about the permanence of the program effect on marijuana use, they arrived at a range of estimates of prevention's effect on later cocaine use. According to these estimates, the percentage reduction in lifetime cocaine consumption due to prevention for a given cohort ranges from 2.9 to 13.6 percent, with a middle-range guess of 7.6 percent.

Of course, the validity of these estimates hinges on the assumption that the correlation between age at first use of marijuana and later cocaine use is due to certain individual propensities to use, and that prevention's effect on marijuana use is due to its effect on this general propensity. Most important for the purpose of this report, the authors note a high degree of uncertainty that surrounds their estimates of the effects of prevention on later cocaine use—hence the title of their report: *An Ounce of Prevention, A Pound of Uncertainty*. More precise estimates of the effects of prevention on illegal drugs requires longitudinal follow-up of program participants and control groups in a large-enough sample to be able to detect mean group differences in very rare behaviors.

Aside from this paucity of data on the effects of prevention efforts on later illegal drug use, there are also differences across studies in the way tobacco, alcohol, and marijuana use are measured. Most studies use self-reports of drug use. Three types of self-report measures are generally used: prevalence, variety, and frequency measures. Prevalence measures assess status as a user in one's life or during a certain time frame. Variety measures are counts of the number of different substances used and are often used to assess multiple drug use, which may be more dangerous than the use of a single substance. Frequency measures assess how often or how much an individual uses drugs.

These measures can be used to differentiate levels of use. For example, some studies have targeted drinking five or more drinks at one sitting as an outcome of interest. Other studies have developed cut-points to differentiate casual from heavy use, or varying degrees of drug involvement (e.g., Kellam et al., 1982). Age at first use is also sometimes measured, so that delays in onset of drug use can be assessed (e.g., Kellam and Anthony, 1998). Prevention studies generally have not assessed effects of programs on the harmful consequences of drug use or drug dependence, for the reasons mentioned above.

Positive effects of prevention programs have been reported on all three types of self-report measures. For example, in the meta-analysis of school-based prevention programs by Gottfredson et al. (forthcoming), roughly a third (36 percent) of the studies that included any measure of substance use included only prevalence measures; another third (32 percent) included only frequency measures. A smaller number (6 percent) included only variety measures, and 20 percent included some combination of these types of measures.

In the committee's view, these distinctions among the many possible outcomes of prevention programs should be the subject of serious debate and study. The field has not yet developed a consensus about which outcome or outcomes are important and reasonable to expect from prevention programs. Currently, differences across prevalence and frequency measures are glossed over in reports about the effectiveness of prevention. Whether a program works to delay onset for a week or a month, to limit the number of different drugs tried, to reduce the amount consumed per occasion, to prevent dependence, or to limit the harmful consequences of use has not been the focus of prevention studies. Only by encouraging research that includes the entire array of outcome measures and by reporting separately on each can the field move toward an understanding of the dimensions of use that are and are not influenced by various types of prevention programs. This information could then be evaluated according to the value placed on each outcome. Because certain of the outcomes of potential interest (e.g., dependence, harmful consequences) come into play years after a prevention program is over, this recommendation also implies that prevention research should include longer-term follow-up periods.

Features of the Most Effective Prevention Strategies

Botvin's (1990) summary of the effectiveness of different kinds of prevention programs has become influential in the prevention field. According to Botvin, four general approaches are largely ineffective for reducing substance use: "information dissemination" approaches, which teach primarily about drugs and their effects; "fear arousal" approaches, which emphasize the risks associated with tobacco, alcohol, and drug use; "moral appeal" approaches, which teach students about the evils of use; and "affective education" programs, which focus on building self-esteem, responsible decision making, and interpersonal growth. Approaches that do reduce substance use include resistance-skills training, which teaches students about social influences to engage in substance use, and specific skills for effectively resisting these pressures alone or in combination with broader-based life-skills training.

Reviews published since 1990 have generally concurred with Botvin's conclusions regarding the relative effectiveness of social skills approaches as opposed to information-only and affective approaches to classroom-based instructional programs. In addition, however, they have raised questions about the use of different modalities (other than classroom instruction), suggested that different content (other than social skills training) might also be effective in classroom instruction, and have suggested that the delivery mechanisms and methods, duration, and timing may be important moderator variables.

Modalities

Table 7.1 presents estimates of the magnitude of effects of different school-based prevention approaches. In addition to showing effect sizes for the major modalities listed above for which more than one study was available, it also shows a separate breakout for the Drug Abuse Resistance Education (D.A.R.E.) program, which is of special interest to policy makers because it is the most widely used classroom instructional program— in 1998 it was used in 48 percent of the nation's elementary schools—and because it enjoys substantial federal support (Gottfredson et al., 2000). The table shows that (a) very few studies are available to assess the effects of modalities other than classroom instruction; (b) the range of average effect sizes observed from study to study is broad; and (c) the mean effect size for each category is in the small range, but this masks considerable variability and most categories include studies with negative as well as positive effects.

Certain of the modalities—counseling, social work and therapeutic interventions that do not use cognitive behavioral or behavioral methods; tutoring, mentoring, and other individual-attention strategies; and recreational, enrichment, and leisure activities—appear ineffective in reducing substance use because the average effect across all studies in these categories is negative and no study shows a positive effect. However, only a small number of studies have examined effects on drug use for these categories of activity.

The average effect size obtained from the 12 studies of D.A.R.E. for which effect sizes could be computed was 0.03—too small to be practically meaningful, but almost identical to the non-D.A.R.E. studies included in the category of skill-building classroom instructional programs that do not emphasize cognitive-behavioral methods.

Also noteworthy is the finding that the magnitude of the effects for changes to the school environment are generally larger than the magni-

TABLE 7.1   Mean Effect Size on Substance Use by Program Category

Program Category	Effect Size			
	Mean[a]	Minimum	Maximum	N[b]
Environmentally focused interventions				
School and discipline management	0.24*	0.15	0.33	2
Interventions to establish norms or expectations for behavior	0.09	−0.23	0.31	12
Classroom or instructional management	0.17*	0.03	0.25	5
Individually focused interventions				
Classroom instruction				
Skill-building instruction using cognitive-behavioral or behavioral instructional methods	0.05*	−0.44	0.37	30
Skill-building instruction without cognitive-behavioral or behavioral instructional methods	0.03	−0.22	0.29	25
D.A.R.E.	0.03	−0.22	0.25	12
Other instructional programs	0.07	−0.26	0.54	5
Cognitive behavioral, behavioral modeling, or behavior modification	0.23	−0.21	0.44	3
Other counseling, social work, and therapeutic	−0.19	−0.39	0.00	2
Mentoring, tutoring, and work study	−0.11	−0.21	0.00	2
All environmentally focused interventions	0.13*	−0.23	0.40	20
All individually focused interventions	0.03*	−0.44	0.54	68

Note: See text for program category descriptions. Substance use outcomes include alcohol, marijuana, and other illicit drugs. Most effects are measured immediately after the completion of the prevention activity, although some are measured months or years later. Source: Gottfredson et al. (forthcoming).
*$p <= .05$.
[a]Inverse variance weighted mean effect size (random effects model).
[b]Number of effect sizes contributing to the analysis.

tude of instructional and other individually focused interventions, which are more often studied and used in schools. Clearly, more research is needed to test the effectiveness of the noninstructional modalities and to understand why so much variability in the magnitude of effects is observed across studies. As discussed in a later section, research is also needed to test the effectiveness of different combinations of modalities.

The need for research on different prevention modalities is particularly crucial with extremely costly and high profile prevention activities.

One such activity is the ongoing National Youth Anti-Drug Campaign of the Office of National Drug Control Policy (ONDCP, July 19, 1999, Media Campaign Update, http://www.mediacampaign.org/newsroom/080299/update.html).

In this media campaign, considerable effort has gone into survey sampling, questionnaire design, and survey administration to evaluate the program. However, because the campaign is being implemented nationwide, there are limits to what can be learned from the evaluation—as the evaluators note in their interim report (Westat, 1999:xiv). Interrupted time-series designs are considerably stronger when the media campaign is varied across media markets. For example, media markets can be randomly assigned to different messages, different initiation dates, or differences in the number and timing of messages (see Cook and Campbell, 1979). This approach was not taken in the National Youth Anti-Drug Campaign. As a result, the evaluation lacks a "counterfactual" condition—an indication of what would have happened to comparable youth in the absence of exposure to the campaign. In addition, a public information campaign of this sort may have fairly small effects on any given individual, even though the aggregate effects may more than justify the expense. Thus, it is likely that the eventual results of the evaluation will be ambiguous.

Content

As reviews of drug prevention have suggested and the results in Table 7.1 document, among instructional programs, those that teach students about social influences to engage in substance use and provide specific skills for effectively resisting these pressures alone or in combination with broader-based life-skills training reduce substance use, particularly when these skills are taught using cognitive-behavioral methods. However, the evidence suggests that, on average, this type of prevention strategy is not likely to have a large or even moderate effect on substance use in the general population, and its effect on subgroups in the population that are at elevated risk for developing substance abuse problems is unknown. Some research suggests that other modalities, including small-group coaching delivered to younger, more vulnerable children (e.g., Lochman's work, described above), or the application of group contingencies for desirable behavior (e.g., Kellam and Anthony, 1998), or broad improvement to school and discipline management (e.g., Gottfredson, 1996), none of which contain any focus on drugs, may be more effective at teaching social competency skills than the universal classroom-based instructional approaches.

Although social competency skill development is one element of effective prevention programming, other content also appears important. Reviews have indicated that approaches aimed at changing normative beliefs about drug use are also effective (Hansen, 1992; Gottfredson, 1997). These approaches often use survey results to correct misperceptions about the prevalence of use, engage youths in discussions to elicit their opinions about the appropriateness, and include testimonials from admired peers emphasizing that use is not acceptable. Instructional programs that incorporate these norm-setting activities have been shown to reduce use (Gottfredson et al., forthcoming; Hansen, 1992), but noninstructional programs that employ these methods outside the context of a broader substance use prevention curriculum are also effective for reducing substance use (Hansen and Graham, 1991; Perry et al., 1996).

Note that these approaches assume that incorrect information about the prevalence or appropriateness of use, rather than poor skills for dealing with social influences to use, increases substance use. On the surface, the effectiveness of these approaches does not square with conclusions of some reviews that programs that provide "information only" about the consequences of substance use do not work. They suggest rather the importance of a credible opinion leader conveying correct information. It may be that the programs giving evidence of harmful effects of providing information only failed to include these key components. Recent commentaries have recommended a return to the information approach, on the assumption that when teens are provided with accurate information, especially from trusted people, they will make good decisions (e.g., Beck, 1998).

The committee recommends additional research to assess the effectiveness of social competency skill development and normative education approaches, which emphasize conveying correct information about the prevalence of drug use and its harmful effects. This research should also assess the interaction between the content of the prevention activity and the risk level of the population targeted, because it is likely that provision of correct information may be especially effective for the subset of the population that is most at risk for higher levels of use. It is likely that research on programs conducted under more tightly controlled or experimental conditions may overestimate the effects that would be observed under normal conditions, and this factor may confound comparisons of the effects of different programs. **Therefore the committee recommends additional research on prevention practices implemented under conditions of normal practice so that variability in effects from study to study may be better understood. Finally, the committee recommends further research on alternative methods and targeting mechanisms for teaching social competency skills.**

Potential Moderators

Several reviews point out the extreme variability in effects across studies of the same type of program and recommend studies of potential moderators of program effectiveness, including the risk level of the population to which the prevention program is delivered, the timing of program delivery in the life-cycle, the duration of the program, and role, skill level, and background of the trainer.

Little is known about the optimal timing of delivery. Because many of the risk factors for later substance use appear at an early age (e.g., impulsive temperament, poor social skills, school failure, peer rejection) or with the behaviors of the parents (e.g., parental drug use and attitudes about drugs, family management practices), it can be argued that prevention should start very early in the life course and target parents as well as children. Many prevention efforts, however, are designed to be delivered during early adolescence, when social influence to use increases. Few studies have assessed effects on later substance use of attempts to alter risk factors that appear at an earlier developmental stage, but they have generally produced positive results. The anger-coping program of Lochman (1992) was an elementary school intervention that reduced substance abuse during adolescence.

The Good Behavior Game is another example of a successful early preventive intervention studies using a randomized control group design (Dolan et al., 1993; Kellam et al., 1994; Kellam and Anthony, 1998). This group-based behavior management program, in which small student teams are formed in each classroom, rewards the teams for achieving behavioral standards. Because the team reward depends on the behavior of each member of the team, peer pressure is used constructively in this program to achieve positive behavior. Early results suggest that the program reduced aggressive behavior, especially among the most aggressive subpopulation. Results from the first follow-up study showed a statistically significant reduction in teacher-rated aggression at 6th grade for certain subgroups. The most recent reports from the project show that by age 14, boys in the classrooms with the program had a lower risk of starting to smoke tobacco than boys in the control classrooms (Kellam and Anthony, 1998).

Other examples of early prevention efforts that have produced positive effects on measures of substance use have been studied using quasi-experimental research designs. They include the Child Development Project (Battistich et al., 1996) and the School Development Program (Comer, 1985). The Child Development Project targets elementary schools and includes the following components, all aimed at creating an environment to support positive youth development:

- "Cooperative learning" activities intended to encourage student discussion, comparison of ideas, and mutual challenging of ideas on academic and social topics;
- A "values-rich" literature-based reading and language arts program intended to foster understanding of diversity;
- "Developmental discipline," a positive approach to classroom management that stresses teaching appropriate behavior rather than punishment, involving students in classroom management, and helping them to learn behavior management and conflict resolution skills;
- "Community-building" activities aimed at increasing appreciation for diversity or students' sense of communal involvement and responsibility; and
- "Home-school" activities to foster parent involvement in their children's education.

Several cohorts of elementary school students in 12 elementary schools were followed for two consecutive years beginning in 1992 to assess effects of this prevention program. Statistically significant positive effects were found on measures of marijuana and alcohol use.

The School Development Program is a comprehensive school organization development intervention seeking to broaden the involvement in school management of stakeholders in the school. The program creates a representative governance and management team composed of school administrators, teachers, support staff, and parents that assesses school problems and opportunities, identifies social and academic goals for the school, plans activities to address the goals, and monitors activities and takes corrective action to keep the activities on track. An evaluation of the program in 10 inner-city Chicago schools over a four-year period found that the rate of increase in substance use was statistically significantly lower in the program than in the comparison schools (Cook et al., 1998).

Although these examples provide evidence that early prevention may work to reduce substance use, little is known about the ideal time or times to deliver preventive interventions, how preventive interventions can be most effectively sequenced over the life course, or how the timing of prevention activities may matter relative to the timing of drug epidemics. Presumably, the effects of cumulative prevention efforts delivered over the entire life course are considerably larger than the relatively short-term efforts that have been studied, and presumably the effects of certain types of prevention are greater during the early stages of an epidemic than when it is in full swing. Clarifying these issues of timing will require additional research.

The duration of programs also varies considerably from study to study. The accumulated wisdom in the prevention field is that longer is better (e.g., Durlak, 1995; Gottfredson, 1997). Programs that provide booster sessions after the initial activity produce more lasting effects than those that do not. These conclusions are based largely on a handful of studies that have compared effects of an instructional program with and without a booster. Botvin et al. (1984b), for example, show that the effects of Life Skills Training (the peer-led version) on self-reports of marijuana use in the past month taken 16 months after the initial pretest are not statistically significantly different from zero for those students in the condition without the booster, but when additional lessons are provided in the following school year to reinforce the initial lessons, effects at 16 months after the pretest are statistically significant and more than doubled in magnitude. However, others have demonstrated both short-term (Eggert et al., 1994) and long-term (e.g., Lochman, 1992) positive effects of one-shot interventions of approximately the same duration as Botvin's initial program. Clearly, booster sessions are not a necessary ingredient of successful prevention, but their timing appears to be important.

For example, research may discover that the total dosage of prevention messages can be traded off against the timing of the messages. Brief messages delivered closer in time to the situation in which an opportunity to use drugs is likely to arise, or small doses delivered continually over the life span, may be more effective than long messages delivered within a short time frame, as is most often the case in drug prevention classes as they are offered today. Mass media campaigns—television and radio advertisements, billboards, and posters—offer this potential advantage over classroom-based messages. More research is needed to sort out these potential trade-offs between timing and dose.

Reviews have also concluded that the role of the deliverer is important. Hansen (1992) suggested that the training and background of the leader and the fidelity of presentation may be more important than the content of the message. Tobler compared programs delivered by different types of leaders: mental health professionals and counselors produced the largest effects, followed by peers; teachers produced the smallest effects. Tobler (1992:20-21) concluded that the leader must be someone who is "competent in group process, who can enhance the interactional process and simultaneously focus and direct the group. Successful leaders have the ability to act as guides, as opposed to being dominant. They are able to tolerate ambivalence, and know when to remain silent to facilitate true dialogue. They are able to empower adolescents to make conscientious decisions and to encourage freedom of choice and individual self determination."

Undoubtedly, the content of the message and the characteristics of the leader interact to produce more or less effective programs. Perhaps the provision of accurate information about the consequences of use by a capable leader with the characteristics described by Tobler would be just as or more effective as a resistance skills training course taught by a teacher.

Timing, duration, and the characteristics of the deliverer are potentially important moderator variables that could explain the wide range of effects observed across studies of prevention activities that are otherwise similar. But at present, we can only guess about which activities and what about each activity is critical to its success. The knowledge base for choosing among the multitude of prevention options is severely limited. Each of the potential moderator variables must be systematically varied in rigorous prevention trials.

Needed Research

Much remains to be learned about the potential of prevention activities for reducing illegal drug use. The committee identified five major areas in which answers from additional research would bridge this knowledge gap. Research is needed to examine

- Which of the noninstructional modalities are effective for reducing drug use.
- Whether prevention activities affect the subsequent drug use of different user groups differently. To what extent do prevention messages spread to individuals and groups not initially targeted, and can this "diffusion effect" be harnessed to reduce drug use in high risk peer groupings?
- Whether prevention activities affect the quantity, frequency or problems associated with use of nongateway substances.
- What prevention content is most effective, with which groups.
- How the timing, duration, and characteristics of the deliverer condition the effects of prevention programs. Does the effectiveness of prevention effects vary relative to the timing of drug epidemics? Are there important trade-offs between total dosage delivered and timing of delivery of prevention messages?

Table 7.2 shows the areas that must be studied for each prevention modality in order to fill in gaps in understanding of the potential of prevention. Most is known about the ideal content of instructional programs, but in the committee's judgment, more research is needed even in that cell.

Once these gaps are filled, the next step will be to explore how effects can be enhanced through combinations of the most effective modalities. A number of studies have combined several modalities (e.g., Battistich et al.,

TABLE 7.2 Gaps in Knowledge about Prevention Effectiveness

Modality	Target Population	Outcomes Affected	Content	Characteristics of Deliverer	Duration	Timing
Mass Media Campaigns	X	X	X	X	X	X
Community Organizing/Coalitions	X	X	X	X	X	X
Family Training, Counseling, or Case Management	X	X	X	X	X	X
Instruction	X	X	X	X	X	X
Behavior Modification and Cognitive/Behavioral Strategies	X	X	X	X	X	X
Other Counseling, Social Work, Psychological, or Therapeutic Strategies	X	X	X	X	X	X
Tutoring, Mentoring, and other Individual-Attention Strategies	X	X	X	X	X	X
Recreational, Enrichment, and Leisure Activities	X	X	X	X	X	X
School/Discipline Management		X	X			X
Establishment of Norms for Behavior	X	X	X	X	X	X
Classroom Management		X				X
Regrouping Students	X	X			X	X
Exclusion of Intruders and Contraband		X				X
Manipulation of School Composition	X	X			X	X

Note – "X" indicates areas in which additional research is needed.

1996; Gottfredson, 1986; Johnson et al., 1990; MacKinnon et al., 1991; Pentz et al., 1990; Pentz et al., 1989; Gottfredson et al., 1996; Skroban et al., 1999). Some of these attempts have been successful, and some have not. The less successful ones have suffered from implementation problems that may have been related to the multimodal nature of the program (e.g., Skroban et al., 1999). These individual studies have not resulted in an accumulation of knowledge about the conditions under which multimodal programs can work and the modes that can and cannot easily be combined. This line of inquiry will have to be carefully designed to control for conditions that may bear on the effectiveness of the activity.

Research should also test the interactive effects of the different elements. That is, combinations may increase the magnitude of effects through the additive effects of each component, but they may also have a multiplicative effect, so that certain strategies are more or less effective in combination with another than they are by themselves. For example, a drug prevention curriculum with a "no use" message may be counterproductive when delivered in a school environment in which norms favor use, or one in which the rules related to the possession of substances are lax or inconsistently applied. Only through research on the additive and multiplicative effects of different strategies can knowledge accumulate that will allow communities to develop portfolios of effective prevention strategies.

CONCLUSIONS AND RECOMMENDATIONS

A wide spectrum of plausible approaches to the prevention of substance use exist in both theory and practice. The effectiveness of most of these approaches for reducing substance use is unknown because the research evidence is nonexistent or inconclusive. Some of the approaches for which we have no evidence of effectiveness include many popular control strategies, such as zero-tolerance policies, the use of security measures such as locker searches, and the presence of police in schools, as well as more innovative approaches that draw on advances in toxicology, molecular biology, genetics, and clinical medicine (e.g., parents' attempts to protect their children via increased use of home test kits to detect drug use, or active immunization of high-risk children with vaccine analogues). Research is needed on a wider array of prevention activities than has been studied to date.

With respect to the prevention approaches that have been studied, the committee makes the following observations:

• Some prevention approaches are effective at delaying the initiation or reducing the frequency of tobacco, alcohol, and marijuana use. The magnitude of these effects are generally small, but the efforts that are generally more effective than other programs are implemented with high fidelity, focus on improving the capability of social organizations such as schools for managing themselves more effectively and communicating clear messages about expected behavior, and use cognitive-behavioral methods to teach skills that youths need to make competent decisions in social situations.

• Considerable heterogeneity in effectiveness is found from study to study in each broad category of prevention activity. Although hints can be gleaned from the literature about factors that might differentiate the more effective from the less effective activities—such as duration, timing, and characteristics of the deliverer—existing research is not capable of isolating these moderating factors.

• Some of the most widely promulgated classroom-based drug prevention programs—such as D.A.R.E. in the 1980s and early 1990s—have been found to have little impact on student drug use. Large amounts of public funds have been and continue to be allocated to prevention activities whose effectiveness is unknown or known to be limited.

• It is not clear that preventing or reducing the use of gateway substances translates into reduced risk of use of cocaine or other illegal drugs. With only a few exceptions, the long-term effects of prevention programs are unknown.

• Some evidence suggests that universal approaches to prevention of drug use have differential effects on different groups, so that students who have already initiated drug use before exposure to the program may escalate it following the program.

In light of these observations, the committee recommends a major increase in current efforts to evaluate drug prevention efforts. Further research is needed to better understand (1) effects of the entire spectrum of plausible approaches to prevention proposed or in use, rather than those that are most easily evaluated; (2) effects of drug prevention programs implemented under conditions of normal practice, outside the boundaries of the initial tightly controlled experimental tests of program efficacy under optimal conditions; (3) effects of different combinations of prevention programs, for example, how they complement each other or detract from one another when used in combination, as they most often are; and (4) the extent to which experimentally induced delays in tobacco, alcohol, and marijuana use yield reductions in later involvement with cocaine and other illegal drugs specifically, and long-term effects of prevention programming more generally.

Until the results of such research are available, policy makers have only a weak information base on which to base policy decisions and are likely to continue to fund and operate ineffective prevention programs and programs of unknown effectiveness.

REFERENCES

Anthony, J.C., and K.R. Petronis
  1991 Epidemiologic Evidence on Suspected Associations Between Cocaine Use and Psychiatric Disturbances. *NIDA Research Monograph* 110:71-94.

Battistich, V., E. Schaps, M. Watson, and D. Solomon
  1996 Prevention effects of the child development project: Early findings from ongoing multisite demonstration trial. *Journal of Adolescent Research* 11(1):12-35.

Beck, J.
  1998 100 years of "just say no" versus "just say know" Reevaluating drug education goals for the coming century. *Evaluation Review* 22:15-45.

Bell, R.M., P.L. Ellickson, and E.R. Harrison
  1993 Do drug prevention effects persist into high school? How project ALERT did with ninth graders. *Preventive Medicine* 22:463-483.

Botvin, G.J., S. Schinke, and M.A. Orlandi
  1995 School-based health promotion: Substance abuse and sexual behavior. *Applied and Preventive Psychology* 4:167-184.

Botvin, G.J.
  1990 Substance abuse prevention: Theory, practice, and effectiveness. Pp. 461-519 in M.Tonry and J.Q. Wilson, eds., *Drugs and Crime.* Chicago: University of Chicago Press.

Botvin, G.J., E. Baker, E.M. Botvin, A.D. Filazzola, and R.B. Millman
  1984a Prevention of alcohol misuse through the development of personal and social competence: A pilot study. *Journal of Studies on Alcohol* 45:550-552.

Botvin, G. J., E. Baker, N.L. Renick, A.D. Filazzola, and E.M. Botvin
  1984b A cognitive-behavioral approach to substance abuse prevention. *Addictive Behaviors* 9:137-147.

Brown, J.H., and I.G.G. Kreft
  1998 Zero effects of drug prevention programs: Issues and solutions. *Evaluation Review* 22(1):3-14.

Brunswick, A.F., and J.M. Boyle
  1979 Patterns of drug involvement: Developmental and secular influences on age at initiation. *Youth and Society* 2:139-162.

Caulkins, J.P., C.P. Rydell, S.S. Everingham, J. Chiesa, and S. Bushway
  1999 *An Ounce of Prevention, A Pound of Uncertainty: The Cost Effectiveness of School-Based Drug Prevention Programs.* Santa Monica, CA: RAND.

Center for Substance Abuse Prevention
  1999 *Here's Proof Prevention Works.* DHHS Publication No. (SMA)99-3300. Rockville, MD: U.S. Department of Health and Human Services.

Comer, J.P.
  1985 The Yale-New Haven primary prevention project: A follow-up study. *Journal of the American Academy of Child Psychiatry* 24(2):54-160.

Cook, T.D., H.D. Hunt, and R.F. Murphy
  1998 *Comer's School Development Program in Chicago: A Theory-Based Evaluation.* Chicago: Institute for Policy Research, Northwestern University.

Cook, T.D., and D.T. Campbell
  1979 *Quasi-Experimentation: Design and Analysis Issues for Field Settings.* Chicago: Rand McNally.

Dishion, T.J., and D.W. Andrews
  1994 Preventing escalation in problem behaviors with high risk young adolescents: Immediate and one year outcomes. *Journal of Consulting and Clinical Psychology* 63(4):538-548.

Dolan, L.J., S.G. Kellam, C.H. Brown, L. Werthamer-Larsson, G.W. Rebok, L.S. Mayer, J. Laudolff, J.S. Turkkan, C. Ford, and L. Wheeler
  1993 The short-term impact of two classroom-based preventive interventions on aggressive and shy behaviors and poor achievement. *Journal of Applied Developmental Psychology* 14:317-345.

Dryfoos, J.G.
  1990 *Adolescents at Risk: Prevalence and Prevention.* New York: Oxford University Press.

Durlak, J.A.
  1995 *School-Based Prevention Programs for Children and Adolescents.* Thousand Oaks, CA: Sage.

Eggert, L.L., E.A. Thompson, J.R. Herting, L.J. Nicholas, and B.G. Dicker
  1994 Preventing adolescent drug abuse and high school dropout through an intensive school-based social network development program. *American Journal of Health Promotion* 8(3):202-215.

Ellickson, P.L., R.M. Bell, and K. McGuigan
  1993 Preventing adolescent drug use: Long-term results of a junior high program. *American Journal of Public Health* 83(6):856-861.

Ellickson, P.L., and R.M. Bell
  1990 Drug prevention in junior high: A multi-site longitudinal test. *Science* 247:1 299-1305.

Ennett, S.T., D.P. Rosenbaum, R.L. Flewelling, G.S. Bieler, C.L. Ringwalt, and S.L. Bailey
  1994a Long-term evaluation of drug abuse resistance education. *Addictive Behaviors* 19(2):113-125.

Ennett, S.T., N.S. Tobler, C.L. Ringwalt, and R.L. Flewelling
  1994b How effective is drug abuse resistance education? A meta-analysis of project D.A.R.E. outcome evaluations. *American Journal of Public Health* 84:1394-1401.

Gilchrist, L.D.
  1991 Defining the intervention and the target population. In C.G. Leukefeld and W.J. Bukoski, eds. *Drug Abuse Prevention Intervention Research: Methodological Issues.* National Institute on Drug Abuse Research Monograph No. 107. DHHS Publication No. (ADM) 91-1761. Washington, DC: U.S. Department of Health and Human Services.

Gilham, S.A., W.L. Lucas, and D. Sivewright
  1997 The impact of drug education and prevention programs: Disparity between impressionistic and empirical assessments. *Evaluation Review* 21(5):589-613.

Gorman, D.M.
  1996 The irrelevance of evidence in the development of school-based drug prevention policy, 1986-1996. *Evaluation Review* 22(1):118-146.

1995   Are school-based resistance skills training programs effective in preventing alcohol misuse? *Journal of Alcohol and Drug Education* 41:74-98.

Gottfredson, D.C.
2001   *Schooling and Delinquency.* New York: Cambridge University Press.
1997   School-based crime prevention. In L.W. Sherman, D.C. Gottfredson, D. MacKenzie, J. Eck, P. Reuter, and S. Bushway, eds., *Preventing Crime: What Works, What Doesn't, What's Promising: A Report to the United States Congress.* Washington, DC: U.S. Department of Justice, Office of Justice Programs.
1986   An empirical test of school-based environmental and individual interventions to reduce the risk of delinquent behavior. *Criminology* 24(4):705-731.

Gottfredson, D.C., G.D. Gottfredson, and S. Skroban
1996   A multimodel school-based prevention demonstration. *Journal of Adolescent Research* 11(1):97-115.

Gottfredson, D.C., D.B. Wilson, and S.S. Najaka
forth-   School-based crime prevention. In D.P. Farrington, L.W. Sherman, and B. Welsh,
coming   eds., *Evidence-Based Crime Prevention.* United Kingdom: Harwood Academic Publishers.

Gottfredson, G.D., D.C. Gottfredson, ? Czeh, D. Cantor, S. Crosse, and I. Hantman
2000   *A National Study of Delinquency Prevention in Schools.* Ellicott City, MD.: Gottfredson Associates, Inc.

Hansen, W.B., and P.M. O'Malley
1996   Drug use. Pp. 161-192 in R.J. DiClemente, W.B. Hansen, and L.E. Ponton, eds., *Handbook of Adolescent Health Risk Behavior.* New York: Plenum Press.

Hansen, W.B.
1992   School-based substance abuse prevention: A review of the state of the art in curriculum: 1980-1990. *Health Education Research* 7:403-430.

Hansen, W.B., and J.W. Graham
1991   Preventing alcohol, marijuana, and cigarette use among adolescents: Peer pressure resistance training versus establishing conservative norms. *Preventive Medicine* 20:414-430.

Hansen, W.B., C.A. Johnson, B.R. Flay, J.W. Graham, and J. Sobel
1988   Affective and social influences approaches to the prevention of multiple substance abuse among seventh grade students: Results from Project SMART. *Preventive Medicine* 17:135-154.

Hawkins, J.D., M.W. Arthur, and R.F. Catalano
1995   Preventing substance abuse. Pp. 343-427 in M. Tonry and D. Farrington, eds., *Building a Safer Society: Strategic Approaches to Crime Prevention.* Chicago: University of Chicago Press.

Hawkins, J.D., R.F. Catalano, D.M. Morrison, J. O'Donnell, R.D. Abbott, and L.E. Day
1992   The Seattle Social Developmental Project: Effects of the first four years on protective factors and problem behaviors. Pp. 141-161 in J. McCord and R.E. Tremblay, eds., *Preventing Antisocial Behavior: Interventions from Birth Through Adolescence.* New York: Guilford Press.

Institute of Medicine
1994   *Reducing Risks for Mental Disorders: Frontiers for Preventive Intervention Research.* Washington, DC: National Academy Press.

Johnson, C.A., M.A. Pentz, M.D. Weber, J.H. Dwyer, N. Baer, D.P. MacKinnon, W.B. Hansen, and B.R. Flay
    1990   Relative effectiveness of comprehensive community programming for drug abuse prevention with high-risk and low-risk adolescents. *Journal of Consulting and Clinical Psychology* 58(4):447-456.

Kandel, D.B.
    1982   Epidemiological and psychosocial perspectives on adolescent drug use. *Journal of the American Academy of Child Psychiatry* 21(4):328-347.
    1975   Stages in adolescent involvement in drug use. *Science* 190:912-914.

Kandel, D., and R. Faust
    1975   Sequences and stages in patterns of adolescent drug use. *Archives of General Psychiatry* 32:923-932.

Kellam, S.G., and J.C. Anthony
    1998   Targeting early antecedents to prevent tobacco smoking: Findings from an epidemiologically based randomized field trial. *American Journal of Public Health* 88: 1490-1495.

Kellam, S.G., G.W. Rebok, N. Ialongo, and L.S. Mayer
    1994   The course and malleability of aggressive behavior from early first grade into middle school: Results of a developmental epidemiologically-based preventive trial. *Journal of Child Psychology and Psychiatry* 35:259-281.

Kumpfer, K.L., V. Molraard, and R. Spoth
    1996   The "Strengthening Families Program" for the prevention of delinquency and drug use. In R. Peters and R. McMahon, eds., *Preventing Childhood Disorders, Substance Abuse, and Delinquency*. Thousand Oaks, CA: Sage Publications.

Lipsey, M.W., and D.B. Wilson
    1993   The efficacy of psychological, educational, and behavioral treatment: Confirmation from meta-analysis. *American Psychologist* 48(2):1181-1209.

Lipsey, M.W.
    1992   Juvenile delinquency treatment: A meta-analytic inquiry into the variability of effects. Pp. 83-127 in T.D. Cook, H. Cooper, D.S. Cordray, H. Hartmann, L.V. Hedges, R.J. Light, T.A. Louis, and F. Mosteller, eds., *Meta-Analysis for Explanation*. New York: Russell Sage Foundation.

Lochman, J.E.
    1992   Cognitive-behavioral intervention with aggressive boys: Three-year follow-up and preventive effects. *Journal of Consulting and Clinical Psychology* 60(3):426-432.

MacCoun, R.
    1998   In what sense (if any) is marijuana a gateway drug? *Drug Policy Analysis Bulletin* 4:5-8.

MacCoun, R., and P. Reuter
    1997   Interpreting Dutch cannabis policy: Reasoning by analogy in the legalization debate. *Science* 278:47-52.

MacKinnon, D.P., C.A. Johnson, M.A. Pentz, J.H. Dwyer, W.B. Hansen, B.R. Flay, and E.Y. Wang
    1991   Mediating mechanisms in a school-based drug prevention program: First-year effects of the Midwestern prevention project. *Health Psychology* 10(3):164-172.

Moffitt, T.E.
    1993   Adolescence-limited and life-course persistent antisocial behavior: A developmental taxonomy. *Psychological Review* 100:674-701.

National Research Council
1993   *Preventing Drug Abuse: What Do We Know?* Committee on Substance Abuse Prevention. D.R. Gerstein and L.W. Green, eds. Washington, DC.: National Academy Press.

Norman, E., and S. Turner
1993   Adolescent substance abuse prevention programs: Theories, models, and research in the encouraging 80's. *Journal of Primary Prevention* 14:3-20.

O'Donnell, J.A., and R.R. Clayton
1979   Determinants of early marijuana use. Pp. 63-110 in G.M. Beschner and A.S. Friedman, eds., *Youth Drug Abuse: Problems, Issues, and Treatment.* Lexington, MA: Lexington Books.

Pentz, M.A., E.A. Trebow, W.B. Hansen, D.P. MacKinnon, J.H. Dwyer, C.A. Johnson, B.R. Flay, S. Daniels, and C. Cormack
1990   Effects of program implementation on adolescent drug use behavior: The Midwestern prevention project (MPP). *Evaluation Review* 14(3):264-289.

Pentz, M.A., J.H. Dwyer, D.P. MacKinnon, B.R. Flay, W.B. Hansen, E.Y.I. Wang, and C.A. Johnson
1989   A multicommunity trial for primary prevention of adolescent drug abuse: Effects on drug use prevalence. *Journal of the American Medical Association* 261(22): 3259-3266.

Perry, C.L., C.L. Williams, S. Veblen-Mortenson, T.L. Toomey, K.A. Komro, P.S. Anstine, P.G. McGovern, J.R. Finnegan, J.L. Forster, A.C. Wagenaar, and M. Wolfson
1996   Project northland: Outcomes of a communitywide alcohol use prevention program during early adolescence. *American Journal of Public Health* 86(7):956-965.

Robins, L.N., and T.R. Przybeck
1985   Age of onset of drug use as a factor in drug and other disorders. In C.L. Jones and R.J. Battjes, eds., *Etiology of Drug Abuse: Implications for Prevention.* National Institute on Drug Abuse Research Monograph No. 56. Washington, DC: U.S. Department of Health and Human Services.

Rosenthal, R., and D.B. Rubin
1982   A simple, general purpose display of magnitude of experimental effect. *Journal of Educational Psychology* 74(2):166-169.

Skroban, S.B., D.C. Gottfredson, and G.D. Gottfredson
1999   A school-based social competency promotion demonstration. *Evaluation Review* 23(1):3-27.

Tobler, N.S., and H.H. Stratton
1997   Effectiveness of school-based drug prevention programs: A meta-analysis of the research. *Journal of Primary Prevention* 18(1):71-128.

Tobler, N.S.
1992   Drug prevention programs can work: Research findings. *Journal of Addictive Diseases* 11(3):1-28.
1986   Meta-analysis of 143 adolescent drug prevention programs: Quantitative outcome results of program participants compared to a control or comparison group. *Journal of Drug Issues* 16(4):537-567.

U.S. Department of Education
1999   *Guidelines and Materials for Submitting Safe, Disciplined, and Drug-Free Schools Programs for Review.* Washington, DC: U.S. Department of Education.

Westat, Inc.
  1999 Evaluation of the National Youth Anti-Drug Media Campaign: Historical Trends in Drug Use and Design of the Phase III Evaluation. Report prepared for the National Institute on Drug Abuse. http:/www.Whitehousedrugpolic.ov/pdf/nida/pdf.

Yamaguchi, K., and D.B. Kandel
  1984 Patterns of drug use from adolescence to young adulthood: III. Predictors of progression. *American Journal of Public Health* 74(7):673-681.

8

Treatment of Drug Users

The past decade has seen a wealth of new research-based resources for drug and alcohol treatment providers. Numerous scholarly reviews of various aspects of the treatment literature were published in the 1990s (e.g., Anglin and Hser, 1990; Carroll, 1996; Higgins, 1999; Meyer, 1992; O'Brien, 1996; Platt, 1995; Van Horn and Frank, 1998). In addition, the decade saw a succession of consensus statements on the state of the science of drug treatment, produced by blue-ribbon panels of experts convened by the Institute of Medicine (1990, 1995, 1996, 1998), the Office of National Drug Control Policy (1996, 1998), the American Psychiatric Association (1995), and the National Institutes of Health (National Consensus Development Panel on Effective Medical Treatment of Opiate Addiction, 1998). The National Institute on Drug Abuse (1999) recently produced an accessible 54-page guide to research-based principles of drug addiction treatment. And the Center for Substance Abuse Treatment now distributes *Treatment Improvement Protocols*, providing best-practice guidelines for drug abuse treatment (see http://www.treatment.org/Externals/tips.html).

We make no attempt in this chapter to review the substantive findings of the growing empirical literature on drug treatment outcomes. Our task is somewhat different. We articulate here recommendations for continuous improvement of the science of drug treatment. In particular, there is a need for better information on the potential benefits and costs of drug treatment as an adjunct to, or an alternative to, traditional criminal justice sanctions and coerced treatment regimes.

Reviewing the evidence, we conclude that the randomized controlled trial has not yet been used to full advantage in treatment evaluation research. Other reviews have stressed the clear value of non-experimental observational studies to evaluate treatment. Without gainsaying the value of these studies, this committee's emphasis is different. Some very informative randomized control trials have been completed, but more trials are needed to fill gaps in evidence that cannot be filled definitively with nonexperimental studies. This chapter reviews the research literature with special emphasis on this important gap.

INTRODUCTION

Information Needed for Policy Guidance

We begin with three observations about the kinds of information that policy makers need.

First, there is no single entity or process called "drug treatment." Rather, there are a plethora of therapies, modalities, and delivery systems: public and private, in-patient and outpatient, voluntary and coerced, talk-based and psychopharmacological, individual and group, cognitive and behavioral, and so on. Clients, family members, and practitioners need guidance as to the most effective strategies for a given client and setting, at an affordable cost. Policy makers and treatment funders need guidance as to the most cost-effective strategies or combinations of strategies.

Second, a very large fraction of the most heavily involved drug users come into contact with the criminal justice system, and many are incarcerated or under the supervision of probation or parole officers. For example, in 1996, 24 percent of jail inmates reported using cocaine or crack in the month before their most recent offense; 9 percent reported heroin or opiate use, and 10 percent reported stimulant use (Sourcebook of Criminal Justice Statistics, 1998, Table 6.33, http://www.albany.edu/sourcebook/1995/ pdf/t633.pdf). Policy makers need better information on the benefits of drug treatment as an adjunct to, or an alternative to, traditional criminal justice sanctions.

Third, somewhere between 3.5 and 6.7 million people in the United States are in need of effective drug treatment (see Woodward et al., 1997; Epstein and Gfroerer, 1995). Only a minority of those who need drug treatment are currently receiving it—somewhere between 20 percent (Lamb et al., 1998) and 48 percent (Woodward et al., 1997). Fewer than 200,000 individuals currently receive methadone maintenance,[1] yet it is believed that there are 600,000 to 1,000,000 heroin addicts in the United

States (Wright et al., 1997). Policy makers urgently need to know the feasibility and possible benefit of expanding the size and coverage of the drug treatment system to reach individuals not currently receiving treatment.

With these points in mind, we offer in this chapter recommendations for continuous improvement of the science of drug treatment, but also for improved estimation of drug treatment effect sizes to support cost-effectiveness and benefit-cost analyses that can inform policy makers. Both goals require increased attention to potential threats to the validity of inferences from treatment outcome studies.

Rationale for Treatment Interventions

When complete and permanent abstinence is used as a criterion of success, between 60 and 90 percent of clients relapse to drug use within 12 months of treatment; relapse rates are similarly high for tobacco and alcohol treatment (Phillips, 1987). Thus, many outside the treatment community have expressed skepticism about the benefits of funding drug treatment.

To some extent, this skepticism is based on unrealistic expectations. In addition to their drug abuse, heavy drug users frequently suffer from various other "co-morbid" conditions—other mental and physical health problems, economic and family problems—that greatly complicate treatment. Moreover, epidemiological, behavioral, genetic, and neuropsychological research suggest that many of those at highest risk for drug dependence and other patterns of antisocial behavior show early and persistent deficits of cognitive functioning and impulse control that may reflect neurological deficits (e.g., Moffitt, 1993). Finally, as we note in Chapter 2, it has become clear that psychoactive drugs have profound and possibly chronic effects on brain functioning, which leaves the person biologically vulnerable to relapse long after the immediate signs of addiction have been alleviated (Leshner, 1997).

Thus, drug dependence is increasingly seen as a chronic relapsing brain disorder (O'Brien and McLellan, 1996; Leshner, 1997), for which

---

[1]According to the Treatment Episodes Data Set (TEDS), heroin and other opiates accounted for 16 percent of the approximately 1.5 million annual treatment admissions in 1997—the largest category of admissions (Substance Abuse and Mental Health Services Administration, 1999, http://www.samhsa.gov/oas/TEDS/TEDSReport97.pdf). Of these, 42 percent (approximately 100,000) were assigned to methadone maintenance treatment. The Uniform Facility Data Set (Substance Abuse and Mental Health Services Administration, 1997, p. 36) indicates that 138,000 of all clients in treatment (15 percent) were receiving either methadone or LAAM. The American Methadone Providers Association cites a higher figure on the number of people currently on methadone maintenance: 170,000.

permanent abstinence may not a realistic goal of any single round of treatment for heavy long-term users. From this perspective, drug dependence requires long-term management comparable to those of other chronic relapsing disorders, such as hypertension, diabetes, and asthma. Drug treatment is a fairly modest intervention relative to the history of conditioned associations, situational stressors, and peer supports that reinforce a pattern of drug use. Thus, without major neuropharmacological breakthroughs, it is unrealistic to expect treatment to provide dramatic short-term results.

At the same time, claims for the effectiveness of drug treatment are sometimes based on misleading or ambiguous results. Many authors have cited observational studies comparing pretreatment and posttreatment drug use consistently find that between a quarter and a half of clients show significant reductions in their frequency of drug use. These reductions are interpreted as evidence for the effectiveness of drug treatment. The U.S. General Accounting Office (1998) has argued persuasively that the heavy reliance on self-report outcome measures in treatment outcome research may inflate estimates of the effectiveness of drug treatment. In this chapter, we argue that these estimates are often vulnerable to various other methodological biases.

A common argument is that even if drug treatment has less than perfect success rates, it is still a good investment. Many authors have cited the CALDATA estimate (Gerstein et al., 1994) that drug treatment has a benefit-cost ratio in the $3 to $7 range, or RAND's analysis (Rydell and Everingham, 1994) suggesting that it is considerably cheaper to reduce cocaine use using drug treatment than to use source-country interventions, interdiction, or drug law enforcement. The committee agrees that drug treatment should not be evaluated according to a standard of perfect abstinence, but rather by its ratio of benefits to costs, and its cost-effectiveness relative to other interventions. Unfortunately, the CALDATA benefit-cost ratio and the RAND cost-effectiveness estimates are based on problematic estimates of treatment effectiveness drawn from uncontrolled observational studies. At present, there is little firm basis for estimating the benefit-cost ratio or relative cost-effectiveness of drug treatment.

We begin by articulating a philosophy of constant treatment improvement through the use of successive randomized controlled clinical trials. We then offer several illustrative examples of compelling experimental research programs. We note the inferential limitations of controlled trials that lack a no-treatment control group. We describe potential opportunities for supplementing existing treatment versus treatment trials with treatment versus no-treatment experiments. We then examine one such domain of opportunity—treatment as an alternative or adjunct to criminal justice sanctions. Finally, we note the potential loss of clinical utility in highly constrained randomized trials and describe analytic methodologies for the more powerful use of nonexperimental observational studies of drug treatment in realistic (and often difficult to study) clinical settings.

CONSTANT IMPROVEMENT OF TREATMENT EFFECTIVENESS VIA A PROGRESSION OF RANDOMIZED TRIALS

In modern medicine, treatments intended to benefit human subjects are evaluated in randomized controlled trials (Peto et al. 1977a, 1977b; Freidman et al., 1985; Meinert, 1986; Piantadosi, 1997; Pocock, 1996). Typically, a new treatment innovation that aims to improve outcomes is compared with an effective, current standard treatment by assigning subjects at random, using random numbers, to either the new treatment or the standard treatment. Random assignment ensures that comparable patients receive competing treatments. The current standard treatment may, in some instances, be no treatment at all, as may occur if no treatment is known to be effective, and if patients are willing to be randomly assigned to no treatment. (The latter condition is often a major obstacle to successful randomization.) A sequence of randomized trials increases the likelihood and rapidity with which improved treatments will replace less effective treatments.

Perhaps the most famous and most instructive example of a randomized trial involves prevention rather than treatment. It is the 1954 trial of the Salk vaccine for poliomyelitis (Meier, 1978). More than 400,000 children were randomly assigned to either the vaccine or a placebo. In the randomized trial, the rate of polio was more than 2.5 times higher in the placebo group than in the vaccine group (Meier, 1978:Table 1), and this finding quickly led to the widespread adoption of the vaccine. Randomized trials quickly create scientific consensus, and often scientific consensus is needed if scientific evidence is to affect public policy.

The Salk trial is instructive not only because of its enormous size and immediate impact on public policy and public health, but also for methodological reasons. Some states refused to participate in the randomized trial. Instead, these states compared vaccinated 2nd graders to 2nd graders who were not vaccinated and to 1st and 3rd graders who were not offered the vaccine. These comparisons were less satisfactory than the comparisons in the randomized trials, for three reasons. First, random assignment of treatments provides a tangible reason to believe the difference in outcomes in vaccinated and placebo groups was caused by the vaccine (Fisher, 1935). Second, in the states that refused to randomize, the vaccine appeared less effective, with unvaccinated second graders having rates of polio only 1.76 times higher than vaccinated 2nd graders, and 1st and 3rd graders having rates of polio only 2.16 higher than vaccinated

2nd graders (Meier, 1978:Table 1). Third, in the states that refused to randomize, the two possible control groups did not agree with each other: the 1st and 3rd graders had a 20 percent higher risk of polio than unvaccinated 2nd graders. In the states that refused to randomize the effects of the vaccine were more ambiguous in principle, smaller in apparent size, and internally inconsistent.

Before randomized trials became the norm in medicine, costly innovations were regularly introduced into standard medical practice, only to discover, years later, that the innovations were ineffective or harmful (Barnes, 1977). The Salk vaccine trial is typical, not atypical: carefully controlled studies often reach different conclusions from poorly controlled studies, and the carefully controlled studies, even if few in number, have the greatest impact on scientific consensus (Chalmers et al., 1972, 1983).

There is considerable debate about the ethics of randomized trials, but certain principles are widely endorsed; see Piantadosi (1997:Chapter 3) for a survey of this literature. Randomized trials are typically ethical when there is no clearly effective treatment, or when there is genuine and realistic uncertainty, reflected in a lack of scientific consensus and limited evidence, as to which of two treatments confers greater benefits with fewer harms. Randomized trials are typically ethical when haphazard circumstances might, in the normal course of events, assign patients to either of two treatments, both of which are realistically hoped to be beneficial. Randomized trials are typically ethical when a new treatment holds realistic promise of substantially improved outcomes but is as yet unproven, and so it cannot be made widely available outside experiments. Medical "practice based on unproven treatments is not ethical" (Piantadosi, 1997:33).

RECENT EXAMPLES OF STRONG TREATMENT EVALUATIONS

There have been a number of randomized controlled trials of treatments for opiate dependence (e.g., Woody et al., 1987) and cocaine dependence (e.g., Silverman et al., 1996; Crits-Christoph et al., 1999). In this section, we briefly summarize five recent treatment evaluation studies that, in the committee's view, exemplify the methodological state of the art in drug treatment research. This selection is intended to be illustrative, not exhaustive. We do not assert that the conclusions of these studies are beyond reproach; indeed, in a later section, we discuss inferential shortcomings of these studies and methodological steps that might address them.

The highlighted studies are randomized trials, and they demonstrate that such experiments are possible in this field. They are noteworthy for the attention the investigators devoted to random treatment assignment, treatment fidelity, measurement reliability and validity, and the use of research design and statistical analysis in an attempt to rule out possible alternative explanations. With respect to measurement, each study utilized continuous measures of success rather than a crude categorical "abstinent or not abstinent" outcome classification. To use abstinence as the only goal would be as erroneous as using complete absence of pain as the only goal of an arthritis treatment. In the real-world situation, the goal should be improvement.

1. **G.E. Woody, A.T. McLellan, L. Luborsky, and C.P. O'Brien (1987) Twelve-month follow-up of psychotherapy for opiate dependence.** *American Journal of Psychiatry* **144:590-596.**[2] A total of 120 male veterans who were addicted to opiates were randomly assigned to one of three treatments while maintained on a level dose of methadone: (a) paraprofessional drug counseling only, (b) counseling plus professional supportive-expressive psychotherapy, or (c) counseling plus professional cognitive behavioral psychotherapy. They were evaluated at a 12-month follow-up using a battery of assessment instruments, including the Addiction Severity Index and several psychiatric diagnostic instruments. Though all three groups showed improvement at follow-up, the two groups receiving professional psychotherapy showed greater improvement by various criteria.

2. **G.E. Woody, A.T. McLellan, L. Luborsky, and C.P. O'Brien (1995) Psychotherapy in community methadone programs: A validation study.** *American Journal of Psychiatry* **152:1302-1308.** This study conceptually replicated the research team's previous counseling only versus counseling plus supportive-expressive comparison in three community-based methadone programs. This study also addressed a confounding factor in the original design—specifically, that the psychotherapy groups received attention from two therapists while the counseling only group received the attention of only one therapist. In this second study, data at a 6-month follow-up showed significantly better improvement in the supportive-expressive psychotherapy condition than in the counseling-only condition.

3. **P. Crits-Christoph, L. Siqueland, J. Blaine, A. Frank et al. (1999) Psychosocial treatments for cocaine dependence.** *Archives of General Psychiatry* **56:493.** A total of 487 cocaine-dependent patients were randomly assigned to one of four treatment conditions. All groups received

---

[2]Charles O'Brien is both a committee member and a coauthor of two of these studies. Note that these particular studies were selected for inclusion in this discussion by consensus of the committee.

group drug counseling. In addition, one arm received individual drug counseling, one received cognitive therapy, and one received supportive expressive therapy. Outcomes were measured using the Addiction Severity Index, a drug use score, and the number of days of cocaine use in the past month. Outcomes were assessed monthly during treatment period, and at 9, 12, 15, and 18 months after randomization. The best results were found for the group drug counseling + individual drug counseling group. The study and its presentation are noteworthy for the attention paid to protocol violations, with follow-up of violators, analyses of missing data and treatment integrity, assessment of possible unique therapist effects, and so on.

4. **S.T. Higgins et al. (1995) Outpatient behavioral treatment for cocaine dependence: One-year outcome.** *Experimental and Clinical Psychopharmacology* **3:205-212.** This study analyzes 12-month follow-up data from two randomized controlled trials, involving a total of 78 community residents who met DSM-III-R criteria for cocaine dependence. Both trials compared traditional drug abuse counseling to a community reinforcement approach involving spouses, friends, or relatives and employment and other counseling services, and an incentive voucher system in which participants earned retail vouchers of modest monetary value for each negative urinalysis over a 24-week period. The first trial compared traditional counseling and the community reinforcement approach + vouchers; the second compared the community reinforcement approach alone to community reinforcement approach + vouchers. Outcomes included the Addiction Severity Index and urine test results. All conditions showed significant improvement over the course of the trials; community reinforcement approach + vouchers was superior to traditional counseling on various outcome measures, but the community reinforcement approach alone and community reinforcement approach + vouchers did not significantly differ from each other. The authors acknowledge that the small sample size provided adequate statistical power for within-treatment effects but inadequate power for post-treatment follow-up results.

5. **K. Silverman, S.T. Higgins, R.K. Brooner, I.D. Montoya, E.J. Cone, C.R. Schuster, and K.L. Preston (1996) Sustained cocaine abstinence in methadone maintenance patients through voucher-based reinforcement therapy.** *Archives of General Psychiatry* **53:409-415.** This study usefully complements the Higgins et al. study cited above, extending that research in two ways. First, this study examined the effects of a similar voucher-based treatment for cocaine use, but among heroin abusers in a methadone maintenance program rather than community volunteers. Second, this study compared the contingent voucher program to a control condition in which participants were yoked to members of the treatment group; these latter participants thus received vouchers that were not con-

tingent on their own drug use patterns. Those in the contingent voucher condition showed greater reductions in cocaine use than those in the noncontingent vouchers; importantly, the noncontingent vouchers significantly reduced attrition from the study. Thus, it appears that vouchers reduce dropout rates, but that contingent vouchers promote reductions in use that are not solely attributable to remaining in treatment. This study shares a weakness of the Higgins et al. study—a small sample size that limits the statistical power of the analyses.

It is useful to contrast these studies with some of the major American treatment outcome research initiatives of the past 30 years:

- The Drug Abuse Reporting Program (DARP—see Simpson and Sells, 1982, 1990),
- The Treatment Outcome Prospective Study (TOPS—see Hubbard et al., 1989), and
- The Drug Abuse Treatment Outcome Study (DATOS—see Simpson and Curry, 1997).

DARP, TOPS, and DATOS were three large-scale, multisite, multi-investigator initiatives involving tens of thousands of clients, hundreds of clinicians, and a broad range of treatment modalities and therapeutic techniques, client characteristics, and drug abuse patterns. These were ambitious efforts that addressed multiple goals. One goal was descriptive—to attempt to describe the universe of treatment clients, settings, and modalities in the United States. Another goal was inferential—to assess the effects of drug treatment on various client outcomes. Arguably, programs like the Treatment Episodes Data Set (TEDS) and the National Drug and Alcohol Treatment Unit Survey (NDATUS) are better suited for the routine collection of aggregate descriptive statistics about trends in national delivery of drug treatment services. For the second, inferential goal, in the committee's judgment, future research funds would be better spent on a large number of randomized clinical trials, with cross-site extensions and replications. Because they lacked randomized assignment to condition, DARP, TOPS, and DATOS could not provide rigorous evidence on the relative effectiveness or efficacy of particular drug-by-treatment combinations, or for estimating the absolute effect size, cost-effectiveness, or benefit-cost ratio of treatment. **The committee recommends that priorities for the funding of treatment evaluation research should be changed; large-scale, national treatment inventory studies should not be conducted at the expense of greater funding for randomized controlled clinical trials.**

ELIMINATING INFERENTIAL ARTIFACTS AND ESTIMATING ABSOLUTE EFFECT SIZES

Considering the enormous challenges of conducting research in clinical settings, the randomized trials highlighted in the previous section are quite rigorous. They are a powerful source of information for improving drug treatment. But as designed they cannot provide robust estimates of the absolute magnitude and range of treatment effects for various types of clients (especially voluntary versus coerced clients), which are needed for use in cost-effectiveness comparisons, benefit-cost analyses, and simulation modeling of the potential benefits of scaling up or expanding the current treatment system.

The inferential benefits of randomization to experimental condition are well known; see Cook and Campbell (1979) for a comprehensive listing of threats to validity that are reduced or eliminated by randomization. (Note that design limitations create vulnerability to biased inference; they do not guarantee that biased inferences will occur. Whether any bias actually resulted is an empirical question.)

Here, we emphasize the various processes that can differentially bias selection into, or attrition out of, the treatment and control conditions of the study. When other factors are confounded with the treatment variations under study—e.g., addiction severity, motivation to change, life stresses and resources—it is not possible to directly estimate treatment effects by simply examining the difference between mean outcomes in each condition.

Many of these selection biases result from the causal forces that bring clients into treatment. The net directional effect of such biasing processes is rarely clear. Consider a nonexperimental study in which treatment clients are compared with a demographically matched sample of drug users not in treatment. On one hand, one might expect that those who seek and stick with treatment might be more motivated to give up their drug use (see DiClemente, 1999). On the other hand, many if not most clients are in drug treatment not because they voluntarily chose to be, but because they were either formally or informally coerced by a court, law enforcement agency, employer, spouse, or family member. For example, in the 1997 TEDS study, 34.9 percent of all admissions were referred by the criminal justice system (Substance Abuse and Mental Health Services Administration, 1999:Table 3.4). (We briefly examine the literature on coerced treatment below.)

Moreover, at least in the case of tobacco smoking, there is some evidence that smoking cessation clinics disproportionately see the hardest cases—those who were unable to quit smoking on their own (Schachter, 1982). Some selection biases involve client or setting characteristics that are confounded with assignment to or completion of treatment. Others involve dynamic processes of change that are unrelated to treatment, such as external influences that affect drug use (e.g., changes in prices, changes in employment or marital status; see Campbell and Stanley's (1963) discussion of "history" artifacts), autonomous internal processes of change in the individual (what Campbell and Stanley call "maturation" effects), or the statistical effects of random variation in client outcomes over time (regression to the mean).

Regression to the mean is a purely statistical phenomenon that can mask a causal relationship between variables. When the association between an independent variable and a dependent variable (or between measures of a variable at two different points in time) is imperfect, objects or people with extreme scores on the first variable will often be less extreme on the second variable, and vice versa. Hence, predictions from one variable to the other are "regressive." Treatment studies are particularly vulnerable to regression artifacts if clients are most likely to seek treatment when their drug use or related problems become extreme. As Higgins (1999:516) argues: "caution is imperative in interpreting pre- to post-treatment changes. Patients likely enter treatment when drug use and related adverse consequences have reached an uncomfortable intensity (for them and others), and thus the intake interview is likely to represent an extreme estimate. If so, subsequent assessments on average will be less extreme even in the absence of treatment due to the ubiquitous phenomenon of regression to the mean."

Thus, even if treatment had no beneficial effect on clients, one might expect to see the same qualitative decline in drug use reported in most nonexperimental pretreatment/posttreatment comparisons—a chance fluctuation in drug use and problem frequency, followed by a noncausal return to average levels. Note that regression to the mean provides one plausible interpretation—but certainly not the only interpretation—of the widespread belief that alcoholics and other addicts need to hit rock bottom before they will be ready to change their behavior (but see McLellan et al., 1992, for evidence that a small sample of patients on a waiting list reported worsening rather than improving symptoms over time).

Because these various biases can occur in either an upward or downward direction, their net effect on treatment outcome estimates is unclear. Note that the treatment estimate from a single study may reflect biases in both directions, and the relative effect of each bias may differ *across* studies. Randomized clinical trials of the type illustrated in the previous section go a long way toward eliminating concerns about the biasing effects of regression to the mean, biased selection to treatment, and biased attrition. Indeed, such trials greatly reduce biases in estimates of the advantages of one treatment method over another one.

But these trials cannot rule out the possibility of constant biases—
selection biases that affect each condition under study. Constant bias does
not threaten inferences about relative effectiveness of one treatment over
another across randomized conditions. But it does threaten inferences
about the *absolute* size of any treatment effect, relative to zero, making
cost-effectiveness or benefit-cost estimation hazardous. Moreover, constant biases make it difficult to accurately forecast the likely effects of
expanding treatment coverage to include those not currently receiving
services. To some extent, these inferential threats can be addressed
through sophisticated statistical methods (discussed in a later section).
But ultimately, the most persuasive strategy for addressing these concerns is the use of randomized trials with a no-treatment control group.
According to Higgins (1999:517):

> However, even in [recent] controlled trials, the absence of "placebo" or
> no-treatment control groups precludes precise estimates of what pro-
> portion of pre- to post-treatment changes are attributable to treatment.
> The cocaine-dependence treatment field would be well served by care-
> ful consideration of what additional experimental or quasi-experimental
> control conditions might be ethically and practically possible in future
> efficacy and effectiveness studies to help strengthen the validity of caus-
> al inferences and permit more precise estimates of the contribution of
> treatment to any changes observed.

The almost complete lack of no-treatment control groups in drug treatment research is striking. While there are numerous studies of placebo
versus a new medication plus minimal counseling, studies of patients
randomized to nothing at all are lacking. The drug treatment community
has not ignored this issue (e.g., Anglin and Hser, 1990) but has generally
responded with three plausible objections: clients are unlikely to agree to
possible assignment to a no-treatment control group, no-treatment control groups are unethical, and there are alternative methods for achieving
the same inferences.

Will clients agree to randomization to a no-treatment control group? The
committee agrees that this is an important practical concern, but in the
absence of such trials for drug treatment, it is not possible to estimate the
magnitude of the problem. Presumably, this is a greater concern for studies of clients voluntarily seeking treatment than for studies of legally
coerced clients (discussed below).

Are no-treatment control groups unethical? In brief, many clinicians argue that it is unethical to withhold treatment from those in need of it. Of
course, one might counter that this begs the question of whether in fact
drug treatment is beneficial. There is a competing ethical concern—the
missed opportunities involved in failing to discover a more effective treatment because of undue faith in current standards of best practice.

The prevailing standard for judging the ethics of withholding treatment is called the equipose principle (Freedman, 1987, 1990). According to Freedman's original (1987:144) statement of the equipose principle, it is ethically acceptable to withhold treatment if "there is no consensus within the expert clinical community about the comparative merits of the alternatives to be tested" (1987:144). Although it is clear that the drug treatment community lacks consensus on which therapeutic techniques and modalities are most appropriate for cocaine or marijuana dependence, it seems unlikely that treatment experts would question whether treatment is preferable to no treatment. The politics of funding—especially the appearance of a zero-sum budget battle among the various demand- and supply-side programs—creates pressures against actively questioning the effectiveness of one's own interventions. And the history of science shows clearly that expert scientific communities often reach consensus in favor of invalid conclusions (see MacCoun, 1998 for a discussion of the effects of homogeneous bias in research communities).

There are numerous cautionary tales of premature medical consensus reached in the absence of clinical trials. Cohen (1998) cites three examples: the administration of oxygen to premature newborns, the Vineburg procedure for coronary insufficiency (sham cardiac surgery), and superficial temporal to middle cerebral artery anastomosis (the surgical connecting of 2 arteries). Similarly, recent large-scale clinical trials have cast doubt on conventional assumptions about the links between estrogen and female heart attack risk, and between dietary fiber and colon cancer.

These objections are largely addressed by Freedman's subsequent refinement, the clinical equipose principle (1990), which contends that placebo controls are justified when (a) there is no standard treatment, or (b) the standard treatment is no better than a placebo, or (c) the standard treatment is a placebo, or (d) new evidence challenges the net effectiveness of the standard treatment, or (e) an effective treatment is too scarce or too expensive to provide to every patient in need. Regardless of one's views about whether the first four conditions are met for cocaine treatment, it seems clear that the last condition is applicable.

Are no-treatment control groups unnecessary? A second objection to no-treatment control groups is the contention that other sources of evidence render them unnecessary. One might look toward observational data from so-called natural experiments involving the sudden cessation of treatment due to exogenous factors. For example, Anglin and Hser (1990) review evidence on the effects of two methadone clinic closings—a Bakersfield methadone maintenance clinic that was closed by local officials for budgetary and political reasons, and the discharge of clients from the California civil commitment program due to "relatively random legal errors." They argue that in both cases, clients who abruptly ceased treatment fared more poorly than those who received a full course of treatment. Such situations are not conclusive, but they do seem more informative than passive correlational studies that lack such exogenous shocks. Situations in which data collection is ongoing when such shocks occur are rare; we know of no examples involving cocaine treatment or modalities for heroin other than methadone maintenance.

Another line of relevant evidence comes from statistical comparisons of voluntary versus coerced treatment clients. The current consensus is that it does not matter—coerced clients fare no worse (and no better) than voluntary clients (see reviews by Anglin and Hser, 1990; Farabee et al., 1998; Lawental et al., 1996; Silverstein, 1997). Gostin (1991) argues that "the intuition that compulsory treatment will fail because drug dependent people must be self-motivated to benefit . . . simply is not borne out by the data." For example, Silverstein (1997) found no significance outcome differences for court-mandated versus other clients at a semirural drug abuse treatment clinic. Lawental et al. (1996) found comparable improvements for both self-referred and employer-coerced private treatment clients.

These studies help to address concerns about regression and selection artifacts. However, these studies use quasi-experimental, "nonequivalent control group" designs, comparing coerced and noncoerced clients at the same site. Although most of these studies attempted statistical matching, there is no way of knowing whether the coerced and noncoerced groups are otherwise comparable; for all we know, the coerced clients could be individuals who would have benefited even more from treatment in the absence of coercion.

Finally, one could argue for the effectiveness of drug treatment by analogy to other behavior change interventions that have been more rigorously assessed. Other forms of psychotherapy have fared well under randomized, no-treatment control experiments. As discussed in Chapter 7, Lipsey and Wilson (1993) provided a comprehensive review of these literatures, and an enormously ambitious "meta-meta-analysis" of 302 published meta-analyses of treatment interventions. These meta-analyses did not include cocaine or opiate treatment, but they did include arguably similar interventions such as cognitive therapy for depression, tobacco cessation, and weight control. Across the 302 meta-analyses, they reported an average effect size of behavior change interventions of about half a standard deviation; 90 percent were greater than or equal to 0.10, and 85 percent were greater than or equal to 0.20. For smoking cessation, the effect sizes ranged from 0.21 to 0.62 in magnitude; all were reliably above zero. But none of these interventions is perfectly analogous to treatment for psychoactive drug dependence. There are undoubtedly differences across domains in client characteristics, etiology, mechanisms of pathology, legal status, and social stigma that preclude confident generalization to the drug domain.

Moreover, these studies only evaluated the self-selected group of patients who presented for treatment rather than the universe of sufferers in the community. For drug addiction, we would like to know the effects of treatment on all of those with the disorder, including those not presenting for treatment. Because the number of current treatment slots can only accommodate a fraction of those with the disorder, a critical policy question is whether the creation of additional slots is cost-effective. Finding the answer would require a control in the community randomized to no treatment whatsoever.

The meta-analytic data do suggest that nonrandomized trials don't invariably inflate effect sizes. Lipsey and Wilson (1993) found no reliable differences in the effect sizes between experiments (mean = 0.46) and quasi-experiments (mean = 0.41). Shadish and his colleagues (Heinsman and Shadish, 1996; Shadish and Ragsdale, 1996), in more rigorous meta-analyses of data from a sample of the domains covered by Lipsey and Wilson, found that effect sizes tended to be significantly larger in randomized experiments, even after controlling for various confounding differences between experimental and quasi-experimental studies.

In this regard, a study by McKay et al. (1998) is relevant. These authors compared patients either randomly assigned to cocaine treatment and those who "self-selected" into the same treatment settings, finding "greater problem severity at intake among randomized patients coupled with greater improvements by 3-month follow-up relative to the nonrandomized patients" (McKay, 1998:697). The investigators argue that "randomized studies of treatment for cocaine abuse may produce somewhat larger estimates of improvement than what is observed in more typical treatment situations" (see Campbell and Boruch, 1975, for a relevant discussion).

Thus, it is our contention that randomized experiments with no-treatment controls provide more accurate estimates of the efficacy of drug treatment, not necessarily smaller estimates. We do not contend that such no-treatment controls are essential for testing possible improvements in treatment methods; randomized "Treatment A versus Treatment B" trials are a powerful mechanism for that goal. Rather, in the committee's view, no-treatment control groups are necessary to provide the kind of information needed to support policy analyses of the effectiveness and cost-effectiveness of providing drug treatment and of expanding treatment access.

Bias due to incomplete compliance with randomized assignment. In some settings, the experimenter can encourage compliance with the treatment protocol, but some experimental subjects may not comply. Realistically, some proportion of clients in a no-treatment control group may seek out treatment outside the clinical trial; similarly, some fraction of treatment group may fail to attend treatment sessions. Statistically, this noncompliance adds "noise" to the design, and possibly a bias to the estimated treatment effect size. Random assignment of treatments is nonetheless of great value, even though compliance may be imperfect. Recent developments in analytical methodology simultaneously use both the random assignment of intended treatment and the treatment actually received. See Angrist et al. (1996), Balke and Pearl (1997), Manski (1990, 1995), Robins (1989), Rosenbaum (1996, 1999a), Sheiner and Rubin (1995), and Sommer and Zeger (1991) for various approaches.

OPPORTUNITIES FOR RANDOMIZATION WITH NO-TREATMENT CONTROL CONDITIONS

When a pharmaceutical manufacturer makes claims about the efficacy or effectiveness of a new drug product, the U.S. Food and Drug Administration advisory committees looks to the evidence from randomized controlled trials in which eligible participants have been assigned at random to different conditions (e.g., new drug regimen versus usual and customary regimen, new drug regimen versus placebo regimen). In this context, over the long run, randomization is supposed to bring into balance all of the influences on the effects of interest, but for the randomly assigned intervention status. In consequence, randomized designs can provide an especially illuminating body of evidence about the efficacy and effectiveness of newly proposed interventions. It is when the new treatment regiment is compared with a no-treatment control condition that we can gain the most complete evidence of intervention impact. Of course, "no treatment" is rarely an absolute. In reality, new medications are compared against placebo treatment while both placebo and new medication groups receive standard evaluation and non-specific care.

Despite the broadly acknowledged superiority of evidence from randomized designs with no-treatment controls when the task is to assess treatment effects, some observers feel strongly that the benefits of randomization are overstated in studies about the effects of promising therapeutic or preventive interventions (see the next section). These observers argue that randomized trials create impediments to generalizable results of immediate public health significance. In addition, when individuals are seeking treatment for their drug problems, there might be ethical or logistical barriers to the no-treatment control condition that is required to gauge an intervention's effects completely.

It is beyond the scope of this report to settle this issue. However, we do consider some possible situations in which it would be ethical and just to make a random assignment of different interventions, including the no-treatment control condition, in order to gain a more complete, accurate, and precise estimate of the intervention's impact on treatment or prevention of drug problems.

Within the domain of drug intervention research, there may be some missed opportunities for randomized clinical trials, with no-treatment control conditions, that could otherwise be used to assess the efficacy and effectiveness of new treatments or preventive interventions. In this section, we describe several opportunities for research of this type.

In general, the committee has looked into possibilities for placebo-controlled randomized trials that are not being exploited as completely as they otherwise might be. In this context, the first missed opportunity involves the workers (generally unskilled) who now are required by public or private employers to undergo randomly administered drug tests. Many of these workers undergo the tests during an initial review period during which a resume or application has been filed and thereafter periodically during follow-up assessments. Most often, when the workers show a test result that indicates recent drug use, they have not been hired or retained in the job for which they have applied, or they are suspended from their jobs, often without employee assistance or interventions to address underlying drug dependence or other condition that fostered the positive drug test result.

Situations of this type, especially those of preemployment drug testing, represent some missed opportunities for randomized controlled trials to compare drug dependence intervention strategies with no-treatment alternatives. The no-treatment alternative meets most ethical standards because current practice is to provide no treatment to these individuals, but simply to advise them that they have lost the privilege to be hired into the job for which they have applied. In addition, it seems that few of these individuals go out and seek treatment once they have received a positive test result. In situations of this type, an investigator could recruit the prospective employees who have just failed their drug tests, and use randomized designs to test new intervention strategies against the no-treatment alternative. Such patients would have to be evaluated prior to randomization in order to segregate them according to occasional use, abuse, and dependence, since previous studies have found that most of those detected in preemployment drug testing do not meet criteria for dependence.

A second set of opportunities involves health maintenance organizations and managed care practices with health benefits that do not include drug treatment. In these situations, subscribers in need of drug treatment can be offered the chance to enroll in a randomized trial, with a result that some large randomly chosen fraction of those needing treatment receive care subsidized by the health organization, whereas the remainder receive usual and customary care within that practice (namely, no treatment). Here, again, ethical concerns about the research are addressed because at least some individuals will receive subsidized treatment, in a situation in which no one is receiving subsidized treatment.

Another set of opportunities for randomized trials with no-treatment intervention conditions is created by long-standing school policies to expel or suspend students who are found to be drug users. Here again, it is typical to separate the drug-using youth from the rest of the student body, at least for a time. However, it is not standard to provide treatment interventions for the drug dependence that may be prompting continued drug use despite the socially maladaptive consequences of drug use. As such, expelled or suspended students who volunteer to participate in a randomized trial could be randomly assigned to a treatment versus no-treatment condition, allowing estimation of treatment effects against a background of the usual and customary condition of no treatment.

Finally, despite recently advanced federal Office for Protection from Research Risks (OPRR) restrictions on research with prisoners and probationers, the situations of drug-dependent individuals in prison or on probation can sometimes offer an opportunity for randomized trials with no treatment conditions. These situations arise when the prison or probation program is offering no treatment as the usual and customary condition for drug-taking individuals in their custody. In this context, random assignment to a drug treatment condition represents a potentially beneficial departure from the usual and customary condition of no treatment. As such, an array of randomization designs become possible (see further discussion below).

In summary, it often is difficult to argue in favor of randomization designs with no-treatment control conditions when the study participants are being drawn from individuals who are seeking treatment at drug clinics. We have outlined some of the missed opportunities for randomization designs with no-treatment conditions that are created because, at present, many drug users are identified without any formal treatment response.

The committee recommends greater scientific attention to now-missed opportunities to conduct randomized trials of drug treatments with no-treatment control conditions. Certainly, there will be obstacles not mentioned in this chapter. And there are other ethical and legal considerations that must be addressed in the design of such trials, such as protecting the confidentiality of the treatment records and insulating research records from legal or private uses. Nonetheless, the value of evidence based on randomized designs with no-treatment control conditions is sufficiently great to warrant considerable expenditure of effort to overcome these obstacles.

OPPORTUNITIES FOR RANDOM ASSIGNMENT IN THE
CRIMINAL JUSTICE SYSTEM

Apprehension of drug users provides an opportunity to reduce drug use (and future offending) by using the threat of sanctions as a form of leverage to induce arrested or convicted users to participate successfully in treatment programs. In 1973, the National Commission on Marihuana and Drug Abuse concluded that the primary utility of criminal sanctions for consumption-related drug offenses lies in providing therapeutic leverage. During the past three decades, programs linking treatment and the criminal process have been developed and implemented with varying degrees of intensity across the country.

Not all treatment in the criminal justice system is coercive: treatment can be offered on a completely voluntary basis, without any connection to the offender's charges or sentence. Many prison-based programs are of this type. (Conversely, it should be noted, treatment is sometimes compelled without any connection to the criminal justice system, as under a civil commitment statute.) In fact, however, most treatment provided to drug offenders is leveraged, in the sense that it is linked to case outcome or sentence severity.

In thinking about linkages between drug treatment and criminal sanctions, it is important to distinguish between questions of effectiveness and fairness. Supporters of using the criminal justice system for therapeutic leverage typically view treatment participation offered to offenders as an ameliorative device—an opportunity for mitigating the sentence that they would otherwise receive (i.e., probation with treatment is offered in lieu of incarceration, using the threat of incarceration for noncompliance). Others worry that programs of mandated treatment will actually have the effect of increasing the severity of punishment compared with what the offenders would otherwise have received (Covington, Appendix E). As an example, offenders who otherwise would have been sentenced to traditional probation could be subject to treatment conditions that create a risk of imprisonment (for noncompliance) that otherwise would not have existed. Or an offender whose case might otherwise have been dismissed could be sentenced to conditional probation. These are classic "net-widening" concerns, because they widen the reach and deepen the intensity of punishment. This issue should be kept in mind in considering research on coerced treatment.

Legal strategies to coerce drug users into treatment have been used both at the "front end" in diversionary programs and at the "back end" among parole and probation populations. However, experimental designs are rare, and it is difficult to disentangle the effects of treatment from the effects of coercion. Also, many studies have been concerned primarily with treatment retention or length of stay, rather than treatment outcome or posttreatment involvement in drug use or criminal behavior.

Prison-Based Treatment

A number of studies of prison-based programs seem to demonstrate positive postrelease outcomes, including reductions in drug use and crime along with improvements in employment, when inmates who have gone through prison treatment programs are compared with those who have not (Wexler, 1994; Wexler et al., 1999; Inciardi et al., 1997). However, research conducted to date has not yet convincingly demonstrated the effectiveness of prison treatment programs. Even in studies that find a significant relationship between completion of the treatment program and post-release outcomes, the overall positive effect is attenuated by inconsistent findings (e.g., outcomes were not related to dose of treatment, and the no-treatment control group delayed rearrest longer than the treatment groups). Moreover, positive treatment outcomes may be attributable to selection bias (e.g., the high level of commitment of offenders who complete the program rather than the capacity of the program to change their behavior). Also, since most research on effectiveness of prison drug treatment was done on older heroin addicts, the results may not be applicable to younger heroin addicts or to crack cocaine users.

Research on treatment of prisoners incarcerated in the late 1980s and the 1990s is confounded by the influx of tens of thousands of inmates whose drug use has been much less severe than that of earlier generations of prisoners. Positive posttreatment outcomes for these offenders may have less to do with the treatment than with their pretreatment conditions.

Treatment of Probationers

Most people convicted of drug offenses are not in prison. Thus, another key policy question is the effectiveness of using conditional criminal justice dispositions (e.g., pretrial diversion, probation, parole) to mandate drug treatment in the community. At least 60 percent of adults under criminal justice supervision are on probation. Yet the existing literature on probationary drug treatment fails to compare the effectiveness of linking probation to treatment conditions with other community-based criminal justice dispositions or with no intervention at all. The need for such comparisons—between those on probation and a no-supervision control group—becomes more relevant as the net is widened to include drug users who would not have been arrested or put on probation in previous years. The possibility exists that any seeming improvements in the success rates of drug-using probationers over the years could be wrongly attributed to probation itself rather than to the inclusion of offenders with less severe drug and crime problems.

Treatment Alternatives for Street Crime

During the 1970s, the White House Special Action Office for Drug Abuse Prevention and the National Institute on Drug Abuse joined with the Department of Justice to link treatment with criminal justice through a variety of initiatives, the most important of which was Treatment Alternatives to Street Crime (TASC). TASC represents a structured postarrest diversion process under which successful compliance with treatment conditions results in dismissal of the charges without conviction. The effectiveness of TASC was examined using a subsample of subjects drawn from the TOPS study. Hubbard et al. (1988) found that TASC clients stayed in treatment longer and reported less posttreatment drug use than clients who had entered treatment without criminal justice pressure. However, pretreatment differences between the samples and differences in the services received make these findings difficult to interpret. Anglin et al. (1999) used random assignment at two of five study sites. One site showed no beneficial effects of TASC; the other showed reductions in some drug use measures but not on criminal recidivism.

Drug Courts

The substantial increase in drug arrests and of drug-involved offenders in the late 1980s and 1990s stimulated innovative efforts to link the criminal justice system with community treatment programs. Building on the TASC model, hundreds of jurisdictions have established drug courts (usually specialized dockets rather than separate courts) to identify drug users in the criminal justice system, refer them to treatment programs and monitor their progress (Belenko, 1998, U.S. General Accounting Office, 1997). Since all of the drug court initiatives are relatively new, outcome data are limited, and their efficacy remains open to question.

The renascent interest in drug treatment/criminal justice linkages heightens the need for rigorous studies of the therapeutic utility (and cost-effectiveness) of these coercive legal strategies. To what extent, and under what circumstances, does coerced treatment through the criminal justice system achieve beneficial effects, compared with voluntary treatment, through nontherapeutic criminal justice intervention or with no intervention at all? Although more than 20 evaluations have been conducted, various factors make it difficult to draw definitive conclusions

(Belenko, 1998; U.S. General Accounting Office, 1997). First, there are enormous variations in eligibility requirements and program characteristics. Second, the U.S. General Accounting Office found that a majority of programs tended to assess recidivism and not relapse or, less frequently, relapse but not recidivism. Third, most of the existing studies are uncontrolled comparisons involving before-after or nonrandomized comparison groups, with the kind of threats to internal validity discussed earlier in this chapter. While many of these studies report reductions in drug use or criminal recidivism, it is notable that neither result clearly emerged in a rigorous study using random assignment to either drug courts or standard probation (Deschenes et al., 1995).

A Proposed Example

There is a clear need for more rigorous experiments on the effects of drug treatment as an alternative or adjunct to criminal justice sanctions. In the committee's judgment, such experiments are logistically feasible and can be designed to be ethically defensible. Here we offer an example of a possible experiment by way of illustration.

A population of prisoners incarcerated for drug-related crimes could be randomized prior to release from prison. They would be segregated first by drug use category (heroin addicts, cocaine addicts, cocaine/alcohol, cocaine/heroin, etc.). The specific treatments for each category would differ. Subject characteristics to be assessed prior to release would include Addiction Severity Index scores, educational level, prior employment history, marital status, and other risk factors for drug relapse.

Within each category, one group of subjects would be randomized to follow-up as usual by the parole system with no contact with either treatment or research. Evaluation data at each visit would be obtained by a parole officer. Prisoners would be randomly assigned to one of three groups: (1) standard parole; (2) Treatment A; (3) Treatment B. A patient assigned to Treatment A could refuse treatment and receive standard parole instead, but this patient would remain part of the Treatment A group. Similar procedures would be followed for Treatment B. This is Marvin Zelen's (1979) randomized consent design.

It is likely that some subjects assigned to standard parole will enter treatment on their own, and some other assigned to groups A or B will refuse treatment; this fact would have to be considered in the data analysis.

Similarly, the predictor variables obtained prior to randomization would have to be assessed, to determine the comparability of the four groups and for use as covariates in analysis of outcome data.

An advantage of this design is that no one would get less than the standard probation counseling, but only randomly selected subjects would receive treatment. A necessary limitation is that a self-selected group who had been randomized to treatment would refuse to participate, but since they are in the probation system, they could be followed anyway.

The criminal justice component of this design raises complex analytic, legal, and ethical issues above and beyond those in an ordinary treatment experiment. Based on the view that drug dependence is a chronic relapsing disorder, many experts believe that abstinence is inappropriate as a sole or primary evaluative criterion. Yet positive drug tests are typically used as a trigger for sanctioning in mandated treatment regimes. Thus a key concern, from both an ethical and a scientific standpoint—is whether either of the treatment regimes is more restrictive than the baseline parole regime. For example, would the parolees in all groups be subject to monitoring (e.g., drug testing) on the same terms? Would they be subject to revocation on the same terms? Variations on the proposed design might include intensity of monitoring as a treatment variation, or the use of graduated sanctions less severe than a return to prison (see Kleiman, 1997). Another question is whether program effects should be reported while the coercive leverage of parole supervision is still operative, or only after parole supervision has ended. This is both a methodological concern and a question of policy: To what extent is coercive leverage necessary (or even sufficient) for any observed treatment effect? These questions reflect the tensions inherent in a program that combines therapeutic and social control objectives. The relative restrictiveness and punitiveness of traditional vs. treatment-oriented sanctioning options is an important issue that merits careful attention.

The committee recommends that treatment researchers take greater advantage of possible opportunities for randomization to no-treatment control groups. For example, we strongly encourage studies of incarcerated and postincarcerated prisoners as outlined in this report. The committee urges federal and state agencies and private institutions to minimize organizational obstacles to such studies, within ethical and legal bounds.

TOWARD STRONGER OBSERVATIONAL STUDIES

The committee strongly recommends that treatments intended to benefit people be evaluated in carefully conducted randomized controlled experiments. At times, however, such experiments are not possible. For example, it is not possible to experiment with treatments believed to be harmful. For instance, it is important to know the effects on children of cocaine use by their mothers while pregnant, but this cannot be studied in an experiment. In observational or nonexperimental studies of treatment effects, the absence of random assignment of treatments may seriously bias comparisons of treated and control subjects. Many authors in the drug treatment literature recognize these concerns (e.g., Anglin and Hser, 1989), but in the committee's judgment, many observers have too often relied on large observational studies instead of randomized trials to draw conclusions about the effectiveness of treatment.

A detailed discussion of methods for observational studies is not possible in this report. Good discussions of these methods may be found in Cook and Campbell (1979), Manski (1995), and Rosenbaum (1995). Although there is a great deal of agreement about methods for observational studies, there is some disagreement as well. Some of the disagreements are captured by the exchange between Rosenbaum (1999b), Manski (1999), Robins (1999), and Shadish and Cook (1999).

One common argument for nonrandomized studies is that the requirements of a randomized trial make it too artificial to describe treatment as it actually occurs in the field—the "effectiveness versus efficacy" debate. Meta-analyses by Shadish and colleagues (1997, 2000) do find that nonrandomized evaluations of psychotherapy are more clinically representative, but these meta-analyses do not indicate that clinical representativeness is associated with psychotherapy effect sizes.

It may be true that carefully controlled trials are less broadly representative than large-scale observational studies, but even the latter cannot guarantee generalizability across settings and over time. Medical researchers and social scientists alike are increasingly reluctant to rely on single studies, of any sort. There is a growing understanding of the need to look for converging patterns across experiments. In this light, the committee applauds the recent National Drug Addiction Treatment Clinical Trials Network of the National Institute on Drug Abuse that is now conducting large-scale randomized, controlled trials in average treatment programs in communities across the country. These studies should provide a more accurate picture of treatment effectiveness for the nation as a whole. But even in the absence of such an initiative, meta-analytic techniques make it possible to aggregate and compare data across studies (Cook et al., 1992). From a meta-analytic standpoint, heterogeneity across settings, populations, and experimental variations is advantageous for determining whether conclusions are robust, and whether there are important boundary conditions on a phenomenon. The identification of apparent cross-study moderating variables is often a valuable stimulus for theory development, suggesting important variables to test in subsequent experiments.

The committee recommends broader use of meta-analytic techniques for cumulating and comparing findings across treatment outcome studies.

REFERENCES

American Psychiatric Association
  1995   *Practice Guidelines for Treatment of Patients with Substance Use Disorders: Alcohol, Cocaine, Opioids.* Washington, DC: American Psychiatric Association.

Anglin, M.D., and Y.I. Hser
  1990   Treatment of drug abuse. Pp. 393-460 in M. Tonry and J.Q. Wilson, eds., *Drugs and Crime (Crime and Justice: A Review of Research)*, Vol. 13. Chicago: University of Chicago Press.

Anglin, M.D., D. Longshore, and S. Turner
  1999   Treatment alternatives to street crime: An evaluation of five programs. *Criminal Justice & Behavior* 26:168-195.

Angrist, J.D., G. Imbens, and D.B. Rubin
  1996   Identification of causal effects using instrumental variables (with discussion). *Journal of the American Statistical Association* 91:444-469.

Balke, A., and J. Pearl
  1997   Bounds on treatment effects from studies with imperfect compliance. *Journal of the American Statistical Association* 92:1171-1176.

Barnes, B.A.
  1977   Discarded operations: Surgical innovation by trial and error. Pp. 109-123 in *Costs, Risks and Benefits of Surgery*, J.P. Bunker, B.A. Barnes, and F. Mosteller, eds., New York: Oxford University Press.

Belenko, S.
  1998   *Research on Drug Courts: A Critical Review.* New York: National Center on Addiction and Substance Abuse at Columbia University.

Campbell, D.T., and R.F. Boruch
  1975   Making the case for randomized assignment to treatments by considering the alternatives: Six ways in which quasi-experimental evaluations in compensatory education tend to underestimate effects. Pp. 195-296 in C. Bennett and A. Lumsdaine, eds., *Evaluation and Experiment.* NewYork: Academic Press.

Campbell, D.T., and J.C. Stanley
  1963   *Experimental and Quasi-Experimental Designs for Research.* Chicago: Rand McNally.

Carroll, K.M.
  1996   Relapse prevention as a psychosocial treatment: A review of controlled clinical trials. *Experimental and Clinical Psychopharmacology* 4:46-54.

Chalmers, T.C., P. Celano, H.S. Sacks, and H. Smith, Jr.
  1983   Bias in treatment assignment in controlled clinical trials. *New England Journal of Medicine* 309:1358-1361.

Chalmers, T.C., J.B. Block, and S. Lee
  1972   Controlled studies in clinical cancer research. *New England Journal of Medicine* 287:75.

Cohen, P.J.
  1998   The placebo is not dead: Three historical vignettes. *IRB: A Review of Human Subjects Research* 20:6-8.

Cook, T., and D. Campbell
1979   *Quasi-Experimentation: Design and Analysis Issues for Field Settings.* Boston: Houghton Mifflin.
Cook, T.D., H. Cooper, D.S. Cordray, H. Hartmann, et al., eds.
1992   *Meta-Analysis for Explanation : A Casebook.* New York: Russell Sage Foundation.
Crits-Christoph, Paul, L. Siqueland, J. Blaine, A. Frank, et. al.
1999   Psychosocial treatments for cocaine dependence. *Archives of General Psychiatry* 56:493.
Deschenes, E.P., S. Turner, and P.W. Greenwood
1995   Drug court or probation? An experimental evaluation of Maricopa County's Drug Court. *Justice System Journal* 18(1).
DiClemente, C.C.
1999   Motivation for change: Implications for substance abuse treatment. *Psychological Science* 10:209-213.
Epstein, J.F., and J.C. Gfroerer
1995   A Method for Estimating Substance Abuse Treatment Need from a National Household Survey. Paper presented at the 37th International Congress on Alcohol and Drug Dependence, August 20-25, 1995, University of California, San Diego.
Farabee, D.M., Prendergast, and M.D. Anglin
1998   The effectiveness of coerced treatment for drug-abusing offenders. *Federal Probation* 62(n1):3-10.
Fisher, R.A.
1935   *Design of Experiments.* Edinburgh: Oliver and Boyd.
Freedman, B.
1990   Placebo-controlled trials and the logic of clinical purpose. *IRB: Review of Human Subjects Research* 12:1-6.
1987   Equipose and the ethics of clinical research. *New England Journal of Medicine* 317:141-145.
Freidman, L.M., C.D. Furberg, and D.L. DeMets
1985   *Fundamentals of Clinical Trials.* New York: Springer-Verlag.
Gerstein, D.R., R.A. Johnson, H. Harwood, D. Fountain, N. Suter, and K. Malloy
1994   Evaluating Recovery Services: The California Drug and Alcohol Treatment Assessment (CALDATA). California Department of Alcohol and Drug Programs.
Gostin, L.O.
1991   Compulsory treatment for drug-dependent persons: Justifications for a public health approach to drug dependency. *Milbank Quarterly* 69:561-593.
Gottfredson, D.C., and L. Exum
2000   The Baltimore City Drug Treatment Court: First Evaluation Report. Unpublished manuscript, University of Maryland.
Harwood, Henrick J., R.L. Hubbard, J.J. Collins, and V.J. Rachal
1988   *The Costs of Crime and the Benefits of Drug Abuse Treatment: A Cost-Benefit Analysis Using TOPS Data.* National Institute on Drug Abuse: Research Monograph Series, 86: 209-235.
Heinsman, D.T., and W.R. Shadish
1996   Assignment methods in experimentation: When do nonrandomized experiments approximate answers from randomized experiments? *Psychological Methods* 1:154-169.

Higgins, S.T.
  1999 We've come a long way: Comments on cocaine treatment outcome research. *Archives of General Psychiatry* 56:516-518.
Higgins, S.T., et al.
  1995 Outpatient behavioral treatment for cocaine dependence: One-year outcome. *Experimental and Clinical Psychopharmacology* 3:205-212.
Hubbard, R.L., M.E. Marsden, J.V. Rachal, H.J. Harwood, E.R. Cavanagh, and H.M. Ginzburg
  1989 *Drug Abuse Treatment: A National Study of Effectiveness.* Chapel Hill: University of North Carolina Press.
Hubbard, R.L., J.J. Collins, J.V. Rachal, and E.R. Cavanaugh
  1988 *The Criminal Justice Client in Drug Abuse Treatment.* National Institute on Drug Abuse: Research Monograph Series 86: 57-80.
Inciardi, J.A., S.S. Martin, C.A. Butzin, R.M. Hooper, et. al.
  1997 An effective model of prison-based treatment for drug-involved offenders. *Journal of Drug Issues* 27(n2):261-278.
Institute of Medicine
  1990 *Treating Drug Problems*, Vol. 1. D.R. Gerstein and H.J. Harwood, eds. Washington, DC: National Academy Press.
  1995 *Federal Regulation of Methadone Treatment.* Committee on Federal Regulation of Methadone Treatment. R.A. Rettig and A. Yarmolinsky, eds. Washington, DC: National Academy Press.
  1996 *Pathways of Addiction: Opportunities in Drug Abuse Research.* Washington DC: National Academy Press.
  1998 *Bridging the Gap Between Practice and Research.* S. Lamb, M.R. Greenlick, and D. McCarty, eds. Washington, DC: National Academy Press.
Kleiman, M.A.R.
  1997 Coerced abstinence: A neopaternalistic drug policy initiative. Pp. 182-219 in L.M. Mead, ed., *The New Paternalism: Supervisory Approaches to Poverty.* Washington, DC: Brookings Institution.
Lawental, E., A.T. McLellan, G.R. Grissom, P. Brill, et al.
  1996 Coerced treatment for substance abuse problems detected through workplace urine surveillance: Is it effective? *Journal of Substance Abuse* 8:115-128.
Leshner, A.I.
  1997 Addiction is a brain disease, and it matters. *Science* 287:45-47.
Lipsey, M.W., and D.B. Wilson
  1993 The efficacy of psychological, educational, and behavioral treatment: Confirmation from meta-analysis. *American Psychologist* 48:1181-1209.
MacCoun, R.
  1998 Biases in the interpretation and use of research results. *Annual Review of Psychology* 49:259-287.
Manski, C.
  2000a Comment. *Statistical Science* 14:279-281.
Manski, C.
  2000b Identification problems and decisions under ambiguity: Empirical analysis of treatment response and normative analysis of treatment choice. *Journal of Econometrics* 95(2):415-442.
  1995 *Identification Problems in the Social Sciences.* Cambridge, MA: Harvard University Press.

1990   Nonparametric bounds on treatment effects. *American Economic Review* 319-323.

McKay, J.R., A.I. Alterman, A.T. McLellan, C.R. Boardman, et al.
1998   Random versus nonrandom assignment in the evaluation of treatment for co-caine abusers. *Journal of Consulting and Clinical Psychology* 66:697-701.

McLellan, A.T., C.P. O'Brien, D. Metzger, A.I. Alterman, et al.
1992   How effective is substance abuse treatment—Compared to what? In C.P. O'Brien and J.H. Jaffe, eds., *Addictive States*. New York: Raven Press.

Meier, P.
1978   The biggest public health experiment ever: The 1954 field trial of the Salk polio-myelitis vaccine. Pp. 3-15 in *Statistics: A Guide to the Unknown*, J.M. Tanur et al., eds. San Francisco: Holden Day.

Meinert, C.L.
1986   *Clinical Trials: Design, Conduct, and Analysis*. New York: Oxford University Press.

Meyer, R.E.
1992   New pharmacotherapies for cocaine dependence . . . revisited. *Archives of General Psychiatry* 49:900-904.

Moffitt, T.E.
1993   Adolescence-limited and life-course-persistent antisocial behavior: A develop-mental taxonomy. *Psychological Review* 100:674-701.

National Commission on Marihuana and Drug Abuse
1972   *Marihuana: A Signal of Misunderstanding: The Official Report of the National Commis-sion on Marijuana and Drug Abuse*. New York: Signet.

National Consensus Development Panel on Effective Medical Treatment of Opiate Addiction
1998   Effective medical treatment of opiate addiction. *Journal of the American Medical Association* 280:1936-1943.

National Institute on Drug Abuse
1999   *Principles of Drug Addiction Treatment: A Research Based Guide*. Bethesda, MD: Na-tional Institutes of Health.

O'Brien, C.P.
1996   Recent developments in the pharmacotherapy of substance abuse. *Journal of Con-sulting and Clinical Psychology* 64:677-686.

O'Brien, C.P., and A.T. McLellan
1996   Myths about the treatment of addiction. *Lancet* 347:237-240.

Office of National Drug Control Policy
1998   *Breaking the Cycle with Science Based Policy: Conference Proceedings, Consensus Meet-ing on Drug Treatment in the Criminal Justice System*. Washington, DC: U.S. Gov-ernment Printing Office.
1996   Treatment protocol effectiveness study: A white paper of the Office of National Drug Control Policy. *Journal of Substance Abuse Treatment* 13:295-320.

Peto, R., M.C. Pike, P. Armitage, N.E. Breslow, D.R. Cox, S.V. Howard, N. Mantel, K. McPherson, J. Peto, and G. Smith
1977a Design and analysis of randomized clinical trials requiring prolonged observa-tion of each patient. I. Introduction and design. *British Journal of Cancer* 34:585-612.
1977b Design and analysis of randomized clinical trials requiring prolonged observa-tion of each patient. II. Analysis and examples. *British Journal of Cancer* 35:1-39.

Philips, E.L.
   1987   The ubiquitous decay curve: Service delivery similarities in psychotherapy, medi-
          cine, and addiction. *Professional Psychology: Research and Practice* 18:650-652.
Piantadosi, S.
   1997   *Clinical Trials: A Methodologic Perspective.* New York: John Wiley.
Platt, J.
   1995   Vocational rehabilitation of drug abusers. *Psychological Bulletin* 117:416-433.
Pocock, S. J.
   1996   *Clinical Trials: A Practical Approach.* New York: John Wiley.
Robins, J.M.
   1989   The analysis of randomized and nonrandomized AIDS treatment trials. Pp. 113-
          159 in *Health Service Research Methodology: A Focus on AIDS.* Washington, DC: U.S.
          Public Health Service.
Robins, J.
   1999   Comment. *Statistical Science* 14:281-293.
Rosenbaum, P.R.
   1999a Using combined quantile averages in matched observational studies. *Applied Sta-
          tistics* 48:63-78.
   1999b Choice as an alternative to control in observational studies (with Discussion).
          Statistical Science 14:259-304.
   1996   Comment on "Identification of causal effects using instrumental variables" by
          Angrist, Imbens, and Rubin. *Journal of the American Statistical Association* 91:465-
          468.
   1995   *Observational Studies.* New York: Springer Verlag.
Rydell, P., and S. Everingham
   1994   *The Costs of Cocaine Control.* Santa Monica, CA: RAND.
Schachter, S.
   1982   Recidivism and self-cure of smoking and obesity. *American Psychologist* 37:436-
          444.
Shadish, W.R., A.M. Navarro, G.E. Matt, and G. Phillips
   2000   The effects of psychological therapies under clinically representative conditions:
          A meta-analysis. *Psychological Bulletin* 126:512-529.
Shadish, W.R., and T.D. Cook
   1999   Design rules: More steps toward a complete theory of quasi-experimentation.
          Statistical Science 14:294-300.
Shadish, W., G.E. Matt, A.M. Navarro, G. Siegle, et al.
   1997   Evidence that therapy works in clinically representative conditions. *Journal of
          Consulting and Clinical Psychology* 65:355-365.
Shadish, W.R., and K. Ragsdale
   1996   Random versus nonrandom assignment in controlled experiments: Do you get
          the same answer? *Journal of Consulting and Clinical Psychology* 64:1290-1305.
Sheiner, L.B., and D.B. Rubin
   1995   Intention-to-treat analysis and the goals of clinical trials. *Clinical Pharmacology and
          Therapeutics* 57:6-15.
Silverman, K., S.T. Higgins, R.K. Brooner, I.D. Montoya, E.J. Cone, C.R. Schuster, and K.L.
Preston
   1996   Sustained cocaine abstinence in methadone maintenance patients through
          voucher-based reinforcement therapy. *Archives of General Psychiatry* 53:409-415.

Silverstein, M.E.
    1997   The Relationship Among Stages of Change, Attitude Towards Treatment, and Treatment Investment in Court-Mandated Outpatient Substance Abusers. University of Connecticut. UMI, Order Number: AAM9707847, Dissertation Abstracts International: Section B: The Sciences and Engineering. 1997 Apr. 57 (10-B): p. 6594.

Simpson, D.D., and S.J. Curry
    1997   Special issue: Drug Abuse Treatment Outcome Study (DATOS). *Psychology of Addictive Behaviors* 11(entire issue).

Simpson, D.D., and S.B. Sells, eds.
    1990   *Opioid addiction and treatment: A 12-year follow-up.* Malabar, FL: Robert E. Krieger.

Simpson, D.D., and S.B. Sells
    1982   Effectiveness of treatment for drug abuse: An overview of the DARP research program. *Advances in Alcohol and Substance Abuse* 2:7-29.

Sommer, A., and S.L. Zeger
    1991   On estimating efficacy from clinical trials. *Statistics in Medicine* 10:45-52.

Substance Abuse and Mental Health Services Administration
    1999   *Treatment Episode Data Set (TEDS) 1992-1997: National Admissions to Substance Abuse Treatment Services.* Washington, DC: U.S. Department of Health and Human Services.

U.S. General Accounting Office
    1998   *Drug Abuse: Research Shows Treatment Is Effective, But Benefits May Be Overstated.* GAO/HEHS-98-72. Washington, DC: U.S. General Accounting Office.
    1997   *Drug Courts: An Overview of Growth, Characteristics, and Results.* GAO/GGD-97-106. Washington, DC: U.S. General Accounting Office.

Van Horn, D.H.A., and A.F. Frank
    1998   Psychotherapy for cocaine addiction. *Psychology of Addictive Behaviors* 12:47-61.

Wexler, H.K.
    1994   Progress in prison substance abuse treatment: A five year report. *Journal of Drug Issues* 24:349-360.

Wexler, Harry K., G. De Leon, T. George, D. Kressel, et al.
    1999   The Amity prison TC evaluation: Reincarceration outcomes. *Criminal Justice & Behavior* 26(n2):147-167.

Woody, G.E., et al.
    1995   Psychotherapy in community methadone programs: A validation study. *American Journal of Psychiatry* 152:1302-1308.
    1987   Twelve-month follow-up of psychotherapy for opiate dependence. *American Journal of Psychiatry* 144: 590-596.

Woodward, A., J. Epstein, J. Gfroerer, D. Melnick, R. Thoreson, and D. Wilson
    1997   The drug abuse treatment gap: Recent estimates. *Health Care Financing Review* 18:5-17.

Wright, D., J. Gfroerer, and J. Epstein
    1997   Ratio estimation of hardcore drug use. *Journal of Official Statistics* 13:401-416.

Zelen, M.
    1979   A new design for randomized clinical trials. *New England Journal of Medicine* 300:1242-1245.

9

Final Thoughts: Unfinished Business

T
he legal foundation for the nation's drug control policy was put in place nearly a century ago. The Harrison Narcotics Act of 1914 aimed to suppress use of narcotics (defined to include opiates and cocaine) outside approved medical and scientific channels. Over the course of the 20th century, federal prohibition was extended to marijuana (1937) and to a variety of stimulant, depressant, and hallucinogenic drugs (1965, 1968). Meanwhile, parallel prohibitions were adopted by all the state legislatures. Penalties for violating drug laws were significantly increased during the 1950s and then again in the 1980s.

Until the 1970s, the primary instrument of national drug policy was enforcement of state and federal drug laws, and the federal role was relatively minor. Total federal expenditures in fiscal year 1969 were $66.4 million, allocated primarily to federal law enforcement and to the operation of the two federal hospitals for the treatment of addicted prisoners. During the Nixon administration, however, national drug policy was fundamentally reshaped in response to an epidemic of heroin use in several major cities and an explosion of marijuana and other illegal drug use among college and high school students. Major new initiatives were undertaken to diversify the policy portfolio and to establish and coordinate a strong federal presence.

The Controlled Substances Act, enacted in 1970, established an integrated regulatory framework to replace the patchwork of federal statutes that had accumulated over the century. Two years later, Congress established a drug policy office in the White House, the Special Action Office for Drug Abuse Prevention (SAODAP), to spearhead the new demand-reduction initiatives. It also enacted the legal framework for a nationwide program of voluntary, confidential community-based treatment. Over the next several years, federal funds were appropriated for prevention and treatment programs administered through state and local agencies. (After a number of reorganizations, this money is now administered through the Substance Abuse and Mental Health Services Administration). Federal expenditures on all aspects of drug control rose more than 1,000 percent between 1969 and 1973, and two-thirds of this increase was allocated to treatment and prevention (National Commission on Marihuana and Drug Abuse, 1973:280).

In 1972, Congress also established the interagency Strategy Council on Drug Abuse, cochaired by the chief federal drug law enforcement official and the head of the Special Action Office for Drug Abuse Prevention, and directed it to prepare a comprehensive, coordinated strategy for all federal drug abuse and drug trafficking prevention activities. The structure used to coordinate the growing federal effort has changed repeatedly over the past three decades, but national drug control strategy documents have been issued by the White House every year since 1973.

SCIENCE AND DRUG POLICY: RECENT PROGRESS

The first National Drug Control Strategy was sent to the President in March 1973, as was the report of the National Commission on Marihuana and Drug Abuse, *Drug Use in America: Problem in Perspective*. Both of these documents emphasized the urgent need to establish data systems for monitoring drug use and assessing the impact of drug control policies, and the importance of mounting an aggressive program of research to increase understanding of the causes and consequences of drug use and to inform policy. The challenge was set forth in the 1973 National Drug Control Strategy in the following words (Strategy Council on Drug Abuse, 1973:150):

> Much is still unknown. In every area from treatment to prevention, from control of illicit traffic to the long-term consequences of drug use, there are gaps in our knowledge. A rational strategy should include a systematic effort to acquire the needed information. . . . Current priorities include efforts to measure the size and rate of change in the drug-using population, the adverse consequences of use of various drugs, the natural history of drug use and addiction, and new approaches to treatment and early intervention, including the advantages and disadvantages of educational efforts and mass media campaigns.
>
> Research efforts are also needed to improve our capacity to control availability. These take the form of better methods to determine the origins of

samples of illicit drugs, to gather and analyze intelligence on illicit traffic, and to analyze the relationships between enforcement activity, judicial actions and the price and availability of illicit drugs.

Until these gaps are filled, our policies and strategies must be considered tentative and subject to revision.

The national commission summarized its urgent call for research in the following words (National Commission on Marihuana and Drug Abuse, 1973:367-370):

Throughout this report, we have pointed out numerous gaps in knowledge about the causes, consequences and control of drug-using behavior. . . . While research cannot answer all of the questions, much more information is urgently needed, not only to develop more rational policy for the future, but also to implement effectively the policies we now have . . . .

Even a partial listing of the unanswered questions is startling. We do not know: why people choose to use drugs in spite of criminal laws against use and obvious dangers of dependence and disruption; why some individuals who use drugs with high dependence liability become dependent and others do not; why some populations seem much more susceptible to use or to dependence than others; what social forces precipitate the periodic "epidemics" of drug use and what causes the lulls between these increases; how drug law enforcement operates and what effect it has on use and distribution; how, in terms of effectiveness, the various treatment modalities compare and why each seems to work well for some users, and not at all for others; what is the impact of information on the decisions to use or not use drugs. We do not even know the incidence or prevalence of various patterns of drug use . . . even though this knowledge is essential to sensible planning.

Important steps were taken over the next several years to generate the data and research needed to fill the large gaps in knowledge identified by these two major reports in 1973. These initiatives created an infrastructure for monitoring trends in drug use, enhancing understanding of the determinants and consequences of drug use, and evaluating new prevention and treatment programs. All of the information systems described in Chapter 3 used to monitor trends in drug use were created during the 1970s.

Most significantly, a separate research agency, the National Institute on Drug Abuse (NIDA), was created in the National Institutes of Health to establish and maintain an infrastructure of both extramural and intramural research. Over the past 25 years, NIDA funding, which supports 85 percent of the world's research on drug abuse and addiction (Institute of Medicine, 1996), has underwritten substantial advances in the understanding of neurobiological and behavioral aspects of drug use and has stimulated the development and testing of new modalities of treatment and their introduction into clinical practice (Institute of Medicine, 1996, 1998). Other funding streams in SAMHSA and other federal agencies have been developed for evaluating prevention and treatment programs. In recent years, new collaborative research efforts relating to offender populations have been undertaken by the National Institute of Justice and the Office of Juvenile Justice and Delinquency Prevention and the National Institute on Drug Abuse and the Substance Abuse and Mental Health Service Administration. Although, as this report details, the existing data systems need to be strengthened, and knowledge regarding the effectiveness of treatment and prevention activities still has significant gaps, an impressive body of research has emerged in these areas over the past several decades.

UNFINISHED BUSINESS

The nation has failed to make an equivalent investment in data and research on the effects of enforcement. Federal and state drug enforcement expenditures amounted to $19.5 billion in 1991 (the last year for which aggregate figures including state and local enforcement are available). Expenditures for federal enforcement (including interdiction and international enforcement) increased more than tenfold between 1981 and 1999. In 1998, 1.6 million people were arrested for drug offenses, three times as many as in 1980, and 289,000 new drug offenders were incarcerated in state prisons, more than ten times as many as in 1980 (23,900). The benefits and costs of these policies have been the subject of heated and continuing debate for decades. Yet policy makers are in no better position to evaluate the effectiveness of these activities than they were in 1973, when the National Commission on Marihuana and Drug Abuse and the first National Drug Control Strategy called attention to the "startling" gaps in knowledge about the effects of enforcement.

A small number of economists and policy analysts, supported by ONDCP and other agencies, have doggedly attempted to fill the void by developing analytic models and theories of illegal markets and by making efforts to predict the effects of different types of enforcement interventions. These efforts have helped to characterize the complex interactions of producers, dealers, and users and the subtle processes through which enforcement and other drug control policies might affect prices and consumption. However, as the committee noted in its Phase I report (National Research Council, 1999), even the most creative and sophisticated analytic model cannot inform policy making in the absence of sound data. The weaker the data, the less confidence one can have in the inferences generated by the model about policy effectiveness. As this report demonstrates, no significant progress can be made in assessing the effectiveness of enforcement policy (or its cost-effectiveness in relation to other policy instruments) in the absence of better data on drug prices and consumption.

The need for better data is highlighted in the National Drug Control Strategy for 2000, the latest in the series issued annually by federal drug policy officials since the 1973 federal strategy quoted above. In 1998, ONDCP inaugurated its Performance Measures of Effectiveness System to assess the impact of drug control activities on drug use, drug availability, and the consequences of drug use. The system includes 60 quantitative "performance targets," 12 of which (called "impact targets") relate to "ultimate" outcome measures of drug availability, use, and consequences. ONDCP deserves a great deal of credit for taking the first steps to assess the impact of current policies, including enforcement, on availability, use, and consequences. However, the project is still in an embryonic stage.

In its National Drug Control Strategy for 2000, ONDCP reported to Congress on its progress in developing the Performance Measures of Effectiveness System, pointing out that data do not now exist in relation to 20 of the 60 quantitative performance targets identified in the report. With regard to the impact targets, measures are available for four "use" targets—national prevalence, youth prevalence, workplace prevalence and initial age of use—but not for number of chronic users. Some data are available to develop rough aggregate estimates for the two "consequences" targets—drug-related crime and violence and health and social costs. However, as ONDCP acknowledges, data are presently lacking for the availability targets. A method being developed by ONDCP for estimating the flow of cocaine and heroin into the country is still in an early state of development, and the agency concedes that it does not yet have measures of domestic cultivation and production, trafficker success rate, or an aggregated measure of "availability." It should be emphasized that, even if data were available to develop valid outcome measures in all these domains, ONDCP still has no way of assessing the impact of enforcement interventions (or other interventions for that matter) on these impact targets. It is revealing in this connection that none of the many other outcome measures relates to the price of illegal drugs.

THE WAY FORWARD

Data

The central problem, in a nutshell, is that the nation lacks the data needed to inform policy. Nearly all of the uncertainties regarding the effectiveness of drug control policies stem from the limitations of existing data on illegal drugs. Throughout this report, the committee has repeatedly concluded that essential policy-relevant data are missing or inadequate. In some areas, the data are nonexistent—for example, on total consumption or numbers of heavy users—or are nearly useless for policy purposes—for example, on price. In other areas, the existing data are not generalizable to other populations of interest—for example, the Arrestee Drug Abuse Monitoring Program—or are only modestly helpful in informing policy (cross-sectional prevalence estimates).

The top priorities, in the committee's judgment, are to rectify the two major deficiencies in existing data systems: the absence of adequate consumption data and reliable price data. These data are absolutely critical for evaluating the effectiveness of supply-reduction activities. Specifically:

• Better measures are needed of the distribution of consumption, encompassing frequency, amount, and intensity of use (and escalation or de-escalation of use over time). Only if these measures are available will it be possible to estimate total amount consumed at the population level. The simple prevalence data now available may be sufficient for assessing the impact of policy interventions on initiation and termination of use, but they are not sufficient for assessing the responsiveness of users to enforcement, treatment, and other interventions, the relationship between intensity of use and the consequences of use, or the responsiveness of demand to changes in price.

• Reliable data are needed on retail prices in order to assess the impact of supply-reduction activities on the operation of drug markets. Moreover, price data are essential to evaluate the sensitivity of the demand for drugs to the available supply.

Research Infrastructure

The federal investment in research on the causes of drug abuse and the effects of prevention and treatment amounted to approximately $668 million in 1999, representing about $1 for every $7.33 spent on prevention and treatment. In contrast, the investment in research on illegal drug markets and the effects of enforcement was approximately $113 million, representing about $1 for every $107 spent on enforcement. In other words, although the federal government spends more than twice as much on enforcement as it does on prevention and treatment—and the nation spends more than three times as much, taking into account state and local expenditures—it spends only one-fourteenth as much on research designed to assess the effects of enforcement as it does on treatment and prevention research (controlling for size of investment).

A suitable institutional structure needs to be put in place to plan and implement a major new research effort on the effects of drug control laws and their enforcement (including both interdiction and domestic enforcement), on drug use and its consequences, and on the costs and unintended consequences of enforcement activities. At the present time, only a small number of researchers are working in this important area, and only a few research organizations have made a commitment to it. Established career paths for researchers are unavailable. In order to nurture and harness the intellectual resources that will be needed to mount a successful research effort, it will be necessary to recruit talented social scientists and to establish the necessary incentives, including reliable and stable sources of funding, access to data, and scientific independence.

Funding and Sponsorship

The committee recommends that the National Institute of Justice, the National Science Foundation, and the Bureau of Justice Statistics should be assigned joint responsibility and given the necessary funding to build the scientific infrastructure for research on illegal drug markets and the effects of drug control interventions. The committee recommends lead roles for both NIJ and NSF in order to ensure that investigators are drawn to this barren field from all the social sciences, including criminology, economics, operations research, and public policy analysis. The research envisioned by the committee would draw these diverse disciplines into a collaborative effort to investigate all aspects of the market for illegal drugs, the strategies and activities of enforcement agencies, and the adaptations of offenders to these activities. To carry out this challenging program successfully, it will be necessary to draw on NIJ's contacts with criminal justice organizations and research constituencies, access to offender populations, and experience in collaborative work with the National Institute on Drug Abuse. At the same time, however, NSF provides the expertise and research constituencies in economics lacking at NIJ and can also provide a check against the possibility of insularity and political interference that can arise when any operational agency is given complete control over research bearing on the effectiveness of its operations (e.g., enforcement).

In implementing this new research initiative, NIJ and NSF should take advantage of the full array of mechanisms at their disposal, including investigator-initiated proposals, centers, and research consortia. It is essential that both agencies establish strong collaborative partnerships for this program with the National Institute on Drug Abuse, in order to capture the relevant expertise and to connect investigations with its intramural program in drug epidemiology.

Access to Data

The agencies charged with responsibility for establishing the data systems recommended in Chapter 3—the National Institute of Justice, the Centers for Disease Control and Prevention, and the Bureau of Labor Statistics—and for building the research infrastructure outlined above— the National Institute of Justice and the National Science Foundation— will be faced with a common challenge: removing the legal impediments to collecting and using data on illicit activities. Talented and ambitious researchers will not be willing to enlist in the new research initiative envisioned by the committee unless they are assured reasonable access to pertinent data. The statutory authority appears to be in place for the Department of Justice to grant the necessary immunity for collecting data. It should develop and promulgate clear and specific guidelines or instructions regarding the conditions for securing immunity for data collection under existing law and, if the existing authority is insufficient, should seek the necessary authority from Congress.

The paucity of data also bears on funding strategies for research. The funding agencies should be prepared to fund grants for a sufficient period to enable researchers to carry out primary data acquisition, notably surveys. This is essential in an area such as research on illegal drug markets, in which high-quality datasets are not already available. And we point out again that, when large and influential datasets such as Monitoring the Future have been developed with public funds, there is no excuse for allowing data-collecting organizations to curtail access to these data by other investigators. All funding agencies should ensure public access to nonidentified data. The responsible government agencies should take maximum advantage of developing communications technologies to maximize researcher access to available data.

Scientific Independence

In its final report in 1973, the National Commission on Marihuana and Drug Abuse applauded a 400 percent increase in the federal investment in research from 1969-1973, urged intensification of the investment in research, and emphasized the importance of free scientific inquiry in what had been a highly politicized domain (NCMA, 1973:368-370):

> This commitment to research . . . reflects a significant change in official policy. For many years, research into the effects of prohibited drugs and into the behavior of users was viewed as an attempt to question and subvert government policy. In addition, the aura of criminality surrounding drug-using behavior and the overly rigid protocol requirements often made this area unattractive to researchers. When . . . re-

searchers became [interested], they were often hindered by the law enforcement community. . . .

At last, this has begun to change. With the significant increase in drug use during the 1960's the government recognized the need for information which could come only from expanded research efforts. Prohibited drugs have been made available for legitimate research; confidentiality has been extended to research subjects; and now, public resources are being devoted to this important area. . . .

In urging [increased] research, the Commission cautions against research that points in only one direction. In the past, government agencies have sometimes used drug research to support policy rather than shape it. Studies that produced the answers they wanted were promoted and publicized; projects which appeared to document the "wrong" results were quietly buried and not released. [New research] should specifically include studies that examine without bias alternate hypotheses and approaches.

It is no less important in the year 2001 to emphasize the need for scientific independence in research on illegal drugs than it was in 1973.

THE CHALLENGE AHEAD

Three decades ago, Congress decided to diversify the federal response to drug problems, investing in surveillance, biobehavioral and etiological research, and education and treatment. As a result, the nation has the data systems and research infrastructure needed to assess the effectiveness of preventive and therapeutic interventions. Although further improvements are needed in these areas, as explained in this report, the data and research capacity are in place. In stark contrast, neither the data systems nor the research infrastructure needed to assess the effectiveness of drug control enforcement policies now exists. It is time for the federal government to remedy this serious deficiency. It is unconscionable for this country to continue to carry out a public policy of this magnitude and cost without any way of knowing whether and to what extent it is having the desired effect.

REFERENCES

Institute of Medicine
  1996 *Pathways of Addiction.* Washington, DC: National Academy Press.
  1998 *Bridging the Gap Between Practice and Research; Forging Partnerships with Community-Based Drug and Alcohol Treatment.* Washington, DC: National Academy Press.
National Commission on Marihuana and Drug Abuse
  1973 Final Report. *Drug Use in America: Problem in Perspective.* Washington, DC: U.S. Government Printing Office.

National Research Council
1999   *Assessment of Two Cost-Effectiveness Studies on Cocaine Control Policy.* C.F. Manski, J.V. Pepper, and Y.F. Thomas, eds. Washington D.C.: National Academy Press.
Office of National Drug Control Policy.
2000   *National Drug Control Strategy: Budget Summary February 2000.* Washington, DC: U.S. Government Printing Office.
1999   Drug Data Summary. Rockville: *ONDCP Drug Policy Information Clearinghouse.* Available on line at http://www.whitehousedrugpolicy.gov
Strategy Council on Drug Abuse
1973   *Federal Strategy for Drug Abuse and Drug Traffic Prevention.* Washington, DC: U.S. Government Printing Office.

Appendixes

Appendix A

Characteristics of STRIDE Cocaine Data

This appendix provides supplementary information on characteristics of the System to Retrieve Information from Drug Evidence (STRIDE) cocaine data. STRIDE contains data on acquisitions of illegal drugs by the Drug Enforcement Administration (DEA) and the Metropolitan Police of the District of Columbia (MPDC). This discussion, which complements the description of the STRIDE data in Chapter 3, is oriented toward assessing the usefulness of STRIDE for constructing price indices for cocaine. The statistics reported in this appendix are obtained from the version of the STRIDE data that was supplied to the committee by the DEA. The DEA revises the contents of STRIDE from time to time, so the results reported here may not coincide precisely with results that are obtained from other versions of the data. The committee is confident, however, that the main qualitative conclusions reached using its version of STRIDE would also be reached using other versions.

SPARSENESS OF THE DATA

There are over 160 DEA field offices in the United States. Each is responsible for a geographical area surrounding the city in which it is located. In any given year, STRIDE contains few or no records of purchases by most field offices. This is especially true for small purchases. In 1996, for example, 35 percent of the field offices recorded no purchases of cocaine base. Another 34 percent recorded only 1-9 purchases. Moreover, 55 percent of the offices recorded no purchases of cocaine base in quantities of 5 gm or less, and 32 percent recorded only 1-9 such purchases. Only 6 percent of field offices recorded more than 50 purchases of cocaine base, and only 2 percent recorded more than 50 purchases of quantities of 5 gm or less. These statistics vary somewhat among years and forms of cocaine (powder cocaine and cocaine base), but the message they convey remains the same. It is that in any given year, STRIDE contains little or no information about the price of cocaine, especially the price of retail quantities, in most of the geographical areas covered by DEA field offices.

The sparseness of the STRIDE data limits their usefulness for constructing price indices. There are few cities in which there are enough records of purchases to make precise estimates of prices and price functions, especially for retail quantities. One way of dealing with this problem is to construct price indices only for the few cities for which STRIDE contains relatively large numbers of observations. Many policy studies, however, have used STRIDE to construct a price index for the nation as a whole by pooling all of the STRIDE price data for a given time period. Such a procedure would be acceptable if the price functions of interest were the same in all regions of the country and for all forms of cocaine. As discussed later, however, prices recorded in STRIDE differ greatly among cities and forms of cocaine.

Some studies have attempted to compensate for these differences by allowing the levels of the price functions of different cities to be different. That is, the price functions in different cities are assumed to be parallel lines or curves. Some studies also assume that the distances between the price functions of different cities remain constant over time. However, price functions estimated from STRIDE data have different shapes in different cities and for different forms of cocaine, and the distances between different price functions change over time. Compensating for different shapes as well as variations in levels over time requires estimating a different price function for each city and form of cocaine in each year, but this is not possible because of the small number of observations in STRIDE for most cities. Thus, the STRIDE data can be used to construct a national price index for cocaine only by assuming that price functions in different cities are similar in certain ways—but the STRIDE data can be used to show that the required assumptions are false.

VARIABILITY OF SAMPLE CHARACTERISTICS

The characteristics of the STRIDE data vary greatly among the cities in which the number of observations is relatively large. The characteristics also vary among years within these cities. The figures and table that follow illustrate this variation. Figure A.1 shows year-to-year variations in the numbers of recorded purchases of cocaine base in four cities. Until

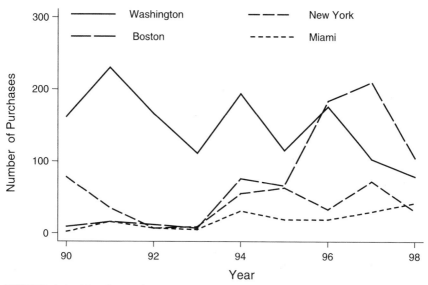

FIGURE A.1   Numbers of purchases of cocaine base in four cities.

1996, there were more purchases in Washington, D.C., than in the other cities.[1] After 1996, there were more purchases in Boston than elsewhere. Throughout the period 1990-1998, there were more purchases in Washington, D.C., than in New York, although Washington, D.C., is a smaller city than New York. Boston is also smaller than New York, but in 1996-1998 there were more purchases in Boston than in New York.

Figure A.2 shows year-to-year variations in the fraction of cocaine purchases of amounts of 5 gm or less in each of four cities. In New York, the fraction of such "small" purchases varies between 5 percent and 47 percent, depending on the year. The fraction of small purchases in Boston increased over the period 1990-1998, whereas there was no strong trend in the other cities. The fraction of small purchases tends to be lower in Detroit than in the other cities except in 1990-1991, when the fraction was lower in Boston.

---

[1]Throughout this and the next two sections, purchases in Washington, D.C., are by agents and informants of the DEA. STRIDE also includes records of purchases by agents and informants of the MPDC. These records are not used in the current discussion to maintain comparability of Washington with other cities, for which records of purchases by the local police are not available. The MPDC data are compared with the DEA data for the Washington area on pp. 9-11.

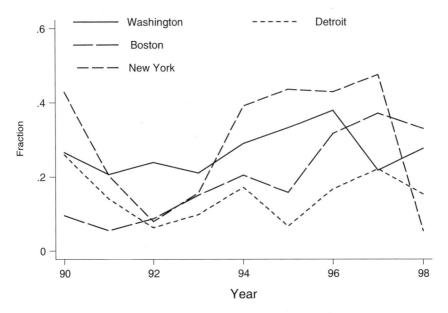

FIGURE A.2   Fractions of cocaine purchases of 5 grams or less in four cities.

Figure A.3 shows the ratio of cocaine seizures to purchases in four cities. Until 1997, the ratio was larger in Miami than in the other cities. The ratio in Chicago increased over the period and exceeded that in Miami in 1998. By contrast, the ratio in Boston decreased over time.

Table A.1 provides further evidence of the variation over time and among cities of the characteristics of the STRIDE data. This table shows year-to-year variations in the median quantities of cocaine base purchased in each of four cities during 1990-1998. The variations in the medians are large within cities over time and among cities. For example, the ratio of the highest to lowest median purchase is 13 in Boston and 20 in New York. In 1996, the median quantity purchased in Detroit was 20 times larger than the median quantity purchased in Boston.

STRIDE does not contain information that reveals the reasons for city-to-city and year-to-year variations in the characteristics of the data. It is likely, however, that much of the variation is due to differences in purchase strategies and law enforcement opportunities among cities and years. Miami, for example, is an important port of entry for cocaine, and this accounts for the large ratio of seizures to purchases there. Chicago has become increasingly important as a transshipment point, and this is likely to account for the increase in the ratio of seizures to purchases

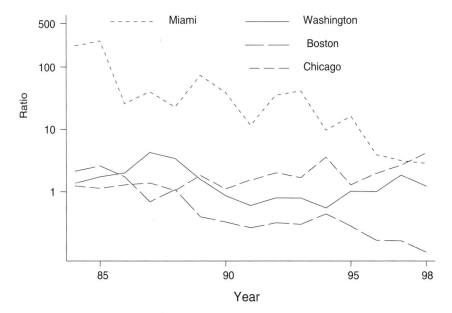

FIGURE A.3   Ratio of cocaine seizures to purchases in four cities.

TABLE A.1   Median Size (gm) of Purchases of Cocaine Base in Four Cities

Year	Boston	Detroit	New York	Washington
1994	26	22	15	14
1995	14	48	7	7
1996	2	41	6	9
1997	3	23	3	26
1998	6	18	60	21

there. In addition, the relatively low proportions of purchases of below 5 gm shown in Figure A.2 and the larger-than-retail-size median purchase sizes shown in Table A.1 reflect the DEA's focus on large cocaine dealing operations. Since nearly all cocaine is ultimately sold to consumers in small quantities (less than 5 gm), the total number of retail-size transactions almost certainly exceeds the total number of transactions involving larger quantities.[2] Thus, the distributions of purchase sizes in the STRIDE data for most of the cities and years shown in Table A.1 are unlikely to be representative of the distributions of purchase sizes in real markets. Similarly, it is likely that year-to-year variations in median purchase sizes of factors of 7 (Boston) to 20 (New York) reflect variations in law enforcement activity, rather than in market characteristics.

In summary, the STRIDE data display characteristics that are consistent with the conclusion that the DEA's data acquisition criteria vary greatly among cities and over time within cities. The characteristics are also consistent with the conclusion that the STRIDE data are not representative of cocaine markets in the cities in which purchases are made. Rather, the data reflect the law enforcement strategies and opportunities of the DEA field offices that made the purchases. Further evidence supporting this conclusion is presented later in this appendix.

DIFFERENCES IN PRICES OF POWDER COCAINE AND COCAINE BASE

Cocaine is sold in several chemically distinct forms, the most important being cocaine powder and cocaine base (crack). Possibly because of the sparseness of the STRIDE data, most existing price indices are based on the assumption that the price of cocaine is independent of its form. Thus, for example, it is assumed that the price of (say) one gram of 65 percent pure cocaine base is the same as the price of one gram of 65 percent pure powder cocaine. This assumption makes it possible to combine the records of purchases of all forms of cocaine in a single dataset for purposes of constructing a price index. The combined dataset is larger than the ones that would be available if the different forms of cocaine were treated separately. However, the practice of combining data on purchases of different forms of cocaine yields misleading results if the different forms have different prices.

As is explained in Chapter 3, there are good reasons for believing that the prices of powder cocaine and cocaine base may be different. The prices of powder cocaine and cocaine base in STRIDE support this belief. The prices of the two forms of cocaine are very different in the STRIDE

---

[2]A simple example illustrates this point. In New York in 1996, the average size of a cocaine purchase of 5 gm or less is 1.3 gm, whereas the average size of all purchases is 179 gm. If all cocaine were ultimately sold to consumers in amounts of 1.3 gm and all wholesale transactions were in amounts of 179 gm, then each wholesale lot of 179 gm would generate 179/1.3 = 138 retail transactions. Therefore, each wholesale lot would have to be sold intact 138 times to equalize the numbers of retail and wholesale transactions.

data. Caulkins (1997) also found differences between the price functions of powder cocaine and cocaine base.

The prices of different forms of cocaine can be compared by estimating a price function for each form. This section reports the results of estimating price functions of the form

(A.1) $\log P = \beta_0 + \beta_1 \log Q + \beta_2 \log \Pi + \beta_3 Z + U,$

where P is the real price of a purchase (in dollars per gram), Q is the amount purchased (in grams), Π is the purity of the purchased cocaine (expressed as a percentage), and Z is a dummy variable that indicates whether the purchase was made in the central city. $Z = 1$ if the purchase was made in the central city, and $Z = 0$ otherwise. U is an unobserved random variable whose median is zero. Thus, (A.1) is a model for the median price conditional on Q, Π, and Z. Logarithmic models similar to (A.1) are widely used for the analysis of the STRIDE data. The median price is estimated here instead of the mean because (1) the median is less sensitive to outlier price observations than the mean is and (2) the use of the median simplifies the conversion of logarithms of prices to prices. However, estimation of mean instead of median prices does not change the conclusion that the prices of powder cocaine and cocaine base are different. The real price, P, is the nominal price (cost/quantity) divided by the consumer price index for the quarter in which the purchase took place.

Model (A.1) was estimated by using the method of least absolute deviations and STRIDE data for the following cities and years: Boston for 1994-1998, San Diego for 1987-1989, and Washington, D.C., for 1989-1992. STRIDE contains relatively large numbers of purchases of both powder cocaine and cocaine base for these city-year combinations. STRIDE contains few records of purchases of powder cocaine or cocaine base or both for other cities and years. The price of a given quantity, purity, and form of cocaine depends on the number of packages that are purchased. To avoid complications arising from this dependence, only single-package purchases were used to estimate (A.1). The model was estimated separately for powder cocaine and cocaine base in each city-year combination.

The estimation results are summarized in Figure A.4. The figure shows predicted median prices of 0.8 gm of 65 percent-pure powder cocaine and cocaine base that is purchased in the central city. The predicted values are obtained from the formula

(A.2) $\hat{P} = \exp[\hat{\beta}_0 + \hat{\beta}_1 \log(0.8) + \hat{\beta}_2 \log(65) + \hat{\beta}_3],$

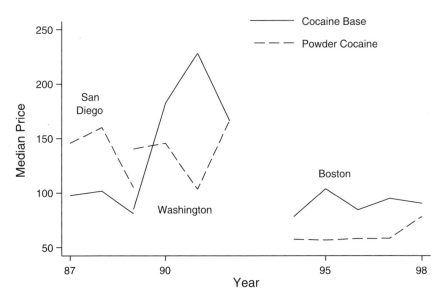

FIGURE A.4   Median prices of powder cocaine and cocaine base in three cities.

where $\hat{P}$ is the predicted median price and $\hat{\beta}_j$ is the estimated value of β_j. It can be seen from the figure that the median prices of powder cocaine and cocaine base are very different.[3] There is no systematic relation between the prices of the two forms of cocaine. The price of powder cocaine was higher than that of cocaine base in San Diego during 1987-1989, but the price of cocaine base was higher in Boston during 1994-1998. In Wash-

---

[3]An asymptotic chi-square test rejects the hypothesis that the coefficients of the models for powder cocaine and cocaine base are equal ($p < 0.01$ for each city). In other words, the test rejects the hypothesis that the price functions of powder cocaine and cocaine base are equal. The test procedure is as follows. The hypothesis has the form H_0: $\beta^{(p)} = \beta^{(b)}$, where $\beta^{(p)}$ and $\beta^{(b)}$, where $\beta^{(p)}$ and $\beta^{(b)}$ are vectors of the coefficients of the models for powder cocaine and cocaine base. Let $b_n^{(p)}$ and $b_n^{(b)}$, respectively, be the estimators of $\beta^{(p)}$ and $\beta^{(b)}$, and let $\Omega_n^{(p)}$ and $\Omega_n^{(b)}$ be the consistent estimators of the covariance matrices of their asymptotic normal distributions. Let d be the dimension of $b_n^{(p)}$ and $b_n^{(b)}$. Then if H_0 is true, $\chi^2 \equiv (b_n^{(p)} - b_n^{(b)})'(\Omega_n^{(p)} + \Omega_n^{(b)})^{-1}(b_n^{(p)} - b_n^{(b)})$ is asymptotically chi-square distributed with d degrees of freedom. The asymptotic chi-square test rejects H_0 at the α level if χ^2 exceeds the $1 - \alpha$ quantile of the chi-square distribution with d degrees of freedom. It is important to note that the p value of a hypothesis test based on the STRIDE data does not have its usual meaning because the data are not a random sample. The p value may, however, be used informally to indicate whether the observed value of a test statistic is likely or unlikely under repeated sampling of a population whose distribution is similar to the empirical distribution of the data.

ington, D.C., the price of cocaine base was below the price of powder cocaine in 1989 but above it in 1990 and 1991. Some of the price differences are very large. For example, the price of cocaine base is 85 percent higher than the price of powder cocaine in Boston in 1995. In Washington in 1989, the price of powder cocaine was 70 percent above the price of cocaine base. In San Diego in 1988, the price of powder cocaine exceeded the price of cocaine base by 62 percent. In addition, the prices of the two forms of cocaine may move in different directions over time. For example, in Washington, D.C., the price of cocaine base increased from 1989-1991, but the price of powder cocaine decreased over this period. Between 1991-1992, however, the price of cocaine base in Washington, D.C., decreased, whereas the price of powder cocaine increased.

In summary, the prices of powder cocaine and cocaine base estimated from STRIDE data can be very different. Price indices that are obtained by combining data on purchases of different forms of cocaine (thereby assuming that the prices of different forms are equal) are likely to be misleading.

DIFFERENT PRICE FUNCTIONS IN DIFFERENT CITIES

As is discussed in Chapter 3, there are good reasons for expecting the price functions of powder cocaine and cocaine base to be different in different cities. Consequently, a price index that is obtained by combining price data from different cities can produce misleading results (see the example in Chapter 3). This section uses STRIDE data for cocaine base to illustrate the differences among the price functions of different cities.

The price functions of different cities can be compared by estimating model (A.1) separately for each city. Earlier in this appendix, model (A.1) was estimated by using the method of least absolute deviations and STRIDE data. Estimates were obtained for Boston, Detroit, New York, and Washington, D.C., for 1994-1998. The use of these cities and years provides a relatively large number of observations for the comparison. Likewise, as earlier, only single-package purchases were used. The model was estimated separately for each city and year. Because the price functions of powder cocaine and cocaine base are different, separate price functions must be estimated for each form of cocaine. The price functions used for the illustrations in this section are for cocaine base.

The estimation results are summarized in Figure A.5. The figure shows predicted median prices of 0.8 gm of 65 percent-pure cocaine base that is purchased in the central city. The predicted values are obtained from equation (A.2). There are large differences among the prices in different cities. In 1995, for example, the price in Washington, D.C., was 2.57

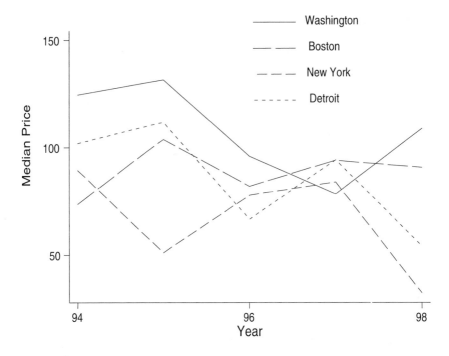

FIGURE A.5   Median prices of cocaine base in four cities.

times the price in New York. Moreover, the relations among the prices in different cities vary from year to year. For example, the price in Detroit was 40 percent above the price in Boston in 1994 and 40 percent below the price in Boston in 1998.[4]

Because of the sparseness of the STRIDE data, existing price indices are obtained by combining data from different cities. Some analysts have attempted to account for differences in prices among cities by including city-specific intercept terms in (A.1). These allow β_0 to be different in different cities. Intercept shifts allow the price in one city to be a constant multiple of the price in another. As shown in Figure A.5, however, the multipliers that relate prices among different cities vary over time and therefore cannot be accounted for by intercept shifts that are not time varying. Moreover, intercept shifts cannot account for differences among cities or over time in the slope coefficients $\beta_1 - \beta_3$. The committee is

_____
[4]The test procedure described in footnote 3 rejects the hypothesis that the price functions are the same in all cities ($p < 0.01$).

aware of only one study in which intercept shifts vary over time and none in which the slope coefficients vary over time and among cities. Thus, no existing studies based on STRIDE fully account for the variation in cocaine price functions among cities and over time. This is probably due to the sparseness of STRIDE data. Fully accounting for all of the variation requires estimating a separate price function for each city and year, but there are not enough observations in STRIDE to permit this for most years and cities. Thus, although combining data from different cities is unavoidable to obtain national-level price indices from STRIDE, such indices are likely to be misleading.

PRICES IN THE STRIDE DATA MAY NOT BE REPRESENTATIVE OF MARKET PRICES

The results presented in the previous sections show that the STRIDE data are sparse, that they reflect variations in law enforcement strategies among cities and over time, that different forms of cocaine have different prices, and that prices are different in different cities. It remains possible, however, that the STRIDE price data for a given city, year, and form of cocaine are representative of market prices for that city, year, and form of cocaine. This section presents evidence suggesting that STRIDE prices are not representative of market prices.

The analysis leading to this conclusion consists of comparing models of the price of cocaine base that are estimated from different subsets of the STRIDE data. The data for the Washington, D.C., area include records of purchases by agents of the DEA and by agents of the Metropolitan Police of the District of Columbia. Separate models of the price of cocaine base can be estimated using the DEA and MPDC purchases. If the DEA and MPDC data were representative of the relations among price, quantity, and purity in the Washington, D.C., area, then the models estimated from each data set would be identical up to the effects of random sampling errors. The evidence presented here, however, suggests that there are large, systematic differences among models estimated from the two datasets.

The estimated model is

(A.3)

$$\log P_{ijt} = \beta_{0jt} + \beta_{1jt}[I(\log Q_{ijt} \leq -1.25)(\log Q_{ijt} + 1.25) - 1.25]$$
$$+\beta_{2jt}(\log Q_{ijt} + 1.25)I(\log Q_{ijt} > -1.25) + \beta_{3jt}\log \Pi_{ijt} + \beta_{4jt}VA_{ijt} + \beta_{5jt}MD_{ijt} + U_{ijt}.$$

In this equation, P_{ijt} denotes the real price of purchase i by agency j ($j =$ MPDC or DEA) in year t. Q_{ijt} and Π_{ijt}, respectively, are the quantity and purity of cocaine base in purchase i by agency j in year t. $VA_{ijt} = 1$ if purchase *ijt* took place in the Virginia suburbs of Washington, D.C., and 0 otherwise. $MD_{ijt} = 1$ if purchase *ijt* took place in the Maryland suburbs and 0 otherwise. Only the DEA makes purchases in the Virginia and Maryland suburbs, so VA_{ijt} and MD_{ijt} are included only if $j = $ DEA. U_{ijt} is an unobserved random variable whose median is zero, and the β's are coefficients that are allowed to be different in different years and in the models for DEA and MPDC purchases.

In equation (A.3), the dependence of log$P$ on log$Q$ has the form of a linear spline with a knot at log$Q = -1.25$. This specification is used because plots of log$P$ vs. log$Q$ or the MPDC data have kinks in the vicinity of log$Q = -1.25$. Plots of log$P$ vs. log$Q$ for the DEA data do not show kinks, but the spline specification is used for the DEA model to facilitate comparisons with the MPDC model.

Table A.2 shows summary statistics for the DEA and MPDC cocaine base data. It is clear that the DEA is oriented toward larger purchases than is the MPDC. The distributions of the amounts purchased by the DEA and MPDC overlap, however. In particular, both datasets contain purchases of quantities that are below and quantities that are above one gram. Moreover, estimating (A.3) by using only observations for which $Q \le 10$ gm does not change the conclusion of this section, which is that that prices estimated from the MPDC and DEA data are systematically different from one another.

The results of estimating (A.3) are shown in Figure A.6. The figure shows the estimated median prices of 0.8 gm of 65 percent pure cocaine base that are obtained using the DEA and MPDC data. The two sets of estimates are very different. The prices estimated from the DEA data exceed those estimated from the MPDC data by 19 percent to 155 percent, depending on the year. Moreover, the DEA and MPDC data produce different estimates of price changes over time. Between 1991 and 1993, the

TABLE A.2   Summary Statistics for Cocaine Base Purchases

Agency	Variable	Median	Mean
Metropolitan Police of the District of Columbia	Cost ($)	20	126
	Quantity (gm)	0.16	2.5
	% of purchases of 5 gm or less	90	
	Purity (%)	81	77
Drug Enforcement Agency	Cost ($)	1,000	1,369
	Quantity (gm)	21	36
	% of purchases of 5 gm or less	30	
	Purity (%)	69	67

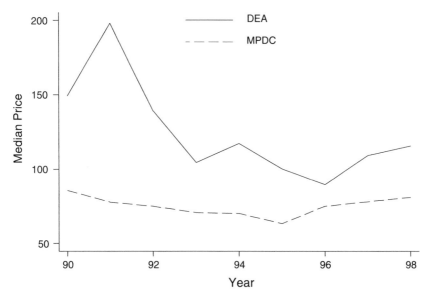

FIGURE A.6   Median prices of cocaine base in Washington, D.C., estimated from Drug Enforcement Agency and Metropolitan Police of the District of Columbia data.

DEA price estimate decreased by 47 percent, whereas the MPDC estimate decreased by only 9 percent.

Conversations with DEA officials have provided a possible explanation for the price differences displayed in Figure A.6. DEA officials believe that agents of the MPDC have better knowledge of local drug markets and greater personal familiarity with retail dealers than do agents of the DEA. Therefore, agents of the MPDC are thought to be able to bargain for lower retail prices than can agents of the DEA. In addition, DEA officials believe that the MPDC has a lower budget for drug purchases than does the DEA, thereby giving MPDC agents a stronger incentive to obtain a low price.

The finding that the DEA and MPDC data lead to different models for the price of cocaine base implies that the DEA and MPDC data on prices of cocaine base cannot both be representative of true market conditions. The data do not provide evidence on whether prices estimated from either data set accurately represent true market conditions. It is possible that one dataset gives a good approximation of true market conditions, whereas the other does not. It is also possible that neither dataset accurately represents true market conditions. Without evidence on this matter, the STRIDE data cannot be relied on to provide accurate estimates of cocaine prices and price changes.

Appendix B

Data Sources

This appendix provides detailed descriptions of several of the more prominent, federally supported data sources on drug use and treatment. The Office of National Drug Control Policy (ONDCP) has identified 25 federal sources of drug data produced by 16 different agencies (see Table B.1 at the end of this appendix). The sources described below are highlighted because of their potential to help improve the empirical foundations for policy on illegal drugs. However, no analysis of methodology similar to that found for the data collections discussed in Chapter 3 was conducted on these data systems. They are included to give the reader a better idea of the breadth of the data sources on drug abuse listed by ONDCP and referenced in this report.

DATA ON CRIMINAL JUSTICE POPULATIONS

Research has documented high levels of illegal drug use among certain institutional populations, especially people held in prisons and jails (Bureau of Justice Statistics, 1994c).[1] These drug users are not covered in the general population surveys described in Chapter 3. However, the

---

[1]In general, prisons are defined as state or federal facilities where inmates whose cases have been adjudicated by the courts are incarcerated for longer than one year. Jails are defined as holding facilities for prisoners awaiting trial or where shorter-term sentences are served by offenders.

Bureau of Justice Statistics (BJS) conducts a range of continuous censuses and surveys of federal, state, and local correctional facilities and their populations, as well as of probation populations. These systems collect data on the number of people sentenced to incarceration (and probation) nationwide, as well as on a wide variety of the features, programs, and services of all correctional facilities in the United States. The systems provide information on the personal characteristics and criminal histories of adjudicated adults, including information on their patterns of past drug use and its proximity to the offense for which they are currently sentenced.

The number of state and federal prisoners in the United States are counted semiannually, through an interagency agreement with the Bureau of the Census. A complete count of state and federal prison facilities is made every five years, also using the Bureau of the Census as the collection agent. A similar jail census and several prison and jail inmate surveys are carried out every five years. The inmate surveys are conducted through in-person interviews with large national probability-based samples of inmates.

In addition to past drug use patterns, these data provide information on the availability and characteristics of drug testing and treatment programs in correctional facilities. Facilities that conduct drug tests are able to report on current drug use for some inmate samples. Information on inmate exposure to treatment, both before and during incarceration, is also available. BJS integrates data from these and other sources to develop detailed reports of trends and descriptive information on the drug involvement of offender populations under correctional supervision (Bureau of Justice Statistics, 2000a, 2000b, 1999b, 1999c, 1998, 1997a, 1997b, 1994a, 1994b, 1993). The most important of the BJS correctional data collections, for purposes of this report, are described below.

Correctional Data Collections

The *National Prisoner Statistics* program produces semiannual (June 30 and December 31) data on the numbers of prisoners in state and federal prison facilities (Beck, 2000a, 2000b). The federal government has published data annually on the prisoner count in each State, the District of Columbia, and the Federal prison system since 1926. This census is an effort to collect comparable data from all states and federal facilities. The data collection form, although brief, provides relatively rich detail. For example, the questionnaire distinguishes among 10 categories of new admissions and 19 categories of release circumstances. Data are also collected on sentence status, the racial and ethnic composition of the inmate population, and their HIV status. In addition to the semiannual prisoner counts, BJS also conducts a periodic Census of State and Federal Prisons every five years. This prison facility census provides the sampling frame for the two nationwide inmate surveys described below:

- The *Survey of Inmates in State Correctional Facilities*, conducted every five years, provides information on individual characteristics of prison inmates (Bureau of Justice Statistics, 1993). In addition to standard elements such as current offenses and sentences, criminal histories, family background, and education level, data are collected on previous drug and alcohol abuse and on exposure to treatment and other in-prison services. Data for this survey are collected through personal interviews with a nationally representative sample of 14,000 inmates in about 300 state prisons and exist for the years 1974, 1979, 1986, 1991, and 1997.
- The *Survey of Inmates in Federal Correctional Facilities*, first conducted in 1991 and again in 1997, collects data on the same variables used in the Survey of Inmates in State Correctional Facilities (Bureau of Justice Statistics, 1997b). These are also self-report data, elicited through personal interviews with a probability-based sample of 4,041 federal inmates. Based on the completed interviews, estimates for the entire correctional population are developed.

Data from the combined inmate surveys are reported as the Survey of Inmates in State and Federal Correctional Facilities. The interview completion rate exceeds 90 percent for both the federal and state surveys.

The *Census of Jails*, conducted every five years, furnishes the sampling frame for the nationwide Survey of Inmates in Local Jails (Bureau of Justice Statistics, 1995). Similar to the Census of State and Federal Prisons described above, these data provide detailed information on each facility, including admissions and releases, court orders, programs that offer alternatives to incarceration, use of space and crowding, staffing, and health care (including prevalence of HIV/AIDS and tuberculosis). The Census of Jails also provides information on drug testing policies and practices. Data exist for the years 1970, 1972, 1978, 1983, 1988, 1993, and 1999.

- The *Annual Survey of Jails* collects intercensal estimates of the number of inmates in the nation's local jails and data on the relationship between jail populations and capacities. These data have been collected annually since 1982, except in the years when the complete Census of Jails, described above, was conducted.
- The *Survey of Inmates in Local Jails* is periodically administered to collect data on the family background and personal characteristics of jail

inmates. It includes detailed data on past drug and alcohol use and history of contact with the criminal justice system. The survey relies on personal interviews with a nationally representative sample of about 6,100 jail inmates. Data are available from this series for years 1972, 1978, 1983, 1989, and 1996.

The *National Survey of Adults on Probation* was conducted for the first time in 1995 (Bureau of Justice Statistics, 1997c). The survey collected data from a nationally representative sample of 5,867 administrative records and conducted follow-up interviews with offenders. The administrative records provide detailed information on current offenses and sentences, criminal histories, levels of supervision and contacts, participation in treatment programs, and disciplinary hearings and outcomes. The offender interviews provide the same information on offender characteristics and drug involvement as that furnished by the jail and prison surveys described above.

The questionnaires for all three inmate surveys and the probation survey include lifetime prevalence for illegal drug use, drug use at the time of the crime (current offense) for which the inmate is currently sentenced, and past-year and past-month prevalence at the time of the current offense. Data also are collected on frequency of drug use prior to both the current offense itself and the arrest for the current offense.

BJS also biennially collects data on courts and sentencing for both federal and state courts. These collections contain detailed information on the demographic characteristics of felons, conviction offenses, type of sentences, sentence lengths, and time from arrest to conviction and sentencing.

• The *National Judicial Reporting Program* surveys a nationwide sample of felony trial courts in 344 counties (Bureau of Justice Statistics, 1996b, 1999a).
• *State Court Processing Statistics* are data on the processing of felony defendants in a representative sample of state courts in the nation's 75 most populous counties, which account for about half the serious crimes nationwide.
• The *Federal Justice Statistics Program* collects information associated with federal criminal cases.

All of the court-related data series collect information on drug felonies, which are divided into two broad offense categories—drug trafficking and other drug offenses. *Drug trafficking* is defined as trafficking, sales, distribution, possession with intent to distribute or sell, manufacturing, and smuggling of controlled substances. The category *Other drug*

offenses includes possession of controlled substances, prescription violations, possession of drug paraphernalia, and other drug law violations.
The other types of felonies detailed in these data systems include a variety
of violent offenses, property offenses, and certain serious public order
offenses (Bureau of Justice Statistics, 1999a, 1999b).

BJS uses all of these data collections to develop descriptive statistics
and trend data across a number of important domains related to illegal
drugs, for example the relationship of drug use to criminal offending, the
use of treatment services by offenders, and trends in drug enforcement.
The following examples provide a small indication of the voluminous
statistical information that is available from these series on these subjects.
The figures cited are the latest available.

Drug Use and Crime

In 1997 the Survey of Inmates in State and Federal Correctional Facilities found that 83 percent of all state inmates reported past drug use, a
figure more than double the reported lifetime prevalence in the general
population for 1997 (Mumola, 1999; Research Triangle Institute, 1997).
However, only one-third of state inmates and one-fifth of federal prisoners admitted using drugs while actually committing their offense. Among
state inmates, a substantially higher proportion of violent and property
offenders reported using alcohol at the time of their offense than reported
illegal drug use. The reverse was true for drug offenders, however. Moreover, only 19 percent of state prisoners reported that they committed their
offense to get money for drugs in 1997 (Bureau of Justice Statistics, 1999e).
Only 16 percent of federal prisoners reported committing their offense to
get money for drugs in 1997.

Drug Treatment

According to the 1997 Survey of State and Federal Prisoners, as many
as one-third of state and one-quarter of federal prisoners reported past
participation in alcohol or drug abuse treatment (defined as residential
treatment, professional counseling, detoxification, or use of a maintenance
drug), and about one in eight state prisoners had participated in these
types of treatment regimes while in prison. Another two-fifths of state
prisoners had participated in some type of self-help program in the past
and one-quarter had taken part in such programs since their admission to
prison (Mumola, 1999). Among probationers, more than two in five were
required as a condition of probation to enroll in some form of substance
abuse treatment, and nearly one-third were subject to mandatory drug
testing (Bureau of Justice Statistics, 1997c).

Drug Enforcement

BJS prison data show that by 1998, the number of state and federal prisoners serving a sentence for a drug offense had grown by nearly 120,000 since 1990. Drug offenders in 1998 accounted overall for 21 percent of state and an astounding 58 percent of federal prisoners (Beck, 2000). For jail inmates, BJS reported that in 1998, 26 percent of all inmates in local facilities had committed a drug offense, and 64 percent of jail inmates had used drugs regularly in the past (Wilson, 2000). State Court Processing Statistics for 1997 also reflect the policy emphasis on enforcement. Drug offenses made up the largest proportion of all felony cases filed in the courts of the nation's largest counties—37 percent of all felonies, compared with 25 percent for violent offenses and 31 percent for property offenses. Drug offenders on pretrial release also engaged in pretrial misconduct at higher rates than other felony offenders (Bureau of Justice Statistics, 1996b). State trial court statistics show similar trends (Bureau of Justice Statistics, 1999d).

Integrated Databases

BJS also develops composite descriptions from their own and other datasets on subjects of special interest. For example, Greenfeld (1998) conducted a new analysis of national data on the impact of alcohol abuse on crime. The report, *Alcohol and Crime*, drew on all of the BJS data series described above, plus the National Crime Victim Survey, the Uniform Crime Reporting Program, and the National Incident Based Reporting Program of the Federal Bureau of Investigation and the Fatal Accident Reporting System of the National Highway Traffic Safety Administration. The findings from this analysis leave no doubt about the magnitude of the public safety problems related to alcohol abuse (Greenfeld, 1998).

Similar efforts could be mounted to develop better information for policy formation on both drug and crime control. One example of the potential for conducting integrated analyses can be found in a current BJS effort to study recidivism among 1994 releasees in 15 states. BJS is integrating a number of datasets to obtain a sample that will be representative of nearly 300,000 persons released from prison. Among other issues, the study will attempt to determine whether drug-involved inmates who were treated in prison have fared better in terms of reoffending than their untreated counterparts upon release (personal communication with Lawrence Greenfeld, Deputy Director, BJS, May 22, 2000). This information will be helpful in developing treatment policies and programs for both active and incarcerated offender populations.

DATA ON YOUTH POPULATIONS

As part of its overall mission to protect the nation's health, the Centers for Disease Control and Prevention (CDC) has developed programs to prevent the most serious health risk behaviors among children, adolescents, and young adults. One part of a four-pronged strategy to accomplish this is the identification and monitoring of both critical health problems among youth and school health policies and programs to reduce them. The *Youth Risk Behavior Surveillance System* (YRBSS) provides national, state, and local-level data on the prevalence of six categories of priority health risk behaviors. The CDC, individual states, and the public can use this vital information to support the design and evaluation of targeted interventions to help young people avoid these high-risk behaviors, one of which is substance abuse.

The school-based components of the Youth Risk Behavior Surveillance system were first implemented in 1990-1991 and conducted biennially during odd-numbered years thereafter. The 1999 survey employed a three-stage cluster design, based on an original sampling frame of 1,270 large counties or groups of smaller adjacent counties, to produce a nationally representative sample of students in grades 9-12. At the second stage of sampling, 187 schools were selected, with probability proportional to school enrollment size. To enable separate analysis by race or ethnicity, schools in the sample with substantial numbers of black and Hispanic students were sampled at higher rates than other schools. The final stage of sampling consisted of randomly selecting one or two intact classes of a required subject, such as English or social studies, from grades 9-12 at each chosen school.

The final sample in the 1999 national survey consisted of 15,349 questionnaires completed in 144 schools. The school response rate was 77 percent and the student response rate was 80 percent, for an overall response rate of 66 percent. All students in classes selected for inclusion in the sample are eligible to participate in the survey. Survey procedures are designed to protect students' privacy by allowing for anonymous and voluntary participation.

State and local jurisdictions participating in this program with their own separate surveys employ the same questionnaire (with some additional or deleted questions based on local needs) and similarly rigorous methods in an attempt to obtain data representative of their public school population in grades 9-12. In the 1999 survey, 22 states and 14 large cities succeeded in obtaining a response rate that allows them to generalize their findings to all public schools in their jurisdiction. Findings from these surveys are subject to two limitations: (1) the data apply only to youth enrolled in school and are not representative of all people in this age group and (2) as with other self-report surveys, the extent of under- or overreporting of behaviors cannot be determined.

The YRBSS survey contains 14 questions about drug use. Self-report information is collected about lifetime, past-year, and past-month use of marijuana, cocaine, heroin, inhalants, methamphetamines, hallucinogens, steroids, and prescription drugs. In addition, there are questions about age of onset for marijuana, about injecting drug use, about drug use at last sexual intercourse, and about access to and use of drugs on school property. These questions measure the level, frequency, and circumstances surrounding youthful drug use, which research has found to be related to a variety of harmful outcomes—teen suicide, early unwanted pregnancy, school failure, delinquency, and transmission of sexually transmitted diseases, including HIV.

While they collect similar information on drug use prevalence and follow nearly identical protocols for administering their questionnaires, there are significant differences between the YRBSS and *Monitoring the Future* (MTF). The surveys have different foci. The YRBSS measures risk behaviors of which drug use is only a single example. MTF's major focus with regard to risk behaviors historically has been on drugs, measuring trends in drug use, the levels of perceived risk, and the degree of personal disapproval associated with each drug.[2] Attitude toward drugs has been shown to be particularly important in explaining trends in use (Johnston et al., 2000). The sample size for the MTF is roughly twice that for the YRBSS, and the MTF survey asks 100 questions on drug use compared with 14 for the YRBSS. The age range covered is similar but not identical: MTF collects data on 8th, 10th, and 12th graders, whereas the YRBSS samples students in grades 9-12. Both surveys collect drug use data on college students and young adults.

Although both surveys utilize a nationally representative sample of youth attending school, the surveys report substantially different prevalence rates for marijuana and cocaine use (see Table B.2). Prevalence rates measured by these surveys for other drugs also may differ. It is not clear whether sampling differences, reporting differences, or some other unknown factors are responsible for the variation in drug use found in these two surveys.

---

[2]MTF also includes about 200 questions on subjects such as attitude toward government, social institutions, race relations, changing roles for women, occupational aims, and marital and family plans.

DATA ON TREATMENT POPULATIONS

The Substance Abuse and Mental Health Services Administration (SAMHSA) of the U. S. Department of Health and Human Services collects data on drug treatment under its *Drug and Alcohol Services Information System* (DASIS). DASIS has three components: (1) the *National Master Facility Inventory*, a continuously updated census of all known substance abuse treatment facilities, serves as the sampling frame for the second and third components; (2) the *Treatment Episodes Data Set* (TEDS) tracks approximately 1.5 million annual admissions to treatment for abuse of alcohol and drugs in facilities that report to individual state administrative data systems; (3) the *Uniform Facility Data Set* (UFDS) annually collects data on the location and use of treatment facilities for alcoholism and drug abuse. Together these three datasets "provide national and state-level information on the numbers and characteristics of individuals admitted to drug treatment and describes the facilities that deliver care to those individuals" (Substance Abuse Mental Health Services Administration, 2000: 15). Here the focus is on TEDS, a continuous data series, in which information on clients receiving substance abuse treatment is collected and analyzed.

The goal of TEDS is to monitor the characteristics of treatment episodes. An event-based system, it identifies the primary as well as secondary substances that lead to each admission and reports the proportion of admissions for each drug including those of greatest interest to the committee—cocaine, opiates, and methamphetamines. It also reports the demographic characteristics of those admitted to drug treatment. It does not, however, represent individuals; thus it cannot measure the total national demand for treatment for any substance of abuse. Measurement of the unmet need for treatment can be accomplished only through comprehensive national and state prevalence surveys.

Analysis of the TEDS data shows that, in 1998, almost half of admissions were for primary abuse of alcohol and 30 percent for primary abuse of cocaine and opiates. Proportions of admissions for cocaine and opiate abuse were equal. Co-occurring abuse of alcohol and hard drugs surfaced as a significant problem, characterizing 42 percent of all admissions (Substance Abuse and Mental Health Services Administration, 2000).

Demographic characteristics of admissions are also of interest. In 1998, most of those admitted to drug treatment were male (70 percent), white (60 percent, although blacks were overrepresented in the admissions sample), and unemployed (65 percent). Those admitted to drug treatment also had less education than the U.S. population as a whole. Over one-third had not graduated from high school, and only 21 percent had attended school beyond the high school years (Substance Abuse and Mental Health Services Administration, 2000).

The 1998 TEDS data indicate changes in substance abuse patterns, but these may merely reflect changing priorities in the treatment system rather than changes in drug abuse behavior. In addition, the TEDS data are aggregated through state systems that have unique characteristics. For example, while TEDS includes a large proportion of treatment facilities, it does not include all such facilities. Most but not all states are able to report admissions to public and private facilities, but some only report admissions supported by public funds. State-to-state variations in data also may include differences in the completeness of reporting, as well as in the ability to distinguish between initial admissions and transfers from one service to another in the course of a single treatment episode. Thus, admission rates for each drug type are available for each state and by geographic region, but state-by-state or regional comparisons must be made with extreme caution.

Special topics can be explored through analysis of TEDS data. Examples include adolescent admissions and their characteristics, multiple drug use and implications for treatment, patterns of use in racial and ethnic subgroups whose members present themselves for treatment, and routes of drug administration, especially for heroin and cocaine.

In addition to TEDS, SAMHSA conducts the *Uniform Facility Data Set Survey*, which provides information on location, characteristics, services, and use of drug and alcohol treatment facilities throughout the United States. It also conducts a single-day census of people in treatment. Data elements that form the core of the survey include organizational setting, service orientation, services available, clients in treatment by type of care, capacity, and annual revenue sources and amounts. The data are used to analyze general treatment services trends and to conduct comparative analyses among regions and states and the nation as a whole. In 1998, these analyses were based on the responses of 13,455 facilities (an increase of 35 percent over the previous year's response rate), and the 1,038,738 people found to be in treatment on the referent date for the single-day census.

SAMHSA and the National Institute on Drug Abuse have also sponsored a series of treatment outcome studies since 1976. These have been single studies conducted over an extended period of time. None of these studies, however, was of clients drawn from a nationally representative sample of treatment facilities.

In 1995, the ONDCP asked SAMHSA to conduct a study that would involve a nationally representative sample of the treatment system. This request was addressed in two stages, the first of which involved a representative probability sample survey drawn from a comprehensive list of organized substance abuse treatment programs, the *Drug Services Research Survey* (DSRS). The second stage was the *Services Research Outcome Study*, designed as a client outcome study based on the DSRS sample. Extensive data was collected on the programs and on a representative sample of discharged clients. The client data included completed interviews and urine specimens. Questions were asked about drug use patterns, criminal activity, employment, health, social support, and other behavior related to treatment goals. The interview covered the life span but focused on the five-year period prior to treatment admission and the period between discharge and the interview.

The interview and other aspects of the research were designed to shed light on who enters treatment, what types of treatment are effective for different types of clients, whether criminal behavior declines and employment increases with treatment, correlates of treatment outcomes, differences in death rates with those of the general population, and characteristics associated with posttreatment mortality (Substance Abuse and Mental Health Services Administration, 1998). The Services Research Outcome Study provides nationally representative data with an extended time perspective to address the question of whether or not treatment works.

<h1 style="text-align:center">REFERENCES</h1>

Beck, A.
2000a *Prison and Jail Inmates at Mid-year 1999.* Washington DC: U.S. Department of Justice, Bureau of Justice Statistics.
2000b *Prisoners in 1999.* Washington DC: U.S. Department of Justice, Bureau of Justice Statistics.
Bureau of Justice Statistics
1990 *National Judicial Reporting Program.* Washington DC: U.S. Department of Justice.
1993 *Survey of State Prison Inmates, 1991.* Washington DC: U.S. Department of Justice.
1994a *Comparing Federal and State Prison Inmates, 1991.* Washington DC: U.S. Department of Justice.
1994b *Correctional Populations in the United States, 1993.* Washington DC: U.S. Department of Justice.
1994c *Drugs and Crime Facts, 1994.* Washington DC: U.S. Department of Justice.
1995 *Jails and Jail Inmates, 1993-94.* Washington DC: U.S. Department of Justice.
1996a *Prison and Jail Inmates, 1995.* Washington DC: U.S. Department of Justice
1996b *Federal Pre-Trial Release and Detention.* Washington DC: U.S. Department of Justice
1997a *Correctional Populations in the United States, 1995.* Washington DC: U.S. Department of Justice.
1997b *Census of State and Federal Correctional Facilities, 1995.* Washington DC: U.S. Department of Justice.
1997c *Characteristics of Adults on Probation, 1995.* Washington DC: U.S. Department of Justice.
1998a *Correctional Populations in the United States, 1996.* Washington DC: U.S. Department of Justice.
1999a *Federal Criminal Case Processing, 1998: With Trends 1982-1998, Reconciled Data.* Washington DC: U.S. Department of Justice.
1999b *Probation and parole in the United States, 1998.* Washington DC: U.S. Department of Justice.

1999c *Time Served in Prison by Federal Offenders.* Washington DC: U.S. Department of Justice.

1999d *Felony Defendants in Large Urban Counties, 1996.* Washington DC: U.S. Department of Justice.

1999e *Substance Abuse and Treatment, State and Federal Prisoners, 1997.* Washington DC: U.S. Department of Justice.

2000a *Drug Use, Testing, Treatment in Jails.* Washington DC: U.S. Department of Justice.

2000b *Prison and Jail Inmates at Midyear, 1999.* Washington D.C. U.S. Department of Justice.

Greenfeld, L.A.

1998 *Alcohol and Crime: An Analysis of National Data on the Prevalence of Alcohol Involvement in Crime.* Washington, DC: U.S. Department of Justice, Bureau of Justice Statistics.

Johnston, L.D., P.M. O'Malley, and J.G. Bachman

2000 *Monitoring the Future: National Results on Adolescent Drug Use: Overview of Key Findings, 1999.* Ann Arbor, MI: Institute for Social Research.

Mumola, C.J.

1999 *Substance Abuse and Treatment, State and Federal Prisons, 1997.* Washington, DC: U.S. Department of Justice, Bureau of Justice Statistics.

Mumola, C.J., and T.P. Bonczar

1998 *Substance Abuse and Treatment of Adults on Probation, 1995.* Washington, DC: U.S. Department of Justice, Bureau of Justice Statistics.

Research Triangle Institute

1997 *National Household Survey on Drug Abuse: Main Findings 1997.* Washington DC: Department of Health and Human Services, Substance Abuse and Mental Health Administration. Available online at http://www.samhsa.gov/oas/NHSDA/1997Main/nhsda1997mfWeb.htm#TopOfPage, October 9, 2000.

Substance Abuse and Mental Health Services Administration

1998 *Services Research Outcomes Study.* Washington, DC: U.S. Department of Health and Human Services.

2000 *Treatment Episode Data Set (TEDS) 1993-1998: National Admissions to Substance Abuse Treatment Services.* Drug and Alcohol Services Information System Series: S-11. Washington, DC: U.S. Department of Health and Human Services.

U.S. Department of Justice, Bureau of Justice Statistics, and Federal Bureau of Prisons.

2000 *Survey of Inmates in State and Federal Correctional Facilities, 1997* [Computer file]. Compiled by U.S. Dept. of Commerce, Bureau of the Census. ICPSR ed. Ann Arbor, MI: Inter-university Consortium for Political and Social Research [producer and distributor]. Available on-line at http://www.icpsr.umich.edu/cgi/ab.prl?file=2598 October 9, 2000.

Wilson, D.J.

2000 *Drug Use, Testing, and Treatment in Jails.* Washington, DC: U.S. Department of Justice, Bureau of Justice Statistics.

308

TABLE B.1 Federal Sources of Drug Data

Title of Dataset	Sponsoring Agency	Information Available	Coverage by Population	Coverage by Geographic Areas	Frequency/ Year Started
Prevalence of Use					
1999 National Household Survey on Drug Abuse	Substance Abuse and Mental Health Services Administration	Presents prevalence for drug and alcohol by age, sex, and region	Household population age 12 and older	National	Annual Started 1976
Monitoring the Future (MTF)	National Institute on Drug Abuse	Reports estimates of drug, alcohol, and tobacco use and attitudes toward drugs of abuse among American youth	6th, 8th, 10th, and 12th graders and young adults age 19	National	Annual Started 1972
Worldwide Survey of Substance Abuse and Health Behaviors Among Military Personnel	U.S. Department of Defense	Measures substance use and health behaviors among military personnel	Active-duty military personnel in the Army, Navy, Marines, and Air Force	U.S. military bases worldwide	Every two to four years Started 1980
Hispanic Health and Nutrition Examination Survey III (HHANES)	National Center for Health Statistics	Assesses health status and drug and alcohol use of Hispanics	Hispanic household members ages 12 to 74	National	1988 to 1994 (last survey was in 1994) Started 1988

Name	Agency	Description	Population	Coverage	Frequency
National Longitudinal Survey of Youth	U.S. Department of Labor	Tracks employment, vocational achievement, family composition, and alcohol and drug use	Individuals ages 14 to 22	National	Annual Started 1979
National Youth Survey	National Institute of Mental Health and the National Institute on Drug Abuse	Assesses family, peer, and other influences on delinquent behaviors and substance abuse	Youths and one parent	National	Annual Started 1976
Community Epidemiology Work Group (CEWG)	National Institute on Drug Abuse	Provides early warning and epidemiology of drug use patterns, trends, and consequences, including risk factors and stages of use	Data gathered from public health agencies, medical and treatment facilities, criminal justice and correctional offices, law enforcement agencies, and other sources unique to local areas	Local, multijurisdictional	Semiannual Started 1976
Arrestee Drug Abuse Monitoring Program (ADAM) (formerly Drug Use Forecasting [DUF]) data 1996	National Institute of Justice	Monitors the extent of drug use among arrestees by demographic characteristics, charge at arrest, treatment history, and socioeconomic characteristics	Adult arrestees and juvenile detainees	Local, multijurisdictional	Annual Started 1997 (DUF 1986 to 1996)

continues

TABLE B.1 Continued

Title of Dataset	Sponsoring Agency	Information Available	Coverage by		Geographic Areas	Frequency/ Year Started
			Population			

Consequences of Drug Use

Title of Dataset	Sponsoring Agency	Information Available	Population	Geographic Areas	Frequency/ Year Started
The Economic Costs of Alcohol and Drug Abuse in the United States	National Institute on Drug Abuse and the National Institute on Alcohol Abuse and Alcoholism	Estimates costs for health care, lost productivity, and criminal justice costs due to drug and alcohol abuse	N/A	National	Initial study started 1992
National Maternal and Infant Health Survey follow up survey 1991	Centers for Disease Control and Prevention and the National Center for Health Statistics	Monitors maternal nutrition and substance abuse as well as infant health	Mothers and infants	National	1988 and 1991 Started 1988
Youth Risk Behavior Surveillance System	Centers for Disease Control and Prevention	Monitors priority health risk behaviors which contribute to the leading causes of mortality and morbidity among youths and adults	School-age youth grades 9 through 12	National	Every two years Started 1990

Drug Abuse Warning Network (DAWN) Drug Abuse Warning Network Year-End 1999 Emergency Department Data 1997 Annual Medical Examiner 1998 Detailed Emergency Department Tables	Substance Abuse and Mental Health Services Administration	Monitors drug abuse patterns and trends and assesses the health hazards associated with drug abuse by involvement of drugs in deaths and emergency department episodes	Drug-related deaths and emergency department episodes	Multijurisdictional	Annual Started 1972

Substance Abuse Treatment and Prevention

Uniform Facility Data Set (UFDS) Survey	Substance Abuse and Mental Health Services Administration	Identifies and describes drug abuse and alcoholism treatment facilities, providing data on facility characteristics, services provided, and single-day census of people in treatment	All alcohol and drug abuse treatment facilities listed on SAMSHA's National Master Facility Register (NMFI).	National	Annual from 1980, excluding 1994

continues

TABLE B.1 Continued

Title of Dataset	Sponsoring Agency	Information Available	Coverage by		Frequency/ Year Started
			Population	Geographic Areas	
Treatment Episode Data Set (TEDS)	Substance Abuse and Mental Health Services Administration	A minimum dataset, reported by states, of demographic and drug history variables on clients admitted to substance abuse treatment. Some states also submit a discharge data set	Admissions to substance abuse treatment, primarily at facilities receiving public funds. Excludes federally-owned facilities	National	Continuous Started 1992
Census of State and Federal Correctional Facilities	Bureau of Justice Statistics	Describes state-operated confinement and community-based facilities including the number of inmates or residents in counseling for drug dependence	State correctional facility inmates	National	Every 5 to 7 years Started 1974

continues

Services Research Outcomes Study (SROS)	Substance Abuse and Mental Health Services Administration and the Department of Health and Human Services	Presents treatment outcomes of persons completing substance abuse treatment programs	Drug abusers discharged from drug abuse treatment facilities	National	One-time study Started 1995
Source and Volume of Illegal Drugs					
1999 International Narcotics Control Strategy Report, U.S. Department of State	U.S. Department of State	Provides production estimates for a variety of illegal drugs by source country		International	Annual
National Narcotics Intelligence Consumers Committee (NNICC), 1997	Drug Enforcement Administration and multiple federal agencies	Collects, analyzes, and disseminates strategic national and international intelligence on the availability of drugs from selected source countries and the supply of illegal drugs to the United States		International	Annual Started 1978

TABLE B.1 Continued

Title of Dataset	Sponsoring Agency	Information Available	Coverage by Population	Geographic Areas	Frequency/ Year Started
Pulse Check	Office of National Drug Control Policy	Describes current trends in illegal drug use and drug markets based on nationwide interviews conducted with ethnographers and epidemiologists, law enforcement officials, and drug treatment providers	Ethnographers, epidemiologists, law enforcement officials, and drug treatment providers	Multijurisdictional	Quarterly until 1996, currently biannual Started 1992
Law Enforcement					
Uniform Crime Reports: Crime in the United States (UCR)	Federal Bureau of Investigation	Presents data on the number of offenses, including drug-related offenses known to the police, arrests, and clearances	98 percent of the total population	Local, state, national	Monthly Started 1930

continues

System to Retrieve Information from Drug Evidence (STRIDE)	Drug Enforcement Administration (DEA)	Analyzes drugs bought or seized by DEA and several states and local agencies	Substances seized or bought by DEA	National	Ongoing Started 1971
Law Enforcement Management and Administrative Statistics (LEMAS)	Bureau of Justice Statistics	Provides national data on the management and administration of law enforcement agencies including the existence of laboratory testing facilities, drug enforcement units, and drug education units	Law enforcement agencies	National	Periodical Started 1987

Processing Drug Offenders

National Corrections Reporting Program (NCRP)	Bureau of Justice Statistics	Tracks prisoners entering and leaving custody or supervision whose most serious offense was drug trafficking or possession	Prison and parole admissions and releases	Multijurisdictional, federal and state	Annual Started 1983

TABLE B.1 Continued

Title of Dataset	Sponsoring Agency	Information Available	Coverage by		Geographic Areas	Frequency/ Year Started
			Population			
Juvenile Court Statistics	Office of Juvenile Justice and Delinquency Prevention	Describes the cases and juveniles processed for drug-related delinquency by the juvenile courts in the United States	Cases disposed of by juvenile courts		National	Annual Started 1929
Institutionalized Offenders and Drugs						
Survey of Inmates in Local Jails	Bureau of Justice Statistics	Describes the characteristics of inmates in local jails by drug and alcohol use, criminal history, current offense, health care, and socioeconomic status	Jail inmates		National	Every 5 to 6 years Started 1972

Survey of Inmates in State Correctional Facilities	Bureau of Justice Statistics	Describes the characteristics of inmates in state correctional facilities by drug and alcohol use, criminal history, current offense, health care, and socioeconomic status	State prison inmates	National	Every 5 to 7 years Started 1974
Juveniles Taken Into Custody	Office of Juvenile Justice and Delinquency Prevention	Monitors juvenile custody facilities and residents with drug-related offenses	Private and public juvenile custody facilities	National	Annual Started 1988

Source: U.S. Office of National Drug Control Policy, "Federal Drug Data Sources," Available at: http://www.whitehousedrugpolicy.gov/drugfact/sources.html [Accessed March 16, 2001].

TABLE B.2   1999 Lifetime and Past-Month Prevalence of Marijuana and Cocaine Use for 10th and 12th Graders

Year in School	Drug	Lifetime Use		Past Month Use	
		MTF	YRBSS	MTF	YRBSS
10th grade	Marijuana	40.9	49.1	19.4	27.8
	Cocaine	7.7	9.9	1.8	3.7
12th grade	Marijuana	49.7	58.4	23.1	31.5
	Cocaine	9.8	13.7	2.6	4.8

NOTE: MTF = Monitoring the Future. YRBSS = Youth Risk Behavior Surveillance System.

SOURCES: Monitoring the Future: National Results on Adolescent Drug Use, Overview of Key Findings. National Institute on Drug Abuse: Washington DC. Available on-line October 9, 2000 at http://monitoringthefuture.org/new.html; and Youth Risk Behavior Surveillance—1999. Centers for Disease Control: Washington DC. Available on-line October 9, 2000 at http://www.cdc.gov/mmwr/preview/mmwrhtml/ss4905a1.htm.

Appendix C

Phase I Report
Executive Summary

The Committee on Data and Research for Policy on Illegal Drugs was formed in early 1998 in response to a request from the Office of National Drug Control Policy (ONDCP) of the Executive Office of the President to study the data and research needed for national policy on illegal drugs. The committee's first task, the subject of this report, was to assess two recent cost-effectiveness studies on cocaine control policy: one by RAND, *Controlling Cocaine: Supply Versus Demand Programs* (Rydell and Everingham, 1994), prepared for ONDCP and the U.S. Army, and one by the Institute for Defense Analyses (IDA), *An Empirical Examination of Counterdrug Interdiction Program Effectiveness* (Crane, Rivolo, and Comfort, 1997), prepared for the Deputy Assistant Secretary of Defense, Drug Enforcement Policy and Support, U.S. Department of Defense. The committee examined the assumptions, data, methods, and findings of the RAND and IDA studies.

The RAND study is best thought of as conceptual research offering a coherent way to think about the cocaine problem. The study documents a significant effort to identify and model important elements of the market for cocaine. It represents a serious attempt to formally characterize the complex interaction of producers and users and the subtle process through which alternative cocaine control policies may affect consumption and prices. The study establishes an important point of departure for the development of richer models of the market for cocaine and for empirical research applying such models to evaluate alternative policies.

However, the RAND study does not yield usable empirical findings on the relative cost-effectiveness of alternative policies in reducing cocaine consumption. The study makes many unsubstantiated assumptions about the processes through which cocaine is produced, distributed, and consumed. Plausible changes in these assumptions can change not only the quantitative findings reported, but also the main qualitative conclusions of the study. Hence the study's findings do not constitute a persuasive basis for the formation of cocaine control policy.

The IDA study is best thought of as a descriptive time-series analysis of statistics relevant to analysis of the market for cocaine in the United States. The study makes a useful contribution by displaying a wealth of empirical time-series evidence on cocaine prices, purity, and use since 1980. Efforts to understand the operation of the market for cocaine must be cognizant of the empirical data. The IDA study presents many of those data and calls attention to some intriguing empirical associations among the various series.

However, the IDA study does not yield useful empirical findings on the cost-effectiveness of interdiction policies to reduce cocaine consumption. Major concerns about data and methods make it impossible to accept the IDA findings as a basis for the assessment of interdiction policies. Numerous problems diminish the credibility of the cocaine price series developed in the study, and an absence of information prevents assessment of the procedure for selecting interdiction events. The conclusions drawn from these data rest on the assumption that all time-series deviations in cocaine price from an exponential decay path should be attributed to interdiction events, not to other forces acting on the market for cocaine. This foundation is too fragile to support the study's conclusions or to serve as a basis for policy.

The process of scrutinizing the specifics of the RAND and IDA studies has helped the committee to frame the questions that it will now address in a broad study of how data and research may, in the future, better serve the objective of informing drug control policy.

SOURCE

National Research Council
    1999 *Assessment of Two Cost-Effectiveness Studies on Cocaine Control Policy.* Committee on Data and Research for Policy on Illegal Drugs. Charles F. Manski, John V. Pepper, and Yonette Thomas, editors. Committee on Law and Justice and Committee on National Statistics, Commission on Behavioral and Social Sciences and Education. Washington, DC: National Academy Press.

Appendix D

How Do Response Problems Affect Survey Measurement of Trends in Drug Use?

John V. Pepper

As discussed in Chapter 2, two databases are widely used to monitor the prevalence of drug use in the United States. Monitoring the Future (MTF) surveys high school students, and the National Household Survey of Drug Abuse (NHSDA) surveys the noninstitutionalized residential population age 12 and over. Each year, respondents from these surveys are drawn from known populations—students and noninstitutionalized people—according to well-specified probabilistic sampling schemes.[1] Hence, in principle, these data can be used to draw statistical inferences on the fractions of the surveyed populations who use drugs.

It is inevitable, however, for questions to be raised about the quality of self-reports of drug use. Two well-known response problems hinder one's ability to monitor levels and trends: nonresponse, which occurs when some members of the surveyed population do not respond, and inaccurate response, which occurs when some surveyed persons give incorrect responses to the questions posed. These response problems occur to some degree in almost all surveys. In surveys of illicit activity, how-

---

[1]The University of Michigan's Institute for Social Research has conducted the MTF survey each year since 1975. Initially the survey focused on high school seniors but expanded to include 8th and 10th grade students in 1991. From 1972 to 1991, the NSHDA was conducted every 2 to 3 years. Since 1992, the Substance Abuse and Mental Health Service Administration has conducted the survey on an annual basis.

ever, there is more reason to be concerned that decisions to respond truthfully, if at all, are motivated by respondents' reluctance to report that they engage in illegal and socially unacceptable behavior. To the extent that nonresponse and inaccurate response are systematic, surveys may yield invalid inferences about illicit drug use in the United States.

In fact, it is widely thought that self-reported surveys of drug use provide downward biased measures of the fraction of users in the surveyed subpopulations (Caspar, 1992; Harrison, 1997; Mieczkowski, 1996). Nonrespondents are likely to have higher prevalence rates than those who respond. False negative responses may be extensive in a survey of illicit activity. While it is presumed that self-report surveys fail to accurately measure levels of use, they are often assumed to reveal trends. The principal investigators of MTF summarize this widely held view when they state (Johnston et al., 1998a:47-48):

> To the extent that any biases remain because of limits in school and/or student participation, and to the extent that there are distortions (lack of validity) in the responses of some students, it seems very likely that such problems will exist in much the same way from one year to the next. In other words, biases in the survey will tend to be consistent from one year to another, which means that our measurement of *trends* should be affected very little by any such biases.

These same ideas are expressed in the popular press as well as in the academic literature. Joseph Califano, Jr., the former secretary of health, education and welfare, summarized this widely accepted view about the existing prevalence measures (Molotsky, *New York Times*, August 19, 1999): "These numbers understate drug use, alcohol and smoking, but statisticians will say that you get the same level of dissembling every year. As a trend, it's probably valid." Anglin, Caulkins, and Hser (1993:350) suggest that "making relative estimates is usually simpler than determining absolute estimates. . . . [I]t is easier to generate trend information . . . than to determine the absolute level."

To illustrate the inferential problems that arise from nonresponse and inaccurate response, consider using the MTF and the NHSDA surveys to draw inferences on the annual prevalence of use rates for adolescents. Annual prevalence measures indicate use of marijuana, cocaine, inhalants, hallucinogens, heroin or nonmedical use of psychotherapeutics at least once during the year. Different conclusions about levels and trends might be drawn for other outcome indicators and for other subpopulations.

Figure D.1 and Table D.1 display a time-series of the fraction of adolescent users as reported in the official annual summaries of the MTF (Johnston et al., 1998b) and the NHSDA (Office of Applied Studies, 1997).

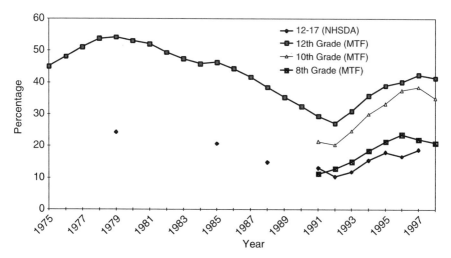

FIGURE D.1 Annual prevalence rate of use of an illegal drug for people ages 12-17, 1975-1999, National Household Survey of Drug Abuse (NHSDA) and Monitoring the Future (MTF). Note: Annual prevalence measures indicate use of marijuana, cocaine, inhalants, hallucinogens, heroin or nonmedical use of psychotherapeutics at least once during the year.
SOURCES: LD Johnston, PM O'Malley, JG Bachman. (Dec. 1998). Drug use by American young people begins to turn downward. University of Michigan News and Information Services: Ann Arbor, MI. [On_line]. Tables 1b and 3. Available: www.isr.umich.edu/src/mtf; accessed 11/16/99.

Data from the MTF imply that annual prevalence rates for students in 12th grade increased from 29 percent in 1991 to 42 percent in 1997. Data from the NHSDA indicate that the annual prevalence rates for adolescents ages 12-17 increased from 13 percent in 1991 to 19 percent in 1997. The level estimates from the two surveys differ, with those from the MTF being more than twice those from the NHSDA.[2] Still, the trends across surveys are generally consistent. Both series suggest that from 1991 to 1997, the fraction of teenagers using drugs increased by nearly 50 percent. Does the congruence in the NHSDA and MTF series for adolescents imply that both surveys identify the trends, if not the levels, or does it merely

---

[2]Similar qualitative differences in levels are generally found if one compares same-age individuals, although the magnitudes are less extreme. Gfroerer et al. (1997b) report that the age-adjusted prevalence rates from the MTF are between 0.92 to 2.24 times the NHSDA rates. In all but one case (8th graders consuming cocaine) these ratios are over 1, with many reaching at least 1.4.

TABLE D.1 Estimated Prevalence Rate of Use of Any Illegal Drugs During the Past Year, National Household Survey of Drug Abuse (NHSDA) and Monitoring the Future (MTF)

Year	MTF 12th Graders	NHSDA, Ages 12-17
1975	45.0	
1976	48.1	
1977	51.1	
1978	53.8	
1979	54.2	24.3
1980	53.1	
1981	52.1	
1982	49.4	
1983	47.4	
1984	45.8	
1985	46.3	20.7
1986	44.3	
1987	41.7	
1988	38.5	14.9
1989	35.4	
1990	32.5	
1991	29.4	13.1
1992	27.1	10.4
1993	31.0	11.9
1994	35.8	15.5
1995	39.0	18.0
1996	40.2	16.7
1997	42.4	18.8

NOTE: These annual prevalence measures indicate use of marijuana, cocaine, inhalants, hallucinogens, heroin or nonmedical use of psycho-therapeutics at least once during the year.

SOURCES: L.D. Johnston, P.M. O'Malley, J.G. Bachman. 1998b. Drug use by American young people begins to turn downward. University of Michigan News and Information Services: Ann Arbor, MI. [On_line]. Tables 1b and 3. Available: www.isr.umich.edu/src/mtf; accessed 11/16/99. Office of Applied Studies National Household Survey on Drug Abuse: Main Findings 1997, Department of Health and Human Services, Substance Abuse and Mental Health Services Administration. Table 2.6. Available:http://www.samhsa.gov/oas/NHSDA/1997Main/Table%20of%20Contents.htm; accessed 11/16/99

indicate that both surveys are affected by response problems in the same way?

This appendix evaluates the potential implications of response problems in the MTF and the NHSDA for assessment of trends in adolescent drug use. Assessment depends critically on the maintained assumptions. After all, the data cannot reveal whether a nonrespondent used drugs or whether a respondent revealed the truth.[3] The data alone cannot reveal the fraction of drug users. Thus, as with all response problems, a fundamental trade-off exists between credibility and the strength of the conclusions. Under the common assumption of stability of error processes, which is implicit in the quotes above, the data identify trends if not levels. This assumption, however, is not innocuous. To the contrary, the assumption that response errors are fixed over time lacks credibility if, for example, the stigma of drug use changes over time. The preferred starting point might instead be to make no assumptions at all, and so obtain maximal consensus (Manski, 1995). In this case, the data do not reveal the trends, but informative bounds may be obtained.

In the drug use context, however, analysis imposing no assumptions at all seems too conservative because there is good reason to believe that observed rates are lower bounds.[4] I take this as a starting point. That is, I assume that in 1991 no less than 29 percent of 12th graders and 13 percent of adolescents ages 12-17 consumed illegal drugs. In 1997 no less than 42 percent of 12th graders and 19 percent of adolescents ages 12-17 consumed illegal drugs.

Under what additional assumptions do these data reveal time trends in the prevalence of drug use, or at least the directions of trends? I find that the necessary conditions depend on the response problem. Given nonresponse alone, the data effectively identify the direction of large changes in prevalence rates and even reveal the direction of smaller year-to-year variations under seemingly modest restrictions on the trends in use among nonrespondents. Drawing inferences given inaccurate response requires stronger assumptions. Given the inaccurate response

---

[3]Throughout this paper I abstract from concerns over sampling variability, focusing instead on the identification problems that arise because the prevalence rate would not be observed even if one obtained a survey of the entire population. Certainly, uncertainty can arise from both identification problems and from sampling variability. Identification problems, however, are the primary hindrance in inference on drug use: without assumptions on misreporting, the data cannot reveal the fraction of users in the population.

[4]There are alternative views, especially with regard to adolescents who in some cases may feel pressure to brag about use. More generally, to the extent that people inclined to give false negative accounts decline to fill out the questionnaire, whereas people inclined to give false positive reports participate in the survey, the observed rates would be biased upward.

problem alone, the data do not reveal the levels, trends, or direction of even the larger changes in the prevalence rates of use. By restricting the variation over time in the accuracy of response and linking inaccurate response to the degree of stigma associated with using drugs, the direction of the trend can be identified.

NONRESPONSE

Nonresponse is an endemic problem in survey sampling. Each year, about 20 to 25 percent of selected individuals do not respond to the NHSDA questionnaire. In the MTF, nearly half of the schools originally surveyed refuse to participate, and nearly 15 percent of the surveyed students fail to respond to the questionnaire.[5] The data are uninformative about nonrespondents. If illegal drug use systematically differs between respondents and nonrespondents, then the data may not identify prevalence levels or trends for the surveyed population.

To see this identification problem, let y_t indicate whether a respondent used drugs in period t, with $y_t = 1$ if the respondent used drugs and 0 otherwise. Let z_t indicate whether a respondent completed the survey in period t. We are interested in learning the fraction of users at time t

(1) $$P[\, y_t = 1 \,].$$

The problem is highlighted using the law of total probability, which shows that

(2) $P[y_t = 1] = P[y_t = 1 \mid z_t = 1] \, P[\, z_t = 1 \,] + P[y_t = 1 \mid z_t = 0] \, P[\, z_t = 0 \,].$

The data identify the fraction of respondents, $P[\, z_t = 1 \,]$, and the usage rates among respondents, $P[y_t = 1 \mid z_t = 1]$. The data cannot reveal the prevalence rates among those who did not respond, $P[y_t = 1 \mid z_t = 0]$.

Likewise, the data alone cannot reveal the magnitude or direction of the trend. For simplicity, assume that the fraction of nonrespondents is fixed over time.[6] Then, to see this identification problem note that

---

[5]These 15-25 percent nonresponse rates are similar to those achieved by the National Survey of Family Growth, which also asks for sensitive information, and not much worse than those achieved in the Current Population Survey, which is used to measure the unemployment rate. The school nonresponse rates in the MTF, however, imply much larger response problems than in the Current Population Survey or the National Survey of Family Growth.

[6]This assumption does not imply that everyone would be either a respondent on both occasions or a nonrespondent on both. Rather, it restricts only the fraction of nonrespondents to be fixed over time. It might be that some persons would respond on one occasion and not the other.

(3) $P[\ y_{t+j} = 1\ ] - P\ [\ y_t = 1\ ] = \{\ P\ [\ y_{t+j} = 1\ |\ z_{t+j} = 1\ ]$
       $- P\ [y_t = 1\ |\ z_t = 1\ ]\}\ P\ [z = 1\ ] + \{\ P\ [y_{t+j} = 1\ |\ z_{t+j} = 0\ ]$
       $- P\ [y_t = 1\ |\ z_t = 0\ ]\}\ P\ [z = 0\ ].$

While the data reveal the trends in use for respondents, $P\ [y_{t+j} = 1\ |\ z_{t+j} = 1\ ] - P\ [y_t = 1\ |\ z_t = 1\ ]$, and the fraction of respondents, $P\ [z = 1\ ]$, the data cannot reveal the trends in use for nonrespondents, $P\ [y_{t+j} = 1\ |\ z_{t+j} = 0\ ] - P\ [y_t = 1\ |\ z_t = 0\ ]$.

Data Missing at Random

The most common assumption used to identify the fraction of users is to assume that, conditional on certain covariates, the prevalence rate for nonrespondents equals the rate for respondents.[7] That is, nonresponse is random conditional on these covariates. This assumption is implicit when researchers use survey weights to account for nonresponse. In fact, the NHSDA includes sampling weights that apply a procedure common to many federal surveys. Nonresponse weights are derived under the assumption that within observed subgroups (e.g., age, sex, and race groups) the fraction of drug users is identical for respondents and nonrespondents. If this missing-at-random assumption is true, weights may correct for survey nonresponse. If false, the estimates may be biased.

I do not find it plausible to assume that the decision to respond to drug surveys is random. In fact, there is some evidence to support this claim. Reporting on a study in which nonrespondents in the NHSDA were matched to their 1990 census questionnaires, Gfroerer and colleagues (1997a:292) conclude that "The Census Match Study demonstrates that response rates are not constant across various interviewer, respondent, household, and neighborhood characteristics. To the extent that rates of drug use vary by these same characteristics, bias due to nonresponse may be a problem." If the missing-at-random assumption applies within the subgroups, these observed differences between respondents and non-respondents might be accounted for using sampling weights. However, since the Census Match Study does not reveal the drug use behavior of nonrespondents, there is no way to evaluate the validity of the missing at random assumption. Even within observed subgroups, nonresponse in surveys of illegal activities may be systematic.

Caspar (1992) provides the only direct evidence on the drug use be-

---

[7]See Horowitz and Manski (1998, 2000) for a review of different methods used to account for nonresponse.

havior of nonrespondents. With a shortened questionnaire and monetary incentives, Caspar (1992) surveyed nearly 40 percent of the nonrespondents to the 1990 NHSDA in the Washington, D.C., area. In this survey, nonrespondents have higher prevalence rates than respondents. Whether these findings apply to all nonrespondents, not just the fraction who replied to the follow-up survey in the Washington, D.C., area, is unknown.

The Monotone Selection Assumption

Rather than impose the missing-at-random assumption, it might be sensible to assume that the prevalence rate of nonrespondents is no less than the observed rate for respondents. Arguably, given the stigma associated with use, nonrespondents have higher prevalence rates than respondents. Formally, this *monotone selection assumption* implies

(4) $P[y_t = 1 \mid z_t = 1] \leq P[y_t = 1 \mid z_t = 0] \leq 1.$

The lower bound results if the prevalence rate for nonrespondents equals the rate for respondents. The upper bound results if all nonrespondents consume illegal drugs. The true rate lies within these bounds.

This restriction on the prevalence rates for nonrespondents implies bounds on the population prevalence rates:

(5) $P[y_t = 1 \mid z_t = 1] \leq P[y_t = 1] \leq P[y_t = 1 \mid z_t = 1] \, P[z_t = 1]$
        $+ P[z_t = 0].^8$

Notice that the lower bound is the fraction of respondents who use illegal drugs in the past year, while the upper bound increases with the fraction of nonrespondents. The width of the bound equals $\{1 - P[y_t = 1 \mid z_t = 1]\}P[z_t = 0]$. Thus, the uncertainty reflected in the bounds increases with the fraction of nonrespondents, $P[z_t = 0]$ and decreases with the prevalence rates of respondents. In the extreme, if all respondents are using drugs, then the monotonicity assumption implies that all nonrespondents would be using drugs as well, so that the prevalence rate would be identified.

Given the MTS assumption in Equation (4), we can also bound the trend from time (t) to time $(t + j)$:

(6) $\{P[y_{t+j} = 1 \mid z_{t+j} = 1] - P[y_t = 1 \mid z_t = 1]\}P[z = 1]$
      $+ \{P[y_{t+j} = 1 \mid z_{t+j} = 1] - 1\} P[z = 0] \leq P[y_{t+j} = 1] - P[y_t = 1] \leq$
      $\{P[y_{t+j} = 1 \mid z_{t+j} = 1] - P[y_t = 1 \mid z_t = 1]\}P[z = 1]$
      $+ \{1 - P[y_t = 1 \mid z_t = 1]\} P[z = 0]$

---

[8]Manski and Pepper (2000) formalize the implications of this assumption.

The upper bound for the trend equals the upper bound for the usage rate at time $t+j$ minus the lower bound at time t. Thus, if the lower bound at time t exceeds the upper bound at time $t+j$, the fraction of users must have fallen over the period. Likewise, if the lower bound at time $t+j$ exceeds the upper bound at time t, then the fraction of users must have risen.

Figures D.2 and D.3 display the estimated bounds from 1975 to 1997 for 12th graders from the MTF survey and for adolescents ages 12-17 from the NHSDA, respectively. For simplicity, I assume the nonresponse rate is fixed at 15 percent in the MTF survey and 25 percent in the NHSDA. I also abstract from concerns about statistical variability and instead focus on the point estimates.

Under the monotone selection assumption, data from the MTF imply that the annual prevalence rate for 12th graders lies between 29 and 40 percent in 1991 and between 42 and 51 percent in 1997.[9] Thus, the data bound the level estimates to lie within about a 10-point range. Notice also that these estimates imply that the fraction of users increased in the 1990s, although the magnitude of these changes and the directions of the year-to-year variations are not revealed. In particular, from 1991 to 1997, the prevalence rate increased by at least 2 points (from 40 to 42 percent), and perhaps by as much as 22 points (from 29 to 51 percent).

The bounds displayed in Figure D.2 reveal the uncertainly implied by student nonresponse to the MTF. These bounds, however, do not reflect school nonresponse. The MTF uses a clustered sampling design whereby schools and then individuals within a school are asked to participate in the study. Each year between 30 to 50 percent of the selected schools decline to participate and are replaced by similar schools in terms of observed characteristics such as size, geographic area, urbanicity, and so forth (Johnston et al., 1998a). In 1995, for example, nearly 38 percent of schools and 16 percent of students declined to participate, so that the overall response rate for the 12th grade survey is only 52 percent (Gfroerer et al., 1997b).

To the extent that nonrespondent schools have drug usage rates that systematically differ from respondent schools, inferences drawn using the survey will be biased. With school nonresponse and replacement rates of nearly 50 percent, this is an especially important nonresponse problem. If incorporated into the bounds developed above, the data no longer even reveal the direction of the largest trends.

Data from the NHSDA imply that the annual prevalence rate of use

---

[9]Using the law of total probability to weight the fraction of respondents and nonrespondents, the upper bound prevalence rates are found by assuming that all nonrespondents use drugs. In 1991, for example, the upper bound rate of 40 = 29*0.85 + 100*0.15.

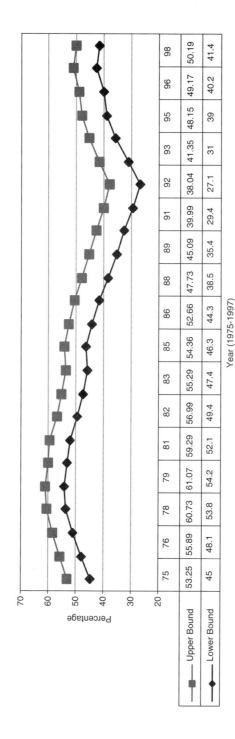

	75	76	78	79	81	82	83	85	86	88	89	91	92	93	95	96	98
Upper Bound	53.25	55.89	60.73	61.07	59.29	56.99	55.29	54.36	52.66	47.73	45.09	39.99	38.04	41.35	48.15	49.17	50.19
Lower Bound	45	48.1	53.8	54.2	52.1	49.4	47.4	46.3	44.3	38.5	35.4	29.4	27.1	31	39	40.2	41.4

Year (1975-1997)

FIGURE D.2 Bounds on annual prevalence rates of use for adolescents in 12 grade in light of survey nonresponse (Monitoring the Future).

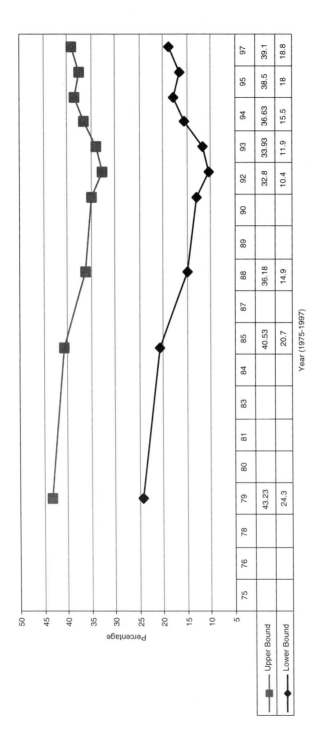

	75	76	78	79	80	81	83	84	85	87	88	89	90	92	93	94	95	97
Upper Bound				43.23					40.53		36.18			32.8	33.93	36.63	38.5	39.1
Lower Bound				24.3					20.7		14.9			10.4	11.9	15.5	18	18.8

Year (1975-1997)

FIGURE D.3 Bounds on annual prevalence rates of use for adolescents ages 12-17 (National Household Survey of Drug Abuse (NHSDA).

for adolescents ages 12-17 lies between 13 and 35 percent in 1991 and between 19 and 39 percent in 1997. Thus, the data combined with the monotone selection assumption bound the prevalence rate to lie within about a 20-point range. In this case, the direction of the trend is not revealed. The fraction of users might have fallen by 16 points (from 35 to 19 percent) or increased by 26 points (from 13 to 39 percent). Thus, in the absence of additional information, the NHSDA data are uninformative about the direction of even large changes over this period. The sharp increase in the fraction of surveyed adolescents using illegal drugs during the 1990s does not rule out a sharp decrease in the rates of use for adolescents who failed to respond to the survey.

The Switching Threshold

There may be informative restrictions on the rate of use among nonrespondents over time that would allow one to identify the direction of the trend. Did the fraction of adolescent users increase in the 1990s? Certainly, that would be the case if we knew that the prevalence rates for respondents and nonrespondents moved in the same direction. More generally, the data could imply a positive trend even if one allowed for the possibility that fewer nonrespondents used illegal drugs, as long as the reduction in the prevalence rate for nonrespondents was not too large. If one is unwilling to rule out the possibility of extreme variation in the behavior of nonrespondents, for example, that all nonrespondents used drugs in 1991 but only 19 percent used drugs in 1997, then the data are less likely to reveal the direction of the trend.

The bound in Equation (6), however, does not impose explicit restrictions on the behavior of nonrespondents over time. Only the monotone selection assumption in Equation (4) applies. Consider, for example, the annual variation in the fraction of users in the early 1990s for adolescents ages 12-17, as revealed in Figure D.3. The bounds on trends allow for the possibility that the usage rate for nonrespondents increased from 10 percent in 1992 to 100 percent in 1993, then back to 12 percent in 1994, and so forth.

Some might argue that such extreme variation in the annual prevalence rate is unlikely. After all, in the NHSDA the reported prevalence rates from one year to the next have never increased by more than 4 percent and never decreased by more than 3 percent. Likewise, the observed annual change in the MTF is bounded between [−3.2, 4.8]. These bounds on the variation in prevalence rates for respondents cannot rule out more extreme volatility in the prevalence rates for nonrespondents. Still, it may be plausible to rule out year-to-year variation in the annual prevalence rates for nonrespondents on the order of the 50 or more points allowed for in Figures D.2 and D.3.

Insight into whether the sign of the trend is identified can be found by evaluating the restrictions on the temporal variation in the prevalence rates of nonrespondents that would be required to identify the direction of change. Suppose that the direction of the trend in prevalence rates for respondents is positive (negative). Then, from Equation (3) we see that the direction of change for the population must also be positive (negative) if the prevalence rate for nonrespondents cannot fall (rise) by more than the switching threshold

$$(7) \qquad ST = -\{P[y_{t+j} = 1 \,|\, z_{t+j} = 1] - P[y_t = 1 \,|\, z_t = 1]\} \frac{P[z=1]}{P[z=0]}.$$

Thus, if it is known that the growth in usage rates for nonrespondents is less (in absolute value) than this switching threshold, the sign of the trend is identified. If, however, the trend in use for nonrespondents might exceed this threshold, the sign of the trend is ambiguous. Notice that to identify the sign of the trend, one need not know the magnitude or direction of the trend for nonrespondents. Rather, one simply needs to rule out the possibility that the trend for nonrespondents exceeds this threshold.

Intuitively, the switching threshold increases with the fraction of respondents and with the prevalence rate of respondents. As the fraction of respondents increases, the behavior of nonrespondents has less impact on the overall prevalence rates; hence the trend in usage rates among nonrespondents must be more exaggerated to switch the sign of the observed trend. Likewise, as the observed prevalence rate of use increases over time, the switching threshold for nonrespondents must also increase.

Table D.2 displays the estimated switching threshold along with the annual trends in usage rates from the MTF. The threshold for the MTF survey is computed by multiplying the observed trend by -5.7 ($= -85/15$). Consider, for instance, the trend from 1992 to 1993. The fraction of respondents using drugs increased 3.9 points, implying a switching threshold of -22.1 ($= -5.7*3.9$). That is, for the annual trend from 1992 to 1993 to fall, the rate of use among nonrespondents must have declined by over 22 points. The monotonicity assumption in Equation (4) does not rule out such large drops among nonrespondents. In fact, the rate of use may have fallen by as much as 69 points, from 100 percent in 1992 to 31 percent in 1993. If, however, it is known that the annual variation in the prevalence rates for nonrespondents cannot exceed 20 points, then the sign of the trend is identified.

Table D.3 displays the estimated switching threshold along with the annual trends in usage rates from the NHSDA. In the NHSDA, there are

TABLE D.2 Observed Annual Trends in Prevalence Rates of Illegal
Drug Use Among 12th Graders and the Switching Threshold for
Nonrespondents, Monitoring the Future.

Year	Observed Trend	Switching Threshold 12th Graders
1976	3.1	−17.6
1977	3.0	−17.0
1978	2.7	−15.3
1979	0.4	−2.3
1980	−1.1	6.2
1981	−1.0	5.7
1982	−2.7	15.3
1983	−2.0	11.3
1984	−1.6	9.1
1985	0.5	−2.8
1986	−2.0	11.3
1987	−2.6	14.7
1988	−3.2	18.1
1989	−3.1	17.6
1990	−2.9	16.4
1991	−3.1	17.6
1992	−2.3	13.0
1993	3.9	−22.1
1994	4.8	−27.2
1995	3.2	−18.1
1996	1.2	−6.8
1997	2.2	−12.5
1991–1997	13.0	73.7

three respondents for every nonrespondent. Thus, uncertainty about the
direction of the trend exists only if one cannot rule out the possibility that
the trend for nonrespondents is three times the negative of the observed
trend. Since the observed prevalence rate increased by 5.7 points from
1991 to 1997, the trend is positive if the usage rates for nonrespondents
did not fall by more than 17.1 points from 1991 to 1997. If one is willing to
assume that the trends in usage rates cannot exceed this threshold, then
the data identify the sign of the trend. Otherwise, the sign of the trend is
indeterminate.

INACCURATE RESPONSE

Self-report surveys on deviant behavior invariably yield some inaccurate reports. Respondents concerned about the legality of their behavior
may falsely deny consuming illegal drugs. Desires to fit into a deviant
culture may lead some respondents to falsely claim to consume illegal

TABLE D.3 Observed Annual Trends in Prevalence Rates of Illegal Drug Use Adolescents Ages 12-17 and the Switching Threshold for Nonrespondents, National Household Survey of Drug Abuse.

Year	Observed Trend	Switching Threshold Adolescents Ages 12-17
1992	-2.7	8.1
1993	1.5	-4.5
1994	3.6	-10.8
1995	2.5	-7.5
1996	-1.3	3.9
1997	2.1	-6.3
1991-1997	5.7	17.1

drugs.[10] Thus, despite considerable resources devoted to reducing misreporting in the national drug use surveys, inaccurate response remains an inherent concern. Surely some respondents fail to provide valid information about whether they consume illegal drugs.

Inaccurate reporting in drug use surveys is conceptually different from the nonresponse problem examined above. While the fraction of nonrespondents is known, the data do not reveal the fraction of respondents who give invalid responses to the questionnaire. It might be that all positive reports are invalid, in which case the usage rate may be zero. Alternatively, it might be that all negative reports are invalid, in which case the entire population may have consumed illegal drugs. Thus, to draw inferences about the fraction of users in the United States, one must impose assumptions about self-reporting errors.

To evaluate the impact of invalid response on the ability to infer levels of use, I introduce notation that distinguishes between self-reports and the truth. Let w_t be the self-reported measure in period t, where $w_t = 1$ if the respondent reported use and 0 otherwise. Let y_t be the truth, where $y_t = 1$ if the respondent consumed drugs and 0 otherwise. We are interested in learning probability of use, $P[\ y_t = 1\ ]$. Formally, we can relate this unobserved prevalence rate to the self-reported usage rates as follows:

$$(8) \quad P[\ y_t = 1] = P[w_t = 1, y_t = 1] + P[w_t = 0, y_t = 1] = P[\ w_t = 1\ ] + P[\ w_t = 0, y_t = 1] - P\ [w_t = 1, y_t = 0].$$

---

[10]While some respondents may falsely claim to consume drugs, the consensus is that false negative reports are more pervasive, even among adolescents. The principal investigators of the MTF summarize this widely held view when they state, "insofar as any reporting bias exists, we believe it to be in the direction of under-reporting. Thus, we believe our estimates to be lower than their true values" (Johnston et al., 1998a:47).

The data identify the fraction of the population who self-report use, $P[\ w_t = 1\ ]$. The data cannot identify the fraction who falsely claim to have consumed drugs, $P\ [w_t = 1, y_t = 0]$, or who falsely claim to have abstained, $P\ [w_t = 0, y_t = 1]$. The data identify prevalence rates if the fraction of false negatives is exactly offset by the fraction of false positive reports, that is, if $P[\ w_t = 0\ , z_t = 0] = P\ [w_t = 1, z_t = 0]$. Otherwise, the fraction of users is not identified.

Magnitude of Inaccurate Response

There is a large literature that provides direct evidence on the magnitude of misreporting in some self-reported drug use surveys. Validation studies have been conducted on arrestees (see, for example, Harrison 1992 and 1997; Mieczkowski, 1990), addicts in treatment programs (see, for example, Darke, 1998; Magura et al., 1987, 1992; Morral et al., 2000; Kilpatrick et al., 2000), employees (Cook et al., 1997), people living in high-risk neighborhoods (Fendrich et al., 1999), and other settings. See Harrison and Hughes (1997) for a review of the literature.

The most consistent information is collected as part of the Arrestee Drug Abuse Monitoring/Drug Use Forecasting (ADAM/DUF) survey of arrestees. To enable inferences on the extent of inaccurate reporting among arrestees, this survey elicits information on drug use from self-reports and urinalysis.[11] Harrison (1992, 1997), for example, compares self-reports of marijuana and cocaine use during the past three days to urinalysis test results for the same period. In general, between 20 and 30 percent of respondents appear to give inaccurate responses. In the 1988 survey, for example, 27.9 percent of respondents falsely deny using cocaine and 1.4 percent falsely claim to have used cocaine. For marijuana, the false negative rates are lower (18.1 percent) and the false positive rates are higher (6.4 percent), but the same basic picture emerges. About half of those testing positive report use, while a substantially higher fraction testing negative report truthfully.

Despite this literature, very little is known about misreporting in the national probability samples. The existing validation studies have largely been conducted on samples of people who have much higher rates of drug use than the general population. Response rates in the validation studies are often quite low and, moreover, respondents are usually not randomly sampled from some known population.

---

[11]The usual assumption is that the urinalysis tests are valid. In fact, however, it is well known that urinalysis tests result in both false negative and positive reports (see Harrison, 1997).

A few notable studies have attempted to evaluate misreporting in broad-based, representative samples. However, lacking direct evidence on misreporting, these studies have to rely on strong, unverifiable assumptions to infer validity rates. Biemer and Witt (1996), for instance, analyze misreporting in the NHSDA under the assumptions that (1) smoking tobacco is positively related to illegal drug use and (2) the inaccurate reporting rate is the same for both smokers and nonsmokers. Under these assumptions, they find false negative rates (defined here as the fraction of users who claim to have abstained) in the NHSDA that vary between 0 and 9 percent. Fendrich and Vaughn (1994) evaluate denial rates using panel data on illegal drug use from the National Longitudinal Survey of Youth (NLSY), a nationally representative sample of individuals who were ages 14-21 in the base year of 1979. Of the respondents to the 1984 survey who claimed to have ever used cocaine, nearly 20 percent denied use and 40 percent reported less frequent lifetime use in the 1988 follow-up. Likewise, of those claiming to have ever used marijuana in 1984, 12 percent later denied use and just over 30 percent report less lifetime use. These logical inconsistencies in the data are informative about validity if the original 1984 responses are correct.

These papers make important contributions to the literature. In particular, they illustrate the types of models and assumptions that are required to identify the extent of misreporting in the surveys.[12] Still, the conclusions are based on unsubstantiated assumptions. Arguably, smokers and nonsmokers may have different reactions to stigma and thus may respond differently to questions about illicit behavior. Arguably, the self-reports in the 1984 NLSY are not all valid.

To evaluate the fraction of users in the population in light of inaccurate response, I begin by imposing the following assumptions on misreporting rates:

IR-1: In any period t, no more than P percent of the self-reports are invalid. That is, $P[\ w_t = 0\ ,\ y_t = 1] + P\ [w_t = 1, y_t = 0] \leq P$.

IR-2: The fraction of false negative reports exceeds the fraction of false positive reports. That is, $P[\ w_t = 0\ ,\ y_t = 1] \geq P\ [w_t = 1, y_t = 0]$.

These assumptions imply that the prevalence rate is bounded as follows:

(9) $$P[\ w_t = 1\ ] \leq P[\ y_t = 1] \leq \min\{P[\ w_t = 1\ ] + P, 1\ \}.$$

The upper bound follows from IR-1, whereas the lower bound follows

---

[12]Biemer and Witt (1996) explicitly note this point when they state that their "objective is to investigate some capabilities and limitations of the methodology and demonstrate its use for surveys such as the NHSDA."

from IR-2. Under these assumptions, the observed trends provide a lower bound for the prevalence rate of use for illegal drugs. The upper bound depends on both the self-reported prevalence rates as well as the largest possible fraction of false negative reports, P.

The upper bound P on the fraction of false reports is not revealed by the data but instead must be known or assumed by the researcher. Suppose, for purposes of illustration, one knows that less than 30 percent of respondents give invalid self-reports of illegal drug use. In this case, the width of the bound on prevalence rates is 0.30, so that the data provide only modest information about the fraction of users. Consider, for instance, estimating the fraction of 12th graders using drugs in 1997. In total, 42.4 percent of respondents in the MTF reported consuming drugs during the year. If as many as 30 percent of respondents give false negative reports, the true fraction of users must lie between 42.4 and 72.4 percent.

Alternatively, one might consider setting this upper bound figure much lower than 30 percent. Suppose, for example, one is willing to assume that less than 5 percent of respondents provide invalid reports of drug use. In this case, the prevalence bounds from Equation 9 will be more informative. The estimated prevalence rate of use for 12th graders in 1997, for instance, must lie between [42.4, 47.4] percent.

Clearly, our ability to draw inferences on the prevalence rate of drug use in the United States depends directly on the magnitude of inaccurate reporting. Without better information, readers may differ in their opinions of the persuasiveness and plausibility of particular upper bound assumptions. A 30-point upper bound may be consistent with the inaccurate reporting rates found in DUF/ADAM, but whether arrestees are more or less likely to hide illegal activities is unknown.[13] A 5-point upper bound may be consistent with the model-based results of Biemer and Witt (1996), but whether the model accurately measures the degree of inaccurate reporting is unknown.

Inaccurate Reporting Rates Over Time

Despite acknowledged uncertainty surrounding the level estimates, many continue to assert that the data do in fact reveal trends. What restrictions would need to be imposed to identify the trend or direction of

---

[13]Two other arguments have been used to suggest that the inaccurate reporting rates from DUF/ADAM might be a conservative upper bound on misreporting in the national surveys. First, there is greater accuracy for annual prevalence of use for all drugs than for within-three-days use measures for stigmatized drugs such as cocaine. Second, survey techniques used in the DUF/ADAM are less advanced than in the national probability samples.

the trend? Assume, for convenience, that the fraction of people falsely reporting that they used drugs is fixed over time. In this case, the trend is revealed if the fraction of people falsely denying use is also fixed over time. The direction of the trend is revealed if one can rule out the possibility that the fraction of respondents falsely denying use changes enough to offset the observed trend. For instance, the reported prevalence rates for adolescents ages 12-17 in the NHSDA increased from 13.1 percent in 1991 to 18.8 percent in 1997. As long as the fraction of respondents falsely denying use did not decrease by more than 5.7 points, the actual prevalence rate increased.

Formally, the trend equals

$$(10) \qquad P[y_{t+j} = 1] - P[y_t = 1] =$$
$$P[w_{t+j} = 1] - P[w_t = 1]$$
$$+ \{ P[w_{t+j} = 0, y_{t+j} = 1] - P[w_{t+j} = 1, y_{t+j} = 0] \}$$
$$- \{ P[w_t = 0, y_t = 1] - P[w_t = 1, y_t = 0] \}$$

The growth in prevalence rates equals the trend in reported use plus the trend in net misreporting, where net misreporting is defined as the difference between the fraction of false negative and false positive reports. Thus, the data identify trends if net misreporting is fixed over time. This assumption does not require the fraction of false negative reports to be fixed over time. Rather, any change in the fraction of false negative reports must be exactly offset by an equal change in the fraction of false positives.

For the drug use surveys, this invariance assumption seems untenable. There is no time-series evidence on inaccurate response that is directly relevant to the national household surveys. Some, however, have argued that the propensity to give valid responses is affected by social pressures that have certainly changed over time. That is, the incentive to give false negative reports may increase as drug use becomes increasingly stigmatized (Harrison, 1997). In this case, inaccurate response is likely to vary over time.

Figure D.4 displays the MTF and NHSDA reported time-series in prevalence rates along with measures of the stigma of drug use elicited from MTF 12th graders and from NHSDA respondents ages 12-17. This stigma index measures the fraction of respondents who either disapprove of illegal drug consumption (MTF) or perceive it to be harmful (NHSDA).[14] The striking feature of this figure is that these prevalence rate

---

[14]The specific question from MTF used to create this index is: "Do you disapprove of people (who are 18 or older) smoking marijuana occasionally?" The NHSDA question used to create the index is: "How much do you think people risk harming themselves physically or in other ways when they smoke marijuana occasionally/once a month?"

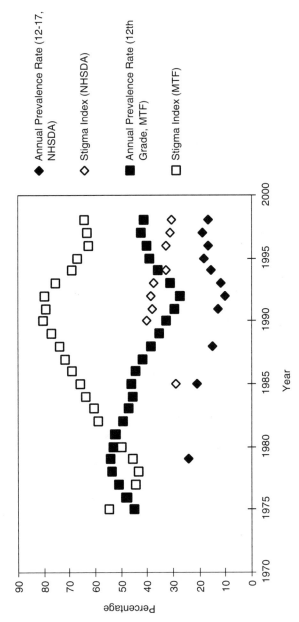

FIGURE D.4 Prevalence of use rates and the stigma index, 1975-1999, National Household Survey of Drug Abuse (NHSDA) and Monitoring the Future (MTF). Note: The specific question from MTF used to create this index is: "Do you disapprove of people (who are 18 or older) smoking marijuana occasionally?" The NHSDA question used to create the index is: "How much do you think people risk harming themselves physically or in other ways when they smoke marijuana occasionally/once a month?" This question is asked of 12-17-year-olds.

SOURCE of Stigma Index: LD Johnston, PM O'Malley, JG Bachman. (Dec. 1998). Drug use by American young people begins to turn downward. University of Michigan News and Information Services: Ann Arbor, MI. [On_line]. Table 9. Available: www.isr.umich.edu/src/mtf; accessed 11/16/99.

and stigma series are almost mirror images of each other. As stigma increases, use decreases. One might interpret these results as evidence that the reported measures are valid. That is, use decreases as perceptions of harm increase. Alternatively, these results are consistent with the idea that changes in stigma are associated with changes in invalid reporting. As stigma increases, false negative reports increase. The consensus view that the data reveal trends seems inconsistent with the view that the fraction of false reports varies with the stigmatization of drugs.

In the absence of an invariance assumption, the data do not identify the trends in illegal drug use. However, the data might reveal the direction of the trend. Consider the level estimates implied by assumption IR-1 and IR-2. Here, if $P = 0.30$, the width of the bound on trends is 60 points—the observed trend plus and minus 0.30. In this case, the sign of the trend is identified if the observed prevalence rates change by more than 30 points over the period.

In practice, this bound implies that the data do not in general reveal the direction of the trend in prevalence rates. Since the observed annual (absolute) change in the prevalence rates never exceeds 5 points, the sign of the annual trend is not identified. Likewise, the observed increase in the fraction of adolescent users during the 1990s is at most estimated to be around 13 points. Thus, if one adopts the restriction that the invalid response rate is less than 30 percent, the observed data would not reveal whether use increased in the 1990s. If one were willing to impose a stronger restriction on misreporting (e.g., $P = 0.05$), the observed data would be able to identify the sign of this trend.

Linking Stigma and Inaccurate Reporting

Imposing explicit restrictions on the behavior of invalid response over time can further narrow the bounds on the trends in prevalence rates. Suppose there is a positive relationship between false negative reporting and the stigmatization of illegal drugs. In particular, assume that

IR-3: the fraction of false positive reports, $P[w_t = 1, y_t = 0]$, is fixed over time,

and that

IR-4: the fraction of users who claim to have abstained, $P[w_t = 0 \mid y_t = 1]$, increases with an index, St, of the degree that illicit drugs are stigmatized. That is, if $S_{t+j} \geq S_t$, then $P[w_{t+j} = 0 \mid y_{t+j} = 1] \geq P[w_{t+j} = 0 \mid y_t = 1]$.

If stigma increases over time, assumptions IR 1-4 imply that

(11) $\text{Min } \{P[w_{t+j} = 1] - P[w_t = 1], (P[w_{t+j} = 1]$
             $- P[w_t = 1])/(1 - K_{max})\}$
             $\leq P[y_{t+j} = 1] - P[y_t = 1] \leq$
             $P[w_{t+j} = 1] - P[w_t = 1] + P,$

where $K_{max} = P/(P + \max(P[w_{t+j} = 1], P[w_t = 1]).$[15] A similar formula applies when stigma falls during the period of interest.

Intuitively, if both the observed trends in stigma and in the fraction of drug users are positive, the data reveal that the prevalence rates increased. In particular, the trend in illegal drug consumption will be no less than the observed trend and no greater than the reported trend plus P. Thus, by imposing assumptions IR-3 and IR-4, the width of the bound on the trend is reduced in half, from 0.60 to 0.30 when $P = 0.30$. If the reported trend is negative, the results are less certain. Here, the lower bound will be less than the reported negative trend, while the upper bound will be positive if the reported prevalence rates from period (t) to ($t+j$) declined by less than P points.

Table D.4 presents the annual trend in the fraction of high school seniors who report using illegal drugs, the direction of change in the stigma index (1 = stigma increased, –1 = stigma decreased) and the estimated bounds for the annual trend under that assumption that no more than 30 percent of respondents misreport drug use. These bounds on trends are much tighter than those derived without imposing the additional assumptions IR-3 and IR-4. In fact, the uncertainty is reduced nearly in half from 60 points to just over 30 points. Even under these stronger assumptions, however, the data do not generally reveal the sign of the annual trend. In only three cases do the data reveal that the annual trend in prevalence rates increases, while in one case the prevalence rate falls. In all other cases, the estimated sign of the annual trend is uncertain, reflecting the fact that the reported trends are almost a mirror image of the trends in the stigma index (see Figure D.4).

Consider, for instance, the bounds on the trend from 1991 to 1992. During this period, the fraction of self-reported users declined by 2.3 points. Over the same period, the stigma index increased. Thus, from Equation (11), we know that the upper bound on the trend equals $-2.3 + P$ and the lower bound on the trend lies slightly below the observed trend. If the maximum possible misreporting rate is greater than 2.3 percent, the data cannot reject the possibility that the trend is positive. In contrast, the fraction of self-reported users from 1990 to 1991 decreased by 3.1 points, while the stigma index also decreased. In this case, the bounds are strictly negative regardless of P.

---

[15]See the technical note at the end of this appendix for a proof of this result.

TABLE D.4 Bounds on Annual Trends in Illegal Drug Consumption for 12th Graders Given Invalid Reporting, Monitoring the Future

Reported Year	Reported Trend	Stigma[a]	LB(30)[b]	UB(30)[b]
1976	3.1	−1	−26.9	5.0
1977	3.0	−1	−27.0	4.8
1978	2.7	−1	−27.3	4.2
1979	0.4	1	0.4	30.4
1980	−1.1	1	−1.7	28.9
1981	−1.0	1	−1.6	29.0
1982	−2.7	1	−4.3	27.3
1983	−2.0	1	−3.2	28.0
1984	−1.6	1	−2.6	28.4
1985	0.5	1	0.5	30.5
1986	−2.0	1	−3.3	28.0
1987	−2.6	1	−4.4	27.4
1988	−3.2	1	−5.5	26.8
1989	−3.1	1	−5.5	26.9
1990	−2.9	1	−5.4	27.1
1991	−3.1	−1	−33.1	−3.1
1992	−2.3	1	−4.6	27.7
1993	3.9	−1	−26.1	7.7
1994	4.8	−1	−25.2	8.8
1995	3.2	−1	−26.8	5.7
1996	1.2	−1	−28.8	2.1
1997	2.2	1	2.2	32.2
1991–1997	13.0	−1	−17.0	22.4

[a]Reported stigma equals 1 if the stigma index increased and −1 if it decreased. The specific question from MTF used to create this index is: "Do you disapprove of people (who are 18 or older) smoking marijuana occasionally?" The NHSDA question used to create the index is: "How much do you think people risk harming themselves physically or in other ways when they smoke marijuana occasionally/once a month?"
[b]UB(z) and LB(z) are the upper and lower bound respectively, under the assumption that no more than z percent of the respondents would give invalid responses.

Source of Stigma Index Data: LD Johnston, PM O'Malley, JG Bachmam, 1998b. Drug use by American young people begins to turn downward. University of Michigan News and Information Services: Ann Arbor, MI. [On_line]. Table 9. Available:www.isr.umich.edu/src/mtf; accessed 11/16/99.

The bounds in Equation (11) may also be used to examine whether the prevalence rate increased from 1991 to 1997. Over this period, the observed rate increased while stigma appeared to be decreasing. Thus, even under the stronger restrictions implied by IR3-4, the data may not reveal whether the large reported increase in use over the 1990s reflects an underlying increase in the number of adolescent users, or if it instead indicates changes in the degree of inaccurate reporting. Depending on the maximum inaccurate reporting rate, P, the sign of the trend may be ambiguous. In fact, if P = 0.30, the lower bound is negative. For the MTF, the bound restricts the trend to lie between –17.0 and 22.4, while for the NSHDA the bound implies that the trend lies between [–24.3, 35.7]. With P = 0.05, however, the lower bound is positive. In this case, the bound for MTF 12th graders is [8.0, 14.6] and for NHSDA adolescents is [0.7, 10.7].

CONCLUSIONS

The Monitoring the Future survey and the National Household Survey of Drug Abuse provide important data for tracking the numbers and characteristics of illegal drug users in the United States. Response problems, however, continue to hinder credible inference. While nonresponse may be problematic, the lack of detailed information on the accuracy of response in the two national drug use surveys is especially troubling. Data are not available on the extent of inaccurate reporting or on how inaccurate response changes over time. In the absence of good information on inaccurate reporting over time, inferences on the levels and trends in the fraction of users over time are largely speculative. It might be, as many have suggested, that misreporting rates are stable over time. It might also be that these rates vary widely from one period to the next.

These problems, however, do not imply that the data are uninformative or that the surveys should be discontinued. Rather, researchers using these data must either tolerate a certain degree of ambiguity or must be willing to impose strong assumptions. The problem, of course, is that ambiguous findings may lead to indeterminate conclusions, whereas strong assumptions may be inaccurate and yield flawed conclusions (Manski, 1995; Manski et al., 2000).

There are practical solutions to this quandary. If stronger assumptions are not imposed, the way to resolve an indeterminate finding is to collect richer data. Data on the nature of the nonresponse problem (e.g., the prevalence rate of nonrespondents) and on the nature and extent of inaccurate response in the national surveys might be used to both supplement the existing data and to impose more credible assumptions. Efforts to increase the valid response rate may reduce the potential effects of these problems.

ACKNOWLEDGMENT

I wish to thank Richard Bonnie, Joel Horowitz, Charles Manski, Dan Melnick, and the members of the Committee on Data and Research for Policy on Illegal Drugs for their many helpful comments on an earlier draft of this paper. Also, I would like to thank Faith Mitchell at the National Research Council for her participation in this project.

TECHNICAL NOTE: STIGMA MODEL

In this appendix, I derive the Equation (11) bounds on the prevalence rate of use implied by assumptions IR 1-4. Recall that

IR-3: the fraction of false positive reports, $P[w_t = 1, y_t = 0]$, is fixed over time,

and

IR-4: the fraction of users who claim to have abstained, $P[w_t = 0 \mid y_t = 1]$, increases with an index, St, of the degree that illicit drugs are stigmatized. That is, if $S_{t+j} \geq S_t$, then $P[w_{t+j} = 0 \mid y_{t+j} = 1] \geq P[w_{t+j} = 0 \mid y_t = 1]$.

The restriction imposed in IR-3 serves to simplify the notation and can be easily generalized. Under this assumption, inferences about trends in illicit drug use are not influenced by false positive reports. That is,

$$(A1) \quad P[y_{t+j} = 1] - P[y_t = 1] = P[w_{t+j} = 1] - P[w_t = 1] \\ + P[w_{t+j} = 0, y_{t+j} = 1] - P[w_t = 0, y_t = 1].$$

Note that this restriction does not contain identifying information. In the absence of additional restrictions, assumptions IR 1-3 imply that in both periods (t) and $(t+j)$ the fraction of false negative reports must lie between $[0, P]$. Thus, the upper bound on the trend in prevalence rates equals the observed trend plus P, while the lower bound is the observed trend minus P. The width of the bound on trend remains $2P$.

By restricting the false negative reports over time, Assumption IR-4 does narrow the bounds. Rewrite Equation (A1) as

$$(A2) \quad P[y_{t+j} = 1] - P[y_t = 1] \\ = P[w_{t+j} = 1] - P[w_t = 1] \\ + P[w_{t+j} = 0 \mid y_{t+j} = 1]P[y_{t+j} = 1] - P[w_t \\ = 0 \mid y_t = 1] P[y_t = 1]$$

and consider the case where the stigma of using drugs increases from period (t) to $(t+j)$.[16] Although assumption IR-4 does not affect the upper bound, it does narrow the lower bound: the fraction of users who claim to have abstained cannot decrease over time. Thus, the lower bound is found by setting the two conditional probabilities equal in which case we know that

---

[16]A similar analysis applies when stigma falls over the period of interest, with assumptions IR1-4 affecting the upper rather than lower bound.

(A3) $P[y_{t+j} = 1] - P[y_t = 1] \ni \{ P [w_{t+j} = 1] - P [w_t = 1] \} / (1 - K),$

where K is the common misreporting rate.

This lower bound depends on the possible value of K, which must lie between

(A4) $0 \le K \le P / (P + \max(P[w_{t+j} = 1], P[w_t = 1]) = K_{max}.$ [17]

Equations (A3) and (A4) imply that if the observed trend is positive, the lower bound is found by setting $K = 0$. If the observed trend is negative, the lower bound is found by setting $K = K_{max}$.

Thus, under assumptions IR 1-4

(A5) $\text{Min } \{ P[w_{t+j} = 1] - P[w_t = 1], (P[w_{t+j} = 1]$
                    $- P[w_t = 1])/(1 - K_{max}) \}$
                    $\le P[y_{t+j} = 1] - P[y_t = 1] \le$
                    $P[w_{t+j} = 1] - P[w_t = 1] + P.$

---

[17]For simplicity, I rule out the case where $(P[w_j = 1] + P) > 1$. Then, from Equation 9, the conditional probabilities in Equation (A2) must lie between $\{0, P/((P[w_{t+j} = 1] + P)\}$ and $\{0, P/((P[w_t = 1] + P)\}$, respectively.

REFERENCES

Anglin, M.D., J.P. Caulkins, and Y.-I Hser
  1993 Prevalence estimation: Policy needs, current status, and future potential. *Journal of Drug Issues* 345-361.

Biemer, P., and M. Witt
  1996 Estimation of measurement bias in self-reports of drug use with applications to the National Household Survey on Drug Abuse. *Journal of Official Statistics* 12(3):275-300.

Caspar, R.
  1992 Followup of nonrespondents in 1990. In C.F. Turner, J.T. Lessler, and J.C. Gfroerer, eds., *Survey Measurement of Drug Use: Methodological Studies.* DHHS Pub. No (ADM) 92-1929.

Cook, R.F., A.D. Bernstein, and C.M. Andrews
  1997 Assessing drug use in the workplace: A comparison of self-report, urinalysis, and hair analysis. In L. Harrison and A. Hughes, eds., *The Validity of Self-Reported Drug Use: Improving the Accuracy of Survey Estimates.* NIDA Research Monograph, Number 167.

Darke, S.
  1998 Self report among injecting drug users: A review. *Drug Alcohol Dependence* 51:253-63.

Fendrich, M., T.P. Johnson, S. Sudman, J.S. Wislar, and V. Spiehler
  1999 Validity of drug use reporting in a high risk community sample: A comparison of cocaine and heroin survey reports with hair tests. *American Journal of Epidemiology* 149(10):955-962.

Fendrich, M., and C.M. Vaughn
  1994 Diminished lifetime substance use over time: An inquiry into differential underreporting. *Public Opinion Quarterly* 58(1):96-123.

Gfroerer, J., J. Lessler, and T. Parsley
  1997 Studies of nonresponse and measurement error in the National Household Survey on Drug Abuse. Pp. 273-295 in L. Harrison and A. Hughes, eds., The Validity of Self-Reported Drug Use: Improving the Accuracy of Survey Estimates. NIDA Research Monograph, Number 167.

Gfroerer, J., D. Wright, and A. Kopstein
  1997 Prevalence of youth substance use: The impact of methodological differences between two national surveys. *Drug and Alcohol Dependence* 47:19-30.

Harrison, L.D.
  1992 Trends in illicit drug use in the United States: Conflicting results from national surveys. *International Journal of the Addictions* 27(7):917-947.
  1997 The validity of self-reported drug use in survey research: An overview and critique of research methods. Pp. 17-36 in L. Harrison and A. Hughes, eds., *The Validity of Self-Reported Drug Use: Improving the Accuracy of Survey Estimates.* NIDA Research Monograph, Number 167.

Harrison, L.D., and A. Hughes, eds.
  1997 *The Validity of Self-Reported Drug Use: Improving the Accuracy of Survey Estimates.* NIDA Research Monograph, Number 167.

Horowitz, J., and C.F. Manski
    1998   Censoring of outcomes and regressors due to survey nonresponse: Identification
            and estimation using weights and imputations. *Journal of Econometrics* 84:37-58.
    2000   Nonparametric analysis of randomized experiments with missing covariate and
            outcome data. *Journal of the American Statistical Association* 95:77-84.

Johnston, L.D., P.M. O'Malley, and J.G. Bachman
    1998a   *National Survey Results on Drug Use from the Monitoring the Future Study, 1975-
            1997*, Vol. I.
    1998b   Drug Use by American Young People Begins to Turn Downward. University of
            Michigan News and Information Services, Ann Arbor, MI. [On line]. Tables 1b
            and 3. Available: www.isr.umich.edu/src/mtf [accessed 11/16/99].

Kilpatrick, K., M. Howlett, P. Dedwick, and A.H. Ghodse
    2000   Drug use self-report and urinalysis. *Drug and Alcohol Dependence* 58(1-2):111-116.

Magura, S., D.Goldsmith, C. Casriel, P.J. Goldstein, and D.S. Linton
    1987   The validity of methadone clients' self-reported drug use. *International Journal of
            Addiction* 22(8):727-749.

Magura, S., R.C. Freeman, Q. Siddiqi, and D.S. Lipton
    1992   The validity of hair analysis for detecting cocaine and heroin use among addicts.
            International Journal of Addictions 27:54-69.

Manski, C.F.
    1995   *Identification Problems in the Social Sciences.* Cambridge, MA: Harvard University
            Press.

Manski, C.F., J. Newman, and J.V. Pepper
    2000   Using Performance Standards to Evaluate Social Programs with Incomplete Out-
            come Data: General Issues and Application to a Higher Education Block Grant
            Program. Thomas Jefferson Center Discussion Paper 312.

Manski, C.F., and J.V. Pepper
    2000   Monotone instrumental variables: With an application to the returns to school-
            ing. *Econometrica* 68(4):997-1010.

Mieczkowski, T.M.
    1996   The prevalence of drug use in the United States. Pp. 347-351 in M. Tonry, ed.,
            Crime and Justice: A Review of Research, Vol. 20.
    1990   The accuracy of self-reported drug use: An evaluation and analysis of new data.
            In R Weisheit, ed., *Drugs, Crime and the Criminal Justice System.*

Molotsky, I.
    1999   Agency survey shows decline last year in drug use by young. *New York Times*,
            August 19.

Morral, A.R., D. McCaffrey, and M.Y. Iguchi
    2000   Hardcore drug users claim to be occasional users: Drug use frequency
            underreporting. *Drug and Alcohol Dependence* 57(3):193-202.

Office of Applied Studies
    1997   National Household Survey on Drug Abuse: Main Findings 1997. U.S. Depart-
            ment of Health and Human Services, Substance Abuse and Mental Health Ser-
            vices Administration. Table 2.6. Available: http://www.samhsa.gov/oas/
            NHSDA/1997Main/Table%20of%20Contents.htm; accessed 11/16/99

Appendix E

Linking Treatment to Punishment: An Evaluation of Drug Treatment in the Criminal Justice System

Jeanette Covington

D rug treatment takes place in a number of different modalities, including therapeutic communities, outpatient drug-free programs, chemical dependency programs, and methadone maintenance programs. The majority of clients who enter and leave these programs do so voluntarily (Substance Abuse Mental Health Services Administration, 1999). However, some clients are referred to these same programs by the criminal justice system and can therefore be punished or threatened with punishment if they fail to respond to treatment and abstain from drugs.

For example, court-based offender management programs, such as Treatment Alternatives to Street Crime and drug courts draw on populations of probationers and refer them to treatment programs in the community. Drug treatment in the criminal justice system takes place among populations of incarcerated prison inmates who are encouraged or required to seek treatment in prison. At least some of these prison-based treatment programs are affiliated with community-based after-care programs that allow inmates to continue therapy when they return to the community on parole. Hence, drug treatment programs in the criminal justice system can in part be distinguished from voluntary programs by the clients they serve. In short, drug treatment programs in the criminal justice system are distinct in that they recruit clients from what are referred to as "captive" populations of prisoners, parolees, or probationers and encourage or require those that they supervise to enter treatment in prison or in the community.

Because treatment clients in criminal justice programs are recruited from these captive populations, they can be distinguished from voluntary treatment clients in that punishment or the threat of punishment is very much a part of any treatment they receive. Presumably, by linking treatment to punishment, criminal justice drug programs can make the consequences of continued drug use more costly for their clients and thereby deter them from continuing drug use once they complete the program. Indeed, it is widely asserted that by linking treatment to punishment or its threat, these programs have done at least as well as voluntary programs in terms of getting users off drugs (Hubbard et al., 1988, 1989).

Not only do criminal justice system-supervised clients differ from voluntary clients because they face punishment or the constant threat of punishment, but they also differ in that system-based programs more narrowly define client success in terms of abstinence. Certainly abstinence is the ideal for programs that treat voluntary clients as well, but staff in these programs typically find that even their most promising graduates routinely relapse and return to treatment. A more significant problem for treatment staff offering therapy to voluntary patients is high dropout rates as many voluntary clients enter treatment, stay very briefly, and then leave without stopping their drug use. In fact, because their clients are voluntary, they cannot be forced to stay in treatment long enough for it to take effect, nor can they be stopped from leaving if they have not achieved abstinence.

Yet in the view of some, a cycle of treatment-seeking followed by relapse and then more treatment-seeking is to be expected, because addiction is a chronic relapsing condition (O'Brien and McClellan, 1996). Thus, there is a presumption that some users will stop and restart their drug use many times before they are able to sustain abstinence. Because recovery after a single treatment episode is rare, therapists who treat voluntary clients often stress other, more modest goals along with abstinence. For example, voluntary clients may be deemed successful if they manage to sustain longer drug-free intervals after a single treatment episode, or if they manage to reestablish ties with nonusing significant others. In fact, both these changes can be important preliminary steps on the road to recovery.

If drug addiction is indeed a chronic relapsing condition that requires multiple treatment episodes before rehabilitation can occur, then the abstinence orientation of criminal justice treatment programs may not be in keeping with the recovery process.[1] Indeed, it might even be said that the

---

[1]For the purposes of this paper, drug addiction is defined as a chronic relapsing *condition*. The author is not confident that drug addiction qualifies as a disease.

probationers, parolees, and prisoners who participate in criminal justice system treatment are being set up to fail because recovery after a single treatment episode is demanded of them. If they fail to sustain abstinence after they leave the program, then they risk additional punishment.

In fact, by linking treatment to punishment, these programs risk having a countertherapeutic effect because they stigmatize the user. Drug users who participate in criminal justice treatment programs are stigmatized because their drug relapses can be punished with short stints in jail or longer stretches in prison. Since would-be employers may refuse to hire users with a record of incarcerations and law-abiding significant others may ostracize such users, punishing drug relapses in these ways may ultimately slow recovery. After all, securing stable employment and establishing ties to law-abiding significant others are crucial in the recovery process (Peters et al., 1999; Biernacki, 1986; Waldorf et al., 1991).

Yet despite these concerns about the limits of criminal justice treatment programs in speeding the recovery process, there is a good deal of research on system-based programs that seems to suggest that they are effective in getting their clients to abstain after a single episode of treatment. Since any claims that system-based programs are effective depend on how these programs are evaluated, this appendix examines the evaluation research on treatment programs in the criminal justice system. Particular attention is paid to research on four programs: in-prison treatment, prison after-care programs, Treatment Alternatives to Street Crime (TASC), and drug courts.

To determine if these programs are effective in bringing about client recovery in a single treatment episode requires some focus on how studies that evaluate these programs are designed. Hence the next section discusses the elements of an appropriate study design that will guide this review.

GUIDELINES FOR EVALUATING SYSTEM-BASED DRUG TREATMENT

To determine if treatment works or not requires that evaluations of treatment effectiveness be well designed. What follows is a list of the elements that contribute to a well-designed study.

Controlling self-selection bias. Among other things, appropriate study designs allow researchers to separate treatment effects from other factors that might influence client outcomes. For example, clients may abstain from drug use after a treatment episode because the program was effective in changing them, or because they themselves are so committed to getting off drugs that they persevere in demanding treatment programs, graduate, and abstain. Hence, clients who successfully abstain may succeed due to treatment effects, or they may be self-selected and succeed independent of treatment effects. Some researchers make an effort to control for this self-selection bias by randomly assigning subjects in their study to either a treatment group or a no-treatment control group. In this way, committed clients will end up in either the treatment group or the control group at random. Often study subjects in evaluation studies of system-based programs are randomly assigned to either a treatment group or a no-treatment control group from a waiting list.

Studies based on comparisons between treatment and no-treatment control groups are important because they can demonstrate if treatment works better than no treatment at all. However, in some evaluation research on system-based treatment programs, clients are randomly assigned to two different types of treatment. This is considerably less desirable than a study design that creates a no-treatment control group, because comparisons between two different types of treatment can determine only if one treatment program works better than another; such study designs cannot establish whether treatment works better than no treatment at all.

Other commonly used study designs in the evaluation research on system-based programs do not use random assignment at all. Instead they set up comparison groups that are matched to the treatment group on a few broadly defined demographic characteristics. Because these studies do not control for self-selection bias, it is often difficult to know how to interpret any findings that are based on such research.

Controlling for a stake in conformity. Apart from a study design that controls for differences in client motivation, there is a need to control for other client characteristics that might influence outcomes, independent of treatment effects. For example, some clients fare better in treatment than others because they have more of a stake in conformity. In particular, clients who have steady jobs or are married tend to fare better in treatment than those who are not because these conventional roles give them some additional incentive to persevere in the difficult recovery process and eventually abstain from drugs (Peters et al., 1999; Biernacki, 1986; Waldorf et al., 1991). Consistent with this research, studies on general populations of drug users indicate that getting married or taking one's first real job figures heavily in users' natural desistance from drugs even without treatment or punishment (Bachman et al., 1997). Fortunately, client characteristics like marital status and employment status are external and easily measured and therefore can be controlled in evaluation studies.

It is important that these individual characteristics be controlled in order to determine how much client success is due to incumbency in these roles prior to treatment and how much is due to treatment program effects. However, it is not enough to simply isolate and control these effects for those who have them before treatment; they should also be controlled in posttreatment follow-ups. After all, some clients may abstain in the posttreatment period because they suddenly acquire a stake in conformity by getting married or beginning to work steadily and not simply due to any previous treatment effects.

Use of credible outcome measures. Apart from controlling for clients' internal commitments and external incentives to recover, it is also important that a study make use of credible outcome measures. Success in most system-based treatment programs is defined in terms of whether or not clients abstain from drugs after they leave treatment, and levels of client abstinence in the follow-up period are variously measured in terms of self-reports, rearrests or reincarceration for the resumption of drug use. Yet there may be reason to question whether these measures provide accurate estimates of drug relapse in the follow-up period. Regular and random urine testing in the follow-up period would seem to be the most accurate method for estimating what percentage of clients relapse.

Identifying appropriate follow-up periods. Apart from the problem of identifying credible outcome measures, a related problem has to do with whether an appropriate follow-up period is selected for measuring client outcomes. Evaluations of drug treatment programs in the criminal justice system often make use of inappropriate follow-up periods, as they only follow clients in the short term, while they are on probation or parole. However criminal justice treatment programs have two components: the therapeutic component, which attempts to change or rehabilitate the client (e.g., counseling, therapeutic community) and the punitive component which attempts to make the client conform to the therapeutic regimen long enough to make needed changes. Hence, criminal justice clients can be said to have completed treatment only after both therapy and the risk of punishment have ended. This means that the appropriate follow-up period for programs that link treatment and punishment *only begins after both the therapeutic and punitive components of treatment have ended.* Probation and parole should not be used as follow-up periods because criminal justice clients are still in the punitive component of the treatment program. It is only after parole and probation, when all program interventions have ceased, that it is possible to tell if the combination of therapy and punishment have somehow changed clients so that they are able to sustain abstinence on their own in the long term.

Linking retention to outcomes. In past research, when program participants have been able to sustain abstinence from drugs after they leave treatment, longer stays in treatment have traditionally predicted these successful outcomes. There is a good deal of evidence that treatment programs in the criminal justice system have been highly effective in using punishment or the threat of punishment to induce their charges to stay in treatment long enough for it to take effect (Wexler et al., 1992; U.S. General Accounting Office, 1997; Belenko, 1998; Hubbard et al., 1988; Hubbard et al., 1989). Hence, evaluations of system-based treatment programs should go a step further and determine whether the longer retention of criminal justice treatment participants somehow translates into positive posttreatment outcomes.

Identifying treatment components that promote recovery. Finally, some evaluation researchers have focused on teasing apart those components of treatment that work. For example, some treatment programs treat clients in several different stages. Prison treatment programs, in particular, are sometimes associated with after-care programs in the community. These multistage programs enable an inmate to begin recovery in the prison treatment program and continue the recovery process in a community-based after-care unit while they are on parole. In such multistage treatment programs, it is important to determine which stage in the treatment process has a greater effect on successful client outcomes.

Teasing apart the components of treatment that work may also involve an effort to identify which therapeutic services contribute most to favorable client outcomes. Some programs can offer an array of services, including counseling, job training and referral, 12-step programs, and group therapy. If certain therapies consistently fail to change clients, that tendency points to a need to explore whether some types of clients might resist particular therapies. In such cases, an effort needs to be made to identify the reasons for client resistance and begin a search for appropriate therapies that might lead to better outcomes.

In the next section, evaluations of in-prison drug treatment and community-based prison after-care programs are reviewed. An effort is made to determine if study designs employed in the evaluations of these programs make it possible to draw firm conclusions about their effectiveness in treating drug-using inmates and parolees. This is followed by a section on system-based treatment programs in the community. Since most drug users in system-based programs in the community are on probation, the section on drug treatment in the community begins with some background on how drug users are supervised on probation. Yet because probation supervision involves large caseloads, probation programs for drug users are often confined to monitoring and punishing drug-using probationers rather than treating them. Special offender management programs like TASC and drug courts often have to be set up to recruit probationers and then link their monitoring and punishment to treatment. Hence, after some background about probation, the evaluation research on these programs is reviewed to determine if they are effective in helping their participants to achieve abstinence.

TREATING DRUG USERS IN PRISON AND AFTER-CARE PROGRAMS

In the past 20 years, prison populations have grown tremendously. The largest increase in the inmate population has occurred due to the rise in the number of persons incarcerated for drug possession and other nonviolent crimes related to drug use. For example, in 1980 there were 23,900 prisoners who had been incarcerated for drug use and drug sales. By 1998, that number had risen tenfold to 236,800 prisoners incarcerated for drug law violations (Blumstein and Beck, 1999; Beck, 2000). Presumably, many of these drug law violators could benefit from treatment while in prison.

Prison-Based Programs

A number of studies of prison-based programs seem to demonstrate positive postrelease outcomes when inmates who have gone through prison treatment programs are compared with those who have not (Wexler et al., 1992, 1996; Inciardi, 1996; Landry, 1997; Mullen, 1996; Wexler, 1996; Field, 1984). In particular, evaluations of one of the better-known prison therapeutic communities, called Stay'n Out, seem to indicate that participants in this prison treatment program experience a number of positive postrelease outcomes when they are compared with a control group that is not exposed to treatment (Wexler et al., 1992, 1996; Landry, 1997).

In an evaluation of Stay'n Out, study subjects were drawn from a waiting list of inmates who had volunteered to participate in the prison therapeutic community. These volunteers were either randomly assigned to the treatment group (who actually enrolled in the therapeutic community) or to the control group who remained on the waiting list and never received treatment. The no-treatment control group included not only those randomly assigned to the waiting list, but also those who volunteered for treatment and were not admitted because they did not have enough time left to serve to complete the 12 months recommended for prison treatment.

Because study subjects in both the treatment and no-treatment control groups volunteered for treatment, any findings from the study can be generalized only to inmates willing to volunteer for prison treatment programs (Wexler et al., 1999). The subjects in this study cannot be said to represent those inmates who do not volunteer for in-prison programs.

Both the treatment group and the no-treatment control group were followed after their release from prison. Outcomes were measured while they were on parole for a period of about 3 years after their release from prison.

When comparisons were made between the male treatment participants and males in the no-treatment control group, subjects in the treatment group were significantly less likely to be rearrested while on parole than the no-treatment controls (Wexler et al., 1992, 1996). However, the findings were mixed as the subjects in the no-treatment control group actually delayed time until arrest longer than the treatment participants (15 months versus 13.1 months), although the differences were not significant. Moreover, the no-treatment control group was more likely to experience a positive parole discharge without technical violations, arrests, or revocation than the treatment group. Again, differences were not significant. The fact that the no-treatment control group fared as well as the treatment group on some measures of success indicates that this in-prison program did not change participants in ways so that they were any more likely to desist from criminal behavior and drug use upon release than a control group who had not received treatment.

Additional problems with this study have to do with the outcome measures selected. Ideally, outcome measures should gauge the impact of in-prison drug treatment on reductions in drug use after release. After all, the effectiveness of in-prison therapeutic communities depends on their ability to change treatment clients in ways so that they will be less likely to use drugs after leaving prison. However, the outcome measures used in the evaluation of Stay'n Out are too global to gauge the impact of prison treatment on postrelease drug use as they include rearrests and parole violations for both drug crimes (drug use, drug sales, etc.) and nondrug crimes (robbery, assault, etc.). To measure the impact of prison drug treatment on postrelease rearrests and parole violations for drug crimes requires that drug crimes be singled out.

Separating drug crimes from nondrug crimes also makes it possible to gauge how much harm paroled prisoners do upon their return to the community. If prisoners are reincarcerated for predatory nondrug crimes like robbery, then it suggests that they continue to pose a threat to the community. If they are rearrested or have their parole revoked for technical violations, like failing a urine test or refusing to attend a drug treatment program, then it is not clear that they necessarily endanger the community. Indeed some have raised questions about the fairness of reincarcerating drug users for such technical violations largely because these violations do not indicate that such users pose a threat to the community (Petersilia and Turner, 1985; Clear and Terry, 2000).

Also problematic from the standpoint of measurement is the use of rearrests and parole discharge as outcome indicators. Because so few episodes of drug use end in an arrest or parole revocation, it is doubtful that counts of study subjects rearrested or deemed parole violators accurately represent all incidents of relapse to drug use in the 3-year post-prison period. (The outcome measures and elements of the study design used in the Wexler et al., 1992 evaluation of Stay'n Out are summarized in Table E.1.)

Apart from the problem with the use of questionable outcome measures, certain of these analyses raise questions about the oft-cited link between longer retention in treatment and more positive outcomes. Prison treatment staff recommend that participants in the prison therapeutic community remain in treatment for 9-12 months to complete each phase of therapy. And, as expected, those who stayed 9-12 months and com-

TABLE E.1 Evaluations of Prison Treatment Programs

	Random Assignment to Prison Treatment	Random Assignment to Aftercare	Outcome Measures	Drug Outcome Measures	Unsupervised Follow-Ups
Stay'n Out Wexler et al., 1996	Yes	Not apply	-Rearrest -Months till rearrest -Positive parole discharge	No	No
Key-Crest Inciardi, 1996 Martin et al., 1999	No	No	-Rearrests (excludes parole violations)	-Self-reports and urine tests are voluntary	No
Amity Wexler et al., 1999	Yes	No	-Reincarceration -Days till incarceration	No	No
Texas In-Prison TC Knight et al., 1999	No	No	-Reincarceration	Urine test for parole supervision	No

pleted treatment were more likely to experience positive outcomes upon release. In particular, they delayed the time until arrest longer than those who had stayed less than 9 months (Wexler et al., 1992). However, ever-longer stays in treatment did not always mean more positive outcomes. While those retained in the prison program for 9-12 months delayed rearrest for 18 months, those who stayed even longer—14 months—actually delayed arrest for only 12 months. Hence, those retained in treatment 9-11 months actually fared better than those retained longer at 14 months. Similarly, those who stayed in treatment 9-11.9 months fared better in terms of positive parole outcomes than those who stayed in treatment more than 12 months. Fully 77 percent of those retained for 9-11.9 months were positively discharged from parole, compared with only 57 percent of those who were retained for more than 12 months (Wexler et al., 1992).

These findings raise questions regarding the time-tested link between retention and positive outcomes, as longer stays do not always translate into less posttreatment criminal behavior. In fact, these inconsistent findings are important enough that replication may be necessary to see if these surprising results show up in evaluations of other system-based treatment programs.

Influence of Community-Based After Care

The findings from the evaluation of Stay'n Out have enormous significance because they are based on comparisons between subjects randomly assigned to treatment or a no-treatment control group. The fact that the study shows that prison treatment has little to no impact on posttreatment outcomes raises doubts about the effectiveness of treatment in prison. However, some have argued that prison-based programs are more likely to bring about improvements if prison treatment participants continue to be involved in a therapeutic community after their release from prison (Inciardi, 1996; Martin et al., 1999; Wexler et al., 1999; Knight et al., 1999). Indeed, it is possible that after-care programs may have more influence on inmate improvements than prison treatment alone. If positive posttreatment outcomes are primarily due to treatment in the community-based after-care unit, it raises the possibility that the very expensive prison-based component is not really necessary.

There may be some support for the notion that the community-based after-care unit is more important than the prison-based component of treatment. In a study of the Key-Crest program that combines a prison therapeutic community and a community-based therapeutic community for after care, Inciardi (1996) was able to determine the importance of prison treatment relative to the after-care program.

As might be expected, the data showed that clients who graduated from both the prison-based Key therapeutic community and the community-based Crest therapeutic community had the most positive outcomes in terms of drug-free and arrest-free status in a 6-month follow-up (Inciardi, 1996; Martin et al., 1999).

The second most successful group included those with *no* prison treatment who underwent work release in the Crest therapeutic community after-care unit only. They were much more likely to be drug free and arrest free than those inmates who participated in the prison treatment program but underwent work release in the community in a unit without a therapeutic community. (The comparison group was the least likely to be arrest free and drug free of the four groups.)

These rankings held in the preliminary 6 month follow-up. In a second follow-up after 18 months, the drug-free and arrest-free scores for all four groups were much lower; however, the rankings remained the same (Landry, 1997; Martin et al., 1999).

The fact that those with community-based after care only outperformed those with prison treatment only raises questions about how much influence prison-based therapeutic communities have on positive outcomes. On the basis of these findings, one could argue that the community-based after-care program was more instrumental in reducing relapse and recidivism than the prison-based program.

Indeed, after examining the follow-up data, the Key-Crest researchers concluded that participation in a prison treatment program alone was not effective in bringing about drug-free or arrest-free status after release. In their view, successful outcomes depended on participation in the community-based after-care program (Martin et al., 1999).

This finding that prison treatment alone was considerably less important than community-based after-care was borne out by research conducted on another prison treatment program called Amity (Wexler et al., 1999). Much like Key-Crest, the Amity program combined a prison-based therapeutic community with a community-based after-care program. Hence it was possible for Amity participants to begin their recovery in the prison-based therapeutic community and continue it in a community-based therapeutic community upon release.

In the Amity program, volunteers for prison treatment were randomly assigned from a waiting list to either treatment or a no-treatment control group (Wexler et al., 1999). In this sense, the Amity program was different from the Key-Crest program as study subjects were not randomly assigned to prison treatment in the Key-Crest study (Wexler et al., 1999). Hence the Amity program controls for selection bias for those who participate in their prison program, whereas the Key-Crest program does not (see Table E.1 for study designs for both Amity and Key-Crest).

The Amity treatment group and no-treatment controls were both followed for 12 months and then 24 months. In both these follow-ups, those who completed both the prison therapeutic community and the after-care component were significantly less likely to be reincarcerated in the 12-month and 24-month follow-ups than the no-treatment controls and those who had not completed both programs. This is consistent with findings from Key-Crest that also show that those who complete both in-prison and after-prison treatment phases do significantly better than all other study subjects (Martin et al., 1999).

However, Wexler et al. (1999) question whether the successes of those who complete both phases of treatment in Amity are due solely to program effects. For while they randomly assign study subjects to prison treatment or a no-treatment control group in the first phase of treatment, they do not randomly assign study subjects in the second phase of treatment when they enter the after-care therapeutic community (see Table E.1). Instead, all those who complete the prison therapeutic community are eligible to volunteer to participate in the after-care program. This means that while self-selection bias is controlled in phase one of the program, it is not controlled in phase two (Wexler et al., 1999). The failure to randomly assign study subjects at phase two means that a self-selection bias is introduced for those participating in the after-care program.

It is possible, then, that prison treatment graduates who self-select to volunteer for after-care and then complete it may be much more motivated to make changes in their lives than those who do not complete both phases of treatment. The possibility exists that such clients might have succeeded due to their own motivation rather than due to the combined effects of in-prison and after-care treatment (Wexler et al., 1999).

All in all, both the Amity and Key-Crest studies seem to suggest that community based after-care programs may be more important than in-prison treatment in helping clients to effect positive changes. This may be so because the after-care programs can help clients while they are in the community and at greatest risk of resuming drug use and criminal behavior. However, the influence of the after-care programs has not yet been demonstrated, as those eligible for after-care were not randomly assigned to treatment and no-treatment control groups in phase two of therapy (see Table E.1).

The effectiveness of the Amity program is also difficult to interpret because global outcome measures are used that include reincarceration for all crimes—both drug crimes and nondrug crimes alike (see Table E.1). In a study such as this in which the effectiveness of drug treatment is being examined, separate measures of reincarceration for drug crimes would have provided more appropriate indicators of drug relapse.

Moreover, there is reason to question the use of reincarceration as an outcome measure, since so few incidents of drug relapse end in reincarceration. In fact, on the face of it, self-reports of drug use or urine tests might seem to provide more accurate estimates of drug relapse than reincarceration.

Self-Reports and Urine Tests as Outcome Measures

At least one study cited in Table E.1 makes use of self-reports of drug relapse. In follow-ups of the Key-Crest program, while study subjects were on parole, they were asked to report on their drug relapses (Martin et al., 1999). However, such self-reports may not provide accurate estimates of drug relapses. After all, while study subjects are on parole, they may be inclined to underreport, since reporting a relapse while on parole could mean additional punishment.

Mindful of the potential for underreporting, Martin et al. (1999) confirmed parolee self-reports with a urine test. However, urine tests were administered only to study subjects who volunteered for follow-up interviews. Urine tests were not administered to those who did not volunteer, which means that the resumption of drug use was not accurately measured for all study subjects.

Urine tests were also used as outcome measures in a study of the Texas in-prison therapeutic community and its after-care program (Knight et al., 1999). Here again, there were problems with the way in which urine tests were administered, as study subjects in the treatment group were subject to more urine testing than subjects in the comparison group (see Table E.1 for the study design of the Texas program). Indeed, the researchers acknowledged this problem and argued that the treatment group seemed to relapse more than the comparison group only because they were subject to more urine testing (Knight et al., 1999).

It is conceivable that urine tests in both these studies could have yielded more accurate estimates of relapse were it not for problems in the way they were administered. Indeed, urine testing of parolees has the potential to provide accurate estimates of relapse. However, even urine testing may have its limits if long-term follow-ups are conducted after parole.

Identifying Appropriate Follow-Up Periods

All the studies cited in this review follow study subjects only while they are being supervised on parole, in work release, or in an after-care therapeutic community. However, none of these studies extends follow-ups to the all-important period after criminal justice supervision has ended. This is unfortunate because the period in which study subjects are on parole is best seen as a part of treatment rather than as a posttreatment follow-up period. In other words, actual or threatened punishment are just as much a part of a program that links treatment to punishment as traditional therapies like therapeutic communities or counseling that are meant to change the client. Hence a client's participation in the program ends only when parole supervision and the risk of punishment ends.

It is important to conduct a follow-up when parole and all other criminal justice treatment interventions have ceased for several other reasons. First, if programs that link treatment to punishment are effective, they have to work in the long term, when drug users are no longer subject to any intervention—either traditional therapy or punishment. Limiting follow-up periods to parole means that program effects are being monitored in the short term while the client is still partially in treatment.

Second, looking at client outcomes after parole also makes comparisons between programs that link treatment to punishment and voluntary programs much simpler. After all, follow-up studies in voluntary programs are typically conducted after the client has left the program and is no longer subject to any therapeutic interventions. Because clients in prison after-care programs are followed only while they are on parole, follow-up comparisons between parolees and voluntary clients after treatment are comparisons between nonequivalent groups. Indeed, such comparisons risk inflating the successes of those being followed on parole, as parolees are still in treatment as long as they are subject to criminal justice supervision. Hence, any claims that parolees in prison after-care programs fare as well or better than voluntary clients will have to await studies based on matching follow-up periods.

Finally, knowing whether prison after-care clients reduce their drug use after leaving parole makes it possible to see if these programs are cost-effective in the long term because of their capacity to change behavior even when clients are no longer subject to parole supervision.

Ideally, urine tests would be conducted after study subjects were released from parole in order to determine how many treatment and control subjects were able to sustain abstinence in long-term follow-ups. However, such tests would probably have to be voluntary in post-parole follow-ups, as clients would no longer be subject to criminal justice supervision. But if urine tests were voluntary in a post-parole follow-up, then it is likely that study subjects who used drugs in the follow-up would refuse to submit a urine test because they might fear they would be subjected to additional punishment. None of the studies cited in this review grapple with the problem of developing long-term outcome measures for a post-parole follow-up, as each of these studies confine their follow-ups to the period when study subjects are on parole (see Table E.1).

Identifying Services That Promote Recovery

In part, the above findings speak to problems in trying to identify which phase in a multiphase treatment process actually works. A related problem has to do with which recovery services offered by a treatment program have the greatest effect. With prison treatment, the program offers individual and group counseling and isolation in a therapeutic community that is meant to resocialize the client to lead a drug-free life. In prison after-care programs, these services can be offered along with staff assistance in helping clients prepare for a job interview, open a checking account, and learn how to budget (Inciardi, 1996). Hence, many of the clients may be working by the time they leave the after-care program. As a variety of services are offered, it is unclear whether the positive outcomes of after-care program completers are due to counseling and resocialization by the therapeutic community or more prosaic services, like job counseling and securing actual employment. If job counseling and actual employment explain positive outcomes, then the therapeutic community component may not be central for client recovery.

It is important to determine exactly which services promote client recovery, because some services may meet with less client resistance than others. In general, the rigorous treatment regimen of therapeutic communities is not very popular in the community, as indicated by the high dropout rates associated with this form of therapy (Institute of Medicine, 1990; Hubbard et al., 1989). Prison-based therapeutic communities may also not be very popular among inmates. This is because inmate subcultures tend to emphasize macho posturing, like being tough and streetwise (Inciardi, 1996). Hence, by prison subcultural standards, the constant confession of personal problems and emotional outpourings, required in therapeutic communities, may seem effeminate. Moreover, low-income and minority clients may resist therapies that require them to reveal intimate details about their lives to a therapist or a group of near strangers (Currie, 1993). This is important, because prison after-care programs draw heavily from low-income and minority populations. If very few inmates are willing to embrace these services, these programs can have only a limited impact on reducing posttreatment crime rates and drug use. By contrast, if much of the success of these programs is due to job training and referral and other services not likely to meet with client resistance, then such services might be deserving of greater emphasis.

Failure to Control for a Stake in Conformity

Both the treatment and criminology literatures consistently show that a stake in conformity speeds recovery from drug use and aging out of crime (Peters et al., 1999; Sampson and Laub, 1993; Steffensmeier and Allan, 1995). Yet the studies reviewed in this section typically fail to control for the effects of employment and marriage. This omission is especially troubling for the posttreatment period, in that it makes it impossible to know if client improvements in the post-treatment period are due to treatment or a client's newly acquired stake in conformity. However, because these studies did not conduct follow-ups that begin after criminal justice supervision has ended, little can be learned about whether prison treatment and after-care help these stigmatized populations to become reintegrated into society independent of their securing a stake in conformity.

SYSTEM-BASED TREATMENT IN THE COMMUNITY

Given the mixed findings, the failure to consistently control for self-selection bias, the problematic outcome measures, and the absence of follow-ups after parole, it is difficult to draw any firm conclusions on whether prison treatment and after-care programs are effective in the long term. Yet even in the absence of firm conclusions, some have soured on treating drug offenders in prison, simply because prison is so expensive (Covington, 2000). For example, even though the costs of a prison-based therapeutic community are modest—$10 to $18 per day—prison itself costs an average of $20,261 per person per year (Mullen, 1996; Camp and Camp, 1999). This makes prison-based treatment the most expensive drug rehabilitation program of all.

The high cost of prison itself is less of a factor with regard to some drug-using offenders who would otherwise be in prison for serious violent crimes. For them, the only relevant expense is the modest added cost of in-prison treatment. However, the more pressing question is whether the large population of drug users imprisoned for drug possession or other nonviolent offenses might be successfully treated in a community-based program. Since they do not represent a threat to the community, requiring them to participate in a treatment program outside prison walls could well lead to reductions in drug use and drug-related crime without the expense associated with incarceration.

Traditional Probation and Intensive Supervision Probation

Mandating treatment in the community is hardly a novel idea, as many drug users and low-level drug sellers are in fact currently being supervised by the criminal justice system in the community because they are on probation. Many persons arrested for drug law violations are either diverted to probation before they are prosecuted, or they are convicted and receive probation as punishment for their crimes. Furthermore, probation is much less expensive than prison, as supervised probation averages a modest $3,000 per person per year (Donziger, 1996).

In theory, at least, probation should be taken seriously as an alternative to prison, since probation officers should be able to mandate treatment or require abstinence of their charges as a condition of probation. For example, they could require probationers to submit to random urine tests to confirm that they are abstaining from drugs. They could also mandate that probationers enter and remain in treatment programs and monitor their progress in the program. If probationers fail to remain abstinent on their own or in treatment, probation officers could make use of graduated punishments, like requiring fines or community service or requiring them to spend two or three days in jail. As the ultimate sanction, they might even send them to jail or prison for much longer.

In practice, however, probation officers cannot conduct routine urine checks or monitor progress in treatment because their caseloads are so large. On average, a single probation officer has an average caseload of 100-300 offenders (Clear et al., 1997; Petersillia and Turner, 1985; Petersilia and Turner 1992). With such large caseloads, many probation officers are reduced to trying to supervise those they deem to be most dangerous and have little to no contact with other probationers defined as less serious.

Because traditional probation programs are likely to remain overextended for the foreseeable future, some have argued for an enhanced form of probation called intensive supervision probation (ISP). While they vary enormously, the one thing these programs should share is a much smaller caseload than traditional probation programs, although in many places there is little difference in caseloads between traditional probation and ISP programs. Smaller caseloads, averaging 30-50 probationers, are important because they allow for much more monitoring and surveillance of probationers. Indeed, in three California counties with such small ISP caseloads, ISP officers met with their charges face-to-face 1-5 times per week and conducted urine tests on a weekly or biweekly basis (Petersilia and Turner, 1985). Clearly, these officers were in a far better position to monitor their offenders' abstinence than traditional probation officers in the same California counties. Due to their smaller caseloads and enhanced surveillance, these ISP programs were more expensive ($6,957-$7,654) than traditional probation ($4,024-$6,122).

Since ISP programs with small caseloads should be capable of engaging in much more surveillance than traditional probation programs, probationers in ISPs should have lower recidivism rates. However, it is often difficult to make comparisons between ISPs and traditional probation because their client populations are so different (Clear, 1999; Clear et al.,

1997; Petersillia and Turner, 1985). Traditional probation programs can include the full range of offenders, from drug users only to drug-using petty criminals to drug-using, serious, repeat offenders. By contrast, because of its enhanced supervision, ISPs should, in theory, include only high-risk offenders, although this is not always the case.

In one California study, probationers were randomly assigned to ISPs or traditional probation, making comparisons easier. Fewer than 10 percent of the offenders in ISPs were rearrested for violent crimes, whereas 15 percent of adult felons on traditional probation throughout the entire state were rearrested for violent crimes (of course, recidivism rates for violent crimes tend to be low) (Petersilia and Turner, 1985; Morgan, 1993).

Although the ISPs had low recidivism rates for serious violent crimes, they had very high rates of technical violations, such as testing positive for drugs or failing to participate in a drug treatment program or failing to meet with a probation officer for a scheduled appointment. As many as 40-46 percent of the offenders in the California ISPs studied had technical violations as their most serious new offense, compared with 26 percent of offenders in traditional probation.

Since testing positive for drugs was one of the technical violations, these findings may suggest that traditional probation programs, with their lower levels of supervision, were actually better than ISPs at preventing drug relapse. However, a more accurate interpretation of these findings is that ISPs were involved in significantly more monitoring and supervision (e.g., urine testing) of their probationers than traditional probation programs, so they were much better able to discover infractions (Petersilia and Turner, 1985). Since the more intensive monitoring of probationer behavior makes ISPs much more likely to find out about continued drug use, it is impossible to determine whether enhanced supervision leads to more or fewer drug relapses than traditional probation.

Fairness Issues

Some question the fairness of punishing probationers for technical violations (Clear and Terry, 2000; Walker, 1994; Petersilia and Turner, 1985). After all, infractions like missing a meeting with a probation officer, testing positive for drugs, or failing to attend drug treatment can be met with real punishments in the form of incarceration or reincarceration (Covington, 1997; Clear and Terry, 2000; Walker, 1994; Petersilia and Turner, 1985). While such infractions certainly violate ISP program rules, they may not indicate that the violator is a danger to the community; hence incarceration or reincarceration may not be justified. Yet as it stands, a burglar can be sentenced to probation and left in the community for his burglary yet find himself being sent to jail or prison on a technical violation for a lesser crime like drug use (Clear and Terry, 2000; Petersilia and Turner, 1985; Petersilia, 1997; Walker, 1994). This is much more likely to happen in an ISP with its enhanced supervision.

Another fairness issue involves meting out real punishments for technical violations such as failing to attend drug treatment, in some cases, even when no local treatment programs are available (Petersilia, 1997). An additional concern has to do with whether *effective* treatment is available, as the effectiveness of self-help programs (e.g., Alcoholics Anonymous, Narcotics Anonymous) and some outpatient drug-free programs has not yet been demonstrated (Landry, 1997; Institute of Medicine, 1990). Since the effectiveness of many system-based treatment programs has not yet been demonstrated, the possibility exists that many of the available programs may not be able to rehabilitate probationers. If so, referral to these programs, in essence, sets them up to fail, and failure can result in punishment.

These concerns about the fairness of probation have become more important in the past 20 years as the probation net has widened to include more and more petty offenders and casual drug users who would have been released in previous years (Walker, 1994; Covington, 1997; Mauer and Huling, 1995). In fact, the population on probation grew by 41.3 percent between 1990 and 1999, and these 1990s increases came after significant growth in the probation population in the 1980s (Bureau of Justice Statistics, 2000; Donziger, 1996). Expanding probation to include more minor offenders means more use of criminal justice resources on nonviolent criminals with little impact on serious crime. Yet as it stands, criminal justice supervision may be expanding to include more and more such people whose offenses do no harm to the community.

Net Widening and the Evaluation of No-Treatment Control Groups

Typically the research on probation does not make use of control groups but rather compares populations subjected to more or less supervision (ISPs versus traditional probation) or samples of probationers with different characteristics (Morgan, 1993; Petersilia and Turner, 1985). Hence it is impossible to determine if those on probation are more likely to age out of using drugs than those not subjected to any criminal justice supervision at all. The need for such comparisons—between those on probation and a no-supervision control group—becomes more relevant as the net is widened to include drug users who would not have been arrested or put on probation in previous years. The possibility exists that any seeming improvements in the success rates of drug-using probationers over the years could be wrongly attributed to probation itself rather than to a net widened to include those with less severe drug and crime problems.

As it turns out, most drug users discontinue drug use on their own after a few years of experimentation, and the vast majority of them do so without being arrested or placed on probation (Bachman et al., 1997; Johnston et al., 1997; Covington, 1997). Since those untouched by the criminal justice system may be little different from those on probation, it may be useful to treat those at large in the community as a comparison group. Comparisons of noncontinuation rates between those who avoid arrest and probation and those on probation may be one way to determine if supervision and coercion really have much impact on desistance from drug use (Walker, 1994).

Another way to determine if supervision and coercion have much impact on reductions in drug use would be to randomly assign a sample of arrestees to either probation or release. The no-supervison control group would be those released, as they would not be subject to monitoring or the threat of punishment that comes with supervision on probation. Comparisons could then be made between those on probation and the no-supervision control group, not subject to either monitoring or coercion, in a follow-up period after probation. If monitoring and coercion alone are sufficient to induce drug users to abstain in the long term, then those subjected to probation supervision should be more likely to abstain from drugs after probation than their age-mates in the control group who could be expected to naturally mature out of drugs at that age without monitoring or the threat of punishment. Of course, such a study might be difficult to implement because sample attrition in the follow-up period would probably be high, especially for the no-supervision controls.

The fact that an authentic control group for probation is one not subject to control, surveillance, or punishment underscores the fact that probation means control, surveillance, and punishment of those who get caught in the criminal justice net. And, while probation programs sometimes link these controls to treatment, they do not do so in any reliable fashion. In fact, if probation supervision expands much more quickly than treatment slots, the real possibility exists that system-based programs for drug users will increasingly come to mean punishment without treatment. It might be wise, then, to consider other system-based programs that do a better job of consistently linking criminal justice sanctions to traditional treatment. Two such programs that were specifically set up to identify probationers, refer them to treatment, monitor their progress, and punish relapses are Treatment Alternatives to Street Crime and drug courts. Evaluations of these two offender management programs are reviewed in the next two sections.

TREATMENT ALTERNATIVES TO STREET CRIME

Established in 1972, Treatment Alternatives to Street Crime (TASC) is explicitly designed to link the coercive tools of the criminal justice system to treatment programs in the community in several ways. First, TASC identifies drug users who come into contact with the criminal justice system and then refers them to appropriate community-based treatment programs (Cook and Weinman, 1988; Inciardi et al., 1996). It then monitors client progress in treatment to determine if the referred clients reduce their crime and drug use and make improvements in their personal and social functioning. If the referred clients fail in treatment, they are returned to the criminal justice system for further sanctioning. If the referred clients successfully complete treatment, then their court cases can be dropped or dismissed. It is hoped that clients who successfully complete treatment will abstain from drugs or reduce their drug intake and thereby their drug-related criminal behavior. Hence, successful treatment outcomes benefit the criminal justice system as they make users, who graduate from treatment, less of a burden.

The effectiveness of TASC was examined using a subsample of clients enrolled in 41 publicly funded treatment programs in the Treatment Outcomes Prospective Study (TOPS), from 1979 to 1981. Hubbard et al. (1988) compared three groups of the TOPS study clients in residential treatment and outpatient drug-free programs: (1) clients referred to treatment by TASC, (2) clients not in TASC who were referred by the criminal justice system (clients on probation, bail, etc.), and (3) self-referrals or clients who had entered residential treatment or outpatient drug-free programs without criminal justice pressures.

As might be expected, the TASC and non-TASC criminal justice referrals stayed in treatment longer than the self-referrals. On average, TASC clients stayed 45 days longer than self-referred clients in outpatient drug-free programs, and the non-TASC criminal justice referrals stayed 17 days longer than the self-referrals (Hubbard et al., 1988, 1989). However, longer treatment retention did not always translate into more successful post-treatment outcomes.

TASC and other criminal justice system-referred clients did report lower levels of drug use following treatment than the self-referred clients. Still, it is difficult to interpret this finding, as the TASC clients, the non-TASC clients referred by the criminal justice system, and the self-referred clients were not randomly assigned to these three groups (see Table E.2 for study design). In addition, no effort was made to match the three groups on background characteristics. Since the three groups were not matched comparison groups, they differed in terms of important pretreatment characteristics. For example, the TASC and non-TASC clients re-

TABLE E.2   Evaluations of TASC Programs

	Random Assignment	Was there a no-treatment control group?	Outcome Measures	Drug Outcome Measures
Hubbard et al. 1988 Hubbard et al. 1989	No	No	Self-reports of predatory crime	Self-reports of drug use in 1-yr. follow-up
Anglin et al.	Yes; in 2 of 5 sites, subjects were assigned to TASC or alternative treatment program	No	Self-reports of crime and arrest records in 6-month follow-up	Self-reports of drug use in 6-month follow-up

ferred by the criminal justice system actually had *lower* drug use levels in the year before treatment than the self-referred clients. Moreover, the TASC and criminal justice system-referred clients were more likely to be users of alcohol and "softer" drugs like marijuana than the self-referrals.

In fact, the two groups of criminal justice system-referred clients differed from the self-referred clients in a number of ways that make differences in posttreatment outcomes difficult to interpret. Both groups of referred clients were younger, included more males, and had more extensive criminal records than the self-referred clients. The referred clients also received *fewer* medical, psychological, and family services while in outpatient drug-free programs than the self-referred clients, perhaps because their drug problems were less severe. This makes it difficult to argue that their greater success in reducing their drug intake following treatment—relative to the self-referred clients—was due to program services. The self-referred clients received more services and yet were more likely to continue their drug use after treatment.

The inconsistent findings, the differences between the criminal justice system-referred and the self-referred clients prior to treatment, and group differences in the services received make it difficult to draw any conclusions regarding differences in post-treatment outcomes among the three groups. These problems also make it difficult to understand the link between the longer stays of the criminal justice system-referred clients and any of their successful posttreatment outcomes. Indeed, these findings suggest that some caution should be exercised in using retention as a proxy measure of successful posttreatment outcomes.

Finally, the fact that the TASC and non-TASC criminal justice system referrals had *less* severe drug problems and more use of alcohol and marijuana than clients who entered treatment without legal pressures raises questions about the way in which TASC and other criminal justice agencies screen drug clients for referral to treatment.

A more recent study by Anglin et al. (1999) also examines the effectiveness of TASC programs, while avoiding many of the problems of the earlier research. Anglin et al. (1999) evaluated the effectiveness of TASC in five programs across the country that at least followed the TASC protocol. Of these five programs, three sites compared TASC clients with a comparison group that had not been randomly assigned. Evaluations in these three sites are difficult to interpret due to the potential for self-selection bias. However, the other two sites in Canton and Portland did use an experimental design. At the Canton and Portland sites, study subjects were randomly assigned either to treatment programs that used the TASC offender management model or to a treatment program that did not use the TASC model. (The alternative program may not have monitored users in treatment as effectively as those in TASC-monitored programs.) Hence Anglin et al. (1999) were comparing clients in two different types of treatment rather than examining TASC clients side by side with a no-treatment control group (see Table E.2).

At one of the two sites located in Portland, TASC clients did no better than those in the non-TASC alternative treatment group. However, TASC clients at the second site in Canton fared better than the clients in the non-TASC treatment alternative on one measure of drug use. TASC clients who reported heavy drug use in the six months prior to intake reduced their drug use much more between intake and follow-up than heavy users in the non-TASC alternative treatment group. On the basis of this finding, Anglin et al. (1999) concluded that TASC could bring about significant reductions in drug use. However, it is important to remember that TASC clients were being compared with clients in the non-TASC alternative treatment group. The TASC clients were not compared with a no-treatment control group, so this study says little about whether TASC is more effective than no treatment at all.

These findings are difficult to interpret for another reason. Measures of drug use for both the intake and follow-up interviews are based on *self-reported* levels of drug use. This makes it difficult to figure out which group was actually more successful. It is conceivable that the TASC clients actually reduced their drug use more between intake and follow-up than the non-TASC alternative treatment group, as the authors concluded. It is also possible that the TASC clients were simply more likely to report large reductions in drug use than those in the non-TASC alternative group. Certainly the TASC clients would have been well aware of the high risk of being punished for repeated drug relapses, in light of their ongoing involvement in the TASC program. This could have easily made them more reluctant to report. In other words, when respondents are asked to report on their drug use in a setting in which they are being heavily monitored and reports of drug use can lead to punishment, the potential for underreporting is quite substantial (Harrison, 1997). This makes it difficult to know what to make of the significant declines in drug use reported by the TASC subjects.

Despite the questionable nature of these two studies on TASC, this research did demonstrate that the program could induce drug users to stay in treatment longer than voluntary clients. This led to renewed interest in the use of punishment or threats of punishment to induce drug users to remain in treatment. With recent increases in the number of drug users brought before the courts, this notion that client recovery is more likely to occur when punishment is linked to treatment is once again a matter of some importance.

DRUG COURTS

Linking treatment to punishment is an issue that is once again garnering some attention as there has been a near tripling of drug arrests in the last 20 years (Flanagan and McLeod, 1983; Bureau of Justice Statistics, 1999). Nearly 80 percent of drug arrests are for possession, and half of current possession arrests involve those caught with small amounts of marijuana. By the late 1980s and early 1990s, the courts became overwhelmed by this huge influx of new drug cases, and some judges began to look for a solution in the form of drug courts. The first drug court was established in Florida in 1989 and, since that time, there has been a rapid expansion in the number of jurisdictions with these courts (U.S. General Accounting Office, 1997; Belenko, 1998). Like TASC, drug courts aim to combine treatment and punishment in an effort to speed client recovery.

Judges were motivated to urge the development of drug courts since they were seeing the same people over and over as they were returned to court for their repeated relapses for drug use or for their rearrests for recurring criminal acts potentially caused by drug use. It was also clear that punishment alone had failed to stop these drug relapses or criminal recidivism, and so there was a renewed emphasis on linking the courts to treatment (Belenko, 1998). The hope was that if the courts required drug offenders to enter and remain in treatment, many would be rehabilitated. If their drug use and their drug-related criminal behavior could be stopped or reduced, they would cease to be a burden on the courts. Moreover, if drug courts could mandate treatment that brought about such positive outcomes, then they could also reduce jail and prison overcrowding. To address these problems, drug courts were set up as designated courtrooms that were specifically geared toward linking drug users to treatment and monitoring their therapeutic progress (Belenko, 1998).

Much like TASC, drug courts identified the drug users in the criminal justice system and referred them to community-based treatment programs. They also monitored participants' progress in treatment and had the option of returning them to court for further sanctions if they failed in treatment. And like TASC participants, drug court participants could see their cases dropped if they completed treatment.

While there are a number of similarities between drug courts and TASC, drug courts are more judge-centered. Drug court participants are regularly required to appear before a judge in a status hearing, in which judges and other court personnel try to help participants address problems with drugs, work, and family life. Drug courts also determine if participants are regularly attending treatment and take reports from treatment providers regarding client progress. Drug court participants are also regularly required to submit urine tests so the courts can determine if they are remaining drug free. If drug court participants miss court hearings, fail to go to treatment sessions regularly, have an excessive number of positive urine tests, or get rearrested while in the drug court program, a number of sanctions are at the judge's disposal (U.S. General Accounting Office, 1997; Belenko, 1998).

Judges can make use of "motivational jail time," in which a participant serves a short stint in jail as punishment for these infractions. The judge may also terminate an errant client from the program and send them back to court. Termination from treatment can have serious implications for the relapsing drug user, as it can mean reinstatement of the original criminal charges. For some users, this could lead to an extended period of incarceration in jail or prison.

Although there have been approximately 20 evaluations of drug court programs (U.S. General Accounting Office, 1997; Belenko, 1998), the programs vary so much in terms of their eligibility requirements, the specified program length, the types of treatment offered, and the degree of coercion they apply, that it is almost impossible to generalize about whether they are effective or to estimate an effect size. Because the data needed to evaluate these programs are often sketchy and incomplete, it is perhaps best to settle on identifying issues that might be addressed in future evaluations rather than attempting to draw any conclusions about their effectiveness based on the data that are currently available:

• *Measuring Drug Court Effectiveness.* Very few studies look at postprogram effects. Moreover, many studies simply compare drug court participants who graduate from the program with drug court participants who drop out. Comparisons between drug court graduates and drug court dropouts introduce self-selection bias, as graduates may fare better than dropouts because of their own commitment to abstaining from drugs rather than program effects. The more appropriate way to measure effectiveness is to compare all drug court participants—graduates and dropouts—to a control group that did not participate in a drug court program (Belenko, 1998; U.S. General Accounting Office, 1997).

Even in the handful of studies that make appropriate comparisons between all drug court participants (dropouts and graduates) and a control group, no mention is typically made of what percentage of those eligible for these programs were willing to participate. Yet if very few persons brought before the courts are willing to volunteer to participate in these programs, they will ultimately do little to relieve overburdened courts. Furthermore, since the willingness to volunteer for a drug court program may vary from court to court, depending on what other options are available with standard adjudication, it may be difficult to generalize any findings on the willingness to volunteer from one court to another.

In addition, very few studies make use of experimental designs in which drug court participants are compared with a no-treatment control group. However, in one study of the Maricopa County drug court, study subjects were randomly assigned to either a drug court or traditional probation and followed over a 3-year period (Turner et al. 1999). In the 3-year follow-up, drug court participants were less likely to be rearrested than those on traditional probation. Indeed, the Maricopa County study compared drug court participants with those on traditional probation in terms of a number of outcome measures, including rearrests for drug crimes and non-drug crimes as well as for convictions or reincarceration in jail or prison during the 3-year follow-up. As noted previously, it is doubtful that outcome measures such as rearrests, convictions and reincarcerations can provide accurate counts of drug use levels or criminal behavior in a follow-up period. After all, many of the subjects in this study could have easily managed some episodes of drug use or criminal behavior in the follow-up period without being rearrested or reincarcerated. Hence it is difficult to know what to make of the drug court participants' lower overall rearrest rates for all crimes.

Not only did the Maricopa County study rely on some of the same questionable outcome measures used in other evaluation studies, but it likewise confined its follow-up period to the 3 years that the subjects were subjected to criminal justice supervision (Turner et al., 1999). Yet follow-ups that occur after criminal justice supervision is over are important because they make it possible to determine if drug court participants are more likely to stay off drugs than those who underwent traditional probation, even when they are not being monitored or subject to the threat of punishment.

Finally, while it is understandable why study subjects in Maricopa were randomly assigned to either a drug court or traditional probation, it should be noted that traditional probation does not qualify as a no-intervention control group. After all, the study subjects on traditional probation were being monitored and punished for any infractions. Hence, this study compares drug court participants, who receive treatment, monitoring, and sanctions, with a traditional probation group that receives the monitoring and sanctions associated with probation. The study does not include a no-treatment/no-supervision control group who experience no criminal justice interventions. This is unfortunate given the fact that the criminal justice net has been widened in recent years to include many minor drug users who look little different from their age-mates who manage to mature out of drugs without treatment or supervision. This study can cast little light on whether any reductions in drug use made by either drug court study subjects or study subjects on traditional probation are due to punishment or treatment or both, or simply the process of maturing out of drug use that occurs at that age.

• *Cost Savings.* It is likely that future evaluations will make an effort to determine if drug courts can achieve cost savings. To achieve cost savings, these programs must significantly reduce the drug use and criminal behavior of program participants. If they succeed, drug court program graduates will be less likely to be sent to jail for extended periods of incarceration, and they will be less likely to be sent to more expensive prisons for longer sentences (Inciardi et al., 1996).

To date, no systematic analysis exists to determine whether drug courts generate cost savings (U.S. General Accounting Office, 1997; Belenko, 1998). However, any attempt to assess cost savings will require some understanding of what types of people end up in drug courts. If drug courts mainly draw people who would otherwise go to prison or jail for extended periods, and if they succeed in reducing their criminal behavior and drug use, then they are likely to generate very impressive cost savings. If they mainly draw people who might otherwise undergo supervision with traditional probation, then they will have to be very successful in reducing post-program drug relapses and criminal recidivism to justify higher costs than those associated with traditional probation. Given the preliminary nature of much of the drug court data, it is difficult to determine if alternative court dispositions for drug court participants would be more or less expensive.

• *Treatment Effectiveness.* Because all drug courts refer clients to treatment and monitor their progress, they do a better job of linking the criminal justice and drug treatment systems than older forms of community supervision, such as traditional probation or intensive probation supervision programs. However, this can be considered a desirable feature only if they link them to effective forms of treatment.

Many drug courts refer clients to self-help programs like Alcoholics Anonymous, Cocaine Anonymous, and Narcotics Anonymous (U.S. General Accounting Office, 1997). Of these three 12-step programs, only Alcoholics Anonymous (AA) has been subjected to a fair amount of evaluation (Landry, 1997). The research on AA suggests that it could be effective; however, efforts to evaluate it are typically stymied by self-selection biases. In short, it is simply not clear whether those involved in AA improve because of their participation in the program or whether they participate in AA because they are already committed to making improvements. The same potential for self-selection bias also limits the capacity to determine the effectiveness of the less-evaluated 12-step programs like Narcotics Anonymous and Cocaine Anonymous.

Drug courts also refer a large number of clients to outpatient drug-free programs (Belenko, 1998). However, the term "outpatient drug-free" refers to a miscellany of programs that vary in terms of the services they offer and may include individual or group counseling, addiction or AIDS education, acupuncture, and/or training in social skills (U.S. General Accounting Office, 1997; Belenko, 1998). This makes it very difficult to determine if the treatment component of drug courts has any lasting and positive effect on outcomes, since it is often unclear which services are offered by different outpatient drug-free programs.

Not only is it unclear which services ensure positive post-program outcomes, but it is also unclear whether retention in drug courts is a predictor of post-program successes. In part, this is because it has been difficult to define retention rates in drug courts (U.S. General Accounting Office, 1997; Belenko, 1998). Estimates suggest that, on average, 43 percent of drug court participants are retained in treatment (U.S. General Accounting Office, 1997). This figure is quite high for treatment programs—especially outpatient drug-free programs, which generally have high dropout rates (see Belenko, 1998). Yet it is not entirely clear whether longer retention translates into more positive outcomes.

Retention certainly has had a close association with positive post-treatment outcomes in earlier literature on voluntary treatment programs that are disengaged from the criminal justice system. But with system-based programs that link treatment and punishment, the meaning of retention may change. It is simply not known whether legal sanctions ad-

ministered by the courts will have the effect of "manufacturing" commitment in people who were not previously committed.

Moreover, there is a possibility that some of the therapeutic services
offered by drug courts may actually generate client resistance to treatment. In particular, the individual and group counseling offered by a
number of outpatient drug-free programs and therapeutic communities
may be inappropriate for some clients. Working-class and low-income
clients, in particular, have been known to resist this type of therapy because they find it difficult to confide personal matters to a stranger or a
group of strangers in counseling sessions (Currie, 1993; Covington, 1997).
For these clients, treatment may be wholly ineffective and yet, if they fail
to attend sessions, they may be punished with "motivational" jail time or
be returned to court to be prosecuted for their original crime. In such
cases, requiring clients to participate in these potentially alienating therapies may set some up to fail in treatment and be subjected to further
sanctions.

Finally, preliminary research suggests that drug courts may do well
with those who already have a stake in conformity. It also suggests that
they are not very effective with those who lack such a stake. In other
words, they fail with the clients who are most likely to fail in other types
of treatment, including the unemployed, the less educated, and those
using hard drugs like cocaine (Peters et al., 1999). If this is borne out in
future research, it means that drug courts may ultimately be incapable of
changing those who are most likely to burden the courts.

CONCLUSION

Clear-cut answers to questions as to whether programs that link treatment to punishment can effect long-term changes in client drug-using
and criminal behavior are difficult to come by. Evaluations of these programs have not been very revealing because many of these studies have
been hobbled by poor study designs. For one thing, study subjects are not
always randomly assigned to treatment or no-treatment control groups,
making it difficult to know whether client successes are due to program
effects or to a client's commitment to abstain from drug use. Equally
worrisome is the problem of identifying valid outcome measures of drug
use and criminal behavior in the follow-up period. While client self-reports of drug use and crime have been used to measure outcomes in the
follow-up, using self-reports with respondents who have recently been
punished for their drug use may result in severe problems with client
underreporting. Rearrests, convictions, or reincarcerations are also questionable measures, because so few episodes of drug use or criminal behavior come to the attention of the criminal justice system and get re-

corded in these official statistics. Furthermore, much of the evaluation research on criminal justice programs makes use of inappropriate follow-up periods while clients are still on probation or parole. It is important that clients in system-based programs be followed after criminal justice supervision has ended because such post-supervision follow-ups make it possible to determine if these programs actually induce users to abstain when they are not being monitored. Design flaws in much of this research preclude any definitive answers regarding program effectiveness.

ACKNOWLEDGMENT

The author wishes to thank Richard Bonnie, Robert MacCoun, and two anonymous reviewers for their comments on earlier drafts of this paper. She is especially grateful to Faith Mitchell at the National Research Council for her participation in this project.

REFERENCES

Anglin, M.D., D. Longshore, and S. Turner
    1999   Treatment alternatives to street crime. *Criminal Justice and Behavior* 26(2):68-195.

Bachman, J., K. Wadsworth, P. O'Malley, L. Johnston, and J. Schulenberg
    1997   *Smoking, Drinking, and Drug Use in Young Adulthood: The Impacts of New Freedoms and Responsibilities.* Mahwah, MJ: Lawrence Erlbaum Associates

Beck, A.
    2000   Prisoners in 1999. *Bureau of Justice Statistics Bulletin.*

Belenko, S.
    1998   Research on drug courts: A critical review. *National Drug Court Institute Review* 1(1):1-42.

Biernacki, P.
    1986   *Pathways from Heroin Addiction: Recovery Without Treatment.* Philadelphia: Temple University Press.

Blumstein, A., and A. Beck
    1999   Population growth in U.S. prisons, 1980-1996. Pp. 17-61 in M. Tonry and J. Petersilia, eds., *Crime and Justice,* Vol. 26, *Prisons.*

Bureau of Justice Statistics
    1999   *Drug and Crime Facts—Drug Law Violations.* Available online at http://www.ojp. usdoj.gov/bjs/dcf/enforce.htm
    2000   *U.S. Correctional Population Reaches 6.3 Million Men and Women, Represents 3.1 Percent of the Adults U.S. Population.* Press Release. Available on-line at http:// www.ojp.usdoj.gov/bjs

Camp, G.M., and C.G. Camp
    1999   *The Corrections Yearbook, 1998.* Middletown, CT: Criminal Justice Institute.

Clear, T.R.
    1999   Leading from and leading toward. *Corrections Management Quarterly* 3(1):14-18.

Clear, T., V. Clear, and A. Braga
    1997   Correctional alternatives for drug offenders in an era of overcrowding. In L. Gaines and P. Kraska, eds., *Drugs, Crime and Justice: Contemporary Perspectives.* Prospect Heights, IL: Waveland.

Clear, T., and K. Terry
    2000   Correction beyond prison walls. In J. Sheley, ed., *Criminology: A Contemporary Handbook,* Third edition. Belmont, CA: Wadsworth.

Cook, L., and B. Weinman
    1988   Treatment Alternatives to Street Crime. In C. Leukefeld and F. Tims, eds., *Compulsory Treatment of Drug Abuse: Research and Clinical Practice.* National Institute on Drug Abuse Research Monograph 86. Rockville, MD: National Institute on Drug Abuse.

Covington, J.
    1997   The social construction of the minority drug problem. *Social Justice* 24(4):117-147
    2000   Incapacitating Drug Offenders. Unpublished paper prepared for the Committee on Data and Research for Policy on Illegal Drugs.

Currie, E.
    1993   *Reckoning: Drugs, The Cities and The American Future.* New York: Hill and Wang.

Donziger, S.
    1996   *The Real War on Crime: The Report of the National Criminal Justice Commission.* New York: HarperCollins.

Field, G.
    1984   The Cornerstone Program: A client outcome study. *Federal Probation* 48(2):50-55.

Flanagan, T., and M. McLeod
    1983   *Sourcebook of Criminal Justice Statistics—1982.* Bureau of Justice Statistics. Washington, DC: U.S. Department of Justice.

Fletcher, B., and F. Tims
    1992   Methodological issues: Drug abuse treatment research in prison and jails. In C. Leukefeld and F. Tims, eds., *Drug Abuse Treatment in Prisons and Jails.* NIDA Research Monograph 118. Rockville, MD: National Institute on Drug Abuse.

Harrison, L.
    1997   The validity of self-reported drug use in survey research: An overview and critique of research methods. In L. Harrison and A. Hughes, eds., *The Validity of Self-Reported Drug Use: Improving the Accuracy of Survey Estimates.* National Institute on Drug Abuse Research Monograph 167. Rockville, MD: National Institute on Drug Abuse.

Hubbard, R., J. Collins, J. Rachel, and E. Cavanaugh
    1988   The criminal justice client in drug abuse treatment. In C. Leukefeld and F. Tims, eds., *Compulsory Treatment of Drug Abuse: Research and Clinical Practice.* NIDA Research Monograph 86. Rockville, MD: National Institute on Drug Abuse.

Hubbard, R.L., M.E. Marsden, J.V. Rachal, H.J. Harwood, E.R. Cavanagh, and H.M. Ginzberg
    1989   *Drug Abuse Treatment: A National Study of Effectiveness.* Chapel Hill: University of North Carolina Press.

Inciardi, J.
    1996   The therapeutic community: An effective model for corrections based drug abuse treatment. In K. Early, ed., *Drug Treatment Behind Bars: Prison-Based Strategies for Change.* Westport, CT: Praeger.

Inciardi, J., D. McBride, and J. Rivers
  1996   *Drug Control and the Courts.* Thousand Oaks, CA: Sage.

Institute of Medicine
  1990   *Treating Drug Problems*, Vol. 1. D. Gerstein and H. Harwood, eds. Washington, DC: National Academy Press.

Johnston, L., P. O'Malley, and J. Bachman
  1997   *National Survey Results on Drug Use from The Monitoring the Future Study, 1975-1995, vols.1,2.* Rockville, MD: National Institute on Drug Abuse.

Knight, K., D. Simpson, and M. Hiller
  1999   Three year re-incarceration outcomes for in-prison therapeutic community treatment. *Prison Journal* 79(3):337-351.

Landry, M.
  1997   *Overview of Addiction Treatment Effectiveness.* Rockville, MD: Substance Abuse and Mental Health Services Administration.

Martin, S., C. Butzin, C. Saum, and J. Inciardi
  1999   Three year outcomes of therapeutic community treatment for drug-involved offenders in Delaware: From prison to work release to after-care. *Prison Journal* 79(3):294-320.

Mauer, M., and T. Huling
  1995   *Young Black Americans and the Criminal Justice System.* Washington, D.C.: The Sentencing Project.

Morgan, K.
  1993   Factors influencing probation outcome: A review of the literature. *Federal Probation* (June):23-29.

Mullen, R.
  1996   Therapeutic communities in prison: Dealing with toxic waste. In K. Early, ed., *Drug Treatment Behind Bars: Prison Based Strategies for Change.* Westport, CT: Praeger.

Mumola, C.
  1999   *Substance Abuse and Treatment, State and Federal Prisoners, 1997.* Special Report. Washington, D.C.: Bureau of Justice Statistics.

O'Brien, C., and A. McLellan
  1996   Myths about the treatment of addiction. *Lancet* 347:237-240.

Peters, R., A. Haas, and M. Murrin
  1999   Predictors of retention and arrest in drug courts. *National Drug Court Institute Review* 2(1):33-60.

Petersilia, J.
  1997   Probation in the United States: Practices and challenges. *National Institute of Justice Journal* (September):2-8.

Petersilia, J., and S. Turner
  1992   An evaluation of intensive probation in California. *The Journal of Criminal Law and Criminology* 82(5):610-658.
  1985   An evaluation of intensive probation in California. *Criminology* 31:18-32.

Sampson, R., and J. Laub
  1993   *Crime in the Making: Pathways and Turning Points Through Life.* Cambridge, MA: Harvard University Press.

Steffensmeier, D., and E. Allan
 1995 Criminal behavior: Gender and age. In J. Sheley, ed., *Criminology: A Contemporary Handbook*. Belmont, CA: Wadsworth.

Substance Abuse, Mental Health Services Administration
 1998 *Treatment Episose Data Set (TEDS): 1992-1997*. Rockville, MD: Substance Abuse, Mental Health Services Administration.

Turner, S., P. Greenwood, T. Fain, and E. Deschenes
 1999 Perceptions of drug court. *National Drug Court Institute Review* 2(1):61-85.

U.S. General Accounting Office
 1997 *Drug Courts: Overview of Growth Characteristics and Results*. Washington, D.C.: U.S. Government Printing Office.

Waldorf, D., C. Reinarman, and S. Murphy
 1991 *Cocaine Changes*. Philadelphia: Temple University Press.

Walker, S.
 1994 *Sense and Nonsense About Crime and Drugs*. Belmont, CA: Wadsworth.

Wexler, H.
 1996 Evaluation of prison substance abuse treatment programs. In K. Early, ed., *Drug Treatment Behind Bars: Prison Based Strategies for Change*. Westport, CT: Praeger.

Wexler, H., G. DeLeon, G. Thomas, D. Kressel, and J. Peters
 1999 The Amity Prison TC evaluation. *Criminal Justice and Behavior* 26(2):147-167.

Wexler, H., G. Falkin, D. Lipton, and A. Rosenblum
 1992 Outcome evaluation of a prison therapeutic community for substance abuse treatment. In C. Leukefeld and F. Tims, eds., *Drug Abuse Treatment in Prisons and Jails*. NIDA Research Monograph 118. Rockville, MD: National Institute on Drug Abuse.

Wexler, H., D. Lipton, and B. Johnson
 1988 A criminal justice system strategy for treating cocaine-heroin abusing offenders in custody. In L. Siegel, ed., *American Justice: Research of the National Institute of Justice*. St. Paul, MN: West Publishing.

Wexler, H., R. Williams, K. Early, and C. Trotman
 1996 Prison treatment for substance abusers: Stay'N Out revisited. In K. Early, ed., *Drug Treatment Behind Bars: Prison Based Strategies for Change*. Westport, CT: Praeger.

Wilson, W.J.
 1987 *The Truly Disadvantaged*. Chicago: University of Chicago Press.
 1996 *When Work Disappears*. New York: Alfred Knopf.

Appendix F

Biographical Sketches

Charles F. Manski (*Chair*) has been Board of Trustees Professor in Economics and Fellow of the Institute of Policy Research at Northwestern University since 1997. Formerly he was a member of the faculty at the University of Wisconsin-Madison (1983-1998), the Hebrew University of Jerusalem (1979-1983), and Carnegie Mellon University (1973-1980). Manski's research spans econometrics, judgment and decision, and the analysis of social policy. He is the author of *Identification Problems in the Social Sciences* (1995) and *Analog Estimation Methods in Econometrics* (1988), coauthor of *College Choice in America* (1983), and coeditor of *Evaluating Welfare and Training Programs* (1992) and *Structural Analysis of Discrete Data with Econometric Applications* (1981). Manski has been editor of the *Journal of Human Resources*, coeditor of the *Econometric Society Monograph Series*, and associate editor of the *Journal of Economic Perspectives, Econometrica*, the *Journal of the American Statistical Association*, and *Transportation Science*. He has served as Director of the Institute for Research on Poverty (1988-1991) and as chair of the board of overseers of the Panel Study of Income Dynamics (1994-1998). At the National Research Council, he has been a member of the Committee on National Statistics, the Commission on Behavioral and Social Sciences and Education, the Committee on the Federal Role in Education Research, the Committee on Research on Law Enforcement and the Administration of Justice, and the Panel on Research on Criminal Careers. Manski is an elected fellow of the Econometric Society, the American Academy of Arts and Sciences, and the American Association for the Advancement of Science. He has B.S. and Ph.D. degrees in economics from the Massachusetts Institute of Technology.

James Anthony is professor at Johns Hopkins University, where he received a faculty appointment in 1978. His professorial appointments are in the Departments of Mental Hygiene and Epidemiology in the School of Hygiene and Public Health and in the Department of Psychiatry and Behavioral Sciences in the School of Medicine. He also is director of the university's Drug Dependence Epidemiology Training Program and co-director of its Psychiatric Epidemiology Training Program. He is an elected member and fellow of the American Psychopathological Association and a member of both the American College of Neuropsychopharmacology and the College on Problems of Drug Dependence. He is also a member of the Society for Epidemiologic Research, the American Public Health Association, the Society for Prevention Research, and the American Association for the Advancement of Science. He has M.Sc. and Ph.D. degrees from the Graduate Schools of the University of Minnesota.

Alfred Blumstein is the J. Erik Jonsson professor of urban systems and operations research and former dean at the H. John Heinz III School of Public Policy and Management of Carnegie Mellon University. He is also the director of the National Consortium on Violence Research, supported by a five-year, $12 million grant from the National Science Foundation. He has had extensive experience in both research and policy with the criminal justice system, serving on the President's Commission on Law Enforcement and Administration of Justice in 1966-1967 as director of its Task Form on Science and Technology. At the National Research Council he was a member of the Committee on Research on Law Enforcement and the Administration of Justice (now the Committee on Law and Justice) from its founding in 1975 until 1986 and was a member of the Commission on Behavioral and Social Sciences and Education. In 1998 he was elected a member of the National Academy of Engineering. His degrees from Cornell University include a Bachelor of Engineering and a Ph.D. in operations research.

Richard J. Bonnie is John S. Battle professor of law at the University of Virginia School of Law and Director of the university's Institute of Law, Psychiatry and Public Policy. He writes and teaches in the fields of criminal law and procedure, mental health law, bioethics, and public health law. His books include *Criminal Law, Marijuana Use and Criminal Sanctions* and *The Marijuana Conviction: A History of Marijuana Prohibition in the United States*. He has served as associate director of the National Commission on Marihuana and Drug Abuse, special assistant to the attorney general of the United States, secretary of the National Advisory Council on Drug Abuse, chair of Virginia's State Human Rights Committee responsible for protecting rights of persons with mental disabilities, and a member of the U.S. State Department delegation charged with investigating psychiatric abuse of human rights in the Soviet Union. He also served on the advisory board for the American Bar Association's Criminal Justice-Mental Health Standards Project and as a member of the John D. and Catherine T. MacArthur Foundation Research Network on Mental Health and the Law. In 1991, he was elected to the Institute of Medicine (IOM) and has been an active participant in the National Academies' work. He currently serves on the IOM Board on Neuroscience and Behavioral Health, the Committee to Assess the Science Base for Tobacco Harm Reduction, and the Committee to Assess the System for Protection of Human Research Subjects. He has previously chaired IOM studies on injury prevention and control and opportunities in drug abuse research and was a member of the IOM Committee on Preventing Nicotine Dependence in Children and Youths.

Jeanette Covington is associate professor in the Department of Sociology at Rutgers University in New Brunswick, New Jersey. Her research and publications have focused on the social ecology of crime, neighborhood change and crime, and fear of crime. She currently serves on the Committee on Law and Justice at the National Research Council. She has also written and conducted research on the causes of drug use, the links between drug use and crime, and an examination of current drug policies. She is currently considering how criminologists construct the variable of race when analyzing data on both crime and drugs. She has B.A., M.A., and Ph.D. degrees from the University of Chicago.

Kathleen Frydl (*Research Associate*) is a staff officer with the Committee on Law and Justice of the Division of Behavioral and Social Sciences and Education at the National Research Council. She holds a Ph.D. in history from the University of Chicago and a B.A. in history and political science from the University of California at Davis.

Denise C. Gottfredson is professor in the Department of Criminal Justice and Criminology at the University of Maryland. Her research interests include delinquency and delinquency prevention, particularly the effects of school environments on youth behavior. After completing graduate school, she worked at the Johns Hopkins University as a researcher on a long-term national evaluation of the Office of Juvenile Justice and Delinquency Prevention's Alternative Education Initiative. She also coauthored a book on school environmental factors related to school disorder and directed several evaluations of violence prevention efforts. She has a Ph.D. in social relations from the Johns Hopkins University, where she specialized in sociology of education.

Darnell F. Hawkins (*Committee on Law and Justice liaison*) is professor of African American studies, sociology, and criminal justice at the University of Illinois at Chicago. He has also held faculty positions at the University of North Carolina, Chapel Hill, and was a visiting scientist at the Centers for Disease Control, Division of Injury Control. His research interests focus primarily on race and crime, homicide among black Americans, and survey research methodology. His numerous publications include *Ethnicity Race and Crime: Perspectives Across Time and Place* (1995), "Race, Social Class, and Newspaper Coverage of Homicide" (with John Johnstone and Arthur Michener), and "Legal and Historical Views on Racial Biases in Prisons" (with Lee E. Ross). He is coeditor for a special issue of *The Journal of Preventive Medicine*, Evaluation of Youth Violence Projects, and serves on the editorial boards of *Crime and Justice: A Review of Research*, *Law and Society Review*, and *Criminology*, among others. He served as a senior consultant to the National Research Council's Committee on the Status of Black Americans and was a member of its Committee on the Assessment of Family Violence Interventions. He has a J.D. degree from the University of North Carolina, Chapel Hill, Law School and a Ph.D. in sociology from the University of Michigan.

Philip Heymann is the James Barr Ames professor at Harvard Law School, director of the Center for Criminal Justice, and professor at the John F. Kennedy School of Government, where he directed the Program for Senior Managers in Government. He has served as assistant attorney general in charge of the Criminal Division of the U.S. Department of Justice, associate Watergate special prosecutor, and, during the 1960s, held the following posts in the U.S. Department of State: executive assistant to the undersecretary of state, deputy assistant secretary of state for international organizations, and head of the bureau of security and consular affairs. As director of the Center for Criminal Justice at Harvard, Heymann has in recent years managed a number of projects designed to improve the criminal justice systems of countries seeking to create or preserve democratic institutions, including Guatemala, Colombia, South Africa, and Russia.

Joel L. Horowitz is the Henry B. Tippie research professor of economics at the University of Iowa. His main focus is theoretical and applied econometrics, and his areas of expertise are econometric theory, semiparametric estimation, bootstrap methods, discrete choice analysis, and analysis of housing markets. His current projects are semiparametric estimation of additive models with unknown links, bootstrap methods for nonsmooth models, and bandwidth selection in semiparametric estimation. He received a B.S. in physics from Stanford University in 1962 and a Ph.D. from Cornell University in 1967.

Robert J. MacCoun is professor of public policy at the Goldman School of Public Policy and Boalt Hall School of Law at the University of California, Berkeley. Trained as a social psychologist, from 1986 to 1993 he was a behavioral scientist at RAND, a nonprofit, nonpartisan private research institution. He has collaborated with economist Peter Reuter on studies of street-level drug dealing in Washington, D.C., comparative research on European and American drug policies, and analyses of the effects of drug laws on drug use and drug-related harms. Their work has appeared in *Science, Psychological Bulletin,* the *Journal of Policy Analysis and Management,* the *Journal of Quantitative Criminology,* and in various book chapters and RAND publications. MacCoun has also conducted numerous studies of jury decision making and civil litigation, with articles in *Science, Psychological Review, Law & Society Review,* and other journals and edited books. Recently, MacCoun has written on bias in the interpretation of research results and on the likely effects of sexual orientation on military cohesion. In 1996, he was selected as distinguished wellness lecturer by the California Wellness Foundation and the University of California.

Mark Harrison Moore is the Guggenheim Professor of Criminal Justice Policy and Management at the John F. Kennedy School of Government, Harvard University. He was the founding chairman of the Kennedy School's Committee on Executive Programs and served in the role for over a decade. He is also the faculty chairman of the school's Program in Criminal Justice Policy and Management, as well as acting director of the Hauser Center for Nonprofit Institutions. His research interests are public management and leadership, criminal justice policy and management, and the intersection of the two. In the area of public management, his most recent book is *Creating Public Value: Strategic Management in Government.* He has written (with others) *Public Duties: The Moral Obligations of Public Officials; Ethics in Government: The Moral Challenges of Public Leadership; Inspectors-General: Junkyard Dogs or Man's Best Friend; Accounting for Change: Reconciling the Demands for Accountability and Innovation in the Public Sector.* In the area of criminal justice policy, he has written *Buy and Bust: The Effective Regulation of an Illicit Market in Heroin;* and *Dangerous Offenders: Elusive Targets of Justice.* In the intersection of public management and criminal justice, he has written (with others) *From Children to*

Citizens: The Mandate for Juvenile Justice and *Beyond 911: A New Era for Policing.*

William Nordhaus is the A. Whitney Griswold Professor of Economics at Yale University and on the staff of the Cowles Foundation for Research in Economics. He has been a member of the Yale faculty and the staff of the Cowles Foundation for Research in Economics since 1967. He has engaged in economic research on a wide range of problems. His early work centered on productivity, inflation, and economic growth, including "Is Growth Obsolete?" His 1982 study was one of the first that pointed to the slowdown in American productivity growth. His studies include a book, *Reforming Federal Regulation*, that examines a "regulatory budget" and other proposals for regulatory reform. Since then, his work has focused primarily on problems of long-run economic growth, energy, natural resources, and the environment.

Charles O'Brien is the chief of psychiatry at the VA Medical Center and professor and vice chair of the Psychiatry Treatment Research Center at the University of Pennsylvania. His research interests are the neurophysiological bases of addictive disorders and their treatment and other mental disorders, particularly from the biological perspective. He was elected as a member of the Institute of Medicine in 1991.

Carol Petrie (*Study Director*) is director of the Committee on Law and Justice, a standing committee within the Division of Behavioral and Social Sciences and Education at the National Research Council. She also served as the director of planning and management at the National Institute of Justice, U.S. Department of Justice, responsible for policy and administration. In 1994, she served as the acting director of the National Institute of Justice. She has conducted research on violence and public policy, and managed numerous research projects on the development of criminal behavior, domestic violence, child abuse and neglect, and improving the operations of the criminal justice system.

Robert Porter is the William R. Kenan, Jr., Professor of Economics at Northwestern University and a research associate of the National Bureau of Economic Research. Previously he held positions at the University of Minnesota and the State University of New York, Stony Brook, and he has been a visiting professor at the Massachusetts Institute of Technology and the University of Chicago. At Northwestern, he teaches graduate courses in industrial organization and undergraduate courses in econometrics and game theory. He has conducted research on a variety of topics in industrial organization, including theoretical and empirical studies of collusion, price wars, and bidders' behavior in auctions. His recent research includes studies of the federal auctions of offshore oil and gas leases and of procurement auctions for highway construction and for school milk, where he has investigated firms' bidding strategies, the formation of bidding consortia and joint ventures, and statistical methods for detecting the presence of a bid rigging scheme. He received an honors B.A. from the University of Western Ontario in 1976 and a Ph.D. in economics from Princeton University in 1981.

Paul R. Rosenbaum is professor of statistics at the Wharton School of the University of Pennsylvania. His research interests include the design and analysis of observational studies, that is, nonexperimental studies of treatment or program effectiveness; psychometrics, particularly latent variable models for item responses; health services research, with particular reference to health care outcomes; and quality design, particularly the design of dispersion experiments. He is the author of the 1995 book, *Observational Studies*, in the Springer Series in Statistics, as well as numerous articles. He is an elected fellow of the American Statistical Association and a member of the National Research Council's Committee on National Statistics. He received a Ph.D. in statistics from Harvard University in 1980.

James Q. Wilson, from 1961 to 1986, was a professor of government at Harvard, and from 1986 to 1997 he was the James Collins professor of management at the University of California, Los Angeles. He is now professor emeritus from the Anderson Graduate School of Management. He is the author or coauthor of 14 books, including *Moral Judgment, The Moral Sense, Thinking About Crime, Varieties of Police Behavior, Crime and Human Nature* (with Richard J. Hernnstein), *Bureaucracy*, and *On Character*. In addition, he has edited or contributed to books on urban problems, government regulation of business, and the prevention of delinquency among children, including *Crime and Public Policy, From Children to Citizens: Families, Schools, and Delinquency Prevention* (with Glenn Loury), *Understanding and Controlling Crime* (with David Farrington and Lloyd Ohlin), and *Drugs and Crime* (with Michael Tonry).

Index

A

ADAM, *see* Arrestee Drug Abuse
    Monitoring program
Adaptive response to enforcement, 5, 157-
    158, 159, 172-174
Addiction, 23, 25, 37, 141-142, 223
    see also Frequency of drug use;
        Treatment programs
    historical response, 17, 18
    neuroscience, 37, 38-42, 51, 243-244, 274
        dose-response relationships, 41, 57-
            60, 62, 230
    price factors, 45-46, 141-142
    social factors, 49, 52, 59
    surveys, 81, 82-83, 85
Addiction Severity Index, 247, 248, 262
Adolescents, 47, 51, 197, 200, 302-303
    see also Monitoring the Future; School-
        based data and approaches
    arrestees, 84, 189-190, 317
    cocaine use, 199-200, 303, 318
    consumption data, 79, 80, 192, 308
    crime associated with drug abuse, 47, 190
    dropouts, 87, 94(n.10)
    employment, 309
    family preventive interventions, 209-210
    historical perspectives, 189-190, 302,
        329, 330-332, 334-344

Juvenile Court Statistics, 316
marijuana use, 192, 199-200, 303, 318
National Longitudinal Survey of Youth,
    98, 169, 309, 337
National Youth Survey, 309
peer influences, 38, 42, 50, 51, 52, 187,
    194, 220, 223-224, 226, 227, 230,
    231, 309
preventive interventions, 138, 209-210,
    217, 220, 223-224, 226, 227, 230,
    231
    school-based, 8, 19, 137, 209, 211-
        213, 219-221, 224-225, 228-229,
        230, 232, 233, 234
    drug testing, 33, 202-203, 233
survey response problems, 8, 30, 82, 93-
    100, 321-344
Youth Risk Behavior Surveillance
    System, 302, 310, 318
African Americans, 179-181, 197, 304
AIDS, 55, 59, 103-104, 105, 298, 303, 376
Alcohol abuse, 8, 23, 308, 316
    adolescent arrestees, 190
    crime associated with, 64, 301
    Drug and Alcohol Services Information
        System, 91, 93, 304
    genetic factors, 49
    illicit drug use and, 9, 23, 34, 217, 218,
        221, 233-234

C

J

K

L

funding, 35, 93, 152, 153, 249, 276
gender factors, 356, 370
heroin users, 242-243, 254, 305
    methadone maintenance, 242-243,
        247, 253-254
historical perspectives, 11, 17-18, 19,
        241, 245, 249, 260, 261, 274
incarcerated persons, 10, 20, 92, 241,
        242, 250, 258, 259-260, 263, 297,
        298, 300, 301, 313, 316, 349-381
marijuana users, 253
methadone, 349
    cocaine user treatment, 248-249
    heroin user treatment, 242-243, 247,
        253-254
multimodal, 19
National Institute on Drug Abuse,
        evaluations, 241, 261, 264, 305
neuroscience and, 39
Office of National Drug Control Policy,
        241, 305-306
opiate users, general, 242, 243(n.1), 246,
        247, 254, 304
organization of data collection, 125
probationers, 242, 256, 259, 260-261,
        262-263, 299, 349, 350-351, 353,
        354-358, 361, 362, 364-373, 374-
        376, 378
racial/ethnic factors, admissions data,
        304
Treatment Episode Data Set (TEDS), 55-
        56, 93, 243(n.1), 249, 250, 304-305
Uniform Facility Data Set, 93, 243, 304,
        305

U

*Under the Influence? Drugs and the American
        Work Force*, 22
Uniform Crime Reports, 301, 341
Uniform Facility Data Set, 93, 243, 304, 305,
        311
Urban areas
    see also specific cities
    drug dealers, police agreements with,
        169-170
    drug dealers' employment
        opportunities, 167-169
    enforcement, 90, 169-179
    price of drugs, 44, 45, 106, 108-109, 113-
        116, 164-166

System to Retrieve Information from
    Drug Evidence (STRIDE), 24,
    106, 108-114, 117, 147, 153, 161,
    164, 283-295, 315
retail drug market, social organization,
    162-165
retail drug market fragmentation, 164,
    165, 166
surveys, 90, 103; *see also* Arrestee Drug
    Abuse Monitoring Program
Urine testing, *see* Drug-testing programs

V

Vaccines
    analogs for drugs, 233
    clinical trials, 245-246
Violence, 1, 63-64, 170, 172, 178
    see also Crime associated with drug use
    child abuse and neglect, 196
    database linkages, 91
    dealers, police agreements with, 169-170
    domestic, 56, 59, 196
    inmate surveys, 92, 298, 300
Voting rights, loss of, 197

W

Washington, D.C., *see* District of Columbia
Welfare benefits, loss of, 33, 196, 197
White House Special Action Office for
        Drug Abuse Prevention, 261,
        271-272
World Wide Web, *see* Internet
Worldwide Survey of Health Related
        Behaviors, 200, 308

Y

Youth Risk Behavior Surveillance System,
        302, 310, 318

Z

Zero tolerance policies, 8, 188, 199, 200, 233
    see also Drug-testing programs
    school-based sanctions, 201-202, 212